Contents

1 Introduction to Sport Governance   1

Managerial Activities Related to Governance   21

Strategic Management and Policy Development   43

GOVERNANCE AND POLICY IN sport ORGANIZATIONS

THIRD EDITION

Mary A. Hums
UNIVERSITY OF LOUISVILLE

Joanne C. MacLean
UNIVERSITY OF THE FRASER VALLEY

Packianathan Chelladurai
CONSULTING EDITOR, SPORT MANAGEMENT SERIES

WITH CONTRIBUTIONS BY
Thierry Zintz
UNIVERSITÉ CATHOLIQUE DE LOUVAIN

Holcomb Hathaway, Publishers
Scottsdale, Arizona

Library of Congress Cataloging-in-Publication Data

Hums, Mary A.
   Governance and policy in sport organizations / Mary A. Hums, Joanne C. MacLean. —
Third edition.
      pages cm. — (Sport management series)
   Includes bibliographical references and index.
   ISBN 978-1-934432-75-4 (print book) — ISBN 978-1-934432-76-1 (ebook) 1. Sports
administration. 2. Sports—Management. I. MacLean, Joanne, 1959- II. Title.
   GV713.H86 2013
   796.06'9—dc23
                                                                            2013006909

Photo credits: *front cover (top to bottom),* Rafał Olechowski/123 RF, Yuri Arcurs/Dreamstime,
Dmitry Naumov/123 RF, Ivan Mikhaylov/123 RF, Glen Jones/123 RF, Methee Wongwuttikom-
jorn/123 RF, Sean Pavone/123 RF; *spine,* Shih-Hao Liao/123 RF; *back cover (top to bottom),*
mikegraffigna/123 RF, Shariff Che\'Lah/Dreamstime, Kitiyud Phornphibul/123 RF, Gehringj/
Dreamstime, Nico Smit/123 RF; *page i,* Danny Hooks/123 RF; *page iii,* Rafał Olechowski/
123 RF; *page xii,* Vladimir Mucibabic/123 RF; *page xiv,* Nicolaas Traut/123 RF; *page xviii,*
Parinya Binsuk/123 RF; *page xx,* Carolina K. Smith, M.D./123 RF; *page 1,* Frank Romeo/
123 RF; *page 21,* Yuri Arcurs/123 RF; *page 43,* Stephen Coburn/123 RF; *page 61,* Konstantin
Pukhov/123 RF; *page 79,* Louis Horch/Dreamstime; *page 111,* Susan Leggett/123 RF; *page
143,* Nuralya/Dreamstime; *page 175,* Herbert Kratky/123 RF; *page 221,* Benis Arapovic/
123 RF; *page 253,* Jeff Crow/123 RF; *page 285,* Sam D'Cruz/123 RF; *page 307,* Richard Kane/
123 RF; *page 333,* Zhang Liwei/Dreamstime; *page 363,* Herbert Kratky/123 RF; *page 381,*
Vichaya Kiatying-Angsulee/123 RF; *page 399,* gemenacom/123 RF

Please note: The authors and publisher have made every effort to provide current website
addresses in this book. However, because web addresses change constantly, it is inevitable
that some of the URLs listed here will change following publication of this book.

Holcomb Hathaway, Publishers, Inc.
8700 E. Via de Ventura Blvd., Suite 265
Scottsdale, Arizona 85258
480-991-7881
www.hh-pub.com

10 9 8 7 6 5 4 3

Print book ISBN: 978-1-934432-75-4
Ebook ISBN: 978-1-934432-76-1

Printed in the United States of America.

Ethics in Sport Organizations   61

Scholastic Sport   79

Intercollegiate Athletics   175

The Major Games in Amateur Sport 221

Olympic Sport 253

11 Paralympic Sport 285

12 Professional Sport Leagues in North America 307

13 Professional Individual Sports   333

14 Professional Sport Beyond North America   363

15 The Future of Sport Governance   381

Foreword

By PACKIANATHAN CHELLADURAI

Troy University

In recent decades scholars have published books on many of the topics suggested in the former guidelines of the National Association for Sport and Physical Education (NASPE) and the North American Society for Sport Management (NASSM), and the current guidelines of the Commission on Sport Management Accreditation (COSMA). Yet there was a deficiency in the list, with few texts on the important topic of governance. Mary Hums and Joanne MacLean filled that gap with this text.

While the research on and the teaching of management topics at the organizational level are legitimate and needed, they tend to overlook the significance and influence of governance organizations, which are at the apex of the organizational network in a given industry segment. In general, these governance organizations serve to achieve the individual and collective goals of the member organizations. They may be authorized to control and regulate the activities of the member organizations. Such organizations also serve the member organizations by generating valued resources and facilitating the interactions and exchange of information among members.

Given the significant role of these governance organizations and the extent and manner of how they govern their respective segments of the sport industry, one would expect that discourse regarding them would have been more extensive than it is now. Notable exceptions are the work of Trevor Slack and his associates, who have studied extensively the national sport governing bodies in Canada, and James Thoma and Laurence Chalip, who have studied governing bodies at the international level. Similarly, the National Collegiate Athletic Association has been the focus of much research and discussion. But such works have been largely confined to governing bodies representing elite sport, just one segment of the sport industry. Hums and MacLean identify and describe this as well as other segments. This book includes chapters on scholastic sport, amateur sport in the community, campus recreation, intercollegiate athletics, major games in amateur sport, Olympic sport, Paralympic sport, North American professional sport (both team and individual), and international professional sport. The conception and selection of these segments is obviously justified by the existence of governing bodies for each of the selected segments. It is also noteworthy that Hums and MacLean cover segments of the industry that encompass participant sport, elite sport, professional/commercial sport, and sport for individuals with disabilities.

The chapters on each of these segments are unique in their inclusion of history of the segment, the governance structures and programming within the segment, and the policy issues faced in each segment. Readers will appreciate and enjoy the presentation in each chapter of the mission statements and financial and membership aspects of the respective governance organizations.

While the chapters on the governance of the segments are the substance of the text, the authors have prefaced these chapters with four introductory chapters. The first chapter is a lucid introduction to the sport industry, its segments, and the concept of governance. The authors argue rightfully that students should gain insight into the "Big Picture" of sport governance in addition to understanding individual organizations within a segment. The second chapter is devoted to a treatise on managerial activities, including planning, organizing, and decision making. The critical concepts of strategic management and policy development are dealt with separately in the third chapter. The fourth chapter is devoted to ethics in sport organizations. This is an important chapter because a major responsibility of governance organizations is to foster ethical conduct by member organizations and the individuals therein. These four introductory chapters lead nicely into the substance of the book. The book's final chapter is fittingly devoted to raising issues that will confront sport governing organizations in the future.

It is a matter of great pleasure and pride to present the credentials of the authors. The pleasure is professional in the sense that I am referring to two outstanding professionals in the field. The pride is personal and stems from the fact that my association with these scholars began as they were developing as academics. Mary Hums and Joanne MacLean were my doctoral students at The Ohio State University. They are not new to the science and art of writing scholarly papers and texts. Each has published in leading journals and each has published texts and/or chapters in texts. And each has been associated with the governance organizations about which they write. These practical experiences have provided them with the insights that they admirably bring to bear on the discussion of the governance of sport industry organizations and segments.

The authors suggest in their preface that the book is written for upper-level undergraduate or graduate students. I am inclined to believe that the substance of the text would be equally appealing to students at all levels. An instructor may adopt the strategy of introducing the industry segments and their governance mechanisms, and then follow it up with classes on management of the governance and member organizations. By the same token, classes on marketing activities of the governance and member organizations may also follow the introduction to industry segments and their governance.

In sum, Hums and MacLean have written an excellent text on the governance of segments of the sport industry. I am not aware of any other book that treats the topic of governance as well as this one. I am pleased and proud to offer this foreword, and I am thankful to the authors and the publisher for granting me this honor.

Preface

As with previous editions, the third edition of *Governance and Policy in Sport Organizations* is designed for use in governance or policy development courses with upper-level undergraduate students, and can also be used with some graduate-level courses that introduce students to business and policy development aspects of the sport industry.

Sport management students entering the workforce will be employed in various sport industry segments. An important part of their training is learning the structure and function of the various sport organizations they will work within or interact with. Successful sport managers understand the big picture of how their sport organizations are structured. They also know what issues their organizations—and they as managers—will have to confront. This book challenges students to integrate management theory with governance and policy development practices. It discusses where the power lies in an organization or industry segment and how individual sport organizations fit into the greater industry.

This third edition of the book reflects industry changes and offers real-world examples. Numerous sport organization websites are highlighted throughout the text, to prompt in-class discussions and facilitate further research. These websites are displayed in the margins of the text and thus are easily referred to. This edition also features new Industry Portraits & Perspectives boxes, with contributions by administrators in a wide variety of sport segments, including campus recreation, Olympic and Paralympic sport, community recreation, and others. For this feature, administrators answered our questions about their jobs and their organizations to give students a glimpse into the practical concerns of sport managers and the impact of governance and policy on their jobs.

In this edition, we continue to explore current topics such as sport and human rights; violence in sport and surrounding sport; use of social media by athletes, coaches, and front office staff; and the evolution of disability sport. Issues such as these will continue to emerge and evolve, and this text will provide a springboard for class discussions and projects.

Knowledge of sport beyond North America yields a well-informed manager and improves chances for success in the increasingly global sport industry. Although this book focuses primarily on North American sport organizations, it presents sufficient information on international sport organizations to provide students with working models and an understanding of these organizations. For example, we highlight how North American scholastic, intercollegiate, and professional sports differ from those in other regions of the world. In this edition, contributions from the French translation of our book, by Thierry Zintz, Université catholique de Louvain, offer additional insight into European sport organizations. In addition, our backgrounds as authors—one American and the other Canadian—contribute to the international scope of this book. Both of us have had hands-on experience in international sport settings as researchers and practitioners. This combination brings a unique skill set and knowledge base to the text. For example, Mary Hums is an internationally recognized researcher in the area of management issues affecting disability sport and contributes her expertise to the Paralympic Sport chapter. Joanne MacLean is an experienced University Athletic Director and Canada's Chef de Mission for the FISU Games, lending her experience to the chapters on Intercollegiate Athletics and Major Games in Amateur Sport.

New to this edition is a chapter on individual professional sport, contributed by Marion Hambrick and Sun Kang, which explores how this industry segment differs from professional sport leagues. Like the other industry segment chapters, it provides readers with an idea of the segment's structure, governing bodies, and the issues facing sport managers working in this area.

Governance and Policy in Sport Organizations is written and organized with the goal of being teacher- and student-friendly so that instructors will be comfortable with the topic and can present the material to students in a clear, organized fashion. To this end, we now include useful information on accreditation standards, on the book's organization and pedagogy, and about the instructor materials available to adopters.

COSMA Curricular Application

As Sport Management educational programs have continued to evolve, the previous NASSM/NASPE approval process has been phased out and new accreditation standards established. Today, Sport Management education programs can be fully accredited by COSMA—the Commission on Sport Management Accreditation. Governance is now included in the COSMA documents as one of the Common Professional Components, in section 3.2 of the *COSMA Self-Study Manual*.

Organization of the Chapters

The book is divided into two main sections. The purpose of this division is to first establish the theoretical knowledge bases related to governance and policy development that sport managers need to operate their sport organizations, and then to present ways the theoretical bases play out in practical sport governance environments.

The first section, Chapters 1 through 4, presents the basics of specific managerial activities necessary for governance and policy development in sport organizations. This section includes material that is more theoretical in nature, covering an introduction to sport governance and the management functions of planning, organizing, decision making, and strategic management. Because sport managers face ethical dilemmas on a regular basis, the book devotes a chapter to ethical decision making and the importance of corporate social responsibility.

The second section of the book, Chapters 5 through 14, details the governance structures of various sport industry segments, including

- scholastic sport
- amateur sport in the community
- campus recreation
- intercollegiate athletics
- major games in amateur sport
- Olympic sport
- Paralympic sport
- North American professional sport leagues
- professional individual sport
- international professional sport

The content of this section is much more applied in nature. These chapters on the specific industry segments include sections on history, governance structures, and current policy issues. Organizational policies often develop as a reaction to current issues faced by sport organizations and sport managers. Because these issues change and evolve over time, for each industry segment the text presents a selection of current policy issues and the strategies that sport managers are implementing to deal with these issues. Often, such organizational policy decisions have ethical underpinnings as well. Throughout the current policy sections, the book addresses the ethical questions sport managers confront when developing policies. Each chapter also contains a case study related to the chapter content, and ethical concerns are integrated into many of these case studies.

Finally, in Chapter 15, with the goal of stimulating student thought and class discussion, we consider challenges with which sport governing bodies may have to grapple in the future.

The Book's Pedagogy

Each chapter includes Chapter Questions, for use either as homework assignments or for class discussion. In addition, chapters contain case studies that have been used successfully in governance classes and have proven useful for students. As mentioned, many of the industry segment chapters include Industry Portraits & Perspectives boxes that provide insight into the job responsibilities of and issues faced by sport managers in that segment. These boxes can be used to stimulate further discussion as readers consider the way the professionals responded to an issue and how they might respond differently. Please note, too, that for easy reference the book's frontmatter includes a table of the many acronyms that students will encounter here and in the field.

Ancillary Materials

Ancillary materials are available to instructors with adoption of this text. These ancillary materials include an Instructor's Manual, a PowerPoint presentation, and a testbank. The Instructor's Manual contains student learning objectives, exam questions (multiple choice, short answer, and true/false, also offered in testbank form), and suggestions for additional assignments. The PowerPoint presentation focuses on key points from the chapters to help instructors deliver the material as effectively as possible. To help readers easily access the many websites cited throughout the book, the ancillary materials also include an electronic document containing active links to the sites. You may distribute this file to your students or post it on your website.

It is our hope that instructors and students will find this book to be an interesting and useful tool for learning the fundamentals of sport governance and its relationship to current policy and ethical issues facing today's sport managers. It is a book designed to help readers understand the big picture of the sport industry, and their place in it as future sport management professionals.

Acknowledgments

A book project is truly a labor of love, and it cannot be undertaken and successfully completed without a great deal of help from others. Thus, many thanks are in order.

First, special thanks to Marion Hambrick and Sun Kang, who stepped up and contributed this edition's chapter on Professional Individual Sport. Our book adopters requested this content, and we are happy to offer this excellent new chapter in response. Our thanks once again to Dr. Chelladurai for contributing his thoughtful foreword to the book. Thanks also to Colette Kelly, Gay Pauley, and all the good people at Holcomb Hathaway for their support and insightful comments throughout the revision process.

Our sincere thanks to the many reviewers who have offered us thoughtful, thorough, and relevant feedback for each edition, making a significant contribution to the book's usefulness. These individuals include *(for the current edition)*: Chad Carlson, Eastern Illinois University; Mark Dodds, SUNY Cortland; Matthew Garrett, Loras College; Harlan L. Johnson, Bacone College; William Kuchler, Methodist University; Rachel Madsen, Niagara University; Robert P. Mathner, Troy University; Jon Oliver, Eastern Illinois University; Chad Seifried, Louisiana State University; Corri Wilson, Southern New Hampshire University; Lonni Wilson, Keiser University; and Athena Yiamouyiannis, Ohio University. *And for prior editions:* Gala Bank, Northwood University; Carol A. Barr, University of Massachusetts; Dennis Bechtol, Northwood University, Florida Campus; Richard C. Bell, Colorado Mesa University; Mel Brennan, Towson University; Susan Brown Foster, Saint Leo University; Karen Danylchuk, University of Western Ontario; Stephen W. Dittmore, University of Arkansas; John Harris, Kent State University; Timothy Henrich, University of the Incarnate Word; Sue Inglis, McMaster University; E. Newton Jackson, Florida State University; Darlene Kluka, Kennesaw State University; John D. McMillan, Bowling Green State University; Steven Ross Murray, Colorado Mesa University; Barry J. Nicholson, Southeast Missouri State University; Jeff Noble, Wichita State University; Cecile Reynaud, Florida State University; James T. Reese, Ohio University; B. David Ridpath, Mississippi State University; Raymond G. Schneider, Bowling Green State University; Robert Taylor, California University of Pennsylvania; Bernadette M. Twardy, Flagler College; Susan Vail, York University; and Michael Wynn, Northwood University.

—*Mary Hums and Joanne MacLean*

I would like to specifically acknowledge my Sport Administration colleagues along the way at the University of Louisville: Chris Greenwell, Dan Mahony, Anita Moorman, Marion Hambrick, Meg Hancock, Gary Bernstein, Alex Lyras, and Simon Pack. Without their ongoing and daily support and encouragement, as academics but more importantly as friends, this project would never have reached completion. I am especially thankful for all they have done for me during the past 15 years. I would also like to thank the student research assistants who helped me with this book in one or all of its editions: Yung Chou (Enzo) Chen, Morgan Fishman, Robert Sexton, Mark Perry, Michael Clemons, and Kathleen Sipe. They put in numerous hours at the computer and in the library searching for information.

My personal thanks to Dr. Chelladurai for his thoughtful foreword and even more for his valuable guidance and mentorship in my academic life. Thanks to David Grevemberg from the Glasgow 2014 Commonwealth Games for his assistance with the chapter on Paralympic sport. I would also like to thank all of our professional colleagues who have adopted the book and made it a success. I sincerely appreciate your support. And to all the students who read it—a big thank you! Without the students, we wouldn't have had the opportunity to write this book.

Finally, I would like to thank my family and friends here and around the world for their support and encouragement. Once again I cannot say enough about the good work of my coauthor, Joanne MacLean. One of the main reasons I asked Joanne if she wanted to team with me on this project was because I knew she was a "do-er," and through each edition she has been a valuable and supportive colleague. She motivated me and kept me going on more occasions than she will ever know! I enjoy working with people like her—people who make me better.

Thanks to all of you!

—MH

I have been challenged by the magnitude of writing each edition of this book and want to thank the many individuals who have assisted and encouraged me. I am fortunate for the support and inquisitiveness of my students and colleagues, first at Brock University and now at the University of the Fraser Valley. I wish to thank graduate student Dan Hess for his hard work researching and checking new content for this edition of the book. I am indebted to Dan for his questions, suggestions, and strong attention to detail.

I continue to be grateful for my family and friends who have always encouraged and shown interest in my academic pursuits. This one's for you Dad!

Finally, I am thankful for my coauthor, Mary Hums. Dr. Hums is known around the world as an accomplished scholar, teacher, and sport manager. To me, she is all of those things while also being an inspiration and a true friend. I am honored to be her co-author.

My thanks to you all!

—JM

About the Authors

Mary A. Hums, Ph.D., received her doctorate in Sport Management from The Ohio State University, an M.A. in Athletic Administration as well as an M.B.A. from the University of Iowa, and a B.B.A. in Management from the University of Notre Dame.

In 2009 Hums was selected as the recipient of NASSM's Earle F. Zeigler Lecture award, the highest academic honor bestowed by the organization. In 2008 she was named an Erasmus Mundus International Visiting Scholar at the Katholieke Universiteit Leuven, Belgium. In 2006, the U.S. Olympic Committee selected her to represent the United States at the International Olympic Academy Educators Session in Olympia, Greece. She was a co-contributor to Article 30.5 (Participation in Cultural Life, Recreation, Leisure and Sport) of the 2006 United Nations Convention on the Rights of Persons with Disabilities. Hums volunteered for the 1996, 2002, and 2010 Paralympic Games. In 2004, she lived in Athens, Greece, working at both the Olympic (Softball) and Paralympic (Goalball) Games.

Hums is currently a Senior Research Fellow for the Institute for Human Centered Design, Advisory Council for the Olympism and Sport Development Center at Brown University, and a NASSM Research Fellow. She received the 2010 University of Louisville Trustees Award and has been a frequent University of Louisville Red and Black Scholar-Athlete Mentor.

In addition to her work on this book, Hums is co-editor of *Principles and Practice of Sport Management* and *Women as Leaders in Sport: Impact and Influence* and is co-author of *Paralympic Sport: All Sports for All People* and *Profiles of Sport Industry Professionals*. Her other scholarly work includes contributions to *The Journal of Sport Management, European Sport Management Quarterly, The Journal of Legal Aspects of Sport, The Journal of Sport and Social Issues, The Journal of Business Ethics, The Cambrian Law Review, The Journal of Career Development, The International Journal of Sport Management,* and *The Recreation Sports Journal.* Hums served as the managing editor for the *Sport Management Education Journal* and was co-editor of two *ICSSPE Bulletin* Special Issues: Sport and Human Rights, and Athletes and Social Change.

Hums is a 1996 inductee in the ASA Indiana Softball Hall of Fame and a 2009 inductee into the Marian High School (Mishawaka, IN) Athletic Hall of Fame.

Joanne MacLean, Ph.D. (The Ohio State University), is Dean of the Faculty of Health Sciences at the University of the Fraser Valley in British Columbia, Canada. From 2002 to 2012 she was professor of Sport Management at Brock University, where she held the positions of department chair (2007–2010) and interim Dean (2010–11). MacLean also has extensive experience in the administration, governance, and human resource management of sport organizations within Canada.

MacLean began her career as a college basketball coach and athletics coordinator before becoming the Athletic Director at the University of Windsor. She was a celebrated university basketball coach, earning Ontario Coach of the Year honors three times in eleven seasons, and being invited to participate as an Assistant Coach with Canada's National Student Team. During this time she was elected to the executive committee of Ontario University Sport and became Vice President for Sport Programming of Canadian Interuniversity Sport.

MacLean has also had a long-term role administering basketball within Canada. She acted as President of the Canadian University Women's Basketball Coaches Association, Chair of the Canadian Women's National Basketball Operations Committee, and was a member of the Board of Directors of Canada Basketball from 2002 to 2008.

In addition to being an experienced administrator in university athletics and national basketball, MacLean has international experience, having represented Canada at three World University (FISU) Games. She was an assistant coach for the women's basketball team at the 1995 FISU Games in Fukuoka, Japan; Assistant Chef de Mission at the 1999 FISU Games in Palma de Mallorca, Spain; and Chef de Mission in Daegu, Korea, in 2003.

MacLean's research interests are in the area of human resource and performance management, sport governance, intercollegiate athletics, and Canada's sport system. She is the author of two books and numerous academic and professional articles in leading sport management publications. MacLean and her colleagues recently completed a three-year research project entitled "Exploring Interdependence in Canada's Sport System," funded by the prestigious Social Sciences and Humanities Research Council of Canada and Sport Canada for more than $71,000. MacLean was named a Research Fellow of the North American Society for Sport Management in 2009.

Acronyms

AAU	Amateur Athletic Union
ABA	American Basketball Association
ACT	American College Test
AD	Athletic Director
ADA	Americans with Disabilities Act
AFC	American Football Conference
AFC	Asian Football Confederation
AFL	American Football League
AFL-CIO	American Federation of Labor–Congress of Industrial Organizations
AGM	Annual General Meeting
AIA	Arizona Interscholastic Association
AIAW	Association for Intercollegiate Athletics for Women
APR	Academic Progress Rate
ASAA	Alaska School Activities Association
ATF	Asian Tennis Federation
ATP	Association of Tennis Professionals
BAA	Basketball Association of America
B.A.S.S.	Bass Anglers Sportsman Society
BUCS	British Universities and Colleges Sport
CAF	Confédération Africaine de Football
CAHPERD	Canadian Association for Health Physical Education Recreation and Dance
CAT	Confederation Africaine de Tennis
CBA	collective bargaining agreement
CCAA	Canadian Collegiate Athletic Association
CCES	Canadian Centre for Ethics in Sport
CEO	Chief Executive Officer
CFAR	Council of Faculty Athletics Administrators
CGF	Commonwealth Games Federation
CIAU	Canadian Interuniversity Athletic Union
CIF	California Interscholastic Federation
CIRA	Canadian Intramural Recreation Association
CIS	Canadian Interuniversity Sport
COC	Canadian Olympic Committee
CoHEASAP	Coalition of Higher Education Association for Substance Abuse Prevention
COI	Committee on Infractions
CONCACAF	Confederation of North Central American and Caribbean Association Football
CONMEBOL	Confederación Sudamericana de Fútbol
COO	Chief Operating Officer
COSAT	Confederación Sudamericana de Tenis
COSMA	Commission on Sports Management Accreditation
COTECC	Central American & Caribbean Tennis Confederation
CP-ISRA	Cerebral Palsy International Sport and Recreation Association
CPR	cardiopulmonary resuscitation
CRH	Commercial Rights Holder
CSR	corporate social responsibility
CU	Cornell University
DI	Division I
DI-FBS	Division I Football Bowl Series
DI-FCS	Division I Football Championship Series
DII	Division II
DIII	Division III
ED	Executive Director
EPC	European Paralympic Committee
EPL	England's Premier League
FA	Football Association of England
FAR	Faculty Athletics Representative
FARE	Football Against Racism in Europe
FIA	Fédération Internationale de l'Automobile
FIBA	Fédération Internationale de Basketball Association
FIFA	Fédération Internationale de Football Association
FISEC	International Sports Federation for Catholic Schools
FISU	Fédération Internationale du Sport Universitaire
FITA	World Archery Federation / International Federation of Archery
FIVB	International Volleyball Federation

GDP	gross domestic product
GDSP	gross domestic sport product
GOC	Games Organizing Committee
GPA	grade-point average
HBCUs	Historically Black Colleges and Universities
HHSAA	Hawaii High School Athletic Association
HSPN	Homeschool Sportnet Incorporated
IAAF	International Association of Athletics Federation
IAAUS	Intercollegiate Athletic Association of the United States
IBSA	International Blind Sports Association
ICSD	International Committee of Sports of the Deaf (ICSD)
ID	identification
IF	International Federation
I–FBS	Football Bowl Subdivision
I–FCS	Football Championship Division
IGF	International Golf Federation
IHF	International Handball Federation
IHSA	Illinois High School Association
IHSAA	Iowa High School Athletic Association
IIS	Institute for International Sport
INAS-FID	International Association of Sport for People with an Intellectual Disability
IOC	International Olympic Committee
IOSDs	International Organizations of Sport for the Disabled
IPC	International Paralympic Committee
IPSFs	International Paralympic Sport Federations
IRL	Indy Racing League
ISHSAA	Indiana State High School Athletic Association
ISOD	International Sport Organization for the Disabled
ITF	International Tennis Federation
ITTF	International Table Tennis Federation
IWAS	International Wheelchair and Amputee Sports Federation
JCC	Jewish Community Centers
JFA	Japan Football Association
JrNBA	Junior National Basketball Association

JrWNBA	Junior Women's National Basketball Association
JSL	Japan Soccer League
KHSAA	Kentucky High School Athletic Association
LLB	Little League Baseball
LOCOG	London Organizing Committee for the Olympic Games
LPGA	Ladies Professional Golf Association
MCAHA	Muskegon (Michigan) County Amateur Hockey Association
MEMOS	Executive Masters in Sports Organization Management
MHSAA	Michigan High School Athletic Association
MIAA	Massachusetts Interscholastic Athletic Association
MLB	Major League Baseball
MLBPA	Major League Baseball Players Association
MLS	Major League Soccer
MPSSAA	Maryland Public Secondary Schools Athletic Association
MVP	most valuable player
NAC	National Administrative Council
NAIA	National Association of Intercollegiate Athletics
NAIB	National Association of Intercollegiate Basketball
NASCAR	National Association of Stock Car Auto Racing
NASPE	National Association for Sport and Physical Education
NASSM	North American Society for Sport Management
NBA	National Basketball Association
NBL	National Basketball League
NBPA	National Basketball Players Association
NCAA	National Collegiate Athletic Association
NCC	National Coordinating Committee
NCCAA	National Christian College Athletic Association
NCHSAA	North Carolina High School Athletic Association
NEA	National Education Association
NFC	National Football Conference
NFHS	National Federation of State High School Associations
NFL	National Football League
NFLPA	National Football League Players Association

NGB	national governing body		RBI	Reviving Baseball in the Inner Cities
NHL	National Hockey League		SAT	Scholastic Aptitude Test
NHLPA	National Hockey League Players Association		SBHCS	Saint Barnabas Health Care System
NHRA	National Hot Rod Association		T&CP	Teaching and Club Professionals
NIA	National Intramural Association		TSSAA	Tennessee Secondary School Athletic Association
NIAAA	National Interscholastic Athletic Administrators Association		UCLA	University of California Los Angeles
NIRSA	National Intramural-Recreational Sports Association		UEFA	Union of European Football Associations
			UFC	Ultimate Fighting Championship
NJCAA	National Junior College Athletic Association		UM	University of Michigan
NMAA	New Mexico Activities Association		UN	United Nations
NOC	National Olympic Committee		UNB	University of New Brunswick
NPC	National Paralympic Committee		UNESCO	United Nations Educational, Scientific and Cultural Organization
NSAA	Nebraska School Activities Association		USADA	United States Anti-Doping Agency
NSCAA	National Small College Athletic Association		USFL	United States Football League
NSOs	Canadian National Sport Organizations		USGA	United States Golf Association
NTC	National Tennis Center		USLTA	United States Lawn Tennis Association
NYSPHSAA	New York State Public High School Athletic Association		USNLTA	U.S. National Lawn Tennis Association
			USNZ	University Sport New Zealand
OCOG	Organizing Committee for the Olympic Games		USOC	United States Olympic Committee
OFC	Oceania Football Confederation		USTA	United States Tennis Association
OFSAA	Ontario Federation of School Athletic Associations		VANOC	Vancouver–Whistler Canada Organizing Committee
OQWIA	Ontario–Quebec Women's Intercollegiate Athletics		VHSL	Virginia High School League
OSAA	Oregon School Activities Association		WADA	World Anti-Doping Agency
OSU	Ohio State University		WFL	World Football League
OTF	Oceania Tennis Federation		WHA	World Hockey Association
OUA	Ontario University Athletics		WIAA	Washington Interscholastic Activities Association
OUAA	Ontario University Athletics Association		WIAU	Women's Intercollegiate Athletic Union
OWIAA	Ontario Women's Intercollegiate Athletic Association		WMSC	World Motor Sports Council
PAs	Players Associations		WNBA	Women's National Basketball Association
PAR-Q	Physical Activity Readiness Questionnaire		WNBPA	Women's National Basketball Players Association
PASO	Pan American Sports Organization		WTA	Women's Tennis Association
PBA	Professional Bowlers Association		WWE	World Wrestling Entertainment
PBR	Professional Bull Riders		XFL	Xtreme Football League
PGA	Professional Golfers' Association		YMCA	Young Men's Christian Association
PHE Canada	Physical & Health Education Canada		YMHA	Young Men's Hebrew Association
PIAA	Pennsylvania Interscholastic Athletic Association		YWCA	Young Women's Christian Association
R&A	Royal & Ancient (golf)		YWHA	Young Women's Hebrew Association

Introduction to
Sport Governance

The National Collegiate Athletic Association (NCAA) passes a new rule about providing payments to student athletes. A Major League Baseball (MLB) player gets suspended for using performance-enhancing drugs. A city's Parks and Recreation Department creates new programs for people with disabilities and those who are overweight or obese. A campus recreation center requires an identification card to enter the facility. The International

Olympic Committee (IOC) changes the sports on the official program of the Olympic Games. These are regular occurrences in the sport industry, each of which deals with issues of membership, regulation, programming, or organizational structure. All are related to governance and policy development in sport organizations. Many organizations in the industry act as governing bodies and make decisions about their everyday operations. This chapter will set the groundwork for you to see governance and policy development in action in the sport industry.

WHAT IS THE SPORT INDUSTRY?

Today's sport industry is continually expanding and evolving on a global scale. Sport is distinctive and remarkable in magnitude and influence, reaching billions of participants and followers. The mass media devote special coverage to the sporting world, recounting competitive, recreational, and leisure-time activities for a variety of age groups and participant levels. The latest stories and trends are the focus of many blogs, Twitter feeds, and other forms of social media. Scholars study sport from each angle as well, including sport history, sport psychology, and sport management.

In your sport management academic career, you are by now well aware of the industry segments of this global industry, including professional sport, intercollegiate athletics, the Olympic and Paralympic Movements, recreational sport, facility management, event management, sport for people with disabilities, health and fitness, sport club management, interscholastic sport, sport marketing, and legal aspects of sport. Considering the numerous segments comprising the sport industry, what is the size and monetary value of this business we call sport?

SCOPE OF THE INDUSTRY

According to a 2011 industry analysis (A. T. Kearney, 2011), the value of the global sport industry was estimated at between $480 billion and $620 billion, a value higher than the gross domestic product (GDP) of many nations. Among the sports that make up this total are football/soccer (43%), U.S. football (13%), baseball (12%), Formula 1 auto racing (7%), basketball (6%), hockey (4%), tennis (4%), and golf (3%) (A. T. Kearney, 2011). Milano and Chelladurai (2011) estimated the size of the gross domestic sport product (GDSP) in the United States as ranging from $168.5 billion to $207.5 billion a year and placing the sport industry among the top 15 to 18 largest industries in the United States.

Despite its size, the sport industry is a people-oriented, service-oriented industry. The importance of treating one's customers and employees in a positive manner has likely been widely discussed throughout all of your

Value of the Sport Industry in Europe

contributed by Thierry Zintz

The White Paper on Sport in Europe by the European Commission (2011) states that "despite the lack of concrete data and comparables on the economic weight of sport, its importance is confirmed by studies and analysis of national accounts, economic aspects of major sport events and the costs of the lack of physical activity, including those associated with the aging population. A study presented in 2006 indicates that sport at large has generated a value added of 407 billion euros in 2004, representing 3.7% of EU GDP, and created 15 million jobs representing 5.4% of the workforce. The contribution of sport should be highlighted and accentuated in the policies of the Union" (European Commission, 2012, Section 3).

The White Paper further states that "a growing share of the economic value of sport is linked to intellectual proper-ty rights. These rights include copyright, commercial communications, trademarks, image rights and media rights. In an industry increasingly global and dynamic, to effectively enforce intellectual property rights in the world is essential to the health of the sport economy. It is also important that the beneficiaries are guaranteed the possibility of having remote access to sporting events in the European Union border" (European Sports Commission, 2012, Section 3).

The White Paper on Sport in Europe argues that "in addition to the overall economic weight of sport, the vast majority of sporting activities are structured as non-profits, many of which depend on public support to ensure all citizens access to sport" (European Commission, 2012, Section 3).

Source: Hums, M. A., MacLean, J. C., Zintz, Th., *La gouvernance au coeur des politiques des organisations sportives,* 1re ed., De Boeck Supérieur, Bruxelles, p. 320. Used with permission.

coursework. Most Sport Management courses deal with a micro approach to the industry, focusing on various specific areas such as marketing, facility management, event management, or financial issues. Governance courses, on the other hand, take a macro view of sport organizations and will help you understand the big picture of how the various sport industry segments work together. Successful sport managers need conceptual skills (Chelladurai, 2009) to see the big picture, an important element in governance. Governance is more closely related to courses dealing with management, organizational behavior, or most especially, legal aspects of sport, which deal specifically with governance-related and policy-oriented issues. What, then, is the definition of *governance?*

DEFINITION OF GOVERNANCE

A common dictionary definition of *governance* is "the exercise of authority." Sometimes people mistakenly think of "governance" as meaning the "government" or elected political officials. It is much more than that. Sport managers must, of course, be aware of legislation or court decisions that affect them. In the sport industry, governance includes regulatory and service organizations. Governance is associated with power, authority, control, and high-level policy making in organizations. People involved in governance make decisions that set the tone for the entire organization.

Sport governance occurs mainly on three different levels—local, national, and international. Examples of a local governance organization are the Kentucky High School Athletic Association (KHSAA) at the state level and the Ontario Federation of School Athletic Associations (OFSAA) at the provincial level. On the national level, examples include the National Football League (NFL), the National Intramural-Recreational Sports Association (NIRSA), USA Hockey, Hockey Canada, and the Hellenic Basketball Federation in Greece. International organizations include the International Olympic Committee (IOC), the International Paralympic Committee (IPC), Fédération Internationale de Football Association (FIFA, the international governing body for soccer), Fédération Internationale de Basketball Association (FIBA, the international governing body for basketball), and the International Association of Athletics Federations (IAAF, the international governing body for track and field, which is known internationally as athletics).

Governance structures within such organizations, while often similar, are not universally the same. Governance structures in North American sport differ from governance structures in European sport. For example, professional leagues in Europe use the promotion and relegation system in which basketball teams that finish at the bottom of a Division I league are relegated to Division II, while the top teams in Division II are promoted to Division I. This system is not used in the professional sport leagues in North America. Even within North America, differences exist between governance structures in Canada and the United States. NCAA rules and regulations governing collegiate sport in the United States are different from the Canadian Interuniversity Sport (CIS) rules and regulations governing collegiate sport in Canada.

The role of a country's government in sport also differs. Some countries may have a separate Ministry of Sport while others may have a sport governing body within a Ministry of Education or Culture. Again, this differs from the United States, where no federal government office exists to oversee sport in the country. There is a White House Office on Olympic, Paralympic, and Youth Sport, but it operates in an advisory capacity rather than as a governing body (White House, 2009).

In the professional sport industry segment, Sharp, Moorman, and Claussen (2010) describe *governance* as being "roughly divided into governance of team sports by professional sport leagues and governance of individual sports by players associations operating professional tours" (p. 262). For international sport managers, according to Thoma and Chalip (1996), governance involves making effective choices among policy alternatives. They suggest three techniques sport managers can use in the international setting: ideology analysis, political risk analysis, and stakeholder analysis.

As you can see from the discussion above, sport governance is often easy to identify but difficult to define. Several authors have offered their thoughts on the subject. According to Kraatz and Block (2008), governance, broadly speaking, is about defining ends and controlling the means to achieve ends. Ferkins, Shilbury, and McDonald (2009) state that sport governance is "the responsibility for the functioning and overall direction of the organization and is a necessary and institutionalized component of all sport codes from club level to national bodies, government agencies, sport service organizations and professional teams around the world" (p. 245). For the purposes of this textbook, the authors of this book define *sport governance* as follows:

> Sport governance is the exercise of power and authority in sport organizations, including policy making, to determine organizational mission, membership, eligibility, and regulatory power, within the organization's appropriate local, national, or international scope.

We will study each element of this definition in this book.

What Is an Organization?

In order for sport governance to take shape, we must first have an organization that needs governing. Certainly, plenty of groups are involved with sport, but what truly identifies a group as an organization rather than just a group of people?

Chelladurai (2009) lists several attributes of an organization, including the following:

1. identity
2. program of activity
3. membership
4. clear boundaries
5. permanency
6. division of labor
7. hierarchy of authority
8. formal rules and procedures

To illustrate how an organization is different from just a group of people, let's attempt to apply these attributes to (1) a professional basketball team and (2) the group of people you met in college and regularly go out with on weekends.

1. IDENTITY.   Teams establish a public identity by their name, whether that name is the Lakers, the Lynx, Real Madrid, or Olympiakos. Teams also have an established corporate identity separate from the players or the fans. In contrast, your group of friends usually does not have a name and is not an established business entity.

2. PROGRAM OF ACTIVITY.   A program of activity implies that an organization has a certain set of goals it wishes to achieve and that these goals are tied to its mission statement and its successful business operation. A basketball team wants to win a championship, and the people who work in its front office want to maximize revenues. A group of friends may have goals (for example, to go to an event), but it does not have a written set of goals it wishes to accomplish or a written mission statement.

3. MEMBERSHIP. Organizations have set rules about membership. In order to play professional basketball, one would need a certain amount of experience at a certain level of play to be considered for "membership" in the league. In a group of friends the rules for membership may depend on who is mad at someone this week, whom you met at a party last week, or whom you have as your current Facebook friends.

4. CLEAR BOUNDARIES. We know who plays on the Lakers or the Lynx because they have published, league-approved rosters. Any claim that "I play for the Lakers" can be easily verified. Groups of friends change from year to year, often from week to week or day to day, depending on who is now dating or mad at whom.

5. PERMANENCY. True organizations have relative permanency, although the organizational members come and go. For example, the Lakers' current players are not the same people as when the franchise was new, but the Lakers' organization still exists. A group of friends also changes over time but is more likely than an organization to cease to exist as a group.

6. DIVISION OF LABOR. Within organizations labor is divided among members. Tasks are determined, and then people are assigned to the tasks. Organizations clearly illustrate division of labor with organizational charts. The front office of a basketball team has specialization areas such as Marketing, Media Relations, Community Relations, and Ticket Sales. On the other hand, a group of friends has no organizational chart with assigned duties, except perhaps for the designated driver.

7. HIERARCHY OF AUTHORITY. An organizational chart also reflects an organization's hierarchy of authority. Who reports to whom is clear from the lines and levels within the chart. At the top of the chart, a basketball team has a General Manager in charge of the day-to-day operations of the club; all others answer to her. In a hierarchy, people higher up are responsible for the actions of the people below them. In a group of friends, one seldom has any personal responsibility for the actions of others in the group.

8. FORMAL RULES AND PROCEDURES. Organizations have formal rules and procedures, such as constitutions, bylaws, and operational manuals. Friends don't have policy manuals outlining how the group will operate, what brand of smartphone everyone will use, or who can come along on Saturday night.

As you see from these very simplified examples, organizations are formalized entities with rules about mission, membership, structure, operation, and authority. You will read about these fundamental concerns of governance in the chapters focusing on the different segments of the sport industry.

Regulatory Power

Another significant aspect of governance is that organizations have regulatory power over members, an ability to enforce rules and impose punishments (sanctions) if necessary. Different governing bodies possess this sanctioning power to different degrees. For example, the National Federation of State High School Associations, referred to as NFHS, establishes set competition rules for individual sports. Failing to follow these rules may prevent a particular school from participating in a certain event. The IOC has the power to ban athletes from competing in future Olympic Games if they test positive for performance-enhancing drugs, and MLB can impose a luxury tax on teams whose payrolls exceed a certain amount. The NCAA determines recruiting rules for coaches, which, if violated, carry sanctions such as loss of scholarships for an ensuing season.

External and Internal Influences on Sport Organizations

Sport organizations do not exist in a vacuum. As part of the greater society in which they exist, they must anticipate changes in both their external and internal environments, preferably before they *must* react. Chelladurai (2009) subdivides the organization's external environment into two categories: (1) the task or operating environment, sometimes referred to as the *proximal* (close) environment, and (2) the general environment, also called the *distal* (further removed) environment. Sport managers must be cognizant of what is happening in their external environments and adapt accordingly. Their internal environments are created through each organization's specific policies and procedures (Chelladurai, 2009).

As open systems with inputs, throughputs, and outputs, sport organizations are in a constant state of interaction with their various environments (Minter, 1998). Governance structures, therefore, must adapt to changes in an organization's internal and external environments. For example, as society increasingly disapproves of the use of performance-enhancing drugs by athletes, more and more sport organizations are toughening their policies and procedures regarding the use of banned substances; as a result, we see the formation of organizations such as the World Anti-Doping Agency (WADA). As another example, as more professional athletes have provided negative public commentary on social media sites such as Twitter, leagues and teams have adapted by creating new social media policies to deal with athletes who engage in such behavior. (See

Chapter 12 for more on this issue.) These *internal* reactions to trends in the sport organization's *external* environment are made to adapt with the times.

The Five R's of Good Governance

For a governing body to operate successfully, it must be structured in such a way that important information can flow throughout the organization and be disseminated externally to others needing this information. But what types of information are most important? According to Grevemberg (1999), sport organizations need to be mindful of what he calls the "Five R's":

1. *Regulations*—systems that report organizational governance structures, constitutions, legal control mechanisms, event selection criteria, and codes of eligibility, conduct, and ethics
2. *Rules*—systems that report technical rules for the officiating and management of the respective sport's competitive events
3. *Rankings*—systems that report and place athlete/team performances based on results and competitive criteria into numerical order from first to last place
4. *Records*—systems that report the best performances ever accomplished by athletes/teams within competitions, time periods, or overall
5. *Results*—systems that report the final standings and performance statistics from competitions (p. 10)

If sport organizations can consistently apply the Five R's across all their operations, they will find that governance can be consistent and efficient.

ORGANIZATIONAL UNITS AND DOCUMENTS IN SPORT GOVERNANCE

G overnance has a certain language, with terms and concepts we must know to understand governance and the inner workings of sport organizations. In terms of sport governance, organizations are made up of distinct units with varying degrees of authority and responsibility. In addition, sport organizations usually maintain a set of documents dealing with governance structures. This section briefly introduces some of these organizational units and documents.

General Assemblies

Many sport organizations (for example, the IOC, IPC, NCAA, and NIRSA) are voluntary in nature. Nevertheless, these organizations employ paid staff members. The size of the headquarters staff can vary widely. NIRSA, for example, has approximately 25 employees, while the NCAA headquarters has approximately 350. The paid staff members handle the day-to-day operations of organizations, although they are not the ones who actually govern the organizations.

The primary governing body is usually called a General Assembly; it may also be called a Congress or a General Business Meeting. In many sport organizations, the members of this governing body are volunteers. According to Chelladurai and Madella (2006), "Voluntary organizations are truly political systems; power is continuously exerted by professionals and volunteers to influence decisions and actions in order to satisfy personal or group needs" (p. 84).

A General Assembly for a sport organization usually convenes on a regular basis (often yearly). The members of the General Assembly, selected in accordance with an organization's constitution and bylaws, vote as a group on legislation, rules, policies, and procedures. This type of governing body generally elects officers such as the President, Vice Presidents, and Secretary. It also has several standing committees assigned specific tasks, as will be discussed later. Its meetings, or sessions, are generally conducted using a common set of rules of operation. One of the most commonly used sets of guidelines for running a meeting is called *Robert's Rules of Order* (Robert, Honemann, Balch & Seabold, 2011). Those of you who are in a fraternity or sorority may recognize these from house meetings you have attended. These rules are often referred to as Parliamentary Procedure, and most organizations designate a person who is familiar with Robert's Rules as the organizational Parliamentarian. It is the Parliamentarian's job to make sure the group members properly follow Robert's Rules of Order so that discussions can proceed in an orderly manner. Meetings organized using Robert's Rules usually follow this order of events:

www

Robert's Rules of Order
www.robertsrules.org

1. call to order
2. approval of the minutes of the previous meeting
3. committee reports
4. old business
5. new business
6. announcements
7. a call to adjourn the meeting

During the meeting, when someone wants to make a suggestion for action by the group, he makes what is called a "motion to take the action." Another person from the group must then second the motion. Then, the meeting chair allows debate on the action to begin. During this time the motion can be amended and if so, the members must then vote on the amended motion. When the debate is complete, the chair calls for a vote.

Votes are taken by a count of hands, by voice, or sometimes by a paper ballot, depending on the topic. If no decision can be reached because, for example, the members need more information, a motion can be tabled—that is, set aside for action at the next meeting. When all the business of the group is complete, someone makes a motion to adjourn the meeting, and after another member seconds that motion, the meeting ends. Using these rules for the standard operation of a business meeting helps ensure fairness and enables all members to voice their opinions in an orderly manner (Introduction to Robert's Rules of Order, n.d.). Often the agendas for General Assembly meetings and the issues on which they vote come from a body known as an Executive Committee or Management Council.

Executive Committees, Governing Boards, and Management Councils

Executive Committees, sometimes called Governing Boards or Management Councils, are small subsets of an organization's General Assembly. Members of the General Assembly select a group, usually from 5 to 20 members, to serve on the organization's Executive Committee. Many believe that the Executive Committee is where the "real power" in a sport organization lies. This group usually generates the agenda action items on which the General Assembly votes. If the Executive Committee does not endorse an idea, it will almost never be brought to the General Assembly for a vote. In addition, this group meets formally more frequently, often two or three times a year, in order to deal with issues that may come up between General Assembly meetings. It may also deal with special issues via video conferences, VoIP calls, web conferencing, conference calls, or through e-mail.

Standing Committees

Sport organizations also designate standing committees with specific responsibilities within their governance structures. The type and number of standing committees vary by organization. The International Table Tennis Federation (ITTF), for example, has committees for the following areas:

- Equipment
- Media
- Merit Awards and Hall of Fame
- Nominations
- Para TT [disabled sport]
- Rules
- Sports Science
- Technical

- Umpires and Referees
- Veterans
- Commissions and Working Groups (Athletes, Juniors, Olympic and Paralympic, Women's Working Group)
- New Technologies & Research Advisory Board (ITTF, 2011)

FIFA (2007), the international governing body for football (soccer), has the following standing committees:

- Finance Committee
- Internal Audit Committee
- Organising Committee for the FIFA World Cup
- Organising Committee for the FIFA Confederations Cup
- Organising Committee for the Olympic Football Tournaments
- Organising Committee for the FIFA World Youth Championships
- Committee for Women's Football and FIFA Women's Competitions
- Futsal Committee [variant form of football]
- Organising Committee for the FIFA Club World Championship
- Referees Committee
- Technical and Development Committee
- Sports Medical Committee
- Players' Status Committee
- Legal Committee
- Committee for Fair Play and Social Responsibility
- Media Committee
- Associations Committee
- Football Committee
- Strategic Committee
- Marketing and Television Advisory Board (p. 30)

Ad Hoc Committees

At times, sport organizations face issues that need to be dealt with on a short-term basis. For example, perhaps the organization is planning to host a special fundraising event or play a home game at a site other than its usual home arena. Because the event may just occur one time, the organization will assemble an *ad hoc,* or temporary, committee that is in charge of the event. Unlike standing committees that deal with ongoing concerns, once the event is over, the ad hoc committee usually ceases to exist. An ad hoc committee usually only operates for a short period of time, generally less than one year. Occasionally, a topic initially addressed by an ad hoc committee will become an ongoing concern and the organization will then establish a standing committee to address it.

Executive Staff

The people who serve on a General Assembly or Executive Council are almost always volunteers. Their business expenses may be paid, but they are not employees of the sport organization. The people who are employed by the sport organization to run the daily operations are called Executive or Professional Staff. People in these positions have titles such as Executive Director, General Manager, Marketing Director, Sport Administrator, Technical Director, or Event Coordinator. These individuals are paid sport management professionals, employed by the governing body. They work in the organization's headquarters, as opposed to volunteers who may be located anywhere in the world. For example, the Executive Staff of the NCAA works daily in offices in Indianapolis, Indiana. The Athletic Directors on NCAA committees, however, are located at their home institutions across the nation and come together only at designated times during the year. As another example, the staff of the World Archery Federation (also known as International Federation of Archery, FITA) works at the headquarters of the organization in Lausanne, Switzerland. The elected Executive Committee members, however, operate from their respective national federations and meet twice a year (Hums, McLean, & Zintz, 2011). Similarly, the Executive Staff for the IPC work in the organization's headquarters in Bonn, Germany. They run the organization on a daily basis, planning events, handling financial matters, and marketing upcoming events. The volunteers, on the other hand, who work with a specific sport such as Ice Sledge Hockey, may be located in Canada, Norway, and the United States. They may meet together at a Sport Technical Committee meeting, for example, at a designated time and place each year or may hold a session during the Paralympic Games.

Constitutions and Bylaws

Almost all sport organizations have documents outlining the basic functions of the organization, usually called the constitution and bylaws. An organization's constitution acts as a governing document that includes statements about the organization's core principles and values. Bylaws, also governing documents, are more operational in nature, outlining how an organization should conduct its business in terms of elections, meetings, and so on. For examples of what these types of documents include, see Exhibit 1.1, a Table of Contents from the Constitution of the International Volleyball Federation (FIVB), and Exhibit 1.2, a Table of Contents from the Bylaws of the International Handball Federation (IHF).

Table of contents of the FIVB constitution.   *exhibit* **1.1**

Source: Condensed from Siekmann, R.C.R., & Soek, J. (1998). *Basic documents of international sports organizations.* The Hague, The Netherlands: Kluwer Law International.

exhibit 1.2 Table of contents of the IHF bylaws.

I	Name, Composition, Domicile
II	Purpose
III	Membership
IV	IHF Bodies
V	Finances
VI	Official Languages, Correspondence, Announcements, and Publications
VII	International Events
VIII	Rules of the Game
IX	Representatives, Officials, Technical Delegates, Referees
X	IHF Adjudicating Bodies
XI	Dissolution of the IHF

Source: Condensed from Siekmann, R.C.R., & Soek, J. (1998). *Basic documents of international sports organizations.* The Hague, The Netherlands: Kluwer Law International.

These different organizational units and documents will be discussed throughout each of the industry segment chapters in this text.

WHY STUDY GOVERNANCE?

With all the areas to study within the academic discipline of Sport Management, why study governance? Three main reasons come to mind: (a) you need to understand the "big picture"; (b) you need to understand how governance fits within the Sport Management curriculum; and

(c) you definitely will use your knowledge of sport governance in whichever industry segment you work.

Understanding the Big Picture

In studying governance, you will truly be challenged to put together all the pieces of the sport industry. As mentioned above, studying sport governance requires the ability to see the big picture, to understand how individual sport organizations fit into the greater industry, and to see the similarities and differences among the various industry segments. Sport governance also prepares you for the global sport industry you will be entering. Sport managers who lack the ability to see how their organizations fit in to the global picture risk having their organizations fall behind. With an understanding of sport governance, you will see how the governing structures of seemingly dissimilar industry segments such as Intercollegiate Athletics and the Olympic Movement have much more in common than you would think.

Governance in the Sport Management Curriculum

As the number of Sport Management academic programs has increased greatly in the past few decades, so have issues of program quality. From the very beginning, governance has been an integral part of Sport Management education. In 1987 two academic organizations, the North American Society for Sport Management (NASSM) and the National Association for Sport and Physical Education (NASPE), formed a task force to develop curricular standards (Parkhouse, 2001). Recognizing the importance of learning governance, the task force included sport governance as one of the content areas required for Sport Management programs to attain NASSM/NASPE approval. The premise was that students must be familiar with governance agencies, their authority, organizational structure, and functions. As Sport Management programs have continued to evolve, the NASSM/NASPE approval process has been phased out and new accreditation standards have been established.

Today, Sport Management education programs can be fully accredited by an organization known as COSMA—the Commission on Sport Management Accreditation. According to NASSM (n.d., para. 1), COSMA "is a specialized accrediting body that promotes and recognizes excellence in sport management education in colleges and universities at the baccalaureate and graduate levels." Governance is now included in the COSMA documents as one of the common professional components.

The educational examples above and in the accompanying box illustrate the international nature of the sport industry. They also reinforce why learning about governing structures on all levels will help develop your understanding of how this worldwide industry operates.

www
COSMA
http://cosmaweb.org/

Sport Management Training Internationally

contributed by Thierry Zintz

Just as training sport managers in good governance practices is important in North American Sport Management programs, it is also important on the international scene. The International Olympic Committee, in collaboration with scholars from around the world, has set up training programs for managers working in the governance of National Olympic Committees (NOCs) and International Federations (IFs). The programs are offered by Olympic Solidarity and culminate in the program known as MEMOS (Executive Masters in Sports Organization Management) (IOC Olympic Studies Center, 2012).

Through this program, Olympic Solidarity provides scholarships for sports leaders supported by their NOCs and accepted by the MEMOS selection committee to take this course. It is recognized internationally and offered by a network of universities partnered with Olympic Solidarity.

MEMOS takes the form of modules, each focusing on one aspect of sport management. The key is for the participants, assisted by a tutor, to complete a project aimed at improving an aspect of the management of their organization. Through a combination of residential modules and distance learning, MEMOS allows participants to learn while continuing their work in their respective sport organizations. MEMOS is offered in English, French, and Spanish.

Source: Hums, M. A., MacLean, J. C., Zintz, Th., *La gouvernance au coeur des politiques des organisations sportives,* 1re ed., De Boeck Supérieur, Bruxelles, p. 320. Used with permission.

Using Knowledge of Governance in Your Career

Understanding governance structures is important for any career in sport management. If you work at a bank, you need to know the rules for your workplace and probably some basic federal and state laws. But for the most part, especially at an entry-level position, you will not be interacting with the people who make the policies for your bank or for the broader banking industry. In sport, however, especially because of the ramifications of enforcement, you will need to be keenly aware of governance structures and issues. You will also need to understand different contexts of governance. There will be governance issues dealing with a given sport and its rules as well as governance issues dealing with the business side of sport. You will need to know where the power lies in your organization, and studying governance can help you understand this. You will need to know which governing bodies you will deal with in your industry segment. If you work in a college athletic department, you must understand how you relate to governance structures of your university, your conference, and the NCAA or CIS. In professional sport, if you deal with players associations or players unions, you will need to know how they relate to the decisions you make. In high school sport, the power rests at the state or provincial level in organizations such as the Indiana State High School Athletic Association (ISHSAA) and the OFSAA. A recreation director in a City Parks and Recreation Department may answer to the mayor or the City Council. If you work for a sport federation such as the Fédération Internationale de l'Automobile (FIA), you will have to be knowledgeable about the federation's rules and regulations dealing with athlete eligibility.

Studying sport governance gives you a perspective on where you fit into your sport organization and where your sport organization fits into its industry segment. For example, if you work in the front office of an MLB team, you will need to understand various levels of governance in your job, from the club's front office to the League Office to the Commissioner's Office. In Olympic and Paralympic Sport, you may be involved in interactions among International Federations, National Governing Bodies, National Olympic Committees, and Organizing Committees of the Olympic Games. In intercollegiate athletics, you will need to know basic NCAA compliance rules to avoid placing your school in danger of NCAA sanctions. If you work for the Commonwealth Games Federation (CGF), you will need to understand eligibility rules for athletes, so that any athletes you are responsible for do not jeopardize their eligibility. In sport, you are likely to have more direct interactions with governing bodies and policy makers than you might in many other industries. In any sport organization you work for or interact with, you need to understand who has the power and where the power lies.

Finally, the importance of sport managers acting in an ethical manner in any sport governance situation cannot be overstated. Sport managers face ethical dilemmas on a daily basis. How they deal with them is a measure of their own ethical nature and that of their organization. For this reason this textbook devotes a chapter to ethical decision making and the importance of corporate social responsibility and discusses various ethical issues sport managers may face in different industry segments.

SUMMARY

The sport industry continues to grow and develop on a global scale. Studying sport governance allows you to take a big-picture approach to this global industry. Learning about the governing structures and documents for sport organizations illustrates where power and authority exist within the industry. This area of study is sufficiently important to be discussed in the COSMA accreditation documentation, reemphasizing the importance of understanding this complex, fascinating aspect of the sport industry.

In your previous Sport Management classes, you learned about basic managerial activities and functions. For purposes of this textbook, we will focus on four of these important areas in Chapters 2 through 4—planning, decision making, strategic management and policy development, and ethical decision making. These activities are the heart and soul of the governance process and have separate chapters devoted to them, further explaining their roles in the governance of sport organizations.

The remainder of the text guides you through selected industry segments and explains how sport governance is implemented in those segments, using numerous examples to illustrate governance in action. It is our hope that you will enjoy these challenging and interesting areas of study within sport management.

caseSTUDY

INTRODUCTION TO GOVERNANCE

You are the Sport Director for the State Summer Games in your home state. The Games take place every year, and the program of sports and events has to be agreed upon by the Games' General Assembly two years in advance. You are part of a group designated to propose the addition of a new sport to the program. How would the organization proceed on deciding whether or not to add a new sport to the program?

1. Research the existing program for your home state and select a sport not currently a part of the program that you would like the group to consider.
2. What type of information should your group gather to help in making this decision?
3. With which organizations and governing bodies will the committee need to interact?
4. When the proposal comes to the General Assembly, describe how Robert's Rules of Order would work at that meeting in making the decision about adding a new sport to the program.

CHAPTER questions

1. Choose a sport organization and then use Chelladurai's model of organizational attributes from this chapter to define the different elements of that organization.
2. Find two sample sport organization constitutions or bylaws. Compare the two for content. Explain why you think they are different or similar.
3. Using the definition of *sport governance* from this chapter, choose a sport organization and identify the different parts of the definition in that organization.

REFERENCES

A. T. Kearney, Inc. (2011). The sports market: Major trends and challenges in an industry full of passion. Retrieved from http://www.atkearney.com/documents/10192/6f46b880-f8d1-4909-9960-cc605bb1ff34

Chelladurai, P. (2009). *Managing organizations for sport and physical activity: A systems perspective* (3d ed.). Scottsdale, AZ: Holcomb Hathaway.

Chelladurai, P., & Madella, A. (2006). *Human resource management in Olympic sport organizations.* Champaign, IL: Human Kinetics.

European Commission. (2012). White Paper on sport—European Union. Retrieved from http://ec.europa.eu/sport/white-paper/whitepaper8_fr.htm

Ferkins, L., Shilbury, D., & McDonald, G. (2009). Board involvement in strategy: Advancing the governance of sport organizations. *Journal of Sport Management, 23,* 245–277.

FIFA. (2007). FIFA statutes. Retrieved from www.fifa.com/mm/document/affederation/federation/fifa_statutes_ 0719_en_14479.pdf

Grevemberg, D. (1999, May). Information technology: A solution for effective Paralympic Sport administration. Paper presented at the VISTA 1999 Paralympic Sport Conference, Cologne, Germany.

Hums, M. A., MacLean, J. C., & Zintz, T. (2011). *La Gouvernance au Coeur des politiques des organisations sportives.* Traduction et adaptation de la 2e édition américaine. Bruxelles, Belgique: Groupe De Boeck.

Introduction to Robert's Rules of Order. (n.d.). Retrieved from www.robertsrules.org/ rulesintro.htm

IOC Olympic Studies Center. (2012). *Post-graduate courses offering Olympic based content.* Author: Lausanne, Switzerland.

ITTF. (2011). Committee nominations 2011. Retrieved from http://www.ittf.com/ittf_misc/nominations_2011.pdf

Kraatz, M. S., & Block, E. S. (2008). Organizational implications of institutional pluralism. In R. Suddaby, R. Greenwood, & K. Sahlin (Eds.), *Handbook of organizational institutionalism* (pp. 243–275). New York: Sage.

Milano, M., & Chelladurai, P. (2011). Gross domestic sport product: The size of the sport industry in the United States. *Journal of Sport Management, 25*(1), 24–35.

Minter, M. K. (1998). Organizational behavior. In J. B. Parks, B. R. K. Zanger, & J. Quarterman (Eds.), *Contemporary sport management* (pp. 79–89). Champaign, IL: Human Kinetics.

NASSM. (n.d.) Program accreditation. Retrieved from http://www.nassm.com/InfoAbout/NASSM/Program Accreditation

Parkhouse, B. L. (2001). *The management of sport: Its foundation and application* (3d ed.). Boston, MA: McGraw-Hill.

Robert, H. M., Honemann, D. H., Balch, T. J., & Seabold, D. E. (2011). *Robert's Rules of Order Newly Revised,* 11th ed., Cambridge, MA: Da Capo.

Sharp, L. A., Moorman, A. M., & Claussen, C. L. (2010). *Sport law: A managerial approach* (2d ed.). Scottsdale, AZ: Holcomb Hathaway.

Thoma, J. E., & Chalip, L. (1996). *Sport governance in the global community.* Morgantown, WV: Fitness Information Technology.

White House. (2009). President Obama announces new White House Office of Olympic, Paralympic, and Youth sport. Retrieved from http://www.whitehouse.gov/the_press_office/President-Obama-Announces-New-White-House-Office-of-Olympic-Paralympic-and-Youth-Sport

Managerial Activities Related to Governance

Sport managers carry out a myriad of managerial activities and functions on a daily basis. The four functions of management have been defined as planning, organizing, leading, and evaluating (Chelladurai, 2009). Sport managers dealing with governance issues must be able to carry out all these functions, but two functions, planning and organizing, are more critical than others and will be discussed in this chapter. Decision making, a subset of leading, is also essential to sport managers dealing with governance issues, and it will also be discussed. Sport managers perform these functions daily. This chapter provides a brief overview of these important managerial activities and their relationship to sport governance.

PLANNING

The Importance of Planning for Sport Organizations

Sport organizations need to plan because the sport industry is a complex entity. Whether it is the Olympic Games bringing together nations or a high school softball tournament featuring local teams, the sport industry requires interaction and cooperation in order for teams, leagues, tours, and events to be successful. What are the specific purposes of planning? According to the Australian Sport Commission (2012), planning serves to help a sport organization:

- become proactive rather than reactive—to clarify club purposes and direction
- initiate and influence outcomes in favour of the club
- exert more control over its destiny—deciding where it wants to be in the future
- adopt a more systematic approach to change and reduce resistance to change
- improve financial performance and use resources effectively
- increase awareness of its operating environment (for example, competitors, government policy, threats)
- improve organisational control and coordination of activities
- develop teamwork off the field. (p. 1)

Given these benefits of planning, why then do some people resist efforts to plan (Bryce, 2008)?

Resistance to Planning

Some people develop comfort zones. They do things a certain way because "We've always done it that way." To these individuals, trying to implement a plan to do something different or new is a challenge they do not wish to undertake. Sometimes people who have worked with an organization for many years respond to planning initiatives with "Why should we do this? We've done this a million times before, and we know no one really looks at these things. Then five years later they ask us to do it again, and they ignore us again." Finally, there are those who simply lack the ability to plan and are intimidated by the process. Good sport managers make planning a priority and learn how to deal effectively with those employees who resist the importance of planning.

Types of Plans

Sport managers must be able to develop both short-term and long-term plans. They must develop timetables so projects and events will take place as smoothly as possible. *Short-term planning* refers to planning projects and events that will occur within the next one to three years. For example, with the Olympic Games, test events in all venues are run within a year or two of the start of the Games. At a new stadium, contracts with concessionaires and security are finalized in the year before the stadium opens.

In contrast, *long-term planning* involves planning that extends three or more years. For example, the Olympic and Paralympic Games are awarded to a host city seven years before the flame is lit to open the Games in that city. Sport teams deciding to build new stadiums must begin working with architects and contractors at least five years before the first beverage is poured at a game. Within these long-term plans, short-term plans must be implemented. Returning to our stadium example, the people who work in Presentation (coordinating the music, announcements, etc., during an event) need to be able to work with the sound system (short-term planning). However, before a sound system in a venue can be checked, all the proper infrastructure for the power must be in place (long-term planning). All these plans must be carefully sequenced for the sport organization to be successful.

Long-term and short-term plans are not the only types of plans sport managers need to develop. For example, there are standing plans and single-use plans (Chelladurai, 2009). *Standing plans* refer to plans that are put in place and then referred to continuously as certain events repeat. For example, a facility manager who develops a plan for a security check of a venue before a home event would implement the plan repeatedly for each home event. *Single-use plans* refer to plans developed for events that may occur just once. For example, executives at a local Sport Commission may develop a parking plan for an event such as a Ryder Cup or Special Olympics World Games, which may be awarded to their city only one time.

The Planning Process

Sport organizations need to follow a set process to establish effective short-term and long-term plans. For some sport organizations, this process may begin with a vision statement. Other organizations will start with a mission statement and then take the following steps (adapted from VanderZwaag, 1998):

1. vision/mission statement
2. goals
3. objectives
4. tactics
5. roles
6. evaluation

The next sections examine each step in the planning process and use examples to illustrate the different steps. The focus is on the sport organization's front-office planning, rather than on-the-field plans such as the Detroit

Tigers' objective to win the World Series and the Stanford University basketball team's objective to win the NCAA women's basketball tournament. As a sport manager, you most likely will be working in off-the-field careers, so the focus of this chapter is on goals and objectives dealing with front-office matters such as increasing ticket sales or securing sponsorship packages. For sport organizations to effectively move into the future, they must establish both long- and short-term plans. Because sport governance issues are generally broad in nature and affect the entire sport organization, any course of action dealing with governance issues must be carefully planned.

Vision statements

A number of sport organizations begin their planning process by developing what is known as a vision statement. According to Heathfield (2007), a *vision statement* is

> a statement about what your organization wants to become. It should resonate with all members of the organization and help them feel proud, excited, and part of something much bigger than themselves. A vision [statement] should stretch the organization's capabilities and image of itself. It gives shape and direction to the organization's future.

Vision statements are different from mission statements in that vision statements focus on the organization's future aspirations and values while mission statements focus on an organization's purpose.

The vision statement for the Special Olympics (2012) is as follows:

> Special Olympics is an unprecedented global movement which, through quality sports training and competition, improves the lives of people with intellectual disabilities and, in turn, the lives of everyone they touch.

The vision statement of the Washington Games (2012) is as follows:

> The SUBWAY Washington Games will be recognized as one of the finest series of amateur sporting events in the Northwest, one of the best state games in the country and an effective sports marketing tool for youth obesity prevention in Washington.

Another useful example of a sport organization's vision statement is that of the International Paralympic Committee, which is presented in Chapter 11.

Mission statements

Sport organizations are a lot like sailboats. Without a rudder to steer, it does not matter how much wind there is; the boat will not go in its intended direction. It will still float, but it will not get where the crew wants it to go. What gives a sport organization its direction?

Direction is established early in the planning process with the organization's mission statement. As previously stated, a *mission statement* focuses on an organization's purpose. More specifically, it

1. describes who we are
2. describes what we do
3. uses concise terms
4. uses language that is understandable to people inside and outside the sport organization
5. communicates the organization's purpose, philosophy, and values

A well-written mission statement does not need to be a lengthy document; it may be only 30 to 40 words, or two or three sentences long. All organizational planning documents should flow from the mission statement. As you read the mission statements in this book, keep in mind they are living documents that are subject to change.

In this section we will use a minor league baseball team as an example, starting with the mission statements of existing franchises. The mission statement for the Mobile BayBears (2012), a AAA minor league baseball team is to

> provide the Gulf Coast Region the ability to enjoy America's National Pastime at Hank Aaron Stadium through cost affordable family fun & entertainment in a safe and enjoyable atmosphere. In addition we are committed to making a positive impact in the community thru our outreach programs and adding to the quality of life in our area.

Here is the mission statement for the Wilmington Blue Rocks (2012), another minor league baseball team:

> To be recognized as the area's best attraction by providing inexpensive family entertainment in a clean, safe, and festive atmosphere. To always work to improve the fan's experience, be regarded as a community leader and set the example of how to operate a successful professional minor league baseball club.

These mission statements are relatively similar. Both clearly state that minor league baseball is about fun and affordable family entertainment. Anyone who has attended a minor league baseball game recently would agree that these statements describe what it is all about—a fun atmosphere, inexpensive food, and between-inning promotional contests for fans of all ages.

Goals

Different textbooks use differing definitions for *goals* and *objectives*. Sometimes the terms are even used interchangeably. In this textbook, however, *goals* are defined as broad, qualitative statements that provide general direction for a sport organization. They are statements of purpose that are achievable (Mulrooney & Farmer, 2001). For example, a minor league base-ball team may have the following goals:

Goal #1 Increase attendance

Goal #2 Increase sponsorship revenues

Objectives

As opposed to goals, which are qualitative in nature, *objectives* are defined as quantitative statements that help a sport organization determine if it is fulfilling its goals. They are measurable, realistic, and clear (Parkhouse, Turner, & Milloch, 2012). Because objectives are quantitative and can be measured (Mulrooney & Farmer, 2001), they are useful tools in evaluating employee and organizational performance. To be measurable, objectives always contain quantifiable measures such as numbers, percentages, or monetary values. Objectives are tied directly to achieving specific goals. For example:

Goal #1 Increase attendance

Objective #1 Increase game-day walk-up sales by 5 percent

Objective #2 Increase group ticket sales by 10 percent

Goal #2 Increase sponsorship revenues

Objective #1 Secure five new corporate sponsors

Objective #2 Increase the value of existing sponsorships by 5 percent

Measurable objectives are important in two ways: First, they can be used in employee and organizational evaluations and, second, they are necessary because it is difficult to manage something you cannot measure!

Tactics

Once sport managers establish their goals and objectives, they must determine specifically how to achieve them. These specific how-to steps are called tactics. (Some textbooks use the term *strategies,* but to avoid confusion with strategic planning principles, *tactics* is the term used here.) *Tactics* are the specific actions sport managers take to achieve organizational objectives. For example:

Goal #1 Increase attendance

Objective #1 Increase game-day walk-up sales by 5 percent

Tactic #1 Add two new promotional nights (bobblehead giveaway and $1 hot dog night)

Tactic #2 Purchase ten 30-second advertising slots on the new local country radio station

Goal #2 Increase sponsorship revenues

Objective #1 Secure five new corporate sponsors

Tactic #1 Have each sales rep contact 10 new local corporations

Tactic #2 Offer special first-year benefits to new sponsors (extra tickets)

Roles

After the tactics have been determined, the responsibilities for carrying out those tactics must be assigned. Roles refer to the organizational units specifically responsible for carrying out the sport organization's tactics and the behaviors needed to achieve success (VanderZwaag, 1998). For example:

Goal #1 Increase attendance

Objective #1 Increase game-day walk-up sales by 5 percent

Tactic #1 Add two new promotional nights (bobble-head giveaway and $1 hot dog night)

Role Ticket Office, marketing

Goal #2 Increase sponsorship revenues

Objective #1 Secure five new corporate sponsors

Tactic #1 Have each sales rep contact 10 new local corporations

Role Marketing, Sales

Evaluation

In the final step in the planning process, sport managers must evaluate the planning process to see if they are fulfilling the organization's mission statement by successfully completing stated goals, objectives, tactics, and roles. For example:

Goal #1 Increase attendance

Objective #1 Increase game-day walk-up sales by 5 percent

Tactic #1 Add two new promotional nights (bobble-head giveaway and $1 hot dog night)

Role Ticket Office, marketing

Evaluation Determine the actual percentage increase and compare to 5 percent target. Reward responsible employees appropriately.

Goal #2 Increase sponsorship revenues

Objective #1 Secure five new corporate sponsors

Tactic #1 Have each sales rep contact 10 new local corporations

Role Marketing, Sales

Evaluation Determine the actual number of new sponsors and compare to target (five new sponsors). Reward responsible employees appropriately.

This brief example shows how the planning process flows from one step to the next. It also shows that the planning process does not consist of a number of separate, fragmented steps but rather is a seamless garment. The process is part of the big picture of the entire organization. Note, too, that all the steps in the process can be traced directly back to, and should be consistent with, the organization's mission statement.

The Role of Planning in Governance

Sport governance is complex and ever-changing. Sport organizations can be as small as a city soccer league or as massive as the Olympic and Paralympic Movements. Whatever the size of the sport organization, those in charge of the governance structures must plan accordingly. Examples of organizations that planned both well and poorly come from the Olympic Games. Local organizing committees for the Montreal 1976 and the Athens 2004 Summer Games ended up running million dollar and euro deficits from construction cost overruns. Meanwhile, the London 2012 Olympic and Paralympic Games came in under budget. An organization without a well-thought-out and organized plan complete with a mission statement, goals, objectives, tactics, roles, and an evaluation system is destined to fail. Remember: If you fail to plan, you plan to fail.

ORGANIZING

The traditional view of organizing revolves around staffing. We usually think of establishing tasks, determining who will be responsible for those tasks, and then placing those people into a hierarchy, commonly illustrated by an organizational chart. *Organizing* can be defined as "the process of delegating and coordinating tasks and resources to achieve objectives" (Lussier & Kimball, 2009, p. 122).

An organizational chart is a diagram showing all positions and reporting relationships within an organization. Sport organizations vary from small units with only a few employees to large, complex organizations with numerous employees. Many of the larger ones are departmentalized into subunits according to the division of labor within the organization and the responsibility of members within each subunit. Exhibit 2.1, an example of an organizational chart for a departmentalized sport organization, depicts the division of labor and coordination of divided tasks among members of the organization. The organization might have been subdivided differently, by business function (Exhibit 2.2), strategic business unit structure (Exhibit 2.3) or geographic region (Exhibit 2.4).

In all cases, well-established structures are important for sport organizations. According to Daft (2010) organizational structure is a "formal

Organizational chart for college athletic department organized by internal department.   *exhibit*   **2.1**

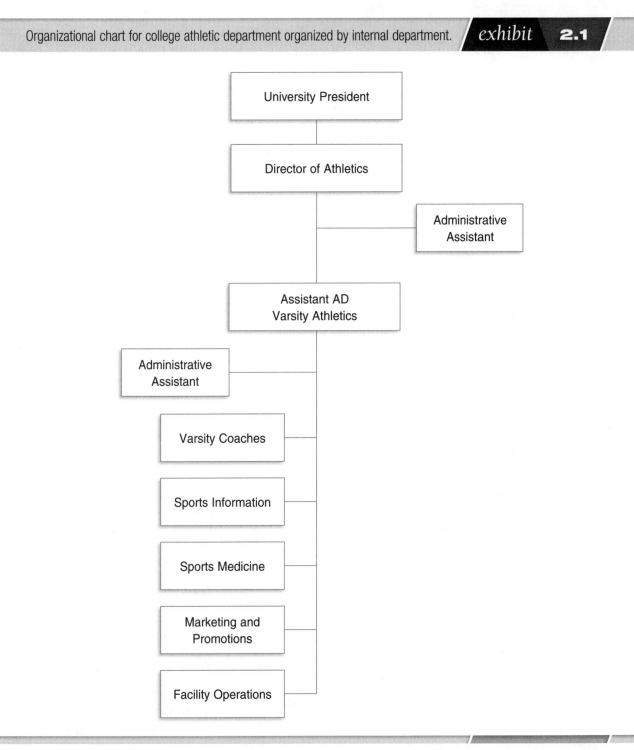

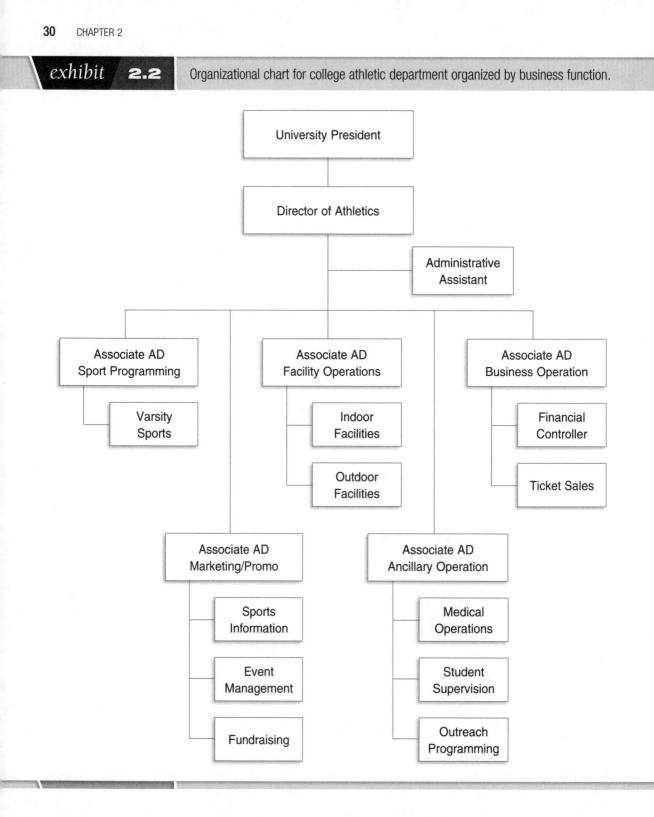

Organizational chart for sporting goods company organized by strategic business unit. *exhibit* 2.3

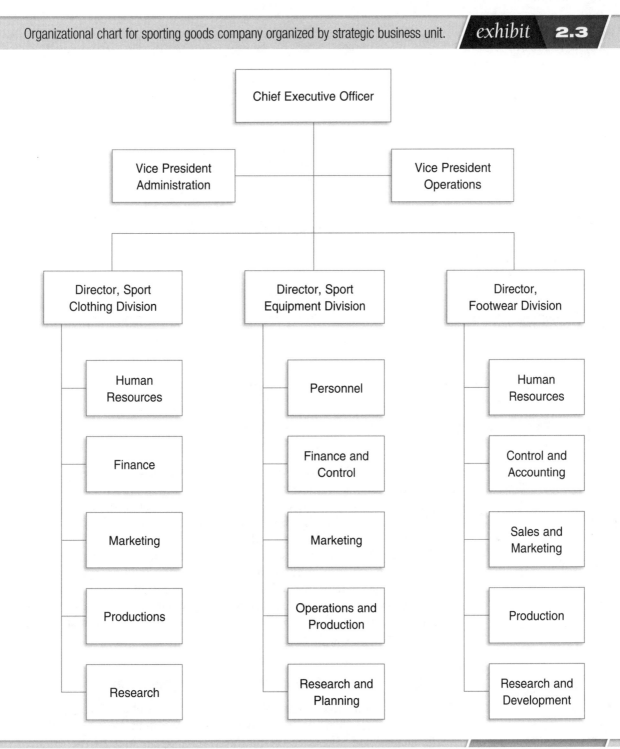

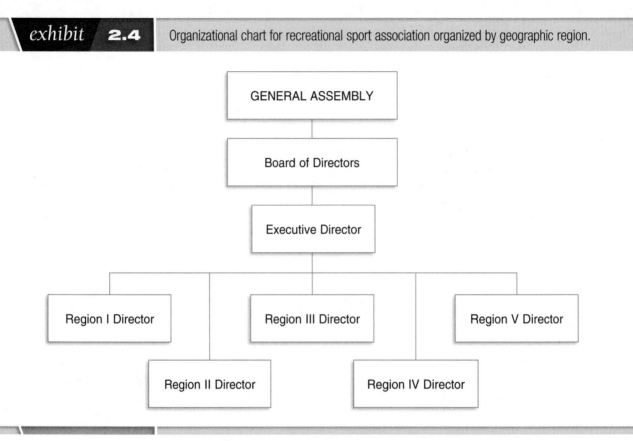

exhibit **2.4** Organizational chart for recreational sport association organized by geographic region.

system of task and authority relationships that control how people coordinate their actions and use of resources to achieve organizational goals" (p. 7). Organizational structure can be examined through the lens of organizational design as well, where organizational design is the method by which sport managers "select and manage aspects of structure and culture" (Jones, 2010, p. 9). This concept of organizational design indicates that structure is not only about the static set of tasks in an organization, but also about what influences the organization's culture. This structural influence can be seen in sport governance organizations. Despite their similarities, the structures of sport organizations also have elements unique to their sport industry segment.

Structural Features of Sport Governance Organizations

Governing organizations generally have several hierarchical levels of work units and subunits. Paid staff members usually maintain the organization's headquarters and take care of the day-to-day operations of the organization. As stated previously, for high school sport, this is the state or provincial athletic association, for example, the Iowa High School Athletic Association (IHSAA). Major professional sport leagues operate league offices such as the National Basketball Association (NBA) League Office in New York City. The headquarters for the IOC resides in Lausanne, Switzerland, while the IPC is housed in Bonn, Germany. The sport managers employed in these offices have titles such as Executive Director, League Vice President, and Marketing Director. These employees keep the organization moving along, and their responsibilities include budgeting, staffing, scheduling tournaments and events, marketing, and media relations. However, this level of the organization does not typically set policies dealing with governance issues. Rather, those sport managers implement the policies determined by another level of the structure.

Most major sport organizations are nonprofit organizations with voluntary membership—not individual people, but institutions or nations. The membership of these organizations—not the paid staff—determines their policies, rules, and regulations. The vehicle for setting these policies usually takes the form of regularly scheduled, often annual, meetings of the membership. Sometimes called General Assemblies or Annual Business Meetings, at these gatherings the members vote to establish policies and rules or to modify existing ones. For example, at the Winter Paralympic Games, Nordic Skiing holds its own Sport Assembly, and the voting members, each representing his or her home nation, vote on issues such as acceptable equipment modifications or the length of various races. While professional sports leagues are for profit, they still have meetings at which they make governance decisions. Every year, for example, at the Baseball Winter Meetings, representatives of minor league baseball teams vote on issues such as draft rules and stadium specifications.

These General Assemblies and Annual Business Meetings often appoint a President for the organization as well as an Executive Committee or Executive Council. Sometimes the organization needs to make adjustments between General Assembly meetings, and so it vests the responsibility and authority to do so in the hands of the President and the Executive Committee. Executive Committees also generate ideas for the Annual General Assemblies to consider. The Executive Committee for the IOC has eight members selected from the Annual General Assembly, plus the President. (Mr. Jacques Rogge of Belgium served as president for over ten years beginning in 2002, and a new president will be elected in September 2013.) For most sport organizations, the true power rests in the hands of the Executive Committee.

Naturally, the governance structures within each industry segment differ. This section merely gives an overview of some important organizational characteristics and shows how organizational charts for sport governance organizations contain elements different from a traditional sport front-office organizational chart (Exhibits 2.1–2.4). In each industry segment chapter, the organizational structures for that industry segment are explained in more detail.

The Role of Organizing in Governance

The organizational structures in any sport governing body dictate the flow of information and the setting of policies and rules and act as philosophical statements about the organization. Power is distributed differently within these structures. Sometimes power rests with the membership, and other times it rests with the Executive Committee or the President. It is important to note that the organizational charts for sport governing structures parallel traditional organizational charts with one difference: In traditional organizational charts we see people or titles in certain places; in governance structures we see governance units. This difference shows us how governing bodies transcend individual responsibility and also shows us the big picture.

DECISION MAKING

The decision-making process is essential in sport governance. We all make decisions every day. Some decisions are very simple. You chose what to wear to class on Monday. What did you consider when deciding what clothes to wear? You probably considered the weather, what was clean, what matched, whom you might sit next to in class, or if you had to give a presentation. Even this simplistic example shows the two basic parts of decision making—gathering and analyzing information. Sport managers must also make decisions on an everyday basis (after they decide what to wear to work).

Routine and Complex Decisions

Sport managers face a variety of decisions in the workplace, some of which are routine and some of which are not routine. *Routine decisions,* sometimes referred to as *programmed decisions,* are straightforward, repetitive, and mundane (The Times 100, 2012). During a Brooklyn Nets basketball game, if a toilet overflows, the decision to call Maintenance to fix it is easy. When the University of Nebraska Sports Information Office is running short of copy paper (a recurring situation), the decision to order more paper is routine.

All decisions are not so easy. Many problems are unique. Complex, nonroutine decisions are novel and referred to as *nonprogrammed decisions* (The Times 100, 2012). For example, baseball stadiums often shoot fireworks after the home team hits a home run. But suppose Stadium Operations personnel discover that some fireworks have been stolen. What types of decisions do they have to make about public safety? Which public safety departments need to be informed? What does the public need to know? Or suppose your local community is struck by a natural disaster such as the 2011 Joplin, Missouri, tornado or Hurricane Sandy in 2012? Do sporting events such as high school, college, or professional games, or even the New York City Marathon go on as scheduled? What about diverting resources to those events from people who may be without power or heat? Or suppose you are a high school athletic director facing budget cuts. How do you decide which teams' budgets will be decreased and which won't, and how will you implement those decisions? These examples illustrate the complex decision making sport managers face.

The Rational Model

One item is of great importance to sport managers when they make decisions: They must have an organized, thoughtful process to follow. Decisions of great magnitude cannot be left to chance. Rather, the sport manager's thought process must be detailed and organized. One such process, the Rational Model based on Robbins (1990), is outlined here:

1. Identify the REAL problem.
2. Identify the decision objective.
3. Gather all pertinent information.
4. Identify any hurdles.
5. Brainstorm for alternatives.
6. Narrow down the options.
7. Examine the pros and cons of each option.
8. Make the decision.
9. Evaluate the decision.

To illustrate this decision-making process, assume that you are the Athletic Director at Big State University (BSU), home of the Fightin' Saugers. Recently, a group of female athletes came to you asking to add rowing and lacrosse to your roster of women's sports. You are aware of the Title IX regulations that pertain to providing appropriate opportunities for female athletes, particularly the "proportionality" interpretation, whereby the ratio of male-to-female athletes must reflect the ratio of male-to-female students in the greater university population. Currently, the student body is 53 percent women and 47 percent men, while the Athletic Department's athlete breakdown is 35 percent female athletes and 65 percent male athletes. You know the financial implications of adding sports, but the group is also threatening legal action if the university does not do as they are asking.

Let's apply the Rational Model:

1. *Identify the REAL problem.* The real problem is that the university is not in compliance with Title IX, which guarantees equal athletic opportunities for men and women athletes.

2. *Identify the decision objective.* The decision objective is to bring the department into compliance.

3. *Gather all pertinent information.* Look at the different program areas Title IX covers, such as facilities, coaches, equipment, travel and per diem, scholarships, and so forth.

4. *Identify any hurdles.* You are aware not only of tangible hurdles, such as budgetary constraints, but also of intangible hurdles, such as people's attitudes toward women's sports.

5. *Brainstorm for alternatives.* Brainstorming is "the process of suggesting many possible alternatives without evaluation" (Lussier & Kimball, 2009, p. 454). The idea is to list all possible ideas now and sort through them later. In this case, the options could include adding sports without increasing the budget, asking the university for additional funding, cutting some men's nonrevenue sports to free up money, dropping football, and finding additional funding sources such as increasing sponsorship dollars, finding new donors, or increasing ticket prices for the major revenue sports. Not all the ideas may be reasonable, but when brainstorming, remember to put all ideas on the table.

6. *Narrow down the options.* Then narrow down your list of options to three or four. Let's say that the best options appear to be finding additional funding sources and dropping some men's nonrevenue sports.

7. *Examine the pros and cons of each option.* Carefully weigh the pros and cons of these options. Dropping men's sports is a quick fix in terms of budgets, but in terms of public relations, it would be a nightmare. Finding additional sponsorship dollars is a possibility as the university is located in a major metropolitan area, but you may be limited in how much you can ask for. Increasing ticket prices will help, but the increase will be limited to how much fans will pay, and the increase will not finance the entire venture.

8. *Make the decision.* You decide on a combination approach, using the tactics of finding additional sponsorship dollars and increasing ticket prices.

9. *Evaluate the decision.* These tactics will have to be evaluated over the coming years. Once the teams are in place, BSU's Athletic Department will need to continually account for sponsorship dollars and fans' responses to increased ticket prices by measuring the impact on tickets sold.

This simplified version of a very complex decision-making process illustrates how an organized approach to decision making can help a sport manager decide on a course of action.

The SLEEPE Principle

Another decision-making method, which takes a more global view of the organization and the implications of sport managers' decisions, is called the SLEEPE Principle. The decisions sport managers make are often very public, subject to scrutiny by the media, fans, and the general public. Therefore, when sport managers make decisions, they must be able to use their conceptual skills to see the big picture. By using the SLEEPE method, decision makers can analyze decisions, especially decisions affecting policy development or interpretation. Originally set up as the SLEEP model by W. Moore at Ohio State University in 1990, this decision-making model has since been modified (Hums, 2006; Hums, Moorman, & Wolff, 2002) and applied in the sport industry to help sport managers see the big picture by analyzing the many different ramifications of their decisions. The components of the SLEEPE Principle are as follows:

S—Social
L—Legal
E—Economic
E—Ethical
P—Political
E—Educational

Using this model helps sport managers understand how their decisions will be viewed in different ways by various constituencies in society. The following example will illustrate this:

You are the Athletic Director at Big State University. Your potential NFL first-round draft pick, star running back Clinton Blanford, has been arrested and is in jail on charges of domestic violence. Your team is headed for a bowl game to determine the national championship. Of course, this story has received extensive national coverage in the press and is the talk of the bowl season. The decision you have to make, in conjunction with your head coach, is whether to allow Blanford to play in the upcoming bowl game. Let's use the SLEEPE Principle to analyze this situation:

S—SOCIAL. Look at the social ramifications of the decision: Allowing Blanford to play makes the statement to society in general that domestic violence is not serious enough to warrant his not playing in the game. This decision could lead to protests by both on- and off-campus groups, including faculty, students, and alumni groups, as well as community organizations opposing domestic violence. It also suggests winning the bowl game is more important to the Athletic Department than standing up against domestic violence by athletes. On the other hand, if you do not allow Blanford to play, many fans and university supporters will be angry, especially if your team loses the game. However, you will have made a statement that BSU will not tolerate this sort of player misconduct.

L—LEGAL.   From the legal standpoint, one may argue that Blanford should be allowed to play because he has not actually been convicted of anything yet. However, extending the definition of legal beyond just the traditional legal system, one can ask, has he violated team or university rules related to such conduct? How would a student who is not an athlete be treated by the university? If he does not play and the team loses, is it possible to hold him in some way legally responsible for the loss of revenue resulting from losing the game (Moorman & Hums, 1999)?

E—ECONOMIC.   The economic ramifications for both the university and Blanford himself are as follows: Allowing him to play maximizes the opportunity to win the game, meaning increased revenue for the university, especially in terms of sales of licensed products and perhaps ticket sales for the upcoming year. Keeping the team highly ranked will help with recruiting and potential future earnings. On the personal level, if Blanford plays well, he could increase his potential professional earnings. On the other hand, if he does not play, there is greater potential that BSU would lose the game, the national championship, and all the revenue streams associated with these events. Blanford's draft status could suffer, costing him money in his contract and potential endorsement deals.

E—ETHICAL.   Next are the ethical considerations. Saying Blanford cannot play takes the ethical stance that domestic violence is wrong and will not be tolerated. It also says athletes are not above the law and must be held accountable for their actions. On the other hand, allowing him to play may make the ethical statement that a person is innocent until proven guilty. He has not yet been tried by a court of law, so he should not be convicted in the court of public opinion. Of all the parts of the SLEEPE Principle, this is the most complex and challenging to sport managers.

P—POLITICAL.   Politically there are a number of constituencies to consider. In this context, the term *political* is not limited to elected officials only; it is broader, including any groups or stakeholders who may exert some type of political power or influence in a given situation. In our example, if Blanford is allowed to play, the university's faculty, staff, and administration will most likely make public statements about the decision. They may exert public pressure on the school's Athletic Department. The school's conference or even the NCAA may also make statements about the decision. Since BSU is a state university, members of the state legislature may also voice their opinions. If he is not allowed to play, some of these same groups may issue supportive comments, publicly supporting and strengthening the Athletic Department's stance.

E—EDUCATIONAL. Finally, there is the educational component to consider. This aspect of the SLEEPE Principle is used only when the decision situation is in an educational setting. If Blanford is allowed to play, it certainly makes the statement that athletics, rather than education, is the primary concern of the Athletic Department and, correspondingly, the university itself. However, not allowing him to play says that, at this university, athletics is not above the law, that education is the primary focus—not winning football games. One can also apply the Educational aspect to evaluate what the sport managers involved learned from this situation and their response to it.

This example illustrates the complexity and public nature of many decisions sport managers face on a daily basis. Athlete misconduct, substance abuse, equity and diversity, violence, economic challenges, and other pressing issues are present in the sport industry just as they are in general society. Because of the far-reaching ramifications of their decisions, forward-thinking sport managers must learn to examine all potential results of and reactions to their decisions before they make them.

This section outlined various decision-making models sport managers can incorporate when solving problems. Often, sport managers' decisions will be ethical in nature. Do the same decision-making models apply? To address the importance of dealing with ethical issues, Chapter 4 discusses ethical decision making.

The Role of Decision Making in Sport Governance

Sport managers dealing with governance issues are faced with decisions that have far-reaching implications. Their decisions, from simple to complex, shape the direction of the organization. The decisions sport managers make are open to public scrutiny and media discussion. As such, sport managers must make sure they have a concrete method for analyzing any decisions they need to make.

SUMMARY

S port managers need to be able to perform the major management functions of planning, organizing, leading, and evaluating. This chapter focused on planning, organizing, and one subset of leading—decision making. It is important to have a solid foundation in these areas before further examining specific industry segments.

Planning is the basis for everything a sport manager does. Sport managers must make both short- and long-term plans. The planning process is sequential: Organizational goals, objectives, tactics, roles, and evaluation all flow from the mission statement. Sport organizations are organized with different levels of responsibility. Determining the tasks an organization needs to accomplish and the people needed to accomplish those tasks is essential for organizational success. Sport managers must make decisions every day. Some of their decisions are routine; others are unique. Two structured methods to help sport managers make solid decisions are the Rational Model of decision making and the SLEEPE Principle. By mastering these important skills, sport managers can successfully conduct the business of governance and policy development in their sport organizations.

case STUDY

MANAGERIAL FUNCTIONS

You are the General Manager for the Elkhart Komets, a struggling AA baseball franchise. Playing in the old, poorly maintained Riverfront Stadium and stuck with a dull logo (a gold star with a silver tail), you need to make some decisions on how to increase revenues. Keep in mind that this is a minor league team, and you have no control over which players you can acquire.

- Use the Rational Model of decision making to determine your course of action.

CHAPTER questions

1. Locate organizational charts for three different sport organizations. Compare and contrast the titles and structures of each. Why are some aspects similar and others different?
2. Choose one of the following:
    - minor league baseball team
    - public assembly facility
    - college or university athletic department
    - high school athletic department
    - charity 5K run/walk
    - campus recreation department
    - sporting goods store

After you choose one of these sport organizations, develop the following:

    a. mission statement

    b. one goal

    c. two objectives for that goal

    d. two tactics for each objective

    e. the roles for each tactic

3. For a sport organization of your choosing, identify two situations that would involve routine decision making and two situations that would involve complex decision making.

REFERENCES

Australian Sports Commission. (2012). Planning. Retrieved from http://www.ausport.gov.au/supporting/clubs/governance/planning

Bryce, T. (2008). Why we resist planning. Retrieved from http://www.articlesbase.com/management-articles/why-we-resist-planning-406566.html

Chelladurai, P. (2009). *Managing organizations for sport and physical activity: A systems perspective* (3d ed.). Scottsdale, AZ: Holcomb Hathaway.

Daft, R. I. (2010). *Organizational theory and design* (10th ed.). Mason, OH: South-Western, Cengage Learning.

Heathfield, S. M. (2007). Build a strategic framework: Mission statement, vision, values. Retrieved from http://humanresources. about.com/cs/strategic planning1/a/strategicplan.htm

Hums, M. A. (2006, May). Analyzing the impact of changes in classification systems: A sport management analysis model. Paper presented at the VISTA 2006 International Paralympic Committee Congress, Bonn, Germany.

Hums, M. A., Moorman, A. M., & Wolff, E. (2002). Examining disability sport from a sport management perspective. *Proceedings of the VISTA 2001 Conference,* Vienna, Austria.

Jones, G. R. (2010). *Organizational theory, design, and change.* Upper Saddle River, NJ: Prentice Hall.

Lussier, R. N., & Kimball, D. (2009). *Applied sport management skills.* Champaign, IL: Human Kinetics.

Mobile BayBears. (2012). Mission statement. Retrieved from http://web.minorleaguebaseball.com/team4/page.jsp?ymd=20110803&content_id=22714656&vkey=team4_t417&fext=.jsp&sid=t417

Moorman, A. M., & Hums, M. A. (1999). Student athlete liability for NCAA violations and breach of contract. *Journal of Legal Aspects of Sport, 9*(3), 163–174.

Mulrooney, A., & Farmer, P. (2001). Managing the facility. In B. L. Parkhouse (Ed.), *The management of sport: Its foundation and application* (3d ed., pp. 272–297). Boston: McGraw-Hill.

Parkhouse, B., Turner, B., & Milloch, K. S. (2012). *Marketing for sport business and success.* Dubuque, IA: Kendall Hunt.

Robbins, S. P. (1990). *Organizational theory: Structure, design and applications* (3d ed.). Englewood Cliffs, NJ: Prentice Hall.

Special Olympics. (2012). Mission/vision. Retrieved from http://info.specialolympics.org/Special+Olympics+Public+Website/English/About_Us/Mission_Vision/default.htm

The Times 100. (2012). Strategy theory. Retrieved from http://businesscasestudies.co.uk/business-theory/strategy/decision-making.html

VanderZwaag, H. J. (1998). *Policy development in sport management.* Westport, CT: Praeger.

Washington Games. (2012). WG about. Retrieved from http://www.washingtongames.org/site223.php

Wilmington Blue Rocks. (2012). Mission statement. Retrieved from http://web.minorleaguebaseball.com/team1/page.jsp?ymd=20090427&content_id=571313&vkey=team1_t426&fext=.jsp&sid=t426

Strategic Management and Policy Development

As discussed in Chapter 1, sport is an industry with considerable reach and impact on consumer-spending indices and the economy in general. Sport is acknowledged as big business, given the sheer numbers of participants, its exponential growth over the past 30 years, and the healthy percentage of the economic marketplace attributed to sport worldwide (DeSchriver & Mahony, 2011). Ozanian's (1995) earlier comment still applies: "What's all the excitement about? Sports is not simply another big business. It is one of the fastest-growing industries in the U.S., and it is intertwined with virtually every aspect of the economy . . . sports is everywhere, accompanied by the sound of a cash register ringing incessantly" (p. 30).

The magnitude and reach of the sport industry is important in terms of economic impact, employment opportunities, and consumer interest. The extent of the business of sport is understandable, considering the vast numbers of both participants and activities involved. The popularity of different sporting activities, for participants and spectators, provides a rationale for the proliferation of organizations delivering the business of sport. Such organizations are involved in providing entertainment (amateur and professional spectator sport) or facilities (gyms and clubs for participation); offering structures within which competitive sport is delivered (minor, scholastic, or college, and club sport leagues and championships); designing and manufacturing equipment used by all levels of participants (clothing, sporting equipment, and other apparel); and promoting and delivering sporting competitions and festivals (World Championships and Paralympic Games). These organizations can be public or private, for-profit or nonprofit. Regardless of the specifics of the business, sport as a consumer product is massive, technological advances occur daily, and focused marketing and promotion efforts are resulting in the further globalization of the sport industry (Markovits & Rensmann, 2010).

Without a doubt, the competition is fierce and the stakes high. For students interested in a career in the sport industry, learning the breadth and depth of the businesses and understanding how these organizations are strategically managed and governed is an important, early step in defining your career. According to Mahony and Howard (2001), the need for effective and strategic management practices and the development of meaningful policy has never been more important for sport organizations. Therefore, the focus of this chapter is the development of business strategy, the implementation of the principles of strategic management, and the development of policy in sport organizations. Even though the 1990s and early 21st century represented a period of expansion in the sport industry, continued growth will only result from the implementation of creative business strategies (Stonehouse, Campbell, Hamill, & Purdie, 2004). It follows, then, that strategic management is an important concept to the sport manager. Future sport managers need to ask themselves:

- Is there a link between the macro approach (assessing the organization as a whole) to strategic management and what a manager does as an individual?
- Will strategic management enable managerial activities to be more successful in defining and setting policy for the organization?
- Is it important to understand strategic management and policy development in order to understand the governance of a sport organization and its pursuit of effectiveness?

The answer to each question is a resounding "Yes." This chapter provides further insight into the importance of strategic management and policy development for sport organizations.

STRATEGIC MANAGEMENT

S *trategy* refers to the plans and actions implemented to achieve a goal in the most efficient and effective manner. Strategy is a common tool used by organizations as a whole or in part to achieve a goal or gain some advantage. Chapter 2 described *tactics* as the specific steps that need to be followed to implement the strategy. You might consider strategy an organization's game plan. Sport is the perfect example to illustrate the concept because strategy is a normal part of competitive sports. A coach develops a game plan or strategy based on her team's strengths and weaknesses in comparison to the competition. The plan, of course, is to negate the opposition's strengths and find ways to capitalize on the strengths of one's own team. Managers of organizations seek these same results. They set goals and strive to realize them through a series of tactics or steps that will help the organization reach a goal. Strategy, then, is an important component in the management of an organization because it helps paint a picture of where the organization is headed. Again, tactics relate to the specific steps used to carry out the broader game plan. Let's focus our attention on the development of overall organizational strategy by first defining *strategic management*.

Defining Strategic Management

The terms *strategic management, business strategy,* and *organizational strategy* are often used synonymously to refer to both a purpose and a plan of action enabling an organization to reach its goals (Belcourt & McBey, 2010). For the purpose of this text, we will use the term *strategic management*. According to Pearce and Robinson (2007), strategic management

- involves decisions and action plans evolving from the organization's mission,
- takes into account both the internal and the external environment,
- involves both short- and long-term objectives (tactics) and plans,
- requires strategic choices in budget resource allocation with respect to tasks, people, structures, technologies, and reward systems.

To summarize, strategic management involves the planning, organizing, leading, and evaluating of an organization's strategy-related decisions and actions (Pearce & Robinson, 2007). On a larger scale, the term *corporate strategy* refers to global strategy for the larger *corporation,* an entity that may include several smaller businesses. Thus, a strategy can be developed in a global organizational sense to deal with corporate-wide plans (corporate-level strategy); it can deal with factors impacting the main organizational mission (business- or management-level strategy); or it can be implemented to enable specific managerial functions such as planning or decision making (functional-level strategy) (Pearce & Robinson, 2007). See Exhibit 3.1.

exhibit   **3.1**   Defining levels of strategy.

Type of Strategy	Definition
Corporate-Level Strategy	General, overall strategic planning for the entire organization and all its business
Business-Level Strategy	Specific, individualized strategic planning for individual products or services
Functional-Level Strategy	Specific, individualized strategic planning concepts implemented by personnel

For example, Maple Leaf Sports & Entertainment Ltd. is the parent company managing the Toronto Raptors basketball and the Toronto Maple Leafs hockey franchises. The organization's corporate strategy might involve a focus on growing the games of basketball and hockey by encouraging grassroots development and opportunities for participation and strengthening the national fan base for these teams. The business-level strategy of the Raptors and Maple Leafs might include a commitment to a certain budget to hire staff and run programming, thereby encouraging the accomplishment of the corporate goals. Partnerships with other sport delivery groups and contributions to both facilities and program development might result. The outcome of these investments will strengthen the functional-level strategies, such as delivering a 3-on-3 mini hoops program for kids prior to an NBA game, by helping to develop a following in a particular sport, widening the fan base, and enabling marketing activities that promote ticket sales. Each level of strategy is critically important and contributes to the overall success of the organization. Then tactics such as advertising, acquiring facilities, and developing rules and regulations are employed to enact the overall strategy.

Strategic management often occurs as a result of some environmental factor impacting the operation of the organization and its ability to achieve defined goals. Specifically, strategy involves creating mission, goals, and objectives statements, along with action plans (tactics) accounting for both the organization's environment and its competition (Stonehouse et al., 2004). With an ultimate goal or several goals in mind, the organization's decision makers will maneuver activities and decisions based upon factors in the organization's environment to achieve them. Strategic management is dynamic, both short and long term in nature, and sometimes results in structural changes to organizational arrangement.

Mintzberg (1988) offered the five Ps of strategy as a way to understand the meaning of strategic management. He suggested that strategic management involves the following:

1. *Planning:* setting a course of action to deal with a situation

2. *Purpose:* actions that are sometimes deliberate and other times emergent that deal with change and opportunity

3. *Ploy:* some specific maneuver to deal with an issue

4. *Position:* the location of the organization relative to its business and competitors

5. *Perspective:* the culture or perspective of the organization

Remember that organizational strategy involves not only goals and objectives but also the tactics by which goals are achieved (Mintzberg, Lampel, Quinn, & Ghoshal, 2002). The chief executives of the organization commonly develop business strategy.

Although defining specific business strategy is important, it is not more important than executing the strategic management plan. According to Belcourt & McBey (2010), this is accomplished by

1. defining the vision or clear purpose

2. converting the vision to measurable objectives

3. defining a plan to achieve the end goal

4. implementing the plan

5. measuring the results and revising the plan based upon actual versus planned events.

The flow of information leading to strategic action involves looking backward and forward prior to assessing the current organizational environment. Managers will evaluate historical, current, and forecasted data in light of the values and priorities of the organization's stakeholders (Pearce & Robinson, 2007). Stakeholders are usually subdivided groups of professionals, volunteers, and customers who have an interest in the product or service being developed.

To be effective, an organization must create a good fit between its strategy, organizational structure, and governance plan (Slack & Parent, 2006). This means the managerial activities related to governance discussed in Chapter 2 are critical to success. If those sport managers responsible for planning, organizing, and decision making are not cognizant of their environment and in tune with the mission and action plans of the organization, then outcomes are bound to be ineffective. Consider the negative results likely to occur if the United States Olympic Committee (USOC) were to work at cross-purposes with the national governing bodies (NGBs). The result of divergent policy or unacknowledged shifts in the environment could lead to chaotic, illogical management illustrated by inconsistent decision making, poor planning, and inadequate organization. For instance, suppose the USOC were to establish a common policy dictating how athletes were selected for the Olympic Teams but not effectively accounting for the differences between selecting an individual athlete in track and field versus a team sport athlete in volleyball. The end result might involve selecting the wrong athletes and might well be illustrated by decreased medal performances at the Olympic Games.

Planning and organizing are critical components of the process, because determining goals and the means to achieve them (tactics) are core items of strategic management. After all, it's hard to achieve success if you cannot define it and the steps needed to achieve it. Developing policies that empower action are equally vital. However, perhaps even more important to the concept of strategic management is strategic decision making. Knowing what to do at the right time is a critical component of strategic management.

Strategic Decision Making

As discussed in Chapter 2, decision making is the act of deciding a course of action based on the available alternatives related to a particular issue. Strategic decision making attaches a global organizational perspective to individual decisions. Strategic decision making usually involves top management decisions related to substantial resources. The long-term prosperity of the organization may even be affected, as strategic decisions sometimes have enduring effects. Strategic decision making involves forecasting both the environment and the effects of a particular decision in the acquisition of long-term goals. Normally, several alternatives and "if–then" scenarios are played out to gain perspective on the results of the decision. Strategic decision making is employed in an attempt to ensure the most profitable decision is made. Follow-up evaluations are used to promptly correct negative outcomes that might accrue once a decision is made. Examples of common strategic decisions in sport organizations include developing partnerships with sponsors or other organizations, long-term planning, establishing the organizational brand, and dramatic shifts in programming.

Decision making in sport organizations is among the manager's most important functions (Chelladurai, 2009). Although some decisions will be routine and repetitive with precedent and policy defining the decision choices, others will involve unique situations with little in the way of established guidelines to assist the decision maker (Amis & O'Brien, 2005). Given the magnitude and importance of the outcome to the entire organization, some decisions require business strategy. In each case, a procedure for framing and solving the problem is critical to ensure a well-thought-out decision. In line with the Rational Model of decision making presented in Chapter 2, Chelladurai (2009) summarizes strategic decision making in the following steps:

1. defining the problem
2. listing all possible alternatives, taking into consideration the internal and external organizational environments
3. assessing the pros and cons of the alternatives

4. considering the global and the long-term impact of the alternatives

5. selecting the best course of action.

Step 4 is included in order that the best and most strategic decision for the overall organization is considered, emphasizing the importance of strategy in sport management.

Good decisions are made when the data is accurate and the means of using it are appropriate. In business, finding and analyzing information and gaining insight from the data to guide decision making is referred to as *analytics*. While coaches and athletes have traditionally used sport statistics to guide decision making in games and events, more recently analytics has been emphasized in managing the sport organization. For example, sport marketing has become a highly data-driven process, and organizations use consumer demographics and perceptions obtained from surveys or other research to develop strategies to enhance the consumption or use of certain products. Sport managers define their general market by using data on size (e.g., numbers of customers), trading radius (e.g., distance customers will travel), demographics (e.g., male vs. female customers, age, income, etc.), psychographics (e.g., personal likes and dislikes), and future trends (e.g., impact of changing game times). Data obtained from sales records, customer comments, account records, complaints, and online interactions may be used in decision making. Organizations may also intentionally source such data through customer questionnaires, mystery shoppers, focus groups, and computerized surveys. Using data from websites and social networking sites gathered via technology also plays an important role in decision making.

The Importance of Strategy in Sport Management

Sport organizations must embrace strategic management practices to maximize their potential for several reasons:

1. TO PLAN EFFECTIVELY.   Strategy is extremely important because sport organizations have historically had reputations for ineffective planning. Many amateur sport groups developed informally and were dominated by volunteer, nonprofessional staff. When the stakes are high, poor management can mean not getting to the medal podium or losing a billion-dollar product line. It is accepted that planning is the foundation of effective strategic management.

2. TO CAPITALIZE ON OPPORTUNITIES.   Capitalizing on opportunity is enhanced by the tenets of strategic management. A turbulent environment can result in a warp-speed, frenetic business climate. Only those organizations with a strategy and an understanding of alternatives will truly capitalize on the opportunities. Suppose that you manage a privately owned fitness club and that you, the owner, and the three investors who provided the original capital to start the club have engaged in regular meetings, charting strategy for the current and future activities of the club. Now suppose that you receive an inside tip that your main competitor who runs three local clubs is about to sell the business. Having a strategic management plan that includes designs for acting relative to both future acquisitions and outselling the competition might well enable you to merge your business with your competitor's. In the absence of such strategic management and planning, you may be ill equipped to make such a decision or to make it in a timely manner. Capitalizing on this opportunity is critical, given the competition among sport organizations for customers, fans, athletes, and consumers.

3. TO MAKE EFFECTIVE DECISIONS.   An organization charting a specific course of action is most likely to make effective decisions. Strategic management will enable strategic decision making by keeping the organization in tune with environmental realities and reducing internal resistance to change.

4. TO ENHANCE THE MANAGER'S ENTREPRENEURIAL ROLE.   Many years ago Mintzberg (1975) described four decisional roles of a manager: entrepreneur, disturbance handler, resource allocator, and negotiator. The sport organization with a clear business strategy has the greatest potential of enhancing the manager's entrepreneurial role, encouraging the development or acquisition of innovative goods and services, and effectively managing organizational change.

In addition to strategic management, effective sport organizations are administered through effective policy. Strategic management involves specific action or patterns of action. The ultimate goal of this action is to achieve objectives defined by the organization while respecting the guiding principles and policies of the organization. Let's turn our attention now to the definition of policy, the importance of policy in the governance of sport organizations, and the concept of policy development.

POLICY

All organizations deal with different types of difficult situations, often issues related to human resources, service delivery, risk management, or finance. The issue could result from deviating from the strategic business plan, straying from past practice, or confronting some new, uncharted ground. It may be difficult or tricky, the answer may not be immediately clear, and the potential consequences could be far-reaching within the organization. Sport organizations require policy in the areas of finance, human resources, facility use and control, equipment, travel, public relations, promotion, and other items related to managing risk. For example, travel is a pressure point in college athletics. How will the college Athletic Director react when an athlete asks to travel to a particular road game on his own? Should this concern the administrator? Are there larger issues to consider? Will granting the request set a precedent? Would it matter if the athlete were to travel with his parents as opposed to his girlfriend? Who would be responsible in the event of an accident? How will the athlete's coach view the situation? Each of these questions, and possibly others defined by the college risk manager and insurance carrier, provides the framework for developing policy to deal with this issue. Let's take a further look at defining policy and answer the questions posed above.

What Is a Policy?

Policies are broad guidelines or procedures an organization follows as it moves toward its goals and objectives. Policies are normally general, written statements providing a framework for enabling decisions while allowing employees some flexibility and discretion in problem solving. These guiding statements are meant to provide common direction for all facets of the organization. It is important to understand that policies are different from objectives, strategies, procedures, or philosophy (VanderZwaag, 1998; see Exhibit 3.2). Policies have wide ramifications and are formal expressions of an organization's standing decisions on important, often recurring, issues. They are different from procedures, which are established to guide the work of an individual or a division within the organization. Policies are also different from goals, objectives, and tactics. They emerge from the organization's philosophy by creating a framework for resolving issues directly and consistently. Effective policies evolve over time in reaction to the environment within which the organization exists. For example, an amateur sport organization often has a fiscal responsibility policy that prevents its departments from spending beyond their budgets. The policy does not dictate how or on what items to spend, but rather creates a bottom line principle specific to the importance of only

Definition of terms related to policy development.   *exhibit*   **3.2**

Philosophy	A set of beliefs used to guide decision making.
Policy	General, usually written statements emerging from an organization's philosophy that express its position on important, recurring issues and used to guide decisions and enable consistent decision making.
Goal	Broad, qualitative statements that provide general direction for an organization (see Chapter 2).
Objective	Quantitative statements that help an organization determine if it is fulfilling its goals (see Chapter 2).
Strategy	A plan to bring about a goal or solution to a problem in the most efficient and effective manner.
Procedure	A step-by-step sequence of activities implemented in order to achieve a task.

spending within the means of the organization. As significant savings occur, the policy might be amended to allow quarterly reports on budget savings to reallocate funds to a list of items not funded in the original budget. Over time, this practice might be changed slightly so that the savings remain within the original department budget to further encourage fiscal responsibility to managers concerned with losing part of their original resources.

Organizations rely upon policy and precedent (or past practice) to solve problems fairly and consistently. In the example of the athlete who wishes to travel by his own means to the college game, the Athletic Director will likely rely on a college policy or a departmental policy for an answer to help ensure consistency when another athlete asks. Furthermore, the administrator will be concerned with the following:

- the college's responsibility for the safety and the behavior of athletes when traveling
- the coach's wishes about team cohesion and togetherness
- the athlete's understanding of his responsibilities and expectations
- the circumstances and rationale surrounding the request.

In such a case, the Department of Athletics may approve the policy shown in Exhibit 3.3 regarding athletes traveling to competitions. In its policy, the department defines an expectation that athletes will travel with their team, but it acknowledges that there are circumstances in which this may not be possible and that such cases will be dealt with on an individual basis. The definition of those circumstances will then be left to the discretion of those involved. Perhaps the athlete has an exam that will not permit him to leave with the team but is able and willing to drive on his own and arrive in time for the game. A parent might be at the game and want to take her son home for the weekend afterward. Together, the case-by-case decisions begin to establish a precedent. An example of the athlete permission form is presented in Exhibit 3.4.

| *exhibit* **3.3** | Sample policy for athletes traveling to competitions. |

It is expected that athletes will travel to and from athletic contests with their teammates on carriers provided by the College. In the event an athlete wishes to make alternate travel plans, he or she must obtain the form "Permission for Alternate Travel Plans—Varsity Athletes" from the Athletic Office. This form requests information regarding the intended mode of transportation and a rationale for the request. Permission may be granted on a case-by-case basis only when the form is signed off by both the head coach and the Athletic Director. Permission requests must be made 48 hours prior to travel.

Sample athlete permission form.

exhibit **3.4**

Department of Athletics
Statement of Personal Responsibility for Alternative
Travel Arrangements Chosen by Student–Athletes

REQUEST   Date: _____

I (_____) request permission to _____

_____

_____

and will not **travel with / return with** the _____ **prior to / following**
                    (circle one)   (team)   (circle one)

the contest played at _____
                                           (location/opponent)

on _____.
             (date)

If my request is approved, I will assume all the responsibilities for my travel, conduct, and well-being while traveling to and/or from the contest. I will not hold the college liable in any way for any harm or injury I may suffer, or for any loss or damage to my property that may occur during this journey.

_____ Date: _____
(Signature of student making request)

Address: _____

_____

_____

Telephone: _____ Birth Date: _____

Permission Granted by Department of Athletics

_____   _____
(Athletic Director)   (Coach)

Date: _____   Date: _____

The Importance of Policy in Sport Organizations

Developing policies permitting effective decision making has never been more important for sport organizations, especially given their current size and complexity. Rapid growth over the past decade coupled with an increase in the complexity and business orientation of sport organizations have made it necessary to expand managers' decision-making responsibilities. This trend toward decentralized decision making means effective policy development is crucial. A policy manual can be an invaluable tool that helps personnel to deal quickly and effectively with issues. Policies also promote fair, equitable decisions supported by rationales that are both reasonable and easy to understand. Policies encourage consistency, ensuring the same answer to a problem is applied between organizational units and over time. Perhaps even more important, policy development enables the organization to link its mission statement and management strategy to its operations, ensuring the business strategy is implemented through overall policies and tactics. Let's consider this point in more detail.

Suppose you become the Athletic Director for a college competing in Division I of the NCAA. You are in the leadership role for directing the department. The mission statement of the department might be "to provide student-athletes opportunities for the pursuit of excellence in a broad range of competitive athletics." You need to ensure that department policies are developed that link to the pursuit of the mission relative to how you operate (management strategy) on a day-to-day basis. The mission clearly reflects the need to offer as many sports as possible and to operate them at the highest possible competitive level in order to win. Policies about funding, recruiting, program breadth, competitive schedules, excellent facilities, and so on will help to link the management and business strategies. This organization wants to offer lots of sport opportunities and to operate them at the highest competitive level. The steps necessary to achieve these goals require following specific tactics. For instance, your tactic might include having a balance of sports that use both indoor and outdoor facilities, with no more than four sports sharing any one facility. This tactic ensures that each team's competitive schedules and necessary practice times can be accommodated.

Remember, too, that sport organizations are held to standards of fairness and principle as defined by law. Policies provide for a systematic framework that aids in decision making. For example, a gender-equity policy may call for an equal number of competitive sport opportunities for females as there are for males within the athletic program. When decisions are being made relative to adding or dropping sports, this policy helps to guide the discussion. Of course, this does not ensure the policy is legally defensible, but it does promote actions based upon reasoned statements of organizational intent, developed for a purpose.

Developing Policy

Armed with an understanding of what a policy is and why it is important, let's now turn our attention to developing policy. *Policy development* is an ongoing process through which a framework for decision making is developed relative to issues broadly encountered throughout the organization. Policy is developed on recurring issues or problems and is usually directed to guiding decision making around critical organizational resources such as finances and personnel (Hoye, Nicholson, & Houlihan, 2009). Policy areas are those parts of an organization's operation where important decisions have surfaced and several alternative actions are possible. The stakes connected to the issues are high; thus the organization forms policy to solve a problem or take a stand on an issue that is likely to recur. Issues or problems that arise, especially those issues that are recurring or that impact a large proportion of organization members or activities, frequently result in the development of policy. Thus policies are active, living documents that can change in response to changes in the environment of the organization. Since policies are meant to clarify actions, embed fairness within operations of what and how things are done, and to help manage risk, it is understandable that policies result from issues that arise. Ultimately, a policy guides the actions of all members of the organization facing a particular issue or dilemma, speeding decision making and unifying the thinking of managers and subordinates.

An effective way to develop policy and to be strategic about it is through the case method analysis for understanding the problem and properly framing the issue (VanderZwaag, 1998). Essentially, the case method analysis is a procedure for looking at a problem, collecting information to assess the available options for solving the problem, and then choosing the alternative most closely aligned with the strategy and philosophy of the organization. This method involves four main steps, as outlined in Exhibit 3.5.

Case method analysis steps for developing policy.   *exhibit* **3.5**

1. Define in detail the issue and the facts describing the scope of the problem and its impact on the organization.

2. Collect and assess information on both sides of the issue. What are the options for action?

3. Evaluate how and to what extent each of these options will ultimately affect the organization.

4. Choose the favored option for solution and specifically define the action. This, then, becomes the written policy statement.

As an example for using the case method analysis outlined, let's consider Major League Soccer (MLS) in the United States and Canada:

1. Define the problem. MLS executives have been aware that soccer, or football as the sport is known around the world, is highly popular worldwide, but does not draw the same fan or media following as other professional leagues in North America, such as the NFL, NHL (National Hockey League), NBA, PGA (Professional Golfers' Association), and LPGA (Ladies Professional Golf Association). In a strategic move, MLS executives decided that increasing the league market share was an issue for the league to strategically manage and that its impact on MLS was a major problem for realizing potential levels of profit.

2. Collect information and formulate options. Those same executives spent considerable time studying the other leagues including England's Premier League (EPL), identifying ways and means for increasing MLS North American profits through team expansion, player acquisitions, promotion and publicity, television, merchandizing, and stadium capacity.

3. Evaluate the options. Evaluate the pros and cons, as well as the potential impact of each of the options identified above.

4. Choose the favored option and define the action. MLS executives identified and pursued player acquisition as a means for increasing the exposure for soccer within the North American professional sport market (Step 4) and thus as a strategic move to increase profit. As an example, in 2007 David Beckham was enticed to join the MLS's Los Angeles Galaxy. The impact of his playing for an MLS team was immediate for virtually all MLS teams in terms of ticket sales, merchandizing, and television revenues.

At the end of each industry segment chapter in this book, a case study gives you an opportunity to deal with real-life policy issues confronting sport managers working in that industry segment. After reading the cases, you may wish to refer to Exhibit 3.5 and follow the steps presented to frame your response to the case.

Once policy is defined, it must be communicated within the organization and properly enforced. This is possible only by developing clearly delineated, written policy (refer to Exhibit 3.5) and a procedure for communicating the policy throughout all levels of the organization. Such a procedure includes the specific communication method (face-to-face meetings, e-mail, or written memo) and the timing for announcing and clarifying the policy, and it identifies exactly who announces what. Commitment and understanding from every level of the organization are necessary for organizational policy to serve its intended purpose. In addition, the developed policy needs to be affiliated with the mission, business pursuits, strategy, and environment of the sport organization. Policies need to remain current and closely aligned with the strategic management activities of the overall management process. In fact, policies play an important role in strategy implementation.

STRATEGIC MANAGEMENT ACTIVITIES AND POLICY DEVELOPMENT

In Chapters 1 and 2 you were introduced to managerial activities related to governance. Planning, organizing, and decision making are actions carried out by sport managers at the *micro,* or departmental, level of analysis. These actions are considered everyday activities performed as the functions of management. The alternative to the micro level of analysis is the *macro* approach to managing the organization. A macro orientation looks at those issues impacting the organization as a whole, assessing things from the perspective of the larger, more complex structure. The content presented earlier in this chapter takes on a macro perspective by investigating the concepts of strategic management and policy development, two concepts that embrace the organization as a whole.

It is important to understand the link between the macro and micro levels of managerial activities guiding an organization. In essence, the managerial activities carried out at the micro level of analysis (planning, organizing, decision making) provide information for the construction of the business strategy and policy development occurring at the macro level of organizational activity. Departmental activities such as planning, organizing, and decision making provide fundamental information for defining organizational strategies. The business strategies then contribute a foundation from which organizational policy is derived. This process should be viewed as a dynamic operation in which information flows both ways in response to the changes that occur in the organizational environment (Exhibit 3.6). Policies empower the action of strategic management.

The interaction of three factors—managerial activities; strategy; and the size, technology, and environment of the organization's structure—is the primary determinant of organizational design (Moorhead, Griffin, Irving, & Coleman, 2000). The structure of an organization reflects the division of labor and the hierarchy of authority and power that exists to maximize the use of available resources (Chelladurai, 2009). The actual structural configuration of the organization can be analyzed from several different perspectives, including (1) its size and shape as depicted on the organizational chart, (2) how it operates via decision making, specialized tasks, and procedures, and (3) the responsibility and authority accorded its members (Moorhead et al., 2000). The chapters that follow describe the governance structures present in several different sport industry segments from these perspectives.

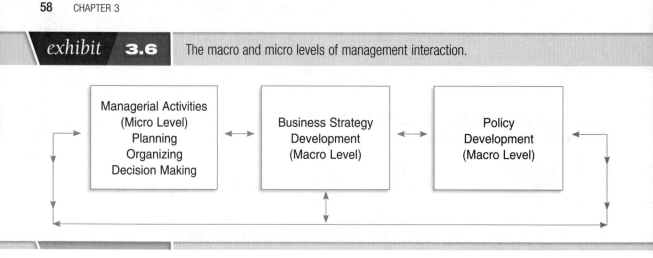

exhibit **3.6** The macro and micro levels of management interaction.

SUMMARY

Sport pervades society, and sports is big business. Organizations delivering the business of sport have grown in response to the interest and economic impact of the sport industry. Accordingly, the importance of effective management has emerged, and the concept of strategic management for sport organizations has evolved. Business strategy involves the development of purposeful plans, actions, and decisions that enable an organization to reach its goals. The strategic level of management involves global, organization-wide strategy dealing with issues that have important financial or human resource consequences for the organization as a whole. Such factors are related to the mission of the organization and are affected by the organizational environment. Strategy involves the creation of mission, goals, and objective statements, along with tactics. Strategy should enable action and decision making as well. Strategic decision making means making the right decision at the right time. Strategic management and decision making are critically important for sport organizations in the pursuit of their organizational goals. Strategy encourages planning, capitalizing on opportunities, and overall competitiveness.

Strategic management is enabled through policy development. A policy is a written statement providing guidelines to solve recurring problems fairly and consistently. Policy is written for issues broadly impacting the organization and its constituent groups. They provide for equitable decision making that can be enacted throughout the organization on a consistent basis. Policy is developed using case method analysis: collecting the facts of the issue, defining and evaluating the options for action, selecting the favored option, and developing the written policy statement.

Including issues of strategy links the micro level of analysis of the organization (the managerial functions of planning, organizing, and decision making) to the macro perspective (strategic management and strategic decision making). The effective sport organization will be structured to embrace both concepts in the pursuit of its organizational goals.

case STUDY

POLICY DEVELOPMENT

As a high school Athletic Director you supervise a large sport program (19 sports) and are determined to be fair to each of the teams. Your problem: 6 sports (girls field hockey, boys football, and boys and girls soccer, lacrosse, and archery) require practice and game time on the only outdoor field you have.

■ Follow the steps in Exhibit 3.5, culminating in writing a policy that (a) covers the use of the field by your teams (you are not in a position to drop any sports) and (b) describes the boundaries for using fields off school property.

CHAPTER questions

1. Suppose you are sitting in an interview for a management position with your favorite professional sport organization. One member of the interview panel says: "The business of sports is fiercely competitive. We have to be very strategic in our management decisions. Tell us what strategic management means to you." List five answers you would provide, given your understanding of this chapter.

2. Consider the following statement: *Timing is everything in strategic decision making.* Is this statement true? Why, or why not? How do you know the best time to make a decision?

REFERENCES

Amis, J., & O'Brien, D. (2005). Organizational theory and the study of sport. In B. L. Parkhouse (Ed.), *The management of sport* (4th ed., pp. 76–95). New York: McGraw-Hill.

Belcourt, M., & McBey, K. J. (2010). *Strategic human resources planning* (4th ed.). Scarborough, Canada: Nelson Thomson Learning.

Chelladurai, P. (2009). *Managing organizations for sport and physical activity: A systems perspective* (3d ed.). Scottsdale, AZ: Holcomb Hathaway.

DeSchriver, T. D., & Mahony, D. F. (2011). Finance and economics in the sport industry. In P. Petersen, J. B. Parks, J. Quarterman, & L. Thibault (Eds.),

Contemporary sport management (4th ed.). Champaign, IL: Human Kinetics.

Hoye, R., Nicholson, M., & Houlihan, B. (2009). *Sport and policy: Issues and analysis.* Oxford, UK: Butterworth-Heinemann.

Mahony, D. F., & Howard, D. R. (2001). Sport business in the next decade: A general overview of expected trends. *Journal of Sport Management, 15*(4), 275–296.

Markovits, A. S., & Rensmann, L. (2010). Gaming the world: How sports are reshaping global politics and culture. Princeton, NJ: Princeton University Press.

Mintzberg, H. (1975). The manager's job: Folklore and fact. *Harvard Business Review, 53,* 49–61.

Mintzberg, H. (1988). *In the strategy process.* Englewood Cliffs, NJ: Prentice Hall.

Mintzberg, H., Lampel, J., Quinn, J., & Ghoshal, S. (2002). *The strategy process: Concepts, context, and cases* (4th ed.). Englewood Cliffs, NJ: Prentice Hall.

Moorhead, G., Griffin, R. W., Irving, P. G., & Coleman, D. F. (2000). *Organizational behavior: Managing people and organizations.* Scarborough, Canada: Nelson Thomson Learning.

Ozanian, M. K. (1995, February 14). Following the money: FW's first annual report on the economics of sports. *Financial World, 164,* 26–27, 30–31.

Pearce, J. A., & Robinson, R. B. (2007). *Strategic management: Formulation, implementation, and control.* Toronto, Canada: Irwin/McGraw-Hill.

Slack, T., & Parent, M. M. (2006). *Understanding sport organizations: The application of organization theory* (2d ed.). Champaign, IL: Human Kinetics.

Stonehouse, G., Campbell, D., Hamill, J., & Purdie, T. (2004). *Global and transnational business: Strategy and management.* Hoboken, NJ: John Wiley & Sons, Inc.

VanderZwaag, H. J. (1998). *Policy development in sport management.* Westport, CT: Praeger.

Ethics in Sport
Organizations

Sales representatives alter receipts to get more money than they are entitled to. Managers lie to their bosses about using company-owned cars. Bosses lie to their employees about company policies. Accountants alter the books to cover up questionable spending practices. Major corporations are forced to close down because of income mismanagement. Large manufacturers violate the human rights of their workers. Organizations use production processes and build facilities that are not environmentally friendly. Such negative news from the corporate world calls into question the ethics we see practiced in business and industry on a daily basis.

The world of sport is a place where we want to believe in fair play and good conduct. But is this world somehow immune to the ethical issues confronting managers and business-people in general society? Unfortunately, the answer is "No," as is illustrated by the following examples:

- NFL players are alleged to have placed monetary awards (bounties) on injuring opposing players.
- NCAA football players who generate millions of dollars for video game companies receive no compensation for the use of their images and likenesses.
- MLB players and Tour de France riders use banned substances to improve performance.
- A state high school athletic association policy on age limits keeps athletes with Down syndrome from being able to participate in their senior year when they are 19.
- A professional athlete tweets racial slurs.
- International officials accept bribes to swing the votes for the selection of a host city for the World Cup.
- The NFL chooses to use replacement officials rather than settle a labor dispute with regular officials.
- A well-known college football coach is accused of sexual misconduct involving children.

Sadly, these types of incidents appear with regularity in the sports pages and are often the lead stories on the evening sports broadcasts. According to Ridinger and Greenwell (2005), "This is problematic as the sport industry prides itself on providing wholesome entertainment, promoting positive values, building character, and creating good role models. Unethical behavior threatens all of the positive benefits" (p. 156). All the above scenarios involve behavior that is considered unethical. As sport managers, you will confront situations that will present you with ethical dilemmas. How, then, should you respond to them?

SPORT AS A MIRROR OF SOCIETY

Every society faces its own unique issues, including violence, substance abuse, domestic abuse, racism, sexism, homophobia, ableism, economic downturns, differential treatment based on religion, and corporate cheating. These issues also appear in all levels and facets of industry, including the sport industry. It has been said that sport is a mirror, a microcosm, or reflection of society, not just in the United States, but other nations as well (Asser, 2000; Eitzen & Sage, 2009; Maguire & Nakayama, 2006; Oprisan, 1999). It should come as no surprise, therefore, that sport managers face the same issues.

According to DeSensi and Rosenberg (2010, p. 2), the following are ethical considerations for sport managers:

- professionalism
- equity
- legal and financial management
- personnel concerns
- governance and policies
- league and franchise issues
- matters of social justice.

Notice that one of the points above mentions governance. Many of the ethical considerations listed above have obvious parallels as societal issues. So how do these societal issues manifest themselves in sport?

The simple diagram in Exhibit 4.1 illustrates how societal issues are reflected in sport. As an example, violence is a daily issue in society, and fighting and killing are often depicted by the media on television, in films, and in video games. Violence, the societal issue, appears on the left-hand side of the model. As the issue is filtered through sport, we see, for example, the fan violence in Vancouver following the 2011 NHL Stanley Cup Playoffs. Another example is the 2011 altercation at the University of Cincinnati college basketball game against Xavier University in which two teams started an all-out brawl. Fights have broken out at Little League baseball games, high school football games, and youth soccer matches. Officials are accosted at an alarming rate, prompting more states to make it a felony offense to strike an official (Sullivan, 2009).

The second example shown in Exhibit 4.1—racism—still exists in society, as evidenced by the disproportionate number of African Americans incarcerated in the United States and by incidents of racial profiling. In sport, the number of African American head coaches in the NCAA Division I football is extremely small. The overwhelming majority of positions with any decision-making power in college sport are held by white people (Lapchick, 2010). In addition, racial taunting and slurs still take place all too often during international soccer matches (Duke, 2011).

The third example illustrated in Exhibit 4.1 is sexual assault. This has occurred across differing levels of sport from high school (KARE-11, 2012), college sport (Huffington Post, 2011), professional sport (Withers, 2010) to elite international competition (CNN, 2012). The coach or general manager must decide whether the player should be allowed to play or should be punished in some way, such as a suspension or fine. Unfortunately, the

exhibit **4.1** Societal issues reflected in sport.

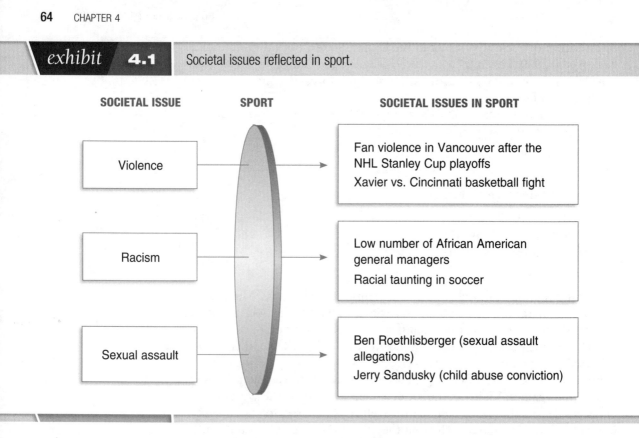

SOCIETAL ISSUE	SPORT	SOCIETAL ISSUES IN SPORT
Violence		Fan violence in Vancouver after the NHL Stanley Cup playoffs Xavier vs. Cincinnati basketball fight
Racism		Low number of African American general managers Racial taunting in soccer
Sexual assault		Ben Roethlisberger (sexual assault allegations) Jerry Sandusky (child abuse conviction)

sport story of the year 2011 was the child sexual abuse scandal at Penn State University involving former assistant coach Jerry Sandusky, which ultimately led to the dismissal of the university's president, chief financial officer, and legendary head coach Joe Paterno.

This diagram could include other examples, but its purpose is not to provide a comprehensive list. Rather, its purpose is to ask, "As sport managers, when we are confronted by these issues, how will we react?" Responding to these incidents is never easy, because sport managers feel pressure from many constituencies to do the right thing. But what is "the right thing," and more important, how should a sport manager decide on carrying out "the right thing"? Remember, too, as mentioned in Chapter 2, the decisions sport managers make will be publicly scrutinized by the media, fans, and casual readers of the news. As a sport manager, you will be faced with ethical dilemmas on a regular basis. But will you know how to recognize an ethical dilemma?

ETHICS DEFINED

here do ethical codes in sport management emanate from, and who is responsible for ethical behavior? The United Nations Educational, Scientific and Cultural Organization (UNESCO) (n.d.) has a Code of Sports Ethics and states that responsibility for ethical behavior lies with those who are involved with sports for children and young adults including (a) governments at all levels and the agencies that work with them; (b) sports and sports-related organizations including sports federations and governing bodies; and (c) individuals including parents, teachers, coaches, referees, officials, sport leaders, athletes who serve as role models, administrators, journalists, doctors, and pharmacists. Clearly, sport managers in general and those working specifically in sport governing bodies are responsible for ethical behavior. While this may sound far away from you as you read this book, ultimately it means as a sport manager you will be responsible for ethics in your sport organization. All sport managers are responsible for ethical behavior, and the higher one moves up in the organization the greater that responsibility becomes. As Lussier and Kimball (2009) point out, "An organization's ethics are the collective behavior of its employees. If each employee acts ethically, the actions of the organization will be ethical, too. The starting place for ethics, therefore, is you" (p. 35).

How does a sport manager recognize when and where ethics will come into play? Sport managers face certain issues and considerations that require ethical analysis. Some of these include (Hums, Wolff, & Morris, 2012):

- Non-discrimination/equity in sporting participation
- Fair play
- Inclusive facilities and equipment
- Protection against abuse and violence
- Safety and security
- Sport-related labor conditions
- Employment and hiring practices
- Right to due process
- Access to information
- Freedom of speech
- Right to privacy
- Environmental violations
- Displacement of persons for sporting events
- Access and availability of resources/financial spending.

Often, when people think of sport ethics they think of conduct and fair play *on* the field. As stated by the Council of Europe Committee of Ministers (2001), "ethical considerations leading to fair play are integral, and not optional elements, of all sports activity, sports policy and management, and apply to all levels of ability and commitment, including recreational as well as competitive sport" (Aims section). Fair play extends to the management of sport as well. From the information above, it is obvious that ethics and ethical concerns spill over into the business aspects of sport. The business venue is where sport managers will encounter myriad ethical issues and dilemmas.

ETHICAL DILEMMAS

What is an ethical dilemma? An *ethical dilemma* occurs "when important values come into conflict, and the decision maker (the leader, in many cases) must make a choice between these values. . . . To further complicate things, ethical dilemmas usually involve multiple stakeholders (those affected by the ultimate decision), and the outcome is marred by uncertainty" (Mullane, 2009, pp. 2–3). According to Wallace (2012), a manager faces a significant ethical conflict when the following exist: "(1) significant value conflicts among differing interests, (2) real alternatives that are equally justifiable, and (3) significant consequences to stakeholders in the situation" (Definition section). For example, a star athlete is arrested for driving while intoxicated one week before the final game for the league championship. Should the player be allowed to play?

- Are value conflicts present? Some people would say the athlete should not play because of the arrest; others would say she has been arrested but not convicted, so let her play.
- Do real alternatives exist that are equally justifiable? Real alternatives may include playing the athlete, not playing the athlete at all, or limiting playing time.
- Are there significant consequences to stakeholders, including owners, sponsors, or investors? If the athlete does not play and the team loses the championship, significant revenue could be lost; if the athlete does play, negative publicity will be significant.

When faced with an ethical dilemma, what is a sport manager to do? What should guide the sport manager when making a decision about an ethical dilemma like this?

ETHICAL DECISION-MAKING MODELS

As discussed in Chapter 2, a sport manager must have an organized and sequential method for making decisions. It is no different when the problem is ethical in nature. The literature on ethical decision making is loaded with different models for managers to use (Low, Ferrell, & Mansfield, 2000). Some very practical models and guidelines have been suggested

(McDonald, 2001; Thornton, Champion, & Ruddell, 2012; Trevino, 1986; Zinn, 1993). These models examine a variety of factors and involve multiple steps. For our purposes, we will identify a straightforward model sport managers can apply in the workplace. The model presented below by Hums, Barr, and Guillion (1999, p. 64) and Hancock and Hums (2011) is an adaptation of Zinn's model:

1. **Identify the correct problem to solve.** When making any type of decision, the decision maker must first identify the *real* problem. Identifying a symptom of the problem and acting on that will not resolve the problem itself.

2. **Gather all pertinent information.** Good decision makers try to be as informed as possible. Is it realistic to think you can gather every piece of information needed? Probably not, but sport managers need to make a good faith effort to find all the information possible to guide them in their decision making.

3. **Explore codes of conduct relevant to one's profession or to this particular dilemma.** More and more sport organizations are developing codes of conduct. Take a look at codes from yours and other sport organizations to see if they provide guidance for your decision.

4. **Examine one's own personal values and beliefs.** We all come to the workplace with our own unique sets of values. Be sure you understand your values and how they could impact your decision. This does not mean every decision has to be in line with your own values. It means you must be keenly aware of your own values and how they may influence your decision.

5. **Consult with peers or other individuals in the industry who may have experience in similar situations.** Sport managers throughout the industry are facing increasing numbers of ethical issues. Perhaps some trusted colleagues have faced a similar dilemma. Talk with them to discuss how they went about solving the issue.

6. **List decision options.** Good decision makers learn to look at as many options as possible so they can make the best choice.

7. **Look for a win–win situation if at all possible.** This is a difficult but critical step. Ethical dilemmas arise when there are questions about the right thing to do. Try to make a decision that maximizes the outcome for the parties involved.

8. **Ask the question, "How would my family feel if my decision and how and why I arrived at my decision appeared on the Internet tomorrow?"** Remember, as a sport manager, your decisions will be publicly analyzed and criticized. Be sure you have done all the right things in making your decision and that there is nothing about your decision you could not be up front about.

9. **Sleep on it.** Do not rush to a decision. In other words, think hard about the situation and the options and consequences you face. You need to make a well-thought-out decision.

10. **Make the best decision possible, knowing it may not be perfect.** At some point, you will have to make your decision. Knowing you have followed the steps listed above will help you reach the best decision possible. In ethical decision making, reasonable people will often reasonably disagree over decisions.

11. **Evaluate the decision over time.** Often overlooked by managers, it is important to reflect on the decision later to see how it is working, or how changes could be made to improve upon it. This step is especially important if the issue or a similar one arises again.

Another useful decision-making technique for examining ethical decisions is the SLEEPE Principle (presented in Chapter 2). This model helps the sport manager look at the big picture before making a decision. Ethical decisions, by their very nature, are bound to have far-reaching and complex ramifications. The SLEEPE Principle helps a sport manager think in broad terms about the ramifications of ethical decisions. In addition, this model has ethical considerations already built in as the second *E* in SLEEPE. Regardless of which model a sport manager chooses to use, each provides a structure to help make decisions (Hums, 2006, 2007).

Up to this point, we have concentrated mainly on ethical situations and how individual sport managers will respond to them. Now we must expand that view and look at sport organizations as a whole and their corporate stance on ethical issues. One way to assess the ethical nature of a sport organization is to examine what kind of "citizen" the sport organization represents. This idea of a sport organization as a "citizen" can be looked at through the concept of corporate social responsibility.

CORPORATE SOCIAL RESPONSIBILITY

Corporate social responsibility (CSR) is a term that often appears in business ethics literature. What does it mean to be a responsible corporate citizen? In general, CSR is

> a concept whereby companies integrate social and environmental concerns in their business operations and in their interaction with their stakeholders on a voluntary basis. Being socially responsible means not only fulfilling legal expectations, but also going beyond compliance and investing "more" into human capital, the environment and the relations with stakeholders. (European Commission, 2001, pp. 4, 6)

Sport management researchers have begun to study the topic of CSR in sport (Babiak & Trendafilova, 2011; Babiak & Wolfe, 2009) and have called for sport managers to be more aware of the power of sport to do good (Darnell, 2012; Hums, 2010; Hums & Hancock, 2012; Thibault, 2009). Social responsibility should become part of who you are and how you do your job on a daily basis once you become a sport manager. It helps to have a few ideas on how to make sure your sport organization acts in a socially responsible manner.

How can CSR be measured? There is no singular measure of good citizenship because by its very nature it can be ascertained only from the perspectives of multiple stakeholders. One of the earliest and still often cited measurements of CSR comes from Carroll (1991), who explained how corporations can operate at four different CSR levels:

1. economic
2. legal
3. ethical
4. philanthropic

He examined corporations and the levels where they existed relative to various organizational stakeholders, including owners, customers, employees, the community, and the public at large (Carroll, 1991). The economic level represents the lowest level of CSR, and the philanthropic represents the highest level of CSR. The concept of CSR is usually applied in business settings; rarely has Carroll's model been applied in a sport industry setting.

Applying CSR in a Sport Setting

For our purposes, let's examine a college Athletic Department and its compliance with Title IX. By law, a college Athletic Department can comply with Title IX by meeting any one prong of the so-called three-prong approach:

1. proportionality—having the same percentage of female athletes and female undergraduates.
2. a continuing history of expanding athletic opportunities for women.
3. demonstrating success in meeting the interests and abilities of female students (Carpenter & Acosta, 2004, pp. 14–15).

Given this information about Title IX compliance, let's apply the four levels of the CSR model to an intercollegiate Athletic Department.

1. ECONOMIC LEVEL. If the department is operating at the economic level, this means it is most interested in achieving purely financial goals. Here the Athletic Department would basically ignore Title IX, doing nothing to comply until forced to do so by outside influences. Using the logic that complying with Title IX is too costly, the Athletic Department would not take any steps to comply with the law unless it became costlier not to comply.

2. LEGAL LEVEL.   If the Athletic Department operates at the legal level, it will attempt to meet the minimum legal criterion for compliance. At this stage, organizations strive to meet legal minimums and basically follow the letter of the law. Most certainly it would only attempt to fulfill one of the three prongs currently used to determine compliance. Since Title IX is not a quota system, this Athletic Department may rely on the so-called proportionality rule. It may make the case for continuing progress in developing opportunities for female athletes, or it could show it is meeting the needs and interests of the female student population. Athletic departments at this level are likely to drop men's sports to be in compliance, a quick and efficient way to come into minimum compliance with the proportionality prong. These same departments may state the reason for dropping the sports was because they needed more resources for women's sport, when in fact the reason was the football "arms race," a football program's increased need for expenditures to keep up with competing teams.

3. ETHICAL LEVEL.   The Athletic Department operating at the ethical level would follow not just the letter of the law, but the spirit of the law as well. The department would not just meet but may exceed the legal minimums because it values providing equal opportunities for women. The department would add emerging sports that attract female participants, such as rowing or lacrosse. Rather than dropping men's sports, the department would find alternative sources of funding or ways to redirect the budget so that female opportunities are increased without adversely affecting opportunities for males.

4. PHILANTHROPIC LEVEL.   Athletic departments operating at the philanthropic level become active advocates for Title IX. They develop model programs for compliance and strive to fulfill all three prongs of the law, instead of the minimal one prong for compliance. These departments actively offer help to athletic departments at other universities as those departments work to comply with Title IX. By presenting their programs as models and perhaps acting in a consultative mode to help other institutions comply with the law, athletic departments can operate at the philanthropic level.

Sport Organizations and Corporate Social Responsibility in Practice

More and more sport organizations are beginning to integrate elements of CSR into their everyday business operations. For example, Nike (much maligned for its labor practices, including unsafe working conditions and low wages) has on its website a section called "Responsibility" that links to pages dealing with community affairs, diversity, environment, manufacturing processes, and reporting. In Nike's *2007–2009 Global Corporate Responsibility Report,* the company's four main goals are to "(1) put investing in sustainability as a key innovation/research and development priority on consumer brands' agendas, (2) fast track innovation through investment and collaboration, (3) launch the GreenXchange as a platform for enabling the sharing of intellectual property to fast track changes efficiently, and (4) build an advocacy agenda to push for large-scale policies and investments in sustainable innovation as a key enabler of global economic competitiveness" (Nike, 2010, p. 23). In addition, Nike is leading the way with the "Stand Up Speak Up" campaign against racism in soccer and was a sponsoring partner of the Changemakers Sport for a Better World Competition. This competition was a "search for innovative ways for sports to promote social change" (Changemakers, 2007, para. 1). Given its past history of controversy with labor practices, Nike seems to be making a concerted effort to publicly present an image of CSR.

The IOC includes several examples of CSR in its required documents for cities bidding to host the Olympic and Paralympic Games. For example, the 2018 Candidature Acceptance Procedure contains suggestions on Olympic Games Impact and on Sustainable Development (IOC, 2009a). Capputo and Pennazio (2006) looked at CSR aspects for the 2006 Torino Winter Olympic Games. They categorized important CSR considerations of the Games, such as economic aspects, environmental sustainability, and social impact. Olympic Games sponsors also have joined in the CSR mind-set. For the 2012 London Games, sustainability was part of the plan from the start, and included areas such as carbon management, sustainable transport, food vision, and waste management (London 2012, n.d.). In addition, corporate sponsors also joined in the environmental sustainability efforts. Coca-Cola, for example, built an environmentally friendly warehouse for the Games, which incorporated roof panels, skylights, and a ground source heat pump (Coca-Cola Ltd., 2011).

Major professional sport organizations also act in a socially responsible manner through various charitable activities. For example, the NFL has partnered for many years with the United Way. The LPGA, Women's National Basketball Association (WNBA), and Major League Baseball (MLB) all work with the Susan G. Komen Breast Cancer Foundation. MLB's Reviving Baseball in the Inner Cities (RBI) program has grown over the last few years. Many universities support local community activities through programs such as the University of Notre Dame's partnership with its campus Center for Social Concerns, where athletes get involved with projects on campus, in the local community, and in other areas around the country.

Finally, numerous sport organizations are beginning to see the importance of crafting codes of ethics (Jordan, Greenwell, Geist, Pastore, & Mahony, 2004). Researchers have studied these codes to examine what types of behaviors such codes should cover. For example, Greenwell, Geist, Mahony, Jordan, and Pastore (2001) examined the codes of ethics for various NCAA conferences. As a follow-up, Jordan et. al. (2004) asked college

www

Nike Corporate Responsibility Report
www.nikeresponsibility.com/report/

coaches their opinions on the contents of NCAA conference codes of ethics. The two studies presented similar findings; namely, that the values (including sportsmanship, healthy environment, professional conduct, compliance with rules, welfare of student-athletes, and equitable treatment) contained in the codes were also the same ideals coaches felt should be included.

Codes of ethics vary in content, length, and complexity. Exhibit 4.2 offers a sample code of ethics from the National Intramural and Recreational Sports Association that is relatively short and concise (NIRSA, 1984). Exhibit 4.3 shows the table of contents of the IOC Code of Ethics (IOC, 2009b).Whether the code is long or short, concise or complex, what is most important is that sport organizations are beginning to develop codes of ethics appropriate for use in their segment of the industry.

ETHICS AND SPORT GOVERNANCE ORGANIZATIONS

Why is it important to include a chapter in this book about ethics? Individual sport managers and sport organizations look to their governing bodies for guidance on a wide range of topics, including legal issues, safety issues, and personnel issues—and ethical issues such as good business practices. Sport governing bodies can set the tone from the top down regarding ethical issues. The stance taken by a governing body will influence decisions you make as a sport manager in any organization under that governing body's umbrella. An example of this relationship is the effect on International Federations and National Sports Organizations when the IOC makes a ruling on banned substances. State and provincial high school athletic associations are taking stronger stances on tobacco use by minors, so individual schools are also instituting such programs. Governing bodies' rulings on ethical issues will hopefully result in behavioral changes and choices by their constituencies as well.

Sport managers need to understand the effects of their decisions and the number of people affected by their decisions (Crosset & Hums, 2012). According to DeSensi (2012), "Is it too much to expect of sport managers that they become ethically, morally and socially responsible professionals? My response is no; I believe they should be at the forefront of this issue. . . . The moral climate of sport has always been in need of improvement, and who better than sport managers to assume this responsibility?" (p. 130). Knowing you will face ethical dilemmas, you will need to employ an ethical decision-making model to deal with them. You will have the opportunity to consider ethical questions in some case studies in this book. You will shape the culture of your organization, impacting its ethical climate and its stance on being a good corporate citizen. In other words, the driving force for a sport organization's level of CSR rests with its employees and, most certainly, with its managers. That means you!

NIRSA Member Code of Ethics.

exhibit   **4.2**

PREAMBLE. An outstanding characteristic of a profession is that its members are continually striving to improve the quality of life for the population they serve. In making the choice to affiliate with a professional association, individuals assume the responsibility to conduct themselves in accordance with the ideals and standards set by the organization. For NIRSA members, this means they will strive to uphold the Bylaws in a manner illustrated in the Code of Ethics.

ARTICLE I

The NIRSA member in fulfilling professional obligations, shall:

1. Seek to extend public awareness of the profession and its achievements.
2. Be true in writing, reporting and duplicating information and give proper credit to the contributions of the others.
3. Encourage integrity by avoiding involvement or condoning activities that may degrade the Association, its members or any affiliate agency.
4. Perform dutifully the responsibilities of professional membership and of any offices or assignments to which appointed or elected.
5. Encourage cooperation with other professional associations, educational institutions and agencies.
6. Practice nondiscrimination on the basis of diversity related to age, disability, ethnicity, gender, national origin, race, religion, and sexual orientation.

ARTICLE II

The NIRSA member in relations with employers and employees staff (sic), shall:

1. Promote and implement the concept of equal opportunity and fairness in employment practices and program administration.

2. Refrain from exploiting individuals, institutions or agencies for personal or professional gain.
3. Secure the trust of employees by maintaining, in confidence, privileged information until properly released.
4. Support the contributions of fellow employees by properly crediting their achievements.
5. Assist and encourage the education of employees in the area of professional development.

ARTICLE III

The NIRSA member in providing programs and services, shall:

1. Endeavor to offer the safest and highest quality program achievable with available resources.
2. Take responsibility for employing qualified individuals in positions that require special credentials and/or experience.
3. Strive to keep abreast of current skills and knowledge and encourage innovation in programming and administration.
4. Promote integrity by accepting gratuities for service of no more than nominal value.
5. Encourage promotion of the ideals of Recreational Sports by incorporating such values as sportsmanship, fair play, participation and an atmosphere which promotes equitable opportunity for all.

Source: NIRSA (1984). Reprinted with permission.

exhibit **4.3**   Table of Contents of the IOC Code of Ethics.

International Olympic Committee Code of Ethics

Preamble

A Dignity

B Integrity

C Resources

D Candidatures

E Relations with States

F Confidentiality

G Implementation

Source: IOC (2009b).

SUMMARY

We see numerous examples of ethical dilemmas in society today. The sport industry is part of that greater society; therefore, we encounter ethical issues and dilemmas in the sport industry as well. When sport managers are faced with ethical dilemmas, they have to make decisions about them. To make sound decisions, sport managers must follow a systematic ethical decision-making process.

When examining ethics, examine ethical activity on the organizational as well as on the individual level. One measure of ethics in a sport organization is CSR, whether it is reflected in a sport organization's stance on a particular issue, its involvement in charitable community events, or its adoption of a code of ethics.

Finally, it is important to examine ethics in the context of governance because of the influence governing bodies have over individual sport organizations. By exhibiting ethical behaviors at the top levels, governing bodies set the ethical tone for their membership.

caseSTUDY

ETHICS

You are an Assistant Athletic Director with Student Academic Services at Big State University. You love baseball and often go to the games; you are known and respected by the players on the team. One day one of the players, Matt, comes to your office and asks to speak with you privately. Matt is a very skilled player and is predicted to be chosen in the early rounds of the draft. Breaking into tears, he tells you, "I recently went to the doctor and found out that I am HIV-positive and I don't know what to do. But please, please, don't tell Coach."

■ Using the ethical decision-making model from this chapter, how do you respond to him, and what course or courses of action can you take after he leaves your office?

CHAPTER questions

1. Using the model presented in Exhibit 4.1, choose three additional societal issues and illustrate how they are seen in sport.
2. Apply Carroll's model of CSR to the following sport organizations:
   a. Your choice of a professional sport franchise
   b. Your college or university Athletic Department
   c. Your nation's National Olympic Committee

   Can organizations exist at different levels in Carroll's model at the same time? Why or why not?
3. Find codes of conduct or codes of ethics from three different sport organizations, each from a different industry segment. Compare the three for similarities and differences.
4. Some organizations have a charitable arm for CSR initiatives, but their business practices may still seem less than ethical. Can Carroll's model be applied to such organizations? Consider whether and how an organization's business practices might be offset by its philanthropic efforts.

REFERENCES

Asser, M. (2000, June 19). Analysis: Soccer violence an international problem. Retrieved from http://news.bbc.co.uk/2/hi/europe/797601.stm

Babiak, K., & Trendafilova, S. (2011). CSR and environmental responsibility: Motives and pressures to adopt green management practices. *Corporate Social Responsibility and Environmental Management, 18*(1), 11–24.

Babiak, K., & Wolfe, R. (2009). Determinants of corporate social responsibility in professional sport: Internal and external factors. *Journal of Sport Management, 23*(6), 717–742.

Capputo, A., & Pennazio, V. (2006). *Corporate social responsibility in sport: Torino 2006 Winter Olympic Games.* Turin, Italy: University Studies of Turin.

Carpenter, L. J., & Acosta, R. V. (2004). *Title IX.* Champaign, IL: Human Kinetics.

Carroll, A. B. (1991, July/August). The pyramid of corporate social responsibility: Toward the moral management of organizational stakeholders. *Business Horizons, 39*–48.

Changemakers. (2007). Sport for a better world. Retrieved from http://www.changemakers.com/competition/sports

CNN. (2012). Two Paralympians, trainer out of London Games over sex assault charges. Retrieved from http://edition.cnn.com/2012/08/23/world/europe/jordan-paralympians-charged/index.html

Coca-Cola, Ltd. (2011). London 2012 Olympic Games. Retrieved from http://www.cokecorporateresponsibility.co.uk/future-challenges/london-2012-olympic-games.aspx

Council of Europe Committee of Ministers. (2001). Code of sport ethics. Retrieved from https://wcd.coe.int/ViewDoc.jsp?Ref=Rec(92)14&Sector=sec CM&Language=lanEnglish&Ver=rev&BackColor Internet=9999CC&BackColorIntranet=FFBB55& BackColorLogged=FFAC75

Crosset, T., & Hums, M. A. (2012). Ethical principles applied to sport management. In L. P. Masteralexis, C. A. Barr, & M. A. Hums (Eds.), *Principles and practice of sport management* (4th ed., pp. 121–140). Sudbury, MA: Jones and Bartlett.

Darnell, S. C. (2012). *Sport for development and peace: A critical sociology.* London: Bloomsbury Academic.

DeSensi, J. (2012). The power of one for the good of many. In A. Gillentine, R. E. Baker, & J. Cuneen (Eds.), *Critical essays in sport management* (pp. 125–132). Scottsdale, AZ: Holcomb Hathaway.

DeSensi, J., & Rosenberg, D. (2010). *Ethics and morality in sport management* (3d ed.). Morgantown, WV: Fitness Information Technology.

Duke, G. (2011, Nov. 3). Can European soccer stamp out racism? Retrieved from http://edition.cnn.com/2011/SPORT/football/11/02/football.racism.europe/index.html

Eitzen, D. S., & Sage, G. H. (2009). *Sociology of North American sport* (8th ed.). Boulder, CO: Paradigm Publishers.

European Commission. (2001). Promoting a European framework for corporate social responsibility. Retrieved from http://eur-lex.europa.eu/LexUriServ/site/en/com/2001/com2001_0366en01.pdf

Greenwell, T. C., Geist, A. L., Mahony, D. F., Jordan, J. S., & Pastore, D. L. (2001). Characteristics of NCAA conference codes of ethics. *International Journal of Sport Management, 2*(2), 108–124.

Hancock, M., & Hums, M. A. (2011). Participation by transsexual and transgender athletes: Ethical dilemmas needing ethical decision making skills. *ICSSPE Bulletin, 68.* Retrieved from http://www.icsspe.org/membersarea_a/bulletin/bulletin_3e18291e.php.html

Huffington Post. (2011, October 28). Marquette University sexual assault. Retrieved from http://www.huffingtonpost.com/2011/10/28/marquette-university-sex-_n_1063472.html

Hums, M. A. (2006, May). Analyzing the impact of changes in classification systems: A sport management analysis model. Paper presented at the VISTA 2006 International Paralympic Committee Congress, Bonn, Germany.

Hums, M. A. (2007, June). The business of the Paralympic Games: Economics and ethics. Paper presented at 7th International Conference on Sports: Economic, Management and Marketing Aspects, Athens, Greece.

Hums, M. A. (2010). The conscience and commerce of sport: One teacher's perspective. *Journal of Sport Management, 24,* 1–9.

Hums, M. A., Barr, C. A., & Guillion, L. (1999). The ethical issues confronting managers in the sport industry. *Journal of Business Ethics, 20*, 51–66.

Hums, M. A., & Hancock, M. (2012). Sport management: Bottom lines and higher callings. In A. Gillentine, B. Baker, & J. Cuneen (Eds.), *Critical essays in sport management: Exploring and achieving a paradigm shift* (pp. 133–148). Scottsdale, AZ: Holcomb Hathaway.

Hums, M. A., Wolff, E. A., & Morris, A. (2012). Human rights in sport checklist. In K. Gilbert (Ed.), *Sport, peace, and development* (pp. 243–254). Champaign, IL: Common Ground.

IOC. (2009a). 2018 candidature acceptance procedures. Retrieved from http://www.gamesbids.com/eng/bid_archives.html#2014

IOC. (2009b). IOC Code of Ethics. Retrieved from http://www.olympic.org/Documents/Reports/EN/Code-Ethique-2009-WebEN.pdf

Jordan, J. S., Greenwell, T. C., Geist, A. L., Pastore, D. L., & Mahony, D. F. (2004). Coaches' perceptions of conference codes of ethics. *Physical Educator, 61*, 131–145.

KARE-11. (2012). Browerville High School athletes charged with sexual assault. Retrieved from http://www.kare11.com/news/article/984633/391/Browerville-High-School-athletes-charged-with-sexual-assault

Lapchick, R. (2010). 2010 *Racial and gender report card: College sport.* Orlando, FL: Institute for Diversity and Ethics in Sport, University of Central Florida.

London 2012. (n.d.). Our responsibility. Retrieved from http://www.london2012.com/about-us/sustainability/our-responsibility/

Low, T. W., Ferrell, L., & Mansfield, P. A. (2000). Review of empirical studies assessing ethical decision making in business. *Journal of Business Ethics, 25*(3), 185–204.

Lussier, R. N., & Kimball, D. C. (2009). *Applied sport management skills.* Champaign, IL: Human Kinetics.

Maguire, J. A., & Nakayama, M. (2006). *Japan, sport and society: Tradition and change in a globalizing world.* London: Routledge.

McDonald, M. (2001). A framework for ethical decision-making: Version 6.0 Ethics shareware. Retrieved from http://www.ethics.ubc.ca/upload/A%20Framework%20for%20Ethical%20Decision-Making.pdf

Mullane, S. P. (2009). Ethics and leadership—White Paper. Coral Gables, FL: University of Miami Johnson Edosomwan Leadership Institute.

Nike. (2010). Corporate responsibility report. Retrieved from http://www.nikebiz.com/crreport/content/pdf/documents/en-US/full-report.pdf

NIRSA. (1984). Professional member code of ethics. Retrieved from http://www.nirsa.org/Content/NavigationMenu/AboutUs/GoverningDocuments/CodeofEthics/Code_of_Ethics.htm

Oprisan, V. (1999). Aspects and tendencies of voluntary work in Romanian sport. In *Papers of the symposium: Volunteers, global society and the Olympic Movement,* Lausanne, Switzerland. Retrieved from www.blues.uab.es/olympic.studies/ volunteers/oprisan.html

Ridinger, L., & Greenwell, T. C. (2005). Ethics in the sport industry. In A. Gillentine & R. B. Crow (Eds.), *Foundations of sport management* (pp. 155–168). Morgantown, WV: Fitness Information Technology.

Sullivan, T. (2009). Fan violence & the law. Retrieved from http://www.youthsportsny.org/2009/12/fan-violence-the-law.html

Thibault, L. (2009). Globalization of sport: An inconvenient truth. *Journal of Sport Management, 23,* 1–20.

Thornton, P. K., Champion, Jr., W. T., & Ruddell, L. S. (2012). *Sports ethics for sport management professionals.* Sudbury, MA: Jones & Bartlett.

Trevino, L. (1986). Ethical decision making in organizations: A personal-situation interactionist model. *Academy of Management Review, 11,* 601–617.

UNESCO. (n.d.). Education: Physical education and sport. Retrieved from http://portal.unesco.org/education/en/ev.php-URL_ID=2223&URL_DO=DO_TOPIC&URL_SECTION=201.html

Wallace, D. (2012). Definition of an ethical dilemma. Retrieved from http://www.scribd.com/raman_panwar_2/d/56047818-Definition-of-an-Ethical-Dilemma

Withers, B. P. (2010). The integrity of the game: Professional athletes and domestic violence. *Harvard Journal of Sport and Entertainment Law, 1*(1), 146–179.

Zinn, L. M. (1993). Do the right thing: Ethical decision making in professional and business practice. *Adult Learning, 5,* 7–8, 27.

Scholastic Sport

On any given Friday night in the fall, the air is filled with the sounds of fans screaming, helmets pounding, and bands playing. On Saturdays in winter, the ball bounces off the court, and skates glide over the ice. In the spring, the starter's gun marks the beginning of the 100-meter dash, and we hear the familiar sound of softballs and baseballs being hit and caught. On fields, courts, and rinks everywhere, it is time for the weekend ritual—high school sports. All across the land, young athletes compete for their schools, their communities, and themselves. Many of you remember those days, no doubt. This chapter will focus on high school sport, a sizable section of the sport industry involving thousands of schools and participants.

Although it may surprise you, this is a primarily North American model. In many nations of the world, young people compete for their local municipality's club teams, not for their high school teams. For example, a young athlete living in the town of Megara, outside of Athens, Greece, will play for the local sports club, not for Megara High School. The high school may not even field any teams, since the schools do not compete against each other in sports like schools in North America. In Amsterdam, a talented young football (soccer) player might compete on a developmental team of the Amsterdam Ajax professional football club. The best young athletes are generally selected early for development by professional clubs. In other countries, high school students participate in sport on the local level—and sometimes even on the national level—as with the high school national baseball championship in Japan. While most of this chapter focuses on the North American model, remember that this is not the only competitive model for youth sport. "The opportunity for boys and girls to represent their school and community as they participate in interscholastic activities is a privilege unique to young people in American education" (PIAA, 2012a, para. 1). How, then, did it happen that North American high school sport developed into the product we see today? To understand this evolution, let us take a look at the history and evolution of sport in high schools.

HISTORY OF HIGH SCHOOL SPORT

The history of high school sport is long and storied. It began simply to develop healthy habits in youngsters and has gained widespread popularity among spectators, with important steps along the way. For purposes of this textbook, we will examine mainly how the governance of high school sport evolved.

Early Development

In the late 1800s, sport was seen as a vehicle to help solve societal ills, such as delinquency and poor health, so schools began to promote sport (Seymour, 1990). In its early days, high school sport was initiated, organized, and operated by students, similar to the way intercollegiate sport started. Also like intercollegiate sport, the need for adult supervision and direction soon became apparent, because the supervising adults did not care for the direction that high school sport was heading. To uphold a certain moral image, administrators felt it necessary to extend their authority over interscholastic sport. In the 1890s, the popularity of high school football soared, and its abuses mirrored those of college sport at the time—overemphasis on winning, using ineligible players, and mismanagement of finances (Rader, 1999).

By the time the 15th Conference on Academies and High Schools met in 1902, faculties controlled sport in several states, and the Conference issued basic recommendations on faculty control of interscholastic sport. Around the same time, state high school associations began to form, with early associations organized in Illinois and Wisconsin (Covell, 2012). In the early 1900s, rules were put in place for high school athletes that defined minimum course loads and satisfactory progress in school, as well as participation eligibility certification. These rules were a progression from those outlined by the Michigan State Teachers' Association's Committee on High School Athletics in 1896 (Forsythe, 1950). As athletics became more integral in a student's academic experience, government-funded educational institutions assumed increased control over the governance of high school athletics (Vincent, 1994).

Development of the National Federation of State High School Associations (NFHS)

In 1920, representatives of five Midwestern states—Illinois, Indiana, Iowa, Michigan, and Wisconsin—met in Chicago to discuss concerns about collegiate and non-school sponsorship of high school events. The result was a plan to ensure the well-being of high school student-athletes in competitive situations. These five state associations banded together to form the Midwest Federation of State High School Athletic Associations. Eventually, more state associations joined this group, and in 1923 they changed their name to the National Federation of State High School Athletic Associations (NFHS, 2011b). By the 1930s, the group assumed responsibility as the rules-writing and rules-publishing body for high school sports. The organization grew throughout the 20th century, adding members until 1969, when all 50 states and the District of Columbia belonged. In the 1970s, the fine arts were added under the organization's umbrella, and the term *Athletic* was removed from the organization's name. The official name became the "National Federation of State High School Associations," as it remains today, and since 1997 the organization has gone by the abbreviation "NFHS" (NFHS, 2007).

Organizational development continued from the 1980s to the present, with increased educational programming, incorporation of debate and spirit programs, and ongoing rules interpretations and publications. In 2000, the NFHS moved its headquarters to Indianapolis, Indiana (NFHS, 2011b).

Development of High School Sport in Europe

contributed by Thierry Zintz

In Europe, school sport evolved from the formation of numerous clubs and sports associations. In many cases, extracurricular sports activities were extended by the creation of clubs involved in competitions organized by sports federations. Alongside school sports, organized on sectarian basis (such as Catholic education based on religious beliefs), political parties in many countries created Christian, liberal, or socialist sport organizations to compete in events organized by sports federations.

By the 1930s, Catholic educational institutions in Europe created the International Sports Federation for Catholic Schools (FISEC). This federation, which organizes international competitions, the FISEC Games, grew gradually, opening to include the Americas and the Middle East. Its religious basis, however, limited its development to countries with a network of Catholic educational institutions.

During the 1960s, international sports contacts between schools of all networks multiplied. The number of competitions, as well as the number of schools, continued to increase. This resulted in the effort to coordinate these events as part of an International School Sport Federation (ISF). The ISF is not specifically linked to networks of educational institutions but organizes world competitions in different sports.

Its mission statement indicates:

The ISF is the International Federation of official school sport organisations in the different countries or of representative organisations where there is no official one. It organises international competitions in different sporting disciplines and encourages contests between school students **with a view to promoting better mutual understanding.** It seeks close collaboration with the school authorities of member countries, with the international sporting federations concerned, and with international organisations having similar aims. (ISF, 2011)

The ISF features competitions in traditional team sports such as basketball, football, handball, and volleyball as well as the individual sports such as athletics, badminton, cross-country, gymnastics, orienteering, skiing, swimming, and table tennis (ISF, 2012).

The ISF is a true movement associated with learning, aimed at raising awareness, and promoting official recognition of good sport and education in schools. The ISF hopes, through its actions, to enable boys and girls to cultivate the ideas of mutual understanding and fair play. It is interesting to note the differences and similarities between North American high school and high school sport around the world. Whenever one looks at high school sport, however, one thing is clear—there are myriad benefits to young people participating.

Source: Hums, M. A., MacLean, J. C., & Zintz, Th., *La gouvernance au coeur des politiques des organisations sportives,* 1re ed., De Boeck Supérieur, Bruxelles, p. 320. Used with permission.

Value of High School Sport Today

The values and benefits of high school sport have been well defined by its advocates. For example, the mission statement of the Alaska School Activities Association (ASAA) (n.d.) is "to advocate participation in cocurricular activities; to regulate interscholastic activities, contests and programs; and to promote the academic and social development of students" (para. 1).

In addition, the ASAA's Strategic Plan is based on the belief that interscholastic activities:

- exist for the intrinsic values they provide for students of member schools;
- are an integral part of the overall educational program;
- provide an opportunity to learn and apply skills beyond the classroom;
- promote character, citizenship, leadership and personal responsibility;
- provide for fair and equitable opportunities for students of member schools;
- provide unique opportunities for students to benefit from cross-cultural contact;
- encourage and enhance the connections between communities and schools, adult and students, and among students;
- promote positive academic growth and healthy lifestyle choices;
- promote the development of good sportsmanship. (ASAA, n.d.)

WWW

Alaska School Activities Association
www.asaa.org

As another example, the Massachusetts Interscholastic Athletic Association (MIAA) states on its website (MIAA, 2011):

> Within high school programs, young people learn the values associated with discipline, performing under stress, teamwork, sacrifice, commitment, effort, accountability, citizenship, sportsmanship, confidence, leadership and organizational skills, participating within rules, physical well-being and healthy lifestyles, striving towards excellence, and many other characteristics that come quickly to the mind of any educator. (p. 2)

WWW

Massachusetts Interscholastic Athletic Association
www.miaa.net

For all these reasons, high school sport has become an important component of many students' total educational experience. To make sure all these worthwhile activities happen in a well-planned and organized environment, governance structures must be in place.

GOVERNANCE

Scholastic sport governance occurs on a number of different levels. As mentioned previously, at the national level there is the NFHS, which includes members from the United States and Canada. But unlike some national-level sport governing bodies, this is not where the real power lies. In high school sport the real power and authority rest at the state and provincial levels, where the regulatory power lies. According to Wong (1994), "the power and authority in high school athletics are in the individual state organizations, which determine the rules and regulations for the sport programs and schools within that state" (p. 22). There is also governance on the local level, meaning the school or school district. Let's look at the organizational structures at these different levels and the scope of their authority.

National Federation of State High School Associations (NFHS)

The NFHS (2011a) is a member-governed, nonprofit national service and administrative organization of high school athletics and fine arts programs in speech, debate, and music. From its offices in Indianapolis, the NFHS serves its 50-member state high school athletic and activity associations, plus those of the District of Columbia. The organization publishes playing rules for 16 sports for boys and girls and provides programs and services that its member state associations can use in working with the 18,500 member high schools and approximately 11 million young people involved in high school activity programs (NFHS, 2011b).

From this information, it is important to note two main points. First, the NFHS is considered a service organization. In contrast to the NCAA, which has strong sanctioning power over members, the purpose of the NFHS is to provide services to its members. Also, the NFHS is not involved solely in athletic competition. Subgroups within the NFHS include not only the National Federation Coaches Association, the National Federation Officials Association, and the National Interscholastic Athletic Administrators Association (NIAAA), but also the National Federation Interscholastic Speech and Debate Association, the National Federation Interscholastic Music Association, and the National Federation Interscholastic Spirit Association. Thus, the organization has a broad base across many high school extracurricular activities. This textbook, however, focuses on those aspects of the NFHS dealing directly with interscholastic athletics.

Mission

The mission statement of the NFHS (presented in Exhibit 5.1) states that its purpose is to promote activities that contribute positively to a student's educational experience. Also apparent is that the organization seeks to develop students into people who will be contributing members of society due to the good lessons they learned from their sport experience. From this mission statement it is clear that high school sport is meant to help students achieve educational goals.

Membership

Who belongs to the NFHS? NFHS membership is made up of state associations, not individuals. "The active members of the National Federation of State High School Associations are the 50 state high school athletic/activity associations, plus the District of Columbia. There are also affiliate members, including associations in the U.S. territories, Canada, and other neighboring nations" (NFHS, 2011d). The affiliated members from outside the United States include Canadian School Sport Federations from Alberta, British Columbia, Manitoba, New Brunswick, Nova Scotia,

www

National Federation of State
High School Associations
www.nfhs.org

www

NFHS Coaches' Association
www.nfhs.org/coach/

NFHS Officials' Association
www.nfhs.org/officials/

National Interscholastic Athletic
Administrators Association
www.niaaa.org/default.asp

www

Canadian School Sport
Federations
www.schoolsport.ca/

| Mission statement of the NFHS. | *exhibit* 5.1 |

The National Federation of State High School Associations serves its members, related professional organizations and students by providing leadership for the administration of education-based interscholastic activities, which support academic achievement, good citizenship and equitable opportunities.

We believe:

- the NFHS is the recognized national authority on interscholastic activity programs.
- interscholastic activity programs enrich each student's educational experience.
- participation in education-based activity programs promotes student academic achievement.
- student participation in interscholastic activity programs is a privilege.
- interscholastic participation develops good citizenship and healthy lifestyles.
- interscholastic activity programs foster involvement of a diverse population.
- interscholastic activity programs promote positive school/community relations.
- the NFHS is the pre-eminent authority on competition rules for interscholastic activity programs.
- national competition rules promote fair play and minimize risks for student participants.
- cooperation among state associations advances their individual and collective well-being.
- properly trained administrators/coaches/directors promote the educational mission of the interscholastic experience.
- properly trained officials/judges enhance interscholastic competition.

Source: NFHS (2011b, p. 6). Reprinted with permission.

Ontario, Prince Edward Island, Quebec, and Saskatchewan. Other affiliates include Guam and the U.S. Virgin Islands (NFHS, 2011d).

Financials

How does the NFHS finance itself? More than half of its income, approximately 52 percent, comes from sales revenue (NFHS, 2007) from its official publications. These publications include rules publications, miscellaneous sports items, sports guides and handbooks, debate item publications, and speech and debate booklets. In addition, the organization earns funds from membership dues and professional organizations; contributions, royalties, and sponsors; meetings and conferences; and a few lesser sources. How is the money spent? The major expense categories for the NFHS are salaries and benefits, professional organizations, rules making and publications, educational and professional development, and management and general (NFHS, 2007).

Organizational structure

The organizational structure of the NFHS indicates that the membership drives the governance of the organization. As illustrated in Exhibit 5.2, the member state associations are at the top of the chart. The organization is divided into eight sections to ensure fair geographic representation. The National Council is the legislative body of the NFHS and is responsible for enacting amendments to the constitution and bylaws in addition to other duties. The National Council consists of one representative from each voting member, that is, from each member state association. The National Council meets two times a year. The Board of Directors of the NFHS is made up of 12 members, one from each geographic section and four additional at-large members. The board is empowered to conduct the business of the NFHS, including activities such as approving the annual budget, overseeing the investment and management of all funds, and establishing the standing rules and special committees (NFHS, 2011b). The next group involved in the governance of the NFHS is the Executive Staff, the organization's paid employees, including an Executive Director and Directors of Marketing, Information Services, Financial Services, Publications and Communications, and Educational Services. Several Assistant Directors are also employed, as well as a General Counsel to handle legal questions and issues. Finally, as with most organizations, a series of committees work in designated areas, such as Rules and Sports Committees, general committees, and special committees (NFHS, 2011b).

State and Provincial High School Athletic Associations

Each state and province has its own high school athletic association. As you will see, they have different names. In the United States, for example, we see the Georgia High School Association, Idaho High School Activities Association, Indiana High School Athletic Association, Maine Principals' Association, Texas University Interscholastic League, and the Wisconsin Interscholastic Athletic Association. In Canada we see the Alberta Schools Athletic Association (ASAA), and the Ontario Federation of School Athletic Associations. Despite their different names, these organizations share common missions and authorities.

State and provincial high school associations serve several important functions. First, they are the regulatory bodies for high school sport in a particular state or province. As noted earlier, the power in high school athletics resides on this level. According to Sharp, Moorman, and Claussen (2010), "Authority to govern interscholastic athletics within a state is granted to the state association by the state legislature or by judicial decision. Each state's

www

Georgia High School Association
www.ghsa.net

Idaho High School Activities Association
www.idhsaa.org

Indiana High School Athletic Association
www.ihsaa.org

Maine Principals' Association
www.mpa.cc

Texas University Interscholastic League
www.uil.utexas.edu

Wisconsin Interscholastic Athletic Association
www.wiaawi.org

Vermont Principals' Association
www.vpaonline.org

Ontario Federation of School Athletic Associations
www.ofsaa.on.ca

Alberta Schools' Athletic Association
www.asaa.ca

exhibit **5.2**

Organizational chart for the National Federation of State High School Associations (NFHS).

MEMBER STATE ASSOCIATIONS

NATIONAL COUNCIL ——————— GENERAL COMMITTEE
Appeal
BOARD OF DIRECTORS ——————— ALL RELATED SUBCOMMITTEES

EXECUTIVE DIRECTOR

NIAAA
Certified Athletic
Administrators Program
Leadership Training Program
Professional Publications

EXECUTIVE STAFF (Support Staff)

GENERAL COMMITTEES
Annual Meeting Advisory
Athletic Directors Advisory
Citizenship
Equity
Hall of Fame Screening
National Records
NFHS Coaches Education
Sports Medicine Advisory

SPECIAL COMMITTEES
Hall of Fame Selection

STAFF COMMITTEE
Sports Rules Review

SPECIAL MEETINGS/EVENTS
Debate Topic Selection Meeting
Hall of Fame Induction
Legal Meeting
National High School Activities Week
Conference for Athletic Directors
NFHS Summer Meeting
NFHS Winter Meeting
NFHS Summit on Current Issues
Professional Development
Conferences
State Music Conference
Student Leadership Conference

PUBLICATIONS
Court and Field Diagram Guide
Forensic Quarterly
High School Sports Record Book
IAA Magazine
Lincoln-Douglas Debate Annual
NFHS Annual Report
NFHS Brochure
NFHS Coaches' Quarterly
NFHS Handbook
NFHS News
NFHS Officials' Quarterly
NFHS Statisticians' Manual
NFHS Catalog
Rules Publications 17 Sports
Speech and Debate Books
Sports Medicine Handbook

EDUCATIONAL SERVICES
NFHS Coaches Education Program
Citizenship Curriculum
Rules Exams and Interpretations
Rules Posters
Sports Transparencies/PowerPoint
Sportsmanship Materials

PROFESSIONAL ORGANIZATIONS
NFCA (Coaches)
NFMA (Music)
NFOA (Officials)
NFSA (Spirit)
NFSDA (Speech and Debate)

17 SPORTS RULES AND
ACTIVITY COMMITTEES
Baseball*
Basketball*
Field Hockey
Football*
Gymnastics Boys/Girls*
Ice Hockey
Lacrosse, Boys
Lacrosse, Girls
Music
Soccer*
Softball*
Speech
Spirit*
Swimming and Diving*/Water Polo
Track and Field/Cross Country*
Volleyball*
Wrestling*

*Interpreters Meetings (11)

VIDEOS
Miscellaneous Videos
Music Videos
Speech and Debate Videos
Sports Videos

OTHER SERVICES
Officials Equipment Center
Corporate Partnership Program
Teleconferences on Critical Issues
Authenticating Mark Program

MEMBER STATE ASSOCIATIONS

Advertising
NFHS Website
Rules Interpretations

Athletic Sanctions
Participation Survey
Rules Interpreters Meetings

Rules Exams
Resource Center
Rules Questionnaires

Legal
Resource for National Issues
Citizenship Programs

Source: NFHS (2011b). Reprinted with permission.

high school athletic association is responsible for implementing and enforcing regulations governing interscholastic athletics participation of the member high schools" (p. 324). This statement clearly establishes that the regulatory power in high school sport governance lies at the state level. Second, they are responsible for organizing state or provincial championships, always the highlight of the year for any sport. Finally, they maintain the educational philosophy for high school athletics in their respective state or province.

State level governance is often vested with power from the state legislature. State or provincial associations have the authority to revoke eligibility for individual students and to disqualify schools from participating in events if the schools break state or provincial association rules. In disputes about eligibility and other questions about the interpretation of rules, the U.S. state high school associations are named in any resulting lawsuits. The reason for this is that in most cases the state association has been found to be a state actor (Altman, 2010), that is, an organization working as if it were empowered by the government to act. You may remember from your Legal Aspects of Sport class that this makes state associations subject to the requirements of the United States Constitution. Whenever a high school athlete feels his or her constitutional rights have been violated because of an association's rule, that athlete names the high school association in the suit. Thus when state associations craft policies, they must be mindful not to enact policies or procedures that could be construed as infringing on a student's fundamental rights, such as the right to due process if a student is denied eligibility for some reason.

Mission

www
Oregon School Activities
Association
www.osaa.org

As mentioned earlier, while the associations differ from state to state or province to province, common ideals are reflected in each association's mission statement. Sample mission statements from the Oregon School Activities Association (OSAA) and the Ontario Federation of School Athletic Associations are presented in Exhibits 5.3 and 5.4, respectively. While these mission statements are somewhat different, one can see similarities between them. Shared themes include the place of athletics in an educational setting, the values and benefits students derive from high school sport, and the provision of service to their members.

Membership

High school associations generally are voluntary, nonprofit organizations whose members are the public and private secondary schools in that particular state or province. In some cases, junior high schools and middle schools may also belong to the association. The size of each association varies, depending on the number of high schools in the state or province. The membership of high school associations is similar to that of the NCAA, where institutions (high schools), not individual people, are the members of the organization.

Mission statement of the Oregon School Activities Association.

exhibit   **5.3**

The mission of the OSAA is to serve member schools by providing leadership and state coordination for the conduct of interscholastic activities, which will enrich the educational experiences of high school students. The OSAA will work to promote interschool activities that provide equitable participation opportunities, positive recognition and learning experiences to students, while enhancing the achievement of educational goals.

Source: OSAA (2012). Reprinted with permission.

Mission statement of the Ontario Federation of School Athletic Associations.

exhibit   **5.4**

The Ontario Federation of School Athletic Associations (OFSAA) is a provincial federation of Associations encompassing volunteer coaches, students, and administrators. OFSAA is dedicated to the promotion and enhancement of the educational value of school sport. As an advocate for school sport, OFSAA provides leadership in advancing the educational benefits of participation through its services, resources and the conduct of secondary school sport Championships.

Source: OFSAA (n.d.). Reprinted with permission.

Financials

The sources of funding for athletic associations vary by state. The Arizona Interscholastic Association (AIA) is primarily financed by membership dues, varsity sport participation fees, officials' registration fees, and sales of items including rule books (AIA, n.d.). The MIAA receives no tax money. Rather, the majority of its income comes from sponsorships and ticket sales at regional and state tournaments (MIAA, 2011). The Nebraska School Activities Association (NSAA) has entered into a corporate partnership with US Bank, allowing the association to maintain and strengthen its programs without shouldering the additional costs (NSAA, n.d.b). Dues from member schools, officials, and a share from the tournament series

WWW

Arizona Interscholastic Association
www.aiaonline.org

Nebraska School Activities Association
www.nsaahome.org

www
Tennessee Secondary School
Athletic Association
www.tssaa.org

support the $2.5 million annual budget of the Tennessee Secondary School Athletic Association (Kreager, 2009; TSSAA, 1999). The Kentucky High School Athletic Association includes financial issues in its Strategic Plan. The specific strategies in this document include the following:

Strategy 1.1   Pursue an aggressive fundraising and promotional strategy seeking additional ancillary revenue for the Association while protecting existing programs.

Strategy 1.2   Continue the practice of fiscal restraint and management controls over the current business operations of the Association.

Strategy 1.3   Exercise control and optimize usage of Association funds.

Strategy 1.4   Analyze event structures and financial management practices. (KHSAA, 2006a, pp. 9–10)

The main sources of funds for the Alberta Schools' Athletic Association include the Alberta Sport, Recreation, Parks and Wildlife Foundation (lottery funds) through the Ministry of Alberta Community Development; membership fees; fundraising; and corporate assistance. The money is spent on transportation and officiating costs for provincial competitions, delegate expenses to meetings, publications and rule books, medals and trophies, office administration, and staff salaries and benefits (ASAA, 2007). As budgets become tighter, associations must come up with more creative means of financing their programs. This topic will be discussed in more detail later in the chapter.

Organizational structure

STATE AND PROVINCIAL ASSOCIATIONS.   During the year, an Executive Committee or Board of Directors meets to deal with any ongoing issues. The Executive Committee is made up of Superintendents, Principals, and Athletic Directors from various high schools around the state or province. In addition, paid Executive Staff members work in the association headquarters year-round. These headquarters are usually located in the capital of the state or province. This provides a central location for members and also access to state and provincial elected officials and education policy makers. While the titles may vary, often the highest-ranking paid staff member is called the Commissioner or the Executive Director. There are also several Associate or Assistant Commissioners or Associate or Assistant Executive Directors, each of whom has distinct responsibilities for certain sports and other areas, such as eligibility, rules interpretation, officials, coaches' clinics, sportsmanship and ethics programs, and trophies and awards. The organizational chart for the Pennsylvania Interscholastic Athletic Association (PIAA) is presented in Exhibit 5.5.

www
Pennsylvania Interscholastic
Athletic Association
www.piaa.org

Organizational chart for the Pennsylvania Interscholastic Athletic Association.   *exhibit*   **5.5**

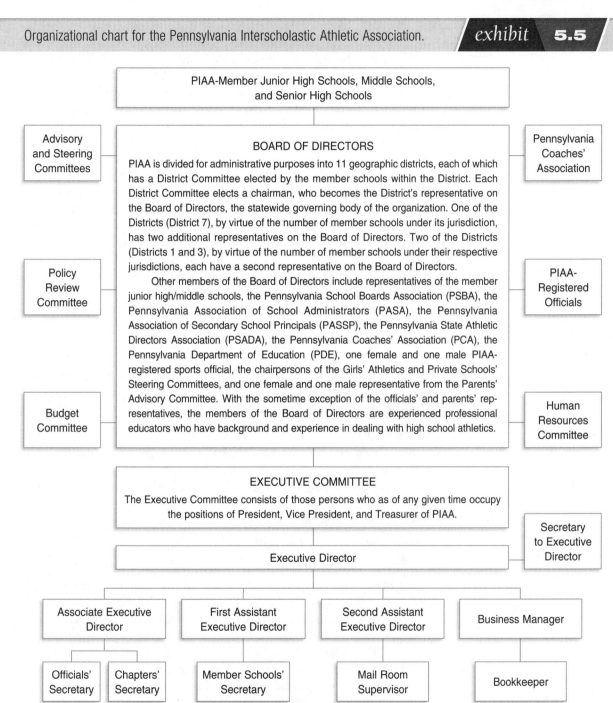

PIAA-Member Junior High Schools, Middle Schools, and Senior High Schools

Advisory and Steering Committees

Pennsylvania Coaches' Association

BOARD OF DIRECTORS

PIAA is divided for administrative purposes into 11 geographic districts, each of which has a District Committee elected by the member schools within the District. Each District Committee elects a chairman, who becomes the District's representative on the Board of Directors, the statewide governing body of the organization. One of the Districts (District 7), by virtue of the number of member schools under its jurisdiction, has two additional representatives on the Board of Directors. Two of the Districts (Districts 1 and 3), by virtue of the number of member schools under their respective jurisdictions, each have a second representative on the Board of Directors.

Other members of the Board of Directors include representatives of the member junior high/middle schools, the Pennsylvania School Boards Association (PSBA), the Pennsylvania Association of School Administrators (PASA), the Pennsylvania Association of Secondary School Principals (PASSP), the Pennsylvania State Athletic Directors Association (PSADA), the Pennsylvania Coaches' Association (PCA), the Pennsylvania Department of Education (PDE), one female and one male PIAA-registered sports official, the chairpersons of the Girls' Athletics and Private Schools' Steering Committees, and one female and one male representative from the Parents' Advisory Committee. With the sometime exception of the officials' and parents' representatives, the members of the Board of Directors are experienced professional educators who have background and experience in dealing with high school athletics.

Policy Review Committee

PIAA-Registered Officials

Budget Committee

Human Resources Committee

EXECUTIVE COMMITTEE

The Executive Committee consists of those persons who as of any given time occupy the positions of President, Vice President, and Treasurer of PIAA.

Executive Director

Secretary to Executive Director

Associate Executive Director

First Assistant Executive Director

Second Assistant Executive Director

Business Manager

Officials' Secretary

Chapters' Secretary

Member Schools' Secretary

Mail Room Supervisor

Bookkeeper

Source: PIAA (2012b). Reprinted with permission.

SCHOOL DISTRICTS.   School districts have various responsibilities, including dealing with high school athletic programs in a limited fashion. For example, local school boards approve all employee contracts, including approving coaches' and athletic directors' contracts. It is important again to note that school district responsibilities differ from state to state. For example, in Indiana, coaches' salaries come from the same general fund as teachers' salaries in that district. Therefore, the school district decides on salaries for coaches from that pool of money. This is not true in all states. In terms of facility construction, decisions on funding sport-related facilities may also be approved by the school district. For example, if a school district decides to fund a gymnasium, the gymnasium is not built just for athletics. It is part of a project benefiting the physical education program, and athletics would share the facility. Finally, school districts may also organize capital campaigns to fund individual projects. Sometimes, depending on the success of the campaign and the immediate needs of the school district, the money raised may or may not go to improving athletic facilities, such as renovating a track or developing an exercise room at a particular school (D. Sullivan, personal communication, June 29, 2002).

INDIVIDUAL SCHOOLS.   Each high school has someone who serves as the Athletic Director. Sometimes this person also works as a coach, although that is not ideal. According to Covell (2012), the responsibilities and tasks of the Athletic Director include:

- hiring, supervising and evaluating coaches;
- coordinating nearly all facets of contest management, including the hiring and paying of officials and event staff; setting . . . training and disciplinary policies; determining . . . budgets; and associated fund-raising;
- determining and verifying game scheduling and athlete eligibility;
- transmitting relevant publicity; and
- handling public relations. (p. 148)

For all of these tasks, the average high school Athletic Director's salary is around $37,000 (Simply Hired, 2012), while other sources project a salary of $50,000–$80,000 depending on if the school is public or private and the assigned duties extend beyond running the athletics program (Nagel, 2012). The Athletic Director is the person who puts forward coaching candidates for the school board's approval. In some states the Athletic Director must also have current teaching certification credentials. In Canada, the setup is usually slightly different. High schools do not have separate Athletic Director positions. The head of the Physical Education Department usually acts as the Athletic Director.

In addition, the Principal has influence in this area as well. The Athletic Director reports directly to the Principal on any matters concerning budget, scheduling, or personnel. If there are conflicts within the department that the Athletic Director cannot resolve, that responsibility may fall to the Principal.

CURRENT POLICY AREAS

A number of policy areas are prominent in the governance of high school athletics, including eligibility; amateurism; gender equity; participation by athletes with disabilities; alcohol, drug, and tobacco use; funding; and home schoolers. Sport managers working in this industry segment must be aware of the constantly changing tides of public opinion about issues surrounding school-age children and young adults as these will impact their policy-making decisions. Several of these issues result from legal challenges to existing or proposed policies. As pointed out earlier in the chapter, because state associations are considered state actors, they cannot violate any students' fundamental rights. The same is true for public school employees, including coaches and athletic directors. Students who believe their rights have been violated can initiate a lawsuit against a coach, an athletic director, a local school board, and the state high school athletic association. The outcomes of these cases can directly affect policies in high school sport, as sometimes the courts mandate that an association change a rule that violated a student's rights.

Eligibility

The policy area receiving the majority of attention is eligibility. Some of you may have attended a high school where an athlete was denied the opportunity to play for a particular reason—maybe his grades were not high enough, or maybe she moved in from a different school district. Perhaps you knew a student who took an eligibility case to the legal system. First, you must remember that playing high school sport is *not* a right guaranteed by law. Attending school until you are a certain age is your right, but participating in interscholastic sport is *a privilege, not a right* (Ness & Colles, 2007). According to Colles and Williams (2010), "Participation is voluntary, and more important, a privilege in the reasoning of the courts, which may be extended at the discretion of the school board" (p. 473). However, even though athletic participation is a privilege, it cannot be taken away arbitrarily. Sport governing bodies must still ensure due process is followed in any decisions they make about eligibility; otherwise, they may end up in litigation. Remember, state associations are state actors, and while their actions are not supposed to violate anyone's constitutional rights, sometimes they do, resulting in litigation. Eligibility discussions most often relate to questions of ethics, academic eligibility, public versus private schools, transfer rules, and age limits for participation.

Ethics and eligibility rules

Eligibility rules in general generate some interesting ethical questions. For example, a high school athletic association may have certain rules about "No pass, no play." While this seems acceptable on the surface, what is the effect on academically struggling students for whom sport is the primary motivation to stay in school? If that chance is taken away, are they more likely to drop out? Although transfer rules are based on the educational premise that a student learns best by staying in the same school for an academic career, should students be "punished" for family problems that may result in relocation to another school district? It is important to make sure the outcome of such rules is, in fact, as fair as possible to the student.

Academic eligibility

All high school associations have policies governing academic eligibility. The reason for this is clear. High school sports are meant to be an extension of a student's educational experience. The purposes of attending high school are to receive an education and earn a diploma so a person can contribute to society in a positive manner. "Overall, academic standards promote educational standards, underscore the educational values of participating in activities, encourage appropriate academic performance and allow the use of interscholastic participation as a motivator for improved classroom performance" (NFHS, 2011b, p. 21).

A focus of discussion in this area is the "No pass, no play" rule. While the specifics differ from state to state, basically this type of rule makes players ineligible to participate for a set number of weeks if they do not meet certain academic standards. For example, students who fail a class in a given term may be ineligible to play sports the following term. Proponents indicate that such rules keep students focused on academics rather than athletics. For athletes seeking college scholarships, these rules also help them stay on a course to meet the NCAA Eligibility Center standards (see Chapter 8). Opponents of such rules mention that for some students, being able to play sports is what motivates them to stay in school, and without the opportunity to participate, those students may drop out. Opponents also point out that this rule may lead students to choose a less-challenging curriculum so they do not put themselves in academic jeopardy. Some states and districts are now revisiting and modifying these rules (McClanahan, 2011).

This matter is determined in a simple way in most European countries. Zintz says, "Being enrolled in and regularly attending classes in a school of secondary education is a primary criterion for eligibility. The second category is age, which cannot of course be waived. When these two conditions are met, the student is eligible to participate in school sport competitions" (Hums, MacLean & Zintz, 2011, p. 105).

Public versus private high schools

Another issue is the public–private school debate. The discussion often centers around private schools' ability to recruit young athletes to play for them. This point raises ethical issues because of the pressures of recruiting young athletes and the possibility of creating a discrepancy between schools with ample resources and those with limited resources and the unlevel playing fields that may result. In some states, private schools dominate state championships, as with volleyball in Kentucky. The KHSAA was the first association to form a Public/Private Task Force to study this debate (KHSAA, 2006b). Ohio, Georgia, and Texas are debating this topic as well, with the Ohio High School Athletic Association forming a Competitive Balance Committee, the Georgia High School Association expanding its divisional structure, and the Texas State Senate discussing the topic (MaxPreps, 2011). Other state associations, such as Missouri, have taken votes to determine whether public school and private school playoff systems should be separate (Wheatley, 2007).

Transfer rules

High school associations have transfer rules for various reasons. These rules keep students from moving from school to school for nonfamily reasons. In other words, these rules are in place to keep students from simply enrolling in whichever school has a successful sports program or a well-known coach. School district boundaries are drawn to ensure fair distribution of students across districts. These distributions are tied to the amount of funding the districts receive from the state or province. Students "jumping" out of district to play sports interrupt this balance. Additionally, transferring schools is generally not easy on high-school-age students, either educationally or socially. If you have ever transferred schools, you may remember the difficulties of making new friends, having new teachers, and learning new rules. In this way, transfer rules work to maintain the ideal of students starting and ending their academic careers in the same school. Another reason for transfer rules is to deter coaches from recruiting students away from other schools. High school athletes, especially the talented ones, have enough pressure on them already. People are wondering where they will go to college, sport apparel companies may already be approaching them, and they still have to maintain their grades for eligibility. Attempting to recruit these students to rival high schools only adds another layer of pressure to their lives. Transfer rules reduce the opportunity for people to exert undue influence and benefit from a student-athlete's prowess (NFHS, 2011b).

Age limits

Traditionally, a student who reached 18 years of age was no longer eligible to participate in high school sport. In Canada, this age limit is usually 19 years of age. According to the NFHS (2011b), the rationale for age eligibility includes the following:

- inhibiting "red shirting" (allowing an extra year of eligibility)
- allowing younger and less-experienced players opportunities to participate
- allowing more students to participate, thus promoting equality
- avoiding overemphasis on athletics
- maintaining safety

Teenagers grow and mature at different rates. Have you ever looked at a room full of high school freshmen boys? They are all shapes and sizes. Now look at a room of seniors. They are much more physically developed. Athletes in their 20s are even more well developed. To keep the size differential under control as much as possible and maintain fair competitive levels, state and provincial athletic associations established age limits to keep more physically developed athletes from injuring the younger, usually smaller athletes. In recent years there have been some modifications in these rules, particularly as they pertain to athletes with cognitive developmental disabilities. The Americans with Disabilities Act (ADA) comes into play here. As you may have learned in your Legal Aspects of Sport class, the two pieces of federal legislation that most directly impact the sport industry in the United States are Title IX and the ADA. Some students with cognitive developmental disabilities, such as Down syndrome, have successfully challenged existing age-limit rules and have been allowed to play past the age of 18 or the prevailing age limit set by their state athletic association. For example, the Michigan High School Athletic Association (MHSAA) recently lifted its age rule under certain circumstances. The new rule states:

- A student's educational progress must have been delayed prior to initial enrollment in the ninth grade solely because of a medically documented disability under the federal Americans with Disabilities Act or Michigan's Persons With Disabilities Civil Rights Act.
- At the time of the waiver request, a student must have a defined disability documented to diminish both physical and either intellectual or emotional capabilities, does not create a health or safety risk to participants and does not create a competitive advantage for the team. (Associated Press, 2012, para. 8)

The age debate is not limited to athletes with disabilities. In Washington state, Darnellia Russell missed a year of school due to her pregnancy. She was then deemed ineligible by the Washington Interscholastic Activities Association (WIAA) because she was 19 years old (Ringer, 2008). The baby's father, however, saw no athletic consequences in the situation. This is another interesting aspect to age limit rules. As evidenced by this section, ongoing debate will continue regarding policy formulation about age limits.

Amateurism

By definition, high school sport means amateur sport. Having limitations on the awards an athlete receives for athletic performance "stimulates participation for the sake of the game itself, prevents exploitation of students, and encourages students to engage in athletic competition for physical, mental and social benefits" (NFHS, 2011b, p. 22). In other words, for high school athletes, sport should be for participation and enjoyment, not a job. Sport should be an extension of the educational mission of the school. To this end, for example, the NFHS has an agreement with professional baseball that professional baseball teams will not sign a high school student to a major or a minor league contract while the student still has high school eligibility (NFHS, 2011b).

Basically, is it in the best interest of the student to leave high school to go directly into the professional ranks? According to NCAA (2011), only .08 percent of boys playing high school football make it to the NFL, and only .03 percent of girls playing high school basketball make it to the WNBA. For the favored few who actually have the talent and the maturity, professional sport can be an option. But what about those who accept the impractical notion that sport is their "way out"? Coaches and athletic directors need to provide realistic information and advice to students who harbor unrealistic hopes and expectations.

Another issue is professionalism in extreme sports. A large number of extreme sport athletes are teenagers who are performing in national and international competitions and often have lucrative sponsorship deals with skateboard or snowboard companies. For example, Olympic Gold Medalist Shawn White "reportedly pulled in a $6 million income while winning all 11 snowboard contests he entered last season. He signed another million-dollar endorsement deal with Red Bull energy drink" (Willoughby, 2007, p. D12). While White is a world-renowned athlete and earned this income at a young age, other young athletes are agreeing to endorse products and become spokespeople for products like Mountain Dew or Sobe. These talented athletes are certainly not competing for their high school teams and would be considered professionals in their respective events. While athletes in other sports such as basketball must wait to become professional athletes, extreme sport competitors are already professionals, even in their teen years.

Gender Equity

Whenever we hear the term *gender equity,* one phrase should come to mind immediately—Title IX. Although most of the publicity generated around Title IX during its 40+ year existence has involved college athletics, this piece of legislation also applies to high school sport. The full title of this historic legislation in the United States is Title IX of the Educational Amendments of 1972. It reads as follows: "No person in the United States shall, on the basis of sex, be excluded from participation in, be denied the benefits of, or be subjected to discrimination under any education program or activity receiving Federal financial assistance" (Carpenter, 2010, p. 540).

While great progress has been made for girls in high school sport, there is still work to be done. A National Women's Law Center (2012) pointed out some of the following:

- Schools are providing 1.3 million fewer chances for girls to play sports in high school as compared to boys. In 1972, only 295,000 girls competed in high school sports, a mere 7.4% of all high school athletes, compared to 3.67 million boys. By the 2010–2011 school year, the number of girls had swelled to 3.2 million, while the number of boys was 4.5 million.
- Less than two-thirds of African-American and Hispanic girls play sports, while more than three quarters of Caucasian girls do. (National Women's Law Center, 2012)

Three quarters of boys from immigrant families are involved in athletics, while less than half of girls from immigrant families are (Sabo & Veliz, 2008).

The courts have repeatedly been asked to rule on different aspects of Title IX legislation, and in 2002 the Bush administration formed a special committee to examine the enforcement, guidelines, and interpretation of the law. Sport managers working in scholastic sport must be aware of any policy interpretations of Title IX issued by the U.S. Department of Education so they can ensure their schools are in compliance with the law.

Gender equity is not a phenomenon limited to the United States. Canada is also dealing with the issue. On the high school level, several provincial associations have policy statements related to gender equity. The OFSAA policy on gender equity (2011) is included in Exhibit 5.6. Discussions about gender equity and fairness in participation opportunities will continue, even as the courts and legislative agencies interpret and reinterpret the laws. The importance of sport participation for girls cannot be overstated. Benefits from participation include greater academic success, increased career opportunities, responsible social behaviors, health benefits, and improved mental health and personal skills (National Women's Law Center, 2012). As outlined in Chapter 4, athletic administrators should consider how they respond to Title IX in terms of corporate social

Gender equity in school sport is the belief and practice which ensure fair access for female student–athletes, coaches, officials and administrators to participate, compete and lead.

Equity does not necessarily mean that all persons must be treated exactly the same. People may need to be treated differently in order to be treated fairly.

VISION

Women and girls will enjoy a full and equitable range of opportunities for participation, officiating, competition and leadership in school sport activities.

GOAL

Through the implementation of this policy, it is our intent to raise awareness, educate, and change attitudes and behaviours which increase and improve the opportunities for girls and women in school sport.

Policy Statements

OFSAA is committed to gender equity as highlighted in the guiding principles of the Federation's Strategic Plan.

OFSAA is committed to educating and providing support to its members through the development and distribution of a gender equity policy.

OFSAA believes that the elimination of barriers to participation will contribute to the achievement of gender equity.

OFSAA believes that gender equity should serve as a guiding principle for all decisions and operations of the Federation and is a key consideration when developing, updating or delivering Federation programs, policies and projects.

Source: OFSAA (2011). Reprinted with permission.

responsibility and whether they are providing opportunities because the law mandates it or because it is the right thing to do.

Participation by Athletes with Disabilities

As mentioned earlier in the section on Eligibility, athletes with disabilities have successfully challenged age limit rules that restrict their full access to participation in high school sport. Beyond that, athletes with disabilities are now gaining opportunities to participate more equally alongside their classmates.

Most notably was a young track athlete from Maryland, Tatyana McFadden. McFadden, born with spina bifida, attended Atholton High School and wanted to compete on the school's track team. A wheelchair racer who had won silver and bronze medals in the 2004 Paralympic Games in Athens, Greece, McFadden was initially blocked from participation. She won the right to compete with able-bodied athletes in track meets after she successfully sued the Howard County Public School System in federal court in 2006. Ultimately, Maryland passed the landmark Fitness and Athletics Equity for Students with Disabilities Act in 2008 (Graham & Seidel, 2010). "The Maryland Public Secondary Schools Athletic Association changed its laws to accommodate those athletes. New language was added . . . to the MPSSAA [Maryland Public Secondary Schools Athletic Association] bylaws, allowing students with disabilities to participate in school sports programs as long as they meet preexisting eligibility requirements, are not ruled to present a risk to themselves or others, and do not change the nature of the game or event" (Graham & Seidel, 2010, para. 1&2). Other states are now following Maryland's lead in providing opportunities for high school athletes with disabilities. According to Mastandrea (2012, para. 1), ". . . the Illinois High School Association (IHSA) announced that it would begin a pilot program of sports events for student athletes with disabilities in cross country, bowling, swimming and diving, and track and field. The plan is to implement state level finals in these sports, and integrate the finals into the IHSA finals for all students during the 2012–2013 school year." Similar discussions are underway in Kentucky, Ohio, and Georgia.

Opportunities for high school students with disabilities took an enormous step forward with the issuance of a Dear Colleague Letter from the Department of Education (DOE) early in 2013; the letter can be found on the government link in the margin. Hailed as the "Title IX for people with disabilities" (Associated Press, 2013), the DOE's guidelines stress that students with disabilities must be treated equitably with regard to interscholastic sport participation opportunities. In summary,

> On January 24, 2013 the Office for Civil Rights issued a Dear Colleague Letter clarifying a school's obligations under the Rehabilitation Act of 1973 to provide extracurricular athletic opportunities for students with disabilities. It creates a clear road for how schools can integrate students with

www

Dear Colleague Letter
http://www2.ed.gov/about/
offices/list/ocr/letters/
colleague-201301-504.html

disabilities into mainstream athletic programs and create adapted programs for students with disabilities. (Active Policy Solutions, 2013, p. 1)

Participation opportunities made available by schools to allow students with disabilities to participate in athletics to the greatest extent possible can include:

- *Mainstream programs*—school-based activities that are developed and offered to all students
- *Adapted physical education and athletic programs*—programs that are specifically developed for students with disabilities
- *Allied or unified sports*—programs that are specifically designed to combine groups of students with and without disabilities together in physical activities

These guidelines were issued as this textbook was being completed. It will be interesting to see how high schools and state high school athletic associations respond to them. This represents a watershed moment for young athletes with disabilities.

Alcohol, Drug, and Tobacco Use

For high school students, who are minors, possessing and consuming alcohol are prohibited by law. Most are also prohibited from purchasing tobacco products due to age restrictions. Possession and use of recreational and some performance-enhancing drugs are illegal, no matter what the person's age. The NFHS

strongly opposes the abuse of anabolic steroids and other performance-enhancing substances by high school student-athletes. Such use violates legal, ethical and competitive equity standards, and imposes unreasonable long-term health risks. The NFHS supports prohibitions by educational institutions, amateur and professional organizations and governmental regulators on the use of anabolic steroids and other controlled substances, except as specifically prescribed by physicians for therapeutic purposes. (NFHS, 2009, para. 1)

In terms of legal action in this area, without a doubt the landmark case is *Vernonia School District 47J v. Acton* (1995). The school Acton attended was having difficulties with student drug use. As administrators looked into the problems, they determined that school athletes appeared to be the leaders of the local drug culture. Because of this, the District proposed a Student Athlete Drug Policy that included drug testing. In the fall of 1997, Acton was denied the opportunity to try out for football because he and his parents refused to sign the drug test consent form. They filed suit against the school district on the basis that the drug-testing policy violated the Fourth and Fourteenth Amendments to the U.S. Constitution, as well as Article 1, Section 9, of the Oregon Constitution. However, the Court ruled that the school district had the right to drug test the athletes: based on "the decreased expectation of privacy, the relative unobtrusiveness of the search, and the severity of the need met by the search—we conclude Vernonia's policy is reasonable and hence constitutional" (*Vernonia School District 47J v. Acton,* 1995). This court decision cleared the way for drug testing of high school athletes.

The NFHS has started its own steroid education program, producing a set of materials called "Make the Right Choice." These materials include DVDs, brochures, and posters (NFHS, 2011c). Today, some states have established their own drug prevention and education programs. For example, the New York State Public High School Athletic Association has a program called Life of an Athlete (NYSPHSAA, 2010).

This issue certainly affects the health and safety of young athletes. It also gives coaches and athletic administrators the opportunity to make a statement about the importance of young people making wise behavioral choices in their lives.

www

NFHS "Make the Right Choice"
www.nfhs.org/content.
aspx?id=3295

NYSPHSAA "Life of an Athlete"
www.nysphsaa.org/
programs/life.asp

Funding

As with all other aspects of education, high school athletics face enormous budgetary pressure. Only a handful of sports generate any income, mostly from ticket sales and concessions. Some athletic programs have booster clubs, made up mostly of parents and alumni, who donate their time and money to help sustain the programs. As mentioned earlier in the chapter, revenue flows into high school associations from various sources, including membership dues, gate receipts, corporate sponsorships, and private donations. Some high school associations are creating new and unique ways to generate funds to ensure their sport programs are financially secure. In addition to the sponsorships mentioned earlier, another source of funding for high school programs that is becoming more popular is corporate donations.

A good example is the Virginia High School League (VHSL), which has established the Virginia High School League Foundation, an endowment fund that relies on tax-free contributions from individuals, businesses, and foundations (VHSL, n.d.). In addition to operating the Foundation, its strategic plan includes this section on Finances and Foundation:

Strategy

The VHSL will increase revenue for support, maintenance and expansion of VHSL services and programs.

Action Plans

1. Identify funding needs in terms of name recognition, student services, reserve fund, recognition program, tournament support, non-revenue activities and team reimbursement.

2. Organize an annual fund drive to build constituency support from individuals and a foundation for a capital campaign.

3. Construct a professionally designed case statement to use as a fundraising tool, as well as a modified version for use in League publications.

4. Increase sponsorships by identifying new sources of revenue and seek additional funds by promoting increased attendance at state events and conducting special events.

5. Build the VHSL Foundation through large annual fund donations and League support, as well as grants from other Virginia foundations. (VHSL, 2007, Finances and Foundation)

Somewhat similar to the VHSL plan, the North Carolina High School Athletic Association (NCHSAA) established an endowment fund in 1991. Recently, the association announced a new capital campaign (NCHSAA, n.d.).

Other associations are directly targeting corporate sponsorships. Often the corporate sponsors' logos appear on the association's website. For example, the Hawaii High School Athletic Association (HHSAA) lists major corporations such as Chevron and Enterprise Rent-A-Car, as well as numerous Hawaii-based corporations such as Hawaiian Airlines and First Hawaiian Bank. The New Mexico Activities Association (NMAA) lists Farmers Insurance, Gatorade, and Sonic among its sponsors; the Iowa High School Athletic Association has the Iowa Farm Bureau; and the Nebraska State Athletic Association has US Bank and the U.S. Marines. The NSAA lists the following as benefits for sponsors in Nebraska:

- Consistently reaching a dominant percentage of the Nebraska student population, coaches, faculty, administrators, friends and family with your corporate identity and message.

- Enhancing your company's community relations program by demonstrating your commitment to educational benefits realized through school activity participation, and ultimately our state communities' youth.

- Increasing and maximizing your products and/or services awareness and ROI by partnering with the organization that produced Nebraska high school championships. (NSAA, n.d.b, para. 3)

The California Interscholastic Federation (CIF) announced it was offering title sponsorships to all of its 450 state and regional championships. A *USA Today* nationwide survey of state associations found 24 that use at least some title sponsorships (Carey & McCarthy, 2012, para. 7). These examples illustrate some tactics high school associations are taking to generate sufficient funds to cover costs and hopefully expand programs when the need arises.

In addition to state associations, individual high schools are also turning to corporate sponsors. Noblesville High School in Indiana secured a $125,000 stadium naming rights deal from a local car dealer Hare Chevrolet (Proffitt, 2012). It is important, however, that schools choose their sponsors

portraits+perspectives

STEVE SILVANO, *Athletic Director*

Moore Traditional High School, Louisville, KY

Our school is a grades 6 through 12 school. My primary job is overseeing and managing both the high school and middle school athletic/activities program. This involves scheduling games, school facilities, and transportation; maintaining eligibility records; working with the principal to hire coaches; and evaluating athletic programs each year.

In my opinion, the most important policy issue confronting high school sport today is year-round sport training. Many middle school and high school athletes now concentrate year-round on one sport. Doing so, they lose out on the advantages of playing multiple sports. Playing more than one sport and exercising various skill sets often will improve aspects of a student's primary sport. For example, a few years ago we had a football lineman who, due to an injury, missed the entire fall season. He later took up wrestling and the following year showed remarkable improvement in his footwork and agility.

I am a member of the state athletic association technology advisory committee. We have met to discuss upgrading the state website. Currently, the coaches' and athletes' pages have been set up to be more user-friendly and to store pertinent information that is easier to process.

High school sport in Jefferson County and the state of Kentucky has many levels and layers of oversight and control. These include the local principal, the director of athletics for the county, the school board, and the state athletic association. One of the best things to come out of this stucture is that it provides a variety of insights and perspectives about a number of issues. This gives us the opportunity to consider viewpoints we otherwise may have overlooked. The biggest drawback of the multi-layered structure is that it's unlikely that every one of the levels will agree. For example, the state may have one set of standards for the number of coaches you may hire for a team while the local school board may cap coaches at a lower level. In such cases, when we follow local rules and standards, someone else in the state following their local rules and standards may have more coaches, possibly giving them an advantage.

High school athletic directors need to stay current as technology continues to evolve. As more individuals and groups get involved in high school athletics, high school athletic directors will need to be vigilant in watching over the best interests of their athletes.

wisely. One could question the selection of a fast-food restaurant as a sponsor, for example, given the obesity epidemic among young people.

Certainly the pressure of finding new alternative funding sources is increasing daily. When seeking corporate sponsors, athletic administrators should research the reputation and products of a potential corporate sponsor. The school's and the corporation's images will be intertwined, so associating with ethical business partners is of the utmost importance.

Home Schoolers

An interesting ongoing debate continues around the issue of whether or not home-schooled students should be eligible to compete in high school athletics. In the United States, close to two million children and young adults are home schooled annually. What happens when home schoolers decide they want to play organized high school sports? With the occasional exception, most home school settings cannot offer competitive high-school-level athletic opportunities, particularly for team sport athletes, so home schoolers who wish to play must make their request to the local public high school they would have attended or, sometimes, to a local private school. Of course, the first athlete who may come to mind is quarterback Tim Tebow, a product of home schooling prior to his college career at the University of Florida. Tebow played high school football for Nease High School in Ponte Vedra Beach, Florida, while being home schooled.

What policies come into play in this situation? This very complex governance and policy area involves the state legislatures, state high school activities associations, occasionally local school districts, and sometimes even the court system. First, there is no one piece of federal legislation in the United States or Canada relative to home schooling. In other words, decisions on all matters involving home schoolers are left up to the individual states and provinces to decide. No wonder there is so much confusion in this area. As of 2011, home schoolers from 34 states were allowed to play high school sport, with criteria for participation varying by state (Home School Legal Defense Association, 2011). This is not to say, however, that there is not some common ground in the discussion. Homeschool Sportnet Incorporated (HSPN) is an organization that considers itself "America's Source for Homeschool Athletics" (HSPN, n.d.). Its mission is presented in Exhibit 5.7.

www

HSPN
www.hspn.net

The issue of home schoolers' eligibility highlights the complex interaction between high school sport governing bodies, state legislations, and the court system (Hums, 1996). Home schooling is a policy area that cuts across several governance levels—local, district, and state. At each level, sport managers need to understand the ethical considerations of letting or not letting home schoolers participate. Is it fair to deny home schoolers the chance to play when their families pay taxes that fund public education? Is it fair for home schoolers to take regularly enrolled students' positions on teams? And what educational message is sent when it is acceptable for home schoolers to play sports with, but not go to school with, other students? Questions continue to emerge and policy continues to evolve in this area as home-schooled students in different states seek the opportunity to participate (Ojalvo, 2012).

SUMMARY

S port governance takes place at a variety of levels, from international to national to state to local. Remember that the real power in scholastic sport lies with the state or provincial associations, although at

Mission statement of the HSPN.

1. To support homeschool parents, athletes, coaches, teams and organizations through means of an interactive web-site, newsletters, workshops and free postings.

2. To provide national athletic events for homeschool students in a Christian environment through the use of venues that are designated as Christian sites and well-known for high ideals.

3. To encourage new start-up teams as well as established organizations by our on-line materials and articles.

4. To offer homeschool teams the best-fit resources from reliable partners in areas such as sports insurance, uniforms, fund raising, web-site support, college recruitment and more.

5. To showcase the talent of homeschool athletes by means of our National Homeschool Scoreboard, n-Perspective Stats Manager, [and] Sports Ticker.

6. To develop a national convention and leadership council.

Source: HSPN, Mission Statement, n.d.

times the courts will mandate their activities if any policies violate students' fundamental rights. The rules-setting and regulatory powers truly reside in these associations. The NFHS acts as a service organization for its state or provincial members. School districts, principals, and athletic directors can set rules on their levels, but they must be in accord with the state or provincial rules. In the United States, high school associations have repeatedly been identified as state actors and therefore subject to the U.S. Constitution for their actions.

The types of governance and policy issues scholastic sport administrators must deal with are vast and complex. The governance decisions they make when setting policy will interact with state as well as federal legislative bodies and laws such as Title IX. They will often come in contact with the judicial system as well, and so they must be prepared for their decisions to be questioned in courts of law. Despite these considerations, scholastic sport administrators have the opportunity to provide programming that has a positive impact on the lives of thousands of young athletes. It is an exciting and personally fulfilling segment of the sport industry.

case STUDY

SCHOLASTIC SPORT

You are the Boys' Basketball Coach at Cheyenne High School. The night you have your preseason organizational meeting for parents and prospective players, you notice a family you have never seen before. After the meeting, the boy and his parents approach you. "We're Mr. and Mrs. Becker and this is our son David. We home school David, but we'd like him to play basketball here at Cheyenne High. We've heard from other parents who home school their children that many states allow it and that in other states, people have challenged for that right in court. We want David to have a chance to play and will pursue whatever avenue is necessary."

1. What do you say to the Beckers this evening?
2. You obviously need to talk to your Athletic Director. What information does the Athletic Director need to gather? What governing bodies should the Athletic Director contact?
3. Should home-schooled students be allowed to participate? Use the SLEEPE Principle to examine all aspects of your decision.
4. How can you and the Athletic Director fairly balance the rights of home schoolers with the rights of students attending the public school daily?

CHAPTER questions

1. How does the North American model of adolescent sport participation differ from that in other countries? What do you consider the advantages and disadvantages of this model compared to others?
2. Where does the main power lie in high school sport? Why?
3. High school sport has a number of goals, including education and participation. Should one of these goals be the preparation of college athletes?
4. One emerging source of funds for high school sport is corporate sponsorship. What are the pros and cons of high school athletic departments pursuing corporate sponsors?

REFERENCES

Active Policy Solutions. (2013). Overview: Disability in sport dear colleague letter. Retrieved from http://www.activepolicysolutions.com/news-resources/

AIA. (n.d.). About AIA. Retrieved from www.aiaonline.org/about/index.php

Altman, S. (2010). State action. In D. J. Cotton, J. T. Wolohan, & T. J. Wilde (Eds.), *Law for recreation and sport managers* (5th ed., pp. 418–427). Dubuque, IA: Kendall-Hunt.

ASAA. (n.d.). Mission statement. Retrieved from http://asaa.org/asaa/about-asaa/mission-statement/

ASAA. (2007). About the Alberta Schools' Athletic Association. Retrieved from www.asaa.ca/new/about asaa.php

Associated Press. (2012, May 31). MHSAA eases age limits for sports eligibility. Retrieved from http://www.battlecreekenquirer.com/viewart/20120531/NEWS/305310012/MHSAA-eases-age-limit-sports-eligibility

Associated Press. (2013, January 25). Sports are a civil right for the disabled, US says. Retrieved from http://www.npr.org/templates/story/story.php?storyId=170221868

Carey, J., & McCarthy, M. (2012, March 15). Title sponsors could be coming to more high school playoffs. Retrieved from http://www.highschoolsports.net/sports/preps/story/2012-03-08/Title-sponsors-could-be-coming-to-more-high-school-playoffs/53540230/1

Carpenter, L. (2010). Gender equity: Opportunities to participate. In D. J. Cotton, J. T. Wolohan, & T. J. Wilde (Eds.), *Law for recreation and sport managers* (4th ed., pp. 538–547). Dubuque, IA: Kendall-Hunt.

Colles, C., & Williams, J. (2010). Voluntary associations and eligibility issues. In D. Cotton & J. Wolohan (Eds.), *Law for recreation and sport managers* (5th ed., pp. 471–482). Dubuque, IA: Kendall-Hunt.

Covell, D. (2012). High school and youth sport. In L. P. Masteralexis, C. A. Barr, & M. A. Hums (Eds.), *Principles and practice of sport management* (4th ed., pp. 141–162). Sudbury, MA: Jones & Bartlett.

Forsythe, L. L. (1950). *Athletics in Michigan schools: The first hundred years.* Englewood Cliffs, NJ: Prentice Hall.

Graham, G., & Seidel, J. (2010, March 25). Public schools open sports to athletes with disabilities. *Baltimore Sun.* Retrieved from http://articles.baltimoresun.com/2010-03-25/sports/bal-va.rule25mar25_1_athletes-mpssaa-disabilities-act

Home School Legal Defense Association. (2011, May). State laws concerning participation of homeschool students in public school activities. Retrieved from http://www.hslda.org/docs/nche/Issues/E/Equal_Access.pdf

HSPN. (n.d.). Home page. Retrieved from http://www.hspn.net/defaultz.asp

Hums, M. A. (1996). Home schooled students' opportunities to participate in interscholastic sport: Legal issues and policy implications for secondary education. *Journal of Legal Aspects of Sport, 6*(3), 169–177.

Hums, M. A., MacLean, J. C., & Zintz, T. (2011). *La Gouvernance au Coeur des politiques des organisations sportives.* Traduction et adaptation de la 2e édition américaine. Bruxelles, Belgique: Groupe De Boeck.

ISA. (2011). Objectives and limits. Retrieved from http://www.isfsports.org/sports/default.asp?id=526

ISF. (2012). About ISF. Retrieved from http://isfsports.org/insideisf/about-isf

KHSAA. (2006a). 2007–2011 Kentucky High School Athletic Association strategic plan. Retrieved from http://www.khsaa.org/strategicplan/20072011/20072011strategicplan.pdf

KHSAA. (2006b, January 10). KHSAA Public/Private update. Retrieved from www.khsaa.org/news/20052006/nr011006.pdf

Kreager, T. (2009, April 6). TSSAA bid policy ups ante for cities. *Daily News Journal.* Retrieved from http://www.timesfreepress.com/news/2009/apr/06/tssaa-bid-policy-ups-ante-cities/?print

Mastandrea, L. (2012). IHSA to pilot events for student athletes with disabilities. Retrieved from http://blog.lindamastandrea.com/2012/06/15/ihsa-to-pilot-events-for-student-athletes-with-disabilities.aspx

MaxPreps. (2011). Ohio highlights private v. public issue in high school sports. Retrieved from http://www.maxpreps.com/news/RLwRo4IdEeCkhgAcxJSkrA/ohio-highlights-private-vs-public-issue-in-high-school-sports.htm

McClanahan, M. (2011, December 19) No-pass, no-play policy suspended in Fairfield. Retrieved from http://www.cbs42.com/content/localnews/story/No-pass-no-play-policy-suspended-in-Fairfield/pmdkBgiGjEGFkWa4G85EFg.cspx

MIAA. (2011, August 20). What is the MIAA? Retrieved from http://www.miaa.net/gen/miaa_generated_bin/documents/menu/ASSOCIATIONPROFILE8202011LATEST.pdf

Nagel, K. (2012, Feb. 26). Athletic directors pull big checks, analysis finds. *Dayton Daily News*. Retrieved from http://www.daytondailynews.com/news/sports/high-school/athletic-directors-pull-big-checks-analysis-finds/nMy6C/

National Women's Law Center. (2012). The battle for equity in athletics in elementary and secondary schools. Retrieved from http://www.nwlc.org/resource/battle-gender-equity-athletics-elementary-and-secondary-schools

NCAA. (2011). Estimated probability of competing in athletics beyond the interscholastic level. Retrieved from http://www.ncaa.org/wps/wcm/connect/public/ncaa/issues/recruiting/probability+of+going+pro

NCHSAA. (n.d.). North Carolina High School Athletic Association endowments. Retrieved from http://www.nchsaa.org/pages/657/Endowment-Fund/

Ness, G., & Colles, C. (2007). Voluntary associations and eligibility issues. In D. J. Cotton & J. T. Wolohan (Eds.), *Law for recreation and sport managers* (4th ed., pp. 467–477). Dubuque, IA: Kendall Hunt.

NFHS. (2007). *National Federation of State High School Associations 2005–2006 annual report*. Indianapolis, IN: Author.

NFHS. (2009). Position statement on anabolic steroids. Retrieved from http://www.nfhs.org/WorkArea/linkit.aspx?LinkIdentifier=id&ItemID=3357&libID=3379

NFHS. (2011a). About us. Retrieved from http://www.nfhs.org/Activity3.aspx?id=3260

NFHS. (2011b). *Handbook 2011–2012*. Indianapolis, IN: Author.

NFHS. (2011c). NFHA steroids awareness. Retrieved from http://www.nfhs.org/content.aspx?id=3295

NFHS. (2011d). State association listing. Retrieved from http://www.nfhs.org/stateoff.aspx

NSAA. (n.d.a). NSAA partnership programs. Retrieved from http://www.nsaahome.org/sponsorship/corpsponsor.pdf

NSAA. (n.d.b). NSAA premier corporate partner: U.S. Bank. Retrieved from http://www.nsaahome.org/sponsor.pdf

NYSPHSAA. (2010). Life of an athlete. Retrieved from http://www.nysphsaa.org/programs/life.asp

OFSAA. (n.d.). What is OFSAA?. Retrieved from http://www2.hts.on.ca/ofsaa/PDFstorage/OFSAA%20info.pdf

OFSAA. (2011). Gender equity policy. Retrieved from http://www.ofsaa.on.ca/sites/default/files/ByLaws%20Sept%202011.pdf

Ojalvo, M. E. (2012). Should home schoolers be allowed to play public school sports? *New York Times*. Retrieved from http://learning.blogs.nytimes.com/2012/02/10/should-home-schoolers-be-allowed-to-play-public-school-sports/

OSAA. (2012). About. Retrieved from http://www.osaa.org/osaainfo/

PIAA. (2012a). Basic philosophy. Retrieved from http://www.piaa.org/about/philosophy.aspx

PIAA. (2012b). Our organization. Retrieved from http://www.piaa.org/about/organization/default.aspx

Proffitt, C. (2012). Noblesville High School turns to corporate sponsorship for football stadium. Retrieved from http://www.wthr.com/story/5328154/noblesville-hs-turns-to-corporate-sponsorship-of-football-stadium?clienttype=printable

Rader, B.C. (1999). *American sports: From the age of folk games to the age of televised sports* (4th ed.). Upper Saddle River, NJ: Prentice Hall.

Ringer, S. (2008). After having baby, gaining eligibility, Roosevelt hoops star is back. *Seattle Times*. Retrieved from http://seattletimes.com/html/highschoolsports/2001812304_ringer11.html

Sabo, D., & Veliz, P. (2008). *Go out and play: Youth sports in America*. East Meadow, NY: Women's Sports Foundation.

Seymour, H. (1990). *Baseball: The people's game*. New York: Oxford University Press.

Sharp, L. A., Moorman, A. M., & Claussen, C. L. (2010). *Sport law: A managerial approach* (2d ed). Scottsdale, AZ: Holcomb Hathaway.

Simply Hired. (2012). High school athletic director salaries. Retrieved from http://www.simplyhired.com/a/salary/search/q-high+school+athletic+director

TSSAA. (1999). TSSAA: History, facts, and figures. Retrieved from http://www.tssaa.org/History/tssaah.htm

Vernonia School District 47J v. Acton. (1995). 515 U.S. 646.

VHSL. (n.d.). VHSL Foundation. Retrieved from http://www.vhsl.org/foundation

VHSL. (2007). Virginia High School League strategic plan. Retrieved from http://www.vhsl.org/files/doc-strategic-plan.pdf

Vincent, T. (1994). *The rise of American sport: Mudville's revenge.* Lincoln: University of Nebraska Press.

Wheatley, T. (2007, May 4). Schools vote against split. *St. Louis Post-Dispatch,* p. D1.

Willoughby, S. (2007, February 13). The crazy world of Senor Blanco. *Denver Post,* p. D12.

Wong, G. M. (1994). *Essentials of sport law.* Westport, CT: Praeger.

Amateur Sport in the Community

6

The term *amateur sport* describes a diverse set of individual and group sporting activities engaged in by millions of people worldwide. Different people play for different reasons. Enjoyment, group affiliation, fitness, healthy living, and the joy of competition are among the most prominent motivations. Amateur athletes do not get paid for their efforts. Rather, a great many amateur sporting activities involve participants who volunteer to play. Participants range from young children to senior citizens to people with disabilities, and their involvement is usually in addition to their primary responsibilities with jobs or schools. Amateur sports include highly competitive events like NCAA playoffs and World Little League Baseball Championships, and they also include less-competitive activities such as organized beach volleyball jamborees and father–daughter golf events. Often lots of media coverage attend the glitz and glitter of highly competitive amateur sporting activities, such as high school and college championship games, but a local weekend beach volleyball tournament with thousands of participants may go unnoticed. Sport study students need an understanding of how community amateur sport entities are organized and governed because many of you will, at some point in your career, be in a leadership position in such organizations. You may be responsible for setting policy and ensuring the effective pursuit of organization goals in this extensive segment of the sport industry.

Organizations delivering amateur sport in the community for youth and adults are both extensive in number and in their variety of activities. In fact, amateur sport in the community has a rich history and an abundance of community structures delivering opportunities for participation. The organizations that govern and establish policy for amateur sport are normally categorized as public or nonprofit. To begin this chapter we will discuss how amateur sport for members of the community first developed and became organized.

HISTORY OF COMMUNITY AND YOUTH SPORT

The roots of modern day amateur sport in North America might be traced to the villages and towns of rural Britain during the industrialization of the 18th and 19th centuries (Kidd, 1999). Mechanization in farming and other industries resulted in the migration of workers from the countryside to cities, and later to North America. Traditionally, farm workers competed in folk games and other precursors to today's athletic events. Although such activities were scarce in overcrowded cities where an expectation of longer work weeks was the norm, games and active forms of recreation continued to be played in elite, all-male schools (Morrow & Wamsley, 2009). As sport for the elite became more popular and better organized, an interest in participating quickly spread to upper-class girls and women and to working-class boys and men. In a similar way, participating in amateur sport emerged and gained momentum in many parts of the world.

In the United States and Canada, adaptation of British sports and development of new games began in the early 1800s. American Indians were accomplished runners, climbers, swimmers, and canoeists, and they participated in many tests of skill and strength. Settlers from England and other parts of Europe brought their own games and tried the indigenous games as well. While working-class men and women had little leisure time to devote to athletic contests, they still participated and spectated during holidays and other special events. By the mid-19th century, North Americans were engaging in a wide variety of athletic contests. An increase in population, the changing nature of work in an increasingly mechanized industrial world, and decreased working hours provided increased leisure time and paved the way for the development of public and nonprofit sport organizations.

Public Sport Organizations

As the urban population increased during the mid- to late-19th century, housing density amplified in urban centers. Municipal activities and private sporting clubs were scrutinized by local governments. Originally, their interest was in regulating leisure practices. Governments declared public holidays, dedicated land for parks and sporting activities, and enacted laws prohibiting what they considered immoral or improper, such as racing and gambling on Sundays. Municipalities subsidized sport competitions such as rifle shooting and banned the rowdiness and immorality thought to be associated with highly publicized prizefights. With increased activities and publicity, along with a greater number of eager participants, public sport organizations developed. Minor sport leagues were formed. Such leagues were managed by groups of individuals who set schedules, adapted and enforced rules and regulations, and promoted and publicized events such as baseball, football, rugby, and track and field. The leagues frequently led to the development of municipal groups, where teams were assembled from the top local talent to represent the entire community. Such a team would then enter into competition by challenging another team from a nearby town. While travel was difficult and kept to a minimum in the early days, teams often endured substantial travel distances in an effort to reap the glory of victory for their hometowns. Competitions between teams from different communities led to the development of sport festivals and jamborees, the precursors to today's state games in the United States and provincial games in Canada. As sport gained interest and became organized by community groups, soon the need for more opportunities and diversity in sport offerings resulted in the development of nonprofit sport organizations.

Nonprofit Sport Organizations

A *nonprofit sport organization* delivers programs and services for a particular sport or group with no intent to gain profit. These types of organizations range from very small (Ontario's London Polo Club) to large professionally run associations (the North Texas Youth Football Association). Nonprofit

www

North Texas Youth Football
Association
http://leaguelineup.com/
welcome.asp?url=ntyfa

sport organizations emerged as an alternative to programs such as recreational sport leagues run by city recreation departments, and in addition to those programs developed with the express intent of making money. In the beginning, nonprofit organizations filled the gap in programming between the two and provided opportunities for participation in sporting events regardless of class or financial background. For-profit organizations offered programming based on business strategies, inevitably providing only the most popular activities. It was impossible for public recreation departments to offer all possible types of sports. Therefore, interested individuals formed their own organizations according to their own interests. Nonprofit sport organizations emerged all over North America for sporting interests as diverse as waterskiing and bicycling, walking and badminton.

Public and nonprofit sport organizations began developing organizational structures, constitutions, positions of leadership with duties and responsibilities, and programs. What are the governance structures for these types of organizations, and how do they develop policy?

GOVERNANCE

www

Climbing Gym Example:
Boise Peak Fitness
www.urbanascent.com

Gymnastic Center Example:
Gold Medal Gymnastics Center
www.gmgc.com

Figure Skating Club Example:
Scarboro Figure Skating Club
www.sfsc.on.ca/

As illustrated by the history of community sport, amateur athletic organizations are structured in a manner consistent with their purpose and mission. While private for-profit ventures exist (such as climbing gyms, gymnastic centers, and figure-skating clubs), most amateur sport in the community is publicly run with funding from some level of government or delivered by nonprofit service organizations. What types of groups fall within these categories, and how are they organized to deliver amateur sport within the community? The following sections will identify the mission, funding, membership, and organizational structure of community amateur sport organizations.

The Governance of Public Sport Organizations

The three main types of public sport organizations delivering amateur sport in our communities are:

1. city parks and recreation departments
2. recreational sport leagues
3. state games and provincial games

City parks and recreation departments

City parks and recreation departments have traditionally housed community sport, recreation, and physical activity programs. Cities provide a wide array of services to their citizens, including utilities such as sewers, water, and gas and electric. Cities also provide public transportation and care for infrastructures such as roads and bridges. In addition to these basic services, many cities also take it upon themselves to offer a wide array of sport and recreation facilities.

MISSION. City parks and recreation department mission statements are as varied as the activities they offer. They usually include themes such as opportunities for leisure-time activities, learning and playing in a safe environment, provision of a wide variety of facilities, and statements of inclusivity and support for diversity. Two sample mission statements, one of the Parks and Recreation Department of the City of Houston and one of the City of Toronto, are presented in Exhibits 6.1 and 6.2.

MEMBERSHIP. Generally these programs are open to any and all residents of a particular city. Established policies deal with participation by nonresidents and guests. The people who take part in physical activities offered by city parks and recreation programs have a wide variety of activities to choose from, including offerings such as swimming, soccer, softball, fitness programs, martial arts, tennis, hiking and biking trails, and many

www

Houston Parks and Recreation Department
http://www.houstontx.gov/parks/aboutus.html

City of Toronto Park and Recreation Department
http://www.toronto.ca/parks/

Mission statement of the City of Houston Parks and Recreation Department.
exhibit **6.1**

To enhance the quality of urban life by providing safe, well maintained parks and offering affordable programming for our community.

Source: City of Houston (2013).

Mission statement of the City of Toronto Parks and Recreation Department.
exhibit **6.2**

The Parks and Recreation Division's mission is to ensure that people in the diverse communities of Toronto have full and equitable access to high-caliber locally responsive recreational programs, efficiently operated facilities, and safe, clean and beautiful parks, open spaces, ravines and forests.

Source: City of Toronto (2011).

others. Activities are not limited to the traditional team sport offerings, as departments try to keep up with trends by offering popular activities. For example, the City of Seattle Parks and Recreation Department offers the following:

> . . . 400 parks and open areas, and over 6200 acres of park land, 204 athletic fields, 151 outdoor tennis courts, an indoor tennis center, 27 community centers, 26 children play areas, 9 gardens, 3 golf courses, more than 60 basketball courts, a variety of places to run & jog, 8 swimming beaches, 2 boating centers, 4 environmental learning centers, 8 indoor pools, 3 outdoor pools, and 30 wading pools. (City of Seattle, 2012)

FINANCIALS. Because these facilities and staff are provided by the city, city residents' tax money underwrites a good portion of the costs. As a result, some facility use and programming may be offered free of charge, for example, swimming at the neighborhood public pool. Other services may require a fee; for example, a city-sponsored softball league may require teams to pay an entrance fee to cover the costs of umpires, field maintenance, and softballs for each game.

The size of a city parks and recreation budget will vary from city to city. For example, the City of Kissimmee, Florida, had a 2010 budget of $4,922,862, which came from ad valorem taxes, impact fees, sales tax, grants, and a utility surcharge (Kissimmee Parks and Recreation, 2011). A much smaller city, Snellville, Georgia, budgeted for $655,782 in expenses in 2011–2012 (City of Snellville, 2013).

ORGANIZATIONAL STRUCTURE. A city parks and recreation department is one of numerous departments within the organizational structure of a city. Exhibit 6.3 shows how parks and recreation fits into the overall organizational chart for the large city of San Diego, California. Exhibit 6.4 illustrates how the organizational chart for the City Park and Recreation Department can become very complex in larger cities like San Diego. By contrast, the parks and recreation department for a smaller city (population 65,000) such as Loveland, Colorado, is presented in Exhibit 6.5.

Recreational sport leagues

Recreational sport leagues provide opportunities for regular participation in sport for both children and adults. Leagues might be established by an interested group of individuals who wish to play basketball on a regular basis, or they may be run by community recreation staffs in city parks and recreation facilities. Leagues are commonly available in a wide variety of sports, like football, baseball, hockey, curling, volleyball, soccer, and bowling. Most recreational sport leagues are considered a public service. They are organized to provide individuals the opportunity to participate in their sport of choice.

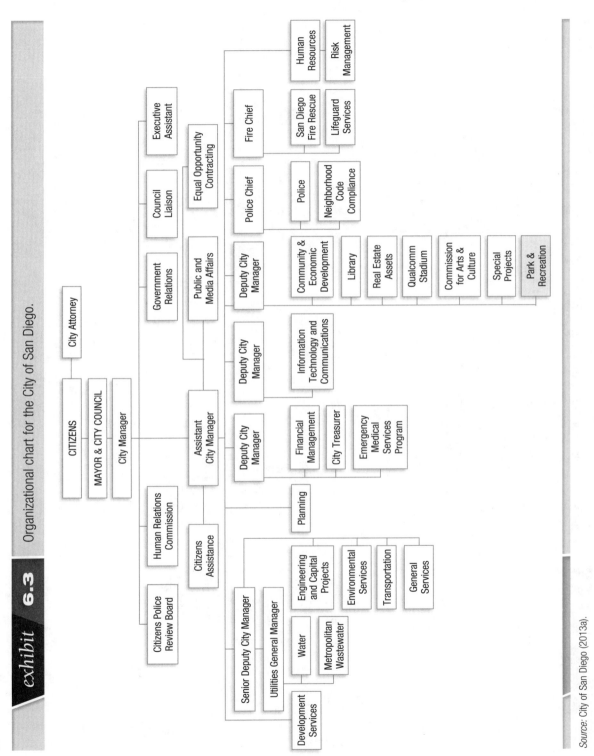

exhibit 6.3   Organizational chart for the City of San Diego.

CITIZENS

MAYOR & CITY COUNCIL

City Manager

City Attorney

Citizens Police Review Board

Human Relations Commission

Citizens Assistance

Assistant City Manager

Government Relations

Council Liaison

Executive Assistant

Public and Media Affairs

Equal Opportunity Contracting

Deputy City Manager

Deputy City Manager

Deputy City Manager

Information Technology and Communications

Financial Management

City Treasurer

Emergency Medical Services Program

Planning

Senior Deputy City Manager

Utilities General Manager

Water

Metropolitan Wastewater

Development Services

Engineering and Capital Projects

Environmental Services

Transportation

General Services

Police Chief

Fire Chief

Police

Neighborhood Code Compliance

San Diego Fire Rescue

Lifeguard Services

Human Resources

Risk Management

Community & Economic Development

Library

Real Estate Assets

Qualcomm Stadium

Commission for Arts & Culture

Special Projects

Park & Recreation

Source: City of San Diego (2013a).

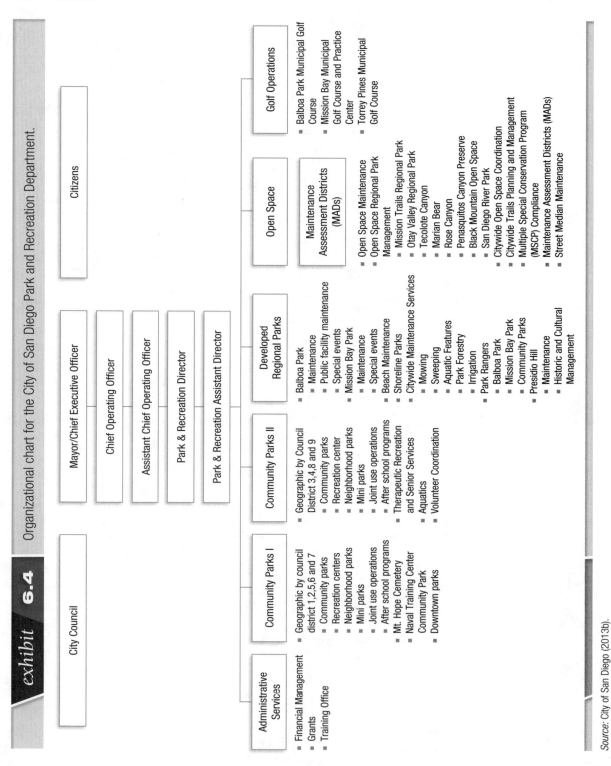

exhibit **6.4** Organizational chart for the City of San Diego Park and Recreation Department.

City Council

Mayor/Chief Executive Officer

Chief Operating Officer

Assistant Chief Operating Officer

Park & Recreation Director

Park & Recreation Assistant Director

Citizens

Administrative Services
- Financial Management
- Grants
- Training Office

Community Parks I
- Geographic by council district 1,2,5,6 and 7
  - Community parks
  - Recreation centers
  - Neighborhood parks
  - Mini parks
  - Joint use operations
  - After school programs
- Mt. Hope Cemetery
- Naval Training Center Community Park
- Downtown parks

Community Parks II
- Geographic by Council District 3,4,8 and 9
  - Community parks
  - Recreation center
  - Neighborhood parks
  - Mini parks
  - Joint use operations
  - After school programs
- Therapeutic Recreation and Senior Services
- Aquatics
- Volunteer Coordination

Developed Regional Parks
- Balboa Park
  - Maintenance
  - Public facility maintenance
  - Special events
- Mission Bay Park
  - Maintenance
  - Special events
  - Beach Maintenance
- Shoreline Parks
- Citywide Maintenance Services
  - Mowing
  - Sweeping
  - Aquatic Features
  - Park Forestry
  - Irrigation
- Park Rangers
  - Balboa Park
  - Mission Bay Park
  - Community Parks
- Presidio Hill
  - Maintenance
  - Historic and Cultural Management

Open Space
- Maintenance Assessment Districts (MADs)
- Open Space Maintenance
- Open Space Regional Park Management
  - Mission Trails Regional Park
  - Otay Valley Regional Park
  - Tecolote Canyon
  - Marian Bear
  - Rose Canyon
  - Penasquitos Canyon Preserve
  - Black Mountain Open Space
  - San Diego River Park
- Citywide Open Space Coordination
- Citywide Trails Planning and Management
- Multiple Special Conservation Program (MSCP) Compliance
- Maintenance Assessment Districts (MADs)
- Street Median Maintenance

Golf Operations
- Balboa Park Municipal Golf Course
- Mission Bay Municipal Golf Course and Practice Center
- Torrey Pines Municipal Golf Course

Organizational chart for the City of Loveland, Colorado, Parks & Recreation Department.

exhibit   6.5

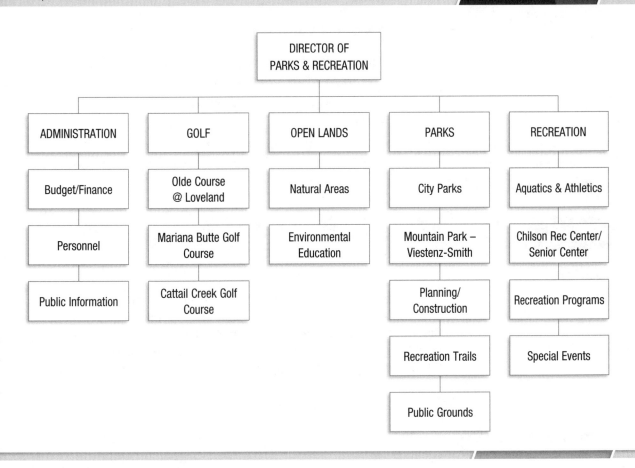

Source: City of Loveland, Colorado (2013).

MISSION. A recreational sport league's mission statement will likely include some comment about what sport the league is delivering and to which level of participant. The league may be highly competitive or designed with more of a recreational focus on fun. Fair play, respect, and ethical conduct are common components of recreational sport league mission statements. See Exhibits 6.6 and 6.7 for the mission statements of the Boise Nationals Soccer Club, in Boise, Idaho, and of the Pickering Hockey Association in Pickering, Ontario.

MEMBERSHIP. Recreational sport leagues are organized for a vast array of participants. Some activities target children and youth groups, other leagues

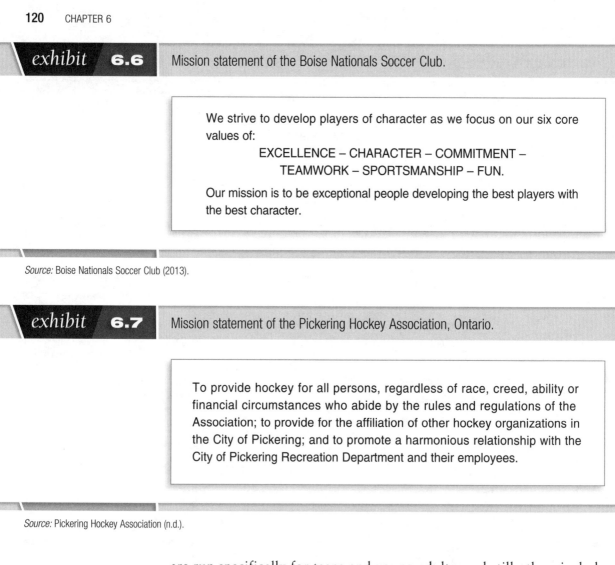

exhibit 6.6   Mission statement of the Boise Nationals Soccer Club.

> We strive to develop players of character as we focus on our six core values of:
>
> EXCELLENCE – CHARACTER – COMMITMENT –
> TEAMWORK – SPORTSMANSHIP – FUN.
>
> Our mission is to be exceptional people developing the best players with the best character.

Source: Boise Nationals Soccer Club (2013).

exhibit 6.7   Mission statement of the Pickering Hockey Association, Ontario.

> To provide hockey for all persons, regardless of race, creed, ability or financial circumstances who abide by the rules and regulations of the Association; to provide for the affiliation of other hockey organizations in the City of Pickering; and to promote a harmonious relationship with the City of Pickering Recreation Department and their employees.

Source: Pickering Hockey Association (n.d.).

are run specifically for teens and young adults, and still others include adults, both young and old. Leagues might be gender specific or coed.

FINANCIALS. Funding for recreational sport leagues is often provided through municipal sources and supplemented by league fees charged to each participant. The salaries of administrators designing and delivering the league may be paid through municipal departments. The costs of facilities are also borne by the community. Often, participants will pay a small fee to generate some revenue toward paying for administrative costs, officials, and equipment. Of course, the "pay for play" fee could be more substantial if the particular sport has expensive requirements, such as ice rental for hockey leagues. The major expense categories for minor sport leagues include facility rental, officials, purchase of equipment, and promotion and publicity.

ORGANIZATIONAL STRUCTURE. A group of officers is usually elected to help organize and govern the activities of the league. These voluntary positions might include a president, vice president, and chairs of a few committees specific to the particular sport. For example, one might expect a Beach Volleyball League to be governed by a League Executive Committee that comprises the President, Vice President, Chair of Scheduling, and Chair of Facilities. The President runs meetings and provides overall direction and leadership, while the Vice President might be responsible for league promotion, complaints, and discipline. The Scheduling Chair develops and communicates all league scheduling, and the Facilities Chair schedules event locations and coordinates with facility staff for equipment. The elected members of the Executive Committee develop policy, and these administrators debate issues and ideas regarding league operation at the Annual Meeting. Policy might be required to guide the league activities in each of the major areas of responsibility and to incorporate where, when, and how the games are played.

State games and provincial games

State games (U.S.) and provincial games (Canada) are amateur sport festivals held every year or two. Individuals and teams may have to qualify to attend the games by successfully advancing through regional competitions or by gaining entry through a lottery or a first-come, first-served basis. These games are usually multisport events, held in both summer and winter. For example, the Iowa Games Annual Sport Festival is held in winter and summer locations each year. Over 65 summer and 24 winter sports are organized for both adult and youth athletes. The Iowa Games are a multisport festival of Olympic-style competition for Iowa's amateur athletes, and in this case age, ability, and gender are not considered criteria for participation.

www

Iowa Games
http://iowagames.org

MISSION. The mission of state and provincial games focuses on delivering a well-organized amateur sport competition for athletes of a variety of ages within the region. The idea of the games is to offer citizens the opportunity to compete, gain experience, and come together in a festival atmosphere. The games are usually multisport and designed for participants, coaches, officials, spectators, volunteers, and sport managers—an experience for everyone. See Exhibit 6.8 for the mission statement of the Iowa State Games.

MEMBERSHIP. The members of summer or winter games hosted by a U.S. state or Canadian province include mostly participants and volunteers. The organization does not have a group of individual members outside the event but is composed of a paid professional staff and a volunteer group that functions as a Board of Directors to organize the events.

FINANCIALS. State and provincial games are funded through both public and private sources, entry fees, and money raised through sponsors and mar-

exhibit   6.8   Mission statement of the Iowa State Games.

> The mission of the Iowa Games is to provide Iowa citizens with a whole-some avenue for positive personal development through sports and physical activity, to recognize their dedication and achievement, to enable all citizens the opportunity to utilize quality sport facilities and to create an amateur sports network of administrators, officials and volunteers throughout Iowa to further the development of amateur athletic programs. In addition, the Iowa Games encourages all Iowans to practice sports-manship, trustworthiness, respect, responsibility, fairness, caring and citizenship, while striving to be a champion on and off the field of play.

Source: Iowa Games (2012). Reprinted with permission.

Iowa Sports Foundation
www.iowasportsfoundation.org

keting initiatives. The Iowa Games, for example, is a project of the Iowa Sports Foundation "made possible because of the financial support from corporate sponsors, in-kind and cash donations" (Iowa Sports Foundation, 2012).

ORGANIZATIONAL STRUCTURE. The paid staff usually comprises an Executive Director, one or more Directors of Sports, Event Operations, and Finance, and a number of assistant positions that help to organize specific components of the games. The Board of Directors, all volunteers, includes a Chair or President, Vice President, Treasurer, Secretary, and a number of board members who may be responsible for specific aspects of the events. The organizational structure of the Iowa Games is presented in Exhibit 6.9.

The Governance of Nonprofit Organizations Involved in Community Sports

The term *nonprofit* aptly describes many community organizations involved in sport. They are organizations developed to deliver activities and services with no intent of making a profit. This type of organization may be large or small and may have a simple or an intricate organizational structure. Prominent examples of nonprofit amateur sport organizations include the Y, formerly the Young Men's Christian Association (YMCA), the Young Women's Christian Association (YWCA), the Boys & Girls Clubs, and the Jewish Community Centers (JCC). Other local nonprofit community groups also provide opportunities for amateur sport.

Organizational structure of the Iowa Games. *exhibit* **6.9**

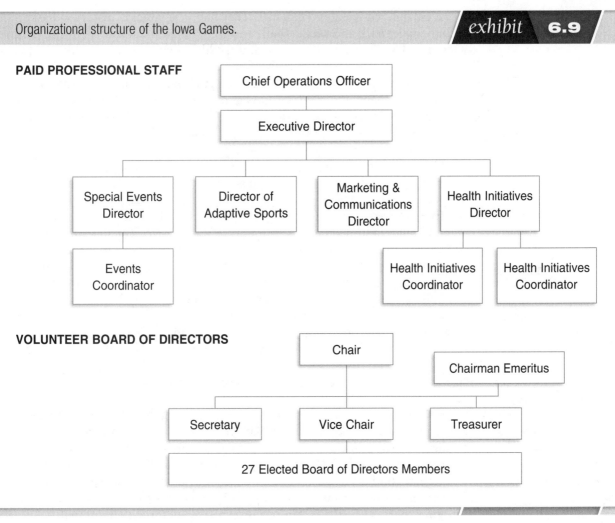

PAID PROFESSIONAL STAFF

Chief Operations Officer

Executive Director

Special Events Director | Director of Adaptive Sports | Marketing & Communications Director | Health Initiatives Director

Events Coordinator

Health Initiatives Coordinator | Health Initiatives Coordinator

VOLUNTEER BOARD OF DIRECTORS

Chair

Chairman Emeritus

Secretary | Vice Chair | Treasurer

27 Elected Board of Directors Members

Source: Iowa Games (2012). Reprinted with permission.

The Y (formerly YMCA)

YMCAs are service organizations, collectively the largest nonprofit community organizations in the United States (Y, 2012). The organization recently rebranded by shortening its name to "the Y" as a way of emphasizing its programs' impact on youth and healthy living. The name change resulted from more than two years of research orchestrated by the national YMCA of America, which revealed that most people do not understand the organization's activities and mission. It will take about 5 years to completely implement the change, giving regional Ys the chance to adapt. Ys provide programming for children and adults, for males and females of all races, abilities, ages, and incomes. They have a significant history in basketball, volleyball, and racquetball, and were the original leaders in camping and fitness, as well as in providing children with swimming lessons (Y, 2012). The Ys serve more than 45 million people in more than 120 countries around the world; there are more than 2,600 Ys located in the United States alone and about 45 YMCAs and 8 Young Women's Christian Associations (YWCAs) located in Canada (YMCA Canada, 2012), where the YMCAs have not yet formally changed their name.

MISSION. A large component of the Y's mandate is delivered via amateur sports programs, including leagues, instructional classes, family nights, youth sports programming, mentoring, and exchange programs. Each Y strives to nurture the healthy development of children and teens, strengthen families, and make the community a better place. The mission involves the development of the "whole body" through programs that often incorporate physical activity. The rebranded organization focuses its activities on youth development, healthy activity, and social responsibility. See Exhibit 6.10 for the mission statement of the Y.

MEMBERSHIP. Ys are a part of community life in neighborhoods and towns across North America. In the United States over 21 million individuals enjoy their services each year. Several types of memberships are available, along with the ability to join only specific programs or groups.

FINANCIALS. Each local Y is an independent, charitable, nonprofit organization required to pay dues to a National Association. Of the total revenue the National Association collects per year, approximately 31 percent comes from program fees, 32 percent from memberships, 19 percent from charitable contributions, 6 percent from resident camping and living quarters, 12 percent from government contracts and grants, and 1 percent from miscellaneous sources (Y, 2012). No one is turned away for inability to pay.

exhibit **6.10**   Mission statement of the Y.

> The Y's mission is "to put Christian principles into practice through programs that build healthy spirit, mind and body for all" through the motto "we build strong kids, strong families and strong communities."

Source: Y (2012).

ORGANIZATIONAL STRUCTURE. Ys have volunteers and professional, full-time, paid staff who help set policy that is then implemented by both employees and volunteers. Most operate with a volunteer Board of Directors, steered by an Executive Committee elected from board members. Other committees work on specific types of programs or initiatives, like youth sports, clubs and camps, and family nights. The local board has jurisdiction over the development of policy for the independent Y, as long as the independent Y meets the following requirements as outlined in the national constitution (Y, 2012):

1. Annual dues are paid by the local Y to the national office, the Y of the U.S.A.
2. The Y refrains from any practices that discriminate against any individual or group.
3. The national mission is supported.

Accordingly, "all other decisions are local choices, including programs offered, staffing, and style of operation" (Y, 2012).

The organizational structure of a typical Y is shown in Exhibit 6.11.

YWCA

The YWCA "advocates for peace, justice, health, human dignity, freedom and care of the environment, and has been at the forefront of raising the status of women since it was founded in 1894 (YWCA, 2012a). It aims to provide safe places for girls and women no matter what their situation. The YWCA USA acts as a voice for women's issues, advocating and lobbying on behalf of pay equity and hate crimes legislation, for example, in order to empower women and girls in our society (YWCA, 2012b).

www

YWCA
www.ywca.org

MISSION. "The YWCA is dedicated to eliminating racism, empowering women and promoting peace, justice, freedom and dignity for all" (YWCA, 2012c), reads the organization's formal mission statement.

MEMBERSHIP. Worldwide there are more than 25 million members in 124 countries, including 2 million members and participants in 250 local associations in the United States and 1 million members in 200 communities in Canada.

FINANCIALS. The total net assets of YWCA USA per year are almost $54 million. Of this amount, revenues accrue from government grants, public support (individuals, foundations, and corporations), membership fees, and program service fees (YWCA, 2010).

ORGANIZATIONAL STRUCTURE. In 2001, YWCA members voted to restructure the national organization. The grassroots Change Initiative reversed the

exhibit   **6.11**   Organization chart for the Harlem YMCA.

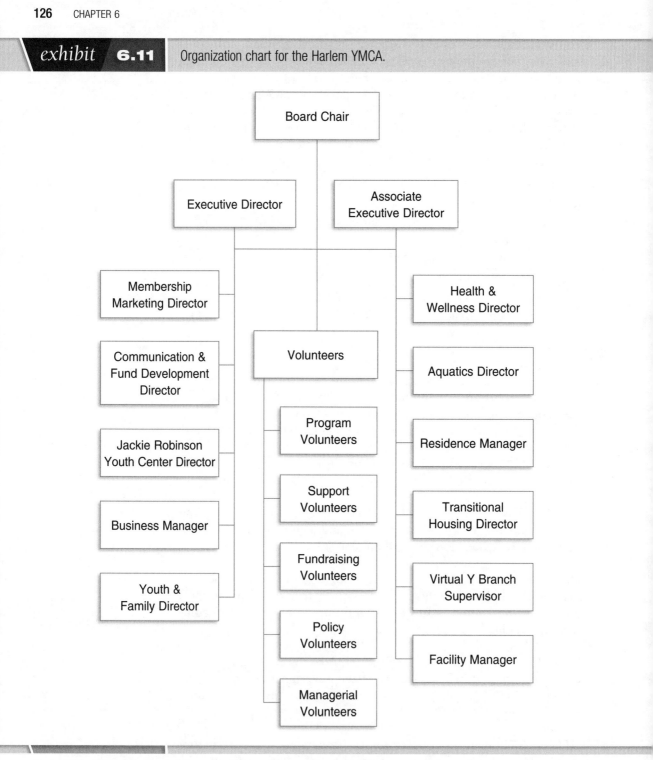

top-down structure to a bottom-up structure grounded in the work of the local associations. Nine separate Regional Councils were created, and each local association became affiliated with a Regional Council. Each local association sends two representatives from their association to serve on the Board of Directors of their Regional Council. The Regional Council in turn elects two representatives to serve on the National Coordinating Board, the governing board of the YWCA. In addition, each Regional Council sends representatives to serve on the national committees, thereby giving extensive local representation on the regional and national level. The national office has been charged primarily with conducting advocacy at the national level and for marketing and branding.

Boys & Girls Clubs

The Boys & Girls Clubs of America is a national association of community boys and girls clubs. Such clubs offer programs and services to promote and enhance the development of boys and girls in a safe, healthy environment. Sports programming is one component of the services provided by Boys & Girls Clubs.

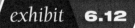

Boys & Girls Clubs of America
www.bgca.org

MISSION. The Boys & Girls Clubs of America acts to provide boys and girls with the following:

- a safe place to learn and grow
- the opportunity for ongoing relationships with caring adult professionals
- life-enhancing programs, opportunities, and character-building experiences.

The Boys & Girls Clubs of America strives to provide opportunities for young people, especially those from disadvantaged backgrounds. See Exhibit 6.12 for its mission statement.

Mission statement of the Boys & Girls Clubs of America.

exhibit **6.12**

The mission of the Boys & Girls Clubs of America is "to enable all young people especially those who need us the most, to reach their full potential as productive, caring responsible citizens."

Source: Boys & Girls Clubs of America (2007).

BOYD WILLIAMS, *Senior Vice President/Chief Operating Officer*

YMCA of the Pikes Peak Region, Colorado Springs, CO

My responsibilities as YMCA Chief Operating Officer cover a broad range of functions. The primary roles are over-all assurance and oversight for the day-to-day operations within the organization, including managing and balancing the organization's operating budget. This work includes all membership and program-related functions, facilities, marketing, member services, financial development, and board/volunteer development. Operationalizing the Association's strategic plan serves to set direction for the organization and ultimately drives decisions that are carried out through the daily execution of operations.

I also work closely with executive staff at each location, offering guidance and supervisory functions. Our priorities include community involvement and ensuring the YMCA is "at the table" for conversations that relate to meeting the community's ever-changing needs.

Interacting with the board of directors and volunteers who serve on standing committees is also an important aspect of my job. Working closely with the board volunteers is necessary because the volunteers are not only fiduciary agents of the organization, but also serve to represent the YMCA within the community and ultimately have the final authority within the not-for-profit structure.

Protecting and sustaining the YMCA's charitable, tax-exempt status remains an important national, state, and local issue for YMCAs throughout the United States. The YMCA earns its tax exemption every day through the quality, life-changing mission work Ys provide to the community. The Y lessens the burden on government through its cause-driven, high impact work, yet many throughout communities where there is a Y presence do not understand the beneficial nature of the Y. The YMCA offers membership and program opportunites for everyone regardless of their ability to pay, through a policy-driven financial assistance program. This policy is just one example of how the Y differentiates itself and remains a significant contributor to the communities it serves.

Local YMCAs must take a more proactive approach in communicating the benefits and differences when being compared to like-providers. Boards play an integral part in setting policy that could affect the Y's charitable status and, equally as important, can help to educate the community on the YMCA's mission and purpose.

Healthcare reform and the continuing decline in the overall health of our nation is and will be a critical factor for Ys in the future. YMCAs are mobilized throughout the country and positioned to affect change through collaborative work with the government, healthcare networks, and other partners with goals of reversing health-related issues.

As a CEO, I was involved in developing strategy and executing a plan to better align the YMCA with its mission and ability to serve all in a more meaningful manner. At the time, the YMCA of the Pikes Peak Region had multiple tiers of membership and the goal was to set a single-tier membership structure. The transition included a change in YMCA policy and thus required board input governance. The change process involved many aspects including determining the financial impact of the membership modification, developing communication strategies, and obtaining board understanding and approval. This policy change was well received after much deliberation and involvement at both the staff and board levels.

I believe the YMCA's governance structure is well-suited for a community based organization that serves specific needs within each local YMCA's service area. Volunteers who serve on YMCA boards are committed individuals who understand the scope of work the Y can provide in meeting current challenges and opportunities. Boards serve in different modes of governance depending on the current issues or focus. Mature YMCA boards have the ability to move from strategic to fiduciary to generative modes of board governance based on the organization's needs, and they provide flexibility in maintaining strong, viable leadership at the volunteer board level.

Challenges under this structure include maintaining YMCA community-relevance that supports the needs of the community and having a board that not only understands the role the Y plays, but also serves as an advocate for the Y at local, state, and national levels. Strong leadership at the board level is a necessity. The board, working with the President/CEO of the YMCA, can help provide the direction needed for the organization and prevent volunteers and the board from becoming misaligned with the organization's mission and strategic direction.

At the local level, I believe the YMCA will continue to struggle with governing in a manner that ensures the YMCA will remain relevant to the community it serves. Identifying individuals within the community fabric who understand the cause-driven focus of the Y will remain critical to building and sustaining strong, volunteer-driven boards.

Today's YMCAs are moving in a direction that has evolved significantly since 1844 and are prepared to address the health issues our nation faces. Continuing to develop policies that address these health issues is critical. The YMCA governance structure has been effective in the past and will continue to play a larger role as YMCAs strive to work collaboratively with entities at the local, state, and even national levels.

MEMBERSHIP. Over 4.1 million youth participated in programs at over 4,000 clubs in the United States, with the gender breakdown at approximately 55 percent male and 45 percent female (Boys & Girls Clubs of America, 2007). The clubs provide a variety of unique sport programming, tournaments, and the JrNBA and JrWNBA programs. Other specialized learning programs, such as the Athletic Director University program, teach youngsters leadership skills to organize and administer their own leagues, clubs, and teams.

FINANCIALS. Boys & Girls Clubs are nonprofit organizations. Revenues to run programming, hire staff, and maintain facilities come from membership dues, private donations, corporate funding, and community partnerships such as the partnership with United Way. Membership rates are kept to a minimum ($10 to $35 per year), and no one is turned away from programming because of an inability to pay. On average, about $300 is spent per youth in a given year.

ORGANIZATIONAL STRUCTURE. There may be as many as 20 clubs in a region, each operating with a small professional staff and many volunteers. The Boys & Girls Clubs of Metro Atlanta, for example, are organized with a volunteer Board of Directors, to which members from each club belong (Boys & Girls Clubs of Metro Atlanta, 2007). The board is elected and is composed of 10 unit board presidents from regions within the geographical area and 49 board members (Boys & Girls Clubs of Metro Atlanta, 2012). The Board of Directors and the association members are responsible for developing policy, such as the policy regarding the division of revenues between each of the metro clubs. Policy may determine that the use of revenues collected by individual clubs be defined without restriction by the club, but that revenues distributed to individual clubs by the over-

www

Boys & Girls Clubs of Metro Atlanta
www.bgcma.org/

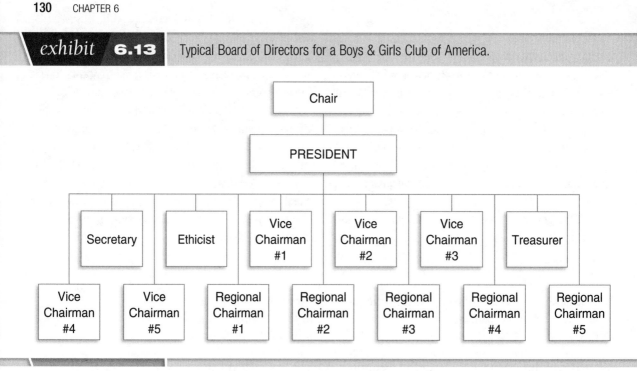

exhibit 6.13   Typical Board of Directors for a Boys & Girls Club of America.

Source: Boys & Girls Clubs of America (2012). Reprinted with permission.

arching Atlanta parent group be used in specific areas such as programming, professional staff, and facilities.

The organizational structure of a typical Boys & Girls Club is shown in Exhibit 6.13.

Jewish Community Centers

www

Jewish Community Center Association of North America
www.jcca.org/

Jewish Community Centers (JCC) are nonprofit organizations under the authority of the Jewish Community Center Association of North America, an umbrella organization including more than 350 JCCs, Young Men's Hebrew Associations/Young Women's Hebrew Associations (YMHAs/YWHAs), and campsites in the United States and Canada (JCCA, 2012). The Jewish Community Center Association offers a wide range of services and resources to help its affiliates provide educational, cultural, social, Jewish identity-building, and recreational programs for people of all ages and backgrounds.

Each year the JCC Association puts together a sporting festival for Jewish teens known as the JCC Maccabi Games. These games are an Olympic-style sporting competition held each summer on multiple sites in North America and is the largest organized sports program for Jewish teenagers in the world (Orange County Maccabi Games, 2012). In addition, the JCC Association helps sponsor the Maccabiah Games, which is essentially the quadrennial Jewish Olympics and is held in Israel the year following the Summer Olympic Games.

MISSION. The mission of the JCC Association of North America is "to encourage and help everyone at the JCC to continue learning, growing, and thriving. It's all about teaching and learning for a lifetime" (JCC, 2012b). The Jewish Community Center of Greater Baltimore, the nation's first JCC, defines its mission as being "dedicated to promoting and strengthening Jewish life and values through its programs and services to individuals, groups, and families" (Jewish Community Center of Greater Baltimore, 2000).

MEMBERSHIP. The JCC Association serves more than 350 JCC, YM/YWHA, and campsites in North America. Each of these organizational members pays annual dues to the association. The association offers its members a wide range of services and resources in educational, cultural, social, Jewish identity-building, and recreational programs for people of all ages and backgrounds (JCC, 2012b).

Individual JCCs offer memberships in various categories. There are individual memberships, family memberships, senior memberships, and some local JCCs even offer full community memberships.

FINANCIALS. In 2010, the JCC Association of North America operated with a budget just below $11 million. Revenues came from the following sources: JCC dues (38%), program revenue (24%), NFC and federation support (21%), foundation grants (10%), corporate sponsorship (5%), and earnings from investments (2%). Association expenses included: program enrichment services (40%), community consultation services (15%), professional leadership (10%), management and finance (10%), marketing and communications (9%), Jewish education (7%), financial resource development (6%), and services to the military (4%) (JCC, 2012b).

In 2010, the JCC of San Francisco had operating revenues of almost $42 million that were derived from the following sources: Maccabi Games 2010, activity income, center membership, gifts and grants, investments, and other income. Expenses included programs, management, building repairs and improvements, and fundraising (JCC of San Francisco, 2010).

ORGANIZATIONAL STRUCTURE. The JCC Association of North America is organized with an Executive Committee and a Board of Directors. The Executive Committee, formed by elected officers, consists of a President, a Chair, seven Vice-Chairs, a Secretary, two Associate Secretaries, a Treasurer, and seven Honorary Chairs. The Board of Directors is very large, consisting of 101 members (JCC, 2012a). The JCC Association has three North American offices, as well as one in Jerusalem, Israel. The North

WWW

JCC Maccabi Games
www.jccmaccabigames.org/

American offices are located in New York City; Austin, Texas; and New Orleans, Louisiana.

The JCC of San Francisco is directed by an Executive Director, a group of elected officers, and a volunteer Board of Directors. Along with the Executive Director, the elected officers include a President, a Vice-President, a Treasurer, and a Secretary. The volunteer Board of Directors is also large, consisting of 25 members (JCC of San Francisco, 2012).

www

JCC of San Francisco
www.jccsf.org

Community groups

Many individuals and groups run nonprofit organizations for sport and physical activity. These may be community based but not run by community government agencies such as city parks and recreation departments, and they usually focus on a single sport or physical activity. Community groups such as the Pacers and Racers Running and Walking Group located in New Albany, Indiana, and the Saskatchewan Road Runners Association have organized themselves to participate in activities related to their sport. The San Juan Sledders Snowmobile Club of Bayfield, Colorado, is another example of a nonprofit amateur sport organization. This group marks and grooms winter trails in the area, encouraging their use for multiple outdoor winter sports such as dogsledding, cross-country skiing, snowshoeing, and snowmobiling.

www

Pacers and Racers Running and Walking Group
www.pacersandracers.com

San Juan Sledders Snowmobile Club
www.sanjuansledders.org

MISSION. The mission of a nonprofit community-based amateur sport organization involves delivering a particular activity by providing facilities and related services, such as arranging for individual participation or competition. Many community groups involve leagues or clubs through which regular activities are scheduled. Encouraging safe, ethical conduct for all participants is a common theme. An excerpt from the mission statement of the Muskegon County Amateur Hockey Association (MCAHA) is presented in Exhibit 6.14.

MEMBERSHIP. Volunteers run community nonprofit amateur sport organizations. Members of the organization are solicited to help organize; in turn, they gain the benefit of services such as events, tournaments, and championships. Membership dues are usually collected on a yearly basis.

FINANCIALS. Nonprofit community groups are typically funded through participant membership fees, sponsorship, and other methods of fundraising. They may also be eligible for grants extended by municipal government agencies or private foundations. For example, a "Fun Run" organized by a city running club might involve municipal support (facilities and race-day logistics), sponsorships (printing costs, post-race refreshments, and awards), and a small entry fee to cover the costs of race T-shirts.

Excerpt from the mission statement of the Muskegon County Amateur Hockey Association.   *exhibit*   **6.14**

> MCAHA is a non-profit youth hockey association open to all youths eighteen (18) and under in the West Michigan area.
>
> MCAHA is organized to provide youths with a recreational amateur hockey development program . . . through skill development and competition. MCAHA recognizes a broad range of ability and commitment amount [to] its participants and strives to provide appropriate instruction and competition within the constraints of cost and ice time. MCAHA does not discriminate on the basis of gender, race, national origin or religious affiliations and seeks to place youths (boys and girls) with similar desires and judged abilities together on teams or in similar groups to maximize enjoyment for all participants.

Source: MCAHA (2013).

ORGANIZATIONAL STRUCTURE. Depending on its size, a community sport organization might be loosely configured or highly structured. A smaller organization such as the San Juan Sledders Snowmobile Club might have a small Executive Committee consisting of a few members in positions such as the President, Vice-President, and Treasurer. Other members of the group are then given tasks, but often they hold no specific titles. More often, the President will provide overall leadership, and the members of the group will complete tasks for each sporting event. An expectation exists for a fair division of labor among all group members. Once initial policy is established for managing the events, the group focuses on service as opposed to being a rules-making or sanctioning body. Conversely, in a larger organization such as the MCAHA, a structured managerial group may provide leadership, with a President, several Vice Presidents, and a number of Committee Chairs.

CURRENT POLICY AREAS

A number of policy areas are prominent for managers of amateur sport organizations in the community. It is important that policy be defined for each of the areas described in this section because the issues are critical to the effective delivery of amateur sport, especially as related to children and children's programming. Effective policy enables effective decision making.

Fundraising

Policy enabling decision making for fundraising is a prominent issue for amateur sport organizations in the community. Community-based amateur sport organizations rely on raising capital for both programming and infrastructure. Public sport organizations compete with every other level of social programming for funding, and government grants often fall short of their needs. As important as fundraising is to public sport organizations, policy that enables effective financial management is even more important with nonprofit sport organizations. Managers in the nonprofit sector are continually concerned with maintaining strict measures for raising money, along with ensuring that budgets are balanced and that spending is effective and shared among as many programs as possible. For instance, the Boys & Girls Clubs of America rely heavily on donations from both the private and the public sectors. While club administrators acknowledge that it takes money to run a Boys & Girls Club (about $300 per youth per year), they point out that the alternative costs of keeping a young adult in jail for a year ($75,000 to $125,000) makes their programming "one of the best bargains in America" (Boys & Girls Clubs of America, 2012). However, high levels of executive compensation and other perks have drawn the attention of the U.S. Senate, as some Boys & Girls Clubs have faced budget shortfalls (Perry, 2010). In fact, the 2005 *Chronicle of Philanthropy* ranked the organization number one among nonprofit youth organizations for efficient use of financial resources, but by 2011 they had dropped to number eighteen (Philanthropy 400, 2012). Notwithstanding the media attention focused on executive compensation, the fundraising policy areas receiving most of the attention are the following:

1. IDENTIFYING FUNDING SOURCES. Most organizations set specific policies that identify sources of funds worth pursuing. Virtually all solicit private donations, government grants, and corporate sponsorships. Specific policy might list donors in order of priority based on which are most likely to enter a partnership and in specific categories of new contacts to pursue. In addition, such policy will certainly outline categories of unacceptable sources of funding. For instance, no Boys & Girls Club would solicit funds from a tobacco company. On the contrary, the club will work hard to disassociate unhealthy practices such as smoking from the club's programming for children and teenagers. The policy might also define special-event types of fundraising (charity dinners, silent auctions, golf tournaments, etc.), and set some parameters on exactly what events will be hosted and what goals will define success.

2. SOLICITING DONATIONS AND SPONSORSHIPS. Other policies will define exactly how donations and sponsorships are solicited and by whom. Will potential donors be called, contacted by mail or e-mail? Will the club website be used to initiate fundraising? How will money be received, and how will records be kept? Such questions can be answered by developing effective policy.

3. SERVICING AND MAINTAINING DONOR RELATIONSHIPS. Ensuring donors and sponsors are "serviced" is very important as well. This means giving back to the donor or sponsor. Once programming has support, every effort must be made to inform, involve, and thank the sponsors for their involvement. Courtesy and reciprocity are critical to building relationships and are the best ways to maintain donor or sponsor involvement from year to year. Newsletters, invitations to see programs in action, thank-you letters from participants, and summarized information outlining the positives resulting from the donation are all effective means of servicing. The Boys & Girls Clubs of America use an extremely prominent National Board of Governors and Officers in their fundraising efforts, whose members include Condoleezza Rice, Ken Griffey Jr., and Denzel Washington.

Inactivity of Youth

Currently, the inactivity of youth generally and the declining numbers of participants in amateur sport have been targeted as problems that community level sport programs can help reverse. Policy is often set to deal with recurring issues and to enable decision making to effect change regarding such issues. All too often, children and youth are less physically active than is optimal for health and wellness because of the prevalence of passive activities, such as video and computer games. Research shows that girls' participation in sport and physical activity declines between ages 5 and 12 (Kernaghan, 2002) and that team sports by both boys and girls have suffered declining participation. Another large drop in participation occurs at the highschool age, where perceived barriers to participation include lack of time, inaccessible or costly facilities, focus on technology-related activities, and body image issues (Dwyer, Allison, Goldenberg, Fein, Yoshida, & Boutilier, 2006).

Some community-based amateur sport organizations are setting policy to ensure that programming exists for all youth age-groups. The goal is to provide a variety of fun-filled, supportive sport and physical activity experiences for youth. Such policy promotes development skills and healthy lifestyles and improves self-esteem. For example, some municipalities have enacted policies to ensure opportunities exist for age-group participants in sports that require the use of already overbooked areas and fields. At times, the policies specify participation for particular groups, such as a girls- or boys-only activity. In many community amateur athletic organizations, such as the City of Vancouver Recreation Department, T-ball programs and Little League Baseball are offered for girls as well as boys. Beyond gender, issues of race, ethnicity, and urban vs. rural further complicate the issue of youth inactivity. The reasons impacting this issue are complicated and involve a mix of societal issues such as culture, income, family responsibilities, and the impact of technology.

Parental Involvement

www
Center for Sports Parenting
www.sportsparenting.org

Institute for International Sport
www.internationalsport.org/
index.cfm

Parental involvement has been a major topic of youth sport over the past several years (Center for Sports Parenting, 2012). Stories of parents being "muzzled" or banned from events are too frequently presented in the media. Adult misbehaviors have become more commonplace: splashing hot coffee in the face of an official; verbally abusing officials, coaches, and kids; and fighting, threatening, and other forms of confrontations. According to Dan Bylsma, former NHL player and Coach of the Pittsburgh Penguins, two questions must be answered: Why have parents become so invested in the progress of their children in sports to the exclusion of other arguably more important endeavors, such as academics? And why does this parental involvement contradict what is best for the child? Amateur sport in the community is about fun, teamwork, dedication, and respect for authority. Excessive parental involvement in amateur sport, especially involvement that overshadows other important aspects of growing up, such as doing homework and chores and gaining experience in a number of activities, teaches children the wrong lessons. Consider the values a child learns when *thousands* of dollars are spent on hockey travel by a parent who would not consider spending tens of dollars on a math tutor (IIS, 2013).

If the purpose of youth sports is to have fun, increase athleticism, and learn the value of teamwork and discipline, then some adults are teaching the wrong lessons. Sport managers and program administrators are working to reverse such involvement by setting policy that curtails "parental over-involvement." Examples include spectator codes of conduct, parental contracts agreeing to acceptable conduct and involvement, and conferences and seminars for parents. The City of Henderson and the Nevada Parks and Recreation Department, for example, encourage parents to get involved and stay involved in amateur sports. They have been proactive by setting policy to educate all participants' parents, which is enacted through YouthFirst, a youth sports orientation program for parents (YouthFirst, 2012). The orientation has been developed by the University of Nevada, Las Vegas, and is designed to encourage parental involvement, emphasize fun, and boost participant retention. The intent is to curb violence in youth sports by orienting all parents to their role, the coach's role, and to what parents can do to foster continued participation by their kids. The program requires parents to complete a certification quiz and sign a code of conduct (YouthFirst, 2012).

www
YouthFirst
www.youthfirst.info

Amateur sport groups in the community are well advised to have policy governing parental involvement. As Dan Bylsma states, "It's long past the time some adults in youth sports clean up their act [and] focus on the wholesome purposes of youth sports and improve the lessons they're teaching their children. Or I fear the next trial for manslaughter will be held in Juvenile Court" (IIS, 2002). Dan Doyle (2007) suggests that "parents must help young athletes understand the meaning of gamesmanship as it applies to their sport(s), and that maintaining one's integrity begins with adhering not only to the rules of the sports, but to the spirit of the rules."

Violence in Sport

Violent behaviors associated with amateur sport are not restricted to parents. Overly aggressive and violent acts by participants and spectators are regularly reported in the media. This includes both physical and verbal acts of aggression. Reducing sport violence involves curtailing both athlete and spectator aggression. Policies dealing with reducing athlete violence strive to achieve the following:

- provide proper, nonaggressive role models for young athletes
- develop rules that allow low tolerance for acts of violence
- apply severe and swift penalties for violence involving the actions of athletes, referees, and coaches
- apply severe and swift penalties for coaches who support and promote violent or aggressive play
- remove stimuli that provoke aggression
- organize referee, coach, parent, and athlete workshops
- provide ample positive reinforcement for appropriate displays of behavior in sport
- teach and practice emotional control (Kids First Soccer, 2007).

Amateur athletic organizations can curtail spectator violence through policies that deal with the following items:

- banning alcoholic beverages
- making it a family affair
- ensuring that the media are not contributing to the buildup of tension
- focusing on achieving excellence rather than fighting the enemy
- fining unruly spectators (Kids First Soccer, 2007).

www

Kids First Soccer
www.kidsfirstsoccer.com

For example, administrators of the Saint Barnabas Health Care System (SBHCS) in New Jersey set policy to curb violence in sport by developing the Rediscovering Youth Sportsmanship program. The key elements of the program are training and education sessions for parents, coaches, officials, facility managers, and sport administrators that provide a system of boundaries, positive reinforcement, and sanctions for certain behaviors,

www
SportSafe Program
www.cscd.gov.bc.ca/sport/
programs/sportsafe.htm

delivered through videos, pledges, surveys, and rewards (SBHCS, 2007). Another example is SportSafe, a program developed by the government of British Columbia, Canada, that aims for a safer environment in sport and recreation. The Anti-Violence Policy for Recreation Facilities enacted as part of SportSafe raises awareness among spectators and parents of their role in creating a positive environment and gives volunteers and staff the mandate and power to deal with violent and antisocial behavior (Government of British Columbia, 2012). The policy defines *violent behavior* as the following:

- loud verbal assaults
- intimidation and threats
- aggressive actions such as approaching another individual or throwing articles
- striking another individual
- attempting to incite violence

Individuals engaging in any of the above activities are immediately ejected from the facility by designated leaders and banned from all local recreation facilities for a period of time defined by the recreation facility staff (Government of British Columbia, 2012).

Selecting Youth Sport Coaches

Good programming for kids depends on having suitable supervision and instruction, the normal role of the coach. Almost 4 million volunteer coaches work with more than 40 million young athletes in the United States alone (Positive Coaching Alliance, 2012). Unfortunately, the large number of volunteer coaches required sometimes results in the hiring of untrained, unprepared coaches. Experts have determined that some 90 percent of youth sports coaches have little to no training (American Coaching Academy, 2008). Far more dangerous is the potential for placing a pedophile or some other criminal in contact with children and youth. To ensure this does not happen, all sport organizations need to use specific criteria for hiring youth coaches and to utilize reference and criminal-background checks before hiring them. All sport organizations must have a personnel policy that contains procedures and requirements for youth sport coaches and volunteers that includes items such as the following:

www
Positive Coaching Alliance
www.positivecoach.org

- required coach training and background
- background information disclosure
- police record check
- coaching expectations and code of conduct
- coaching your own child

- understanding the goals and objectives of the association
- feedback on coaching performance
- dismissing a coach
- an individual's right to appeal

SUMMARY

Thousands of amateur sport organizations are community based. Their mandate is to provide opportunities for sport participation, and such organizations provide a broad spectrum of sports for a broad range of age groups. Such organizations can be categorized as public or non-profit, depending on their purpose and type of funding. Amateur sport at the community level has a rich history and is considered to be one of the foundations of a society in which happiness, health, and well-being are central. Such organizations include leagues, groups, clubs, special-interest groups, and organizations such as the YMCA.

The managers of community-based amateur sport organizations deal with a wide variety of governance and policy issues. Funding is a key area, because fundraising is at the core of the operation of the organization. Programming dependent on both funding and interest and the inactivity of youth are areas of concern and policy development. Inappropriate conduct or interference by parents and violence are other current policy issues concerning amateur sport. Despite these issues, community-based sport managers provide programming that positively impacts the lives of millions of participants. It is an exceptionally important component of the sport industry.

case STUDY

UNBECOMING CONDUCT IN YOUTH SPORT

As the Director of Children's Sport Programming for the town of Clarington, you are organizing a Soccer League for girls and boys from 6 to 10 years old. Experience tells you that the parents and kids of Clarington are a competitive group. At the winter hockey leagues several groups of parents were banned, and suspensions for violent behavior were common among the participants. In an effort to be proactive and eliminate such behaviors in the Soccer League, you have developed a Code of Conduct for both participants and spectators.

1. Describe your Code of Conduct for directing the behavior of (a) participants, (b) parents, and (c) general spectators.
2. How do you plan to communicate the Code of Conduct?

3. How do you plan to enforce the Code of Conduct?

4. How might you go about getting both participants and spectators to buy in to the Code?

5. What ethical dilemmas might you face implementing the policy, and how will you solve them?

CHAPTER questions

1. What is the difference between a public and a nonprofit sport organization? How do the governance structures of the two categories differ? Why do different types of recreational sport organizations exist?

2. Using the Internet, locate a community sport organization, for example, your community's Little League Baseball organization. With which category of those mentioned in this chapter does it most closely align? Summarize its governance structure by describing the following: mission, financials, membership, and organizational structure.

3. You have just been voted President of the Marysville Minor Soccer Association. Your organization provides opportunities for competition for boys and girls in five age groups, with nearly 700 participants on 35 teams. You are dismayed by the recent conduct of both athletes and parents on and off the field, and no policy exists to establish expected behaviors. Address these concerns by doing the following: (a) develop a policy of expected behaviors for players, parents, and coaches; (b) define an overall program of education to ensure that the policy and reasons behind the program are well understood; (c) define a list of sanctions for violating the policy; and (d) decide on a course of action to help you to convince your Executive Committee that the policy is important and that it needs to be implemented next season.

REFERENCES

American Coaching Academy. (2008). Experts say 90% of youth sports coaches have little to no training, thus putting their athletes at risk. Retrieved from http://www.prweb.com/releases/sports/coaching/prweb907124.htm

Boise Nationals Soccer Club. (2013). Idaho's Oldest & Most Successful Soccer Club. Retrieved from http://www.boisenationals.com/aboutbnsc/history/index_E.html

Boys & Girls Clubs of America. (2007). Our mission. Retrieved from www.bgca.org/who weare/mission.asp

Boys & Girls Clubs of America. (2012). The board—who we are. Retrieved from https://www.bgca.org/whoweare/Pages/FactsFigures.aspx

Boys & Girls Clubs of Metro Atlanta. (2007). Boys & Girls Clubs of Metro Atlanta—A positive place for kids. Retrieved from www.bgcma.org

Boys & Girls Clubs of Metro Atlanta. (2012). Board members. Retrieved from http://www.bgcma.org/board_members

Center for Sports Parenting. (2012). CSP hot topic polls. Retrieved from www.sportsparenting.org/polls.html

City of Houston. (2013). Overview of the Parks Department. Retrieved from www.houstontx.gov/parks/AboutUs.html.

City of Loveland, Colorado. (2013). Organizational Chart: Parks & Recreation Department. Retrieved from http://www.cityofloveland.org/index.aspx?page=236

City of San Diego. (2013a). Neighborhood and Customer Services Department. Retrieved from www.sandiego.gov/orgchart/pdf/ncs.pdf.

City of San Diego. (2013b). Parks and Recreation Department. Retrieved from http://www.sandiego.gov/park-and-recreation/pdf/prorgchart.pdf

City of Seattle. (2012). Seattle parks & recreation. Retrieved from http://www.seattle.gov/parks/park-spaces/index.htm

City of Snellville. (2011). General Fund—Budget for fiscal year 2010. Retrieved from http://www.snellville.org/vertical/Sites/%7B2457B773-F66B-45E3-9E9F-57703865A8B2%7D/uploads/%7B183448C0-66CA-432B-95C9-FB91ACF1B901%7D.PDF

City of Toronto. (2011). About us. Retrieved from http://www.toronto.ca/divisions/parksdiv1.htm#mission

Doyle, D. (2007). The practical value of good sportsmanship. Retrieved from www.internationalsport.com/nsd/nsd_letter.cfm

Dwyer, J. M., Allison, K. R., Goldenberg E. R., Fein, A. J., Yoshida, K. K., & Boutilier, M. A. (2006). Adolescent girls' perceived barriers to participation in physical activity. *Adolescence, 41*(161), pp. 75–89.

Government of British Columbia. (2012). Ministry of Community, Sport, and Cultural Development: The SportSafe program. Retrieved from http://www.cscd.gov.bc.ca/sport/programs/sportsafe.htm

IIS. (2002). Untitled article. Retrieved from www.internationalsport.com/nsd/nsd_opeds.cfm?n=bylsma.

IIS. (2013). About Institute for International Sport. Retrieved from http://www.internationalsport.org/about/vision.cfm

Iowa Games. (2012). Iowa Games mission statement. Retrieved from www.iowagames.org/history.aspx

Iowa Sports Foundation. (2012). Becoming a sponsor. Retrieved from http://IowaGames.org/Contact/Becomeasponsor.aspx

JCC. (2012a). Annual report. Retrieved from http://www.jcca.org/about-jcc-association/board-of-directors/

JCC. (2012b). About JCC association. Retrieved from www.jcca.org/about_us.html

JCC of Greater Baltimore. (2000). JCC mission statement. Retrieved from www.jcc.org/template.php?section=AM

JCC of San Francisco. (2010). Independent Auditors Report—2010. Retrieved from https://shamash.jccsf.org/pdf/JCCSF_FS_Final%201208.pdf

JCC of San Franscisco. (2012). Who we are. Retrieved from https://www.jccsf.org/the-centre/who-we-are/board-of-directors/

JCCA. (2012). JCCA annual report 2011. Retrieved from http://d.jcca.org/annual-reports/

Kernaghan, J. (2002). What stops the girls from playing? *Hamilton Spectator.* Retrieved from www.caaws.ca/Whats_New/2002/nov/Hamilton_article.htm

Kidd, B. (1999). *The struggle for Canadian sport.* Toronto: University of Toronto Press.

Kids First Soccer. (2007). Aggression and violence in sport. Retrieved from www.kidsfirstsoccer.com/violence.htm

Kissimmee Parks and Recreation. (2011). Florida Parks and Recreation. Retrieved from http://www.kissimmee.org/modules/showdocument.aspx?documentid=80

MCAHA. (2013). Muskegon County Amateur Hockey Association mission statement. Retrieved from http://www.muskegonchiefs.org/page.php?page_id=469

Morrow, D., & Wamsley, K. (2009). Sport in Canada: A history. Oxford, UK: Oxford University Press.

Orange County Maccabi Games. (2012). JCC Maccabi Experience. Retrieved from http://www.jccoc.org/fitness-recreation/sports-leagues/maccabi-team-oc/

Perry, S. (2010). Senators call on Boys & Girls Clubs of America to justify pay and spending. Retrieved from http://philanthropy.com/article/Senators-Call-On-Boys-Girls/64665/

Philanthropy 400 (2012). America's top fund-raising groups face big struggles. Retrieved from http://philanthropy.com/article/America-s-Top-Charities-Face/129432/

Pickering Hockey Association. (n.d.). PHAinfo. Retrieved from http://www.pickering hockey.com/about/about. html

Positive Coaching Alliance. (2012). The problem and the opportunity. Retrieved from www.positivecoach.org

San Juan Sledders Snowmobile Club. (2007). The San Juan Sledders Snowmobile Club. Retrieved from www.sanjuansledders.org

SBHCS. (2007). Rediscovering youth sportsmanship program. Retrieved from www.discovering sportsmanship.com.

Y. (2012). Welcome to YMCA.net. Retrieved from www.ymca.net/index.jsp

YMCA Canada. (2012). YMCA Canada. Retrieved from www.ymca.ca/eng_ycda.htm

YMCA of Greater New York. (2008). About us. Retrieved from www.ymcanyc. org

YouthFirst. (2012). YouthFirst: Parents Learning About Youth Sports. Retrieved from http://www.youth-first.info/

YWCA. (2010). YWCA of the USA Audited Financial Statements. Retrieved from http://apps.sos.wv.gov/business/charities/readpdf.aspx?DocID=134416

YWCA. (2012a). About the world YWCA. Retrieved from http://www.worldywca.org/About-us/About-the-world-YWCA

YWCA. (2012b). YWCA USA—What We Do. Retrieved from http://www.ywca.org/site/c.cuIRJ7NTKrLaG/b.7521157/k.270E/What_We_Do.htm

YWCA. (2012c). YWCA USA—Mission & Vision. Retrieved from http://www.ywca.org/site/c.cuIRJ7NTKrLaG/b.7515887/k.9633/Mission__Vision.htm

Campus Recreation

Campus recreation is the umbrella term used to describe a myriad of recreation and leisure activity programming on university and college campuses throughout North America. Recreation departments exist on virtually every college and university campus. This segment of the industry has extensive facilities and numbers of personnel, and many of you may want to include campus recreation departments in your career plans. Understanding the organization, governance, and policy issues pertinent to this extensive segment of the sport industry will help you prepare for management positions located on college campuses or within umbrella organizations helping to lead the campus recreation industry.

Historically, college and university administrators have accepted responsibility not only for the education but also for the general welfare of their students. When the promotion of health and well-being was identified as critical for student welfare, campus recreation departments became essential components of institutions of higher learning. In general, the mandate of the Campus Recreation Department is to offer opportunities to participate in both programmed and open-facility recreational activities. This mandate gained momentum because college campuses are often community oriented and can accommodate and serve large populations of students, faculty, and staff members. Today, campus recreation departments aim to enrich student life and are often considered tools for recruiting and retaining college students.

The size of campus recreation departments varies depending upon the campus setting and the size of the institution; however, their purpose is often strikingly similar. Campus recreation provides opportunities to engage in sport and leisure activities. The prime target audience of such programming is the student body. However, programming is usually also accessible to faculty and staff members and sometimes their families. In addition, many activities are made available to the community at large (Mittelstaedt, Robertson, Russell, Byl, Temple, & Ogilvie, 2005). The basic premise underlying campus recreation programming are enjoyment and promotion of a healthy lifestyle through physical activity. The missions and visions of such programs (as referred to in Chapter 2) are represented by slogans such as "Something for Everyone," "Fit for Life," "Intramurals, Where It's Done for Fun," and "Active Living for Health and Happiness."

Many campus recreation department mission statements link the importance of campus facilities to the operation of recreational programming. In addition, the vision of the Campus Recreation Department involves inclusivity, since it operates as a vital part of the university community at large. The mission and vision of campus recreation departments often include a set of values as summarized in Exhibit 7.1.

With this basic understanding of campus recreation, let's look at the roots of campus recreation departments, why they were developed, and how they are organized and governed nationally.

		exhibit 7.1
A summary of the typical values of a campus recreation program.		

Access for all	Provide opportunities for a wide diversity of interests, age groups, abilities, including individuals with a disability.
Customer satisfaction	Develop a friendly, knowledgeable staff and clean, safe, accessible, and attractive facilities.
Awareness	Employ promotional strategies to ensure programs and services are well communicated to new and current participants.
Mutual respect	Ensure a welcoming environment, and promote opportunities for activity in an environment of respect.
Diversity	Create an environment embracing individual differences and reflecting campus diversity.
Variety	Provide opportunities reflecting the diverse interests of the campus community.
Fun	Ensure enjoyment is the mainstay of each programming area.
Development	Provide opportunities for students to guide the programming and gain valuable leadership and management skills.
Evaluation	Maintain a cutting-edge set of programs and facilities reflecting current trends and interests.

THE HISTORY OF CAMPUS RECREATION

Recreation and leisure activities undoubtedly contributed to the early growth of competitive athletics (Langley & Hawkins, 1999). The interest in playing, learning to engage in new activities, or simply getting active is well documented in the history of sport and the pursuit of good health. Early on, goals were likely pure enjoyment, opportunities to socialize with friends, and relief from the boredom of work, study, or everyday life. If physical activity is viewed as a continuum from informal play and recreation that is not necessarily competitive to formal and institutionalized competitive sport (Kane, 2007), it is easy to understand that the early history of recreation on campus is interwoven with campus sport as we know it today.

The First Campus Recreation Programs

Early sport and leisure activities originated with English sport clubs and German gymnastics. Around the midpoint of the 19th century, North Americans were looking for opportunities to be physically active other than in highly competitive sports or in the rigid routine of gymnastics. This interest in pursuing physical and recreational activities and sport was naturally present on college campuses. The campus was an ideal setting for spontaneous games, with divisions already defined by academic class, major, or residence housing. The term *intramural,* used to describe the first programs of campus recreation, comes from the Latin words for "within" (*intra*) and "wall" (*murus*), that is, within the walls of an organization (Brown, 1998).

Competition between different classes soon became commonplace. Colleges and universities embraced the notion that programming for leisure and recreational pursuits, along with competitive athletics, was an important component in the overall education and well-being of their students. In 1904, Cornell University (CU) developed a system of what is known today as instructional sport for students not participating at the varsity level. During the next decade the surge of student interest in recreational sports resulted in the development of a department to manage such student programming. The Ohio State University (OSU) and the University of Michigan (UM) each defined organized intramural departments in 1913 (Mueller & Reznik, 1979). CU quickly followed, along with other colleges and universities in the United States and Canada.

A Rationale for Campus Recreation

When considering the history of higher education, intramural sport is perhaps one of the oldest organized campus activities (Mittelstaedt et al., 2005). Campus recreation emerged as a formal department on campus and recreational programming subsequently experienced extensive growth and popularity for several reasons. A significant factor in legitimizing campus recreation occurred in the early part of the 20th century. In 1918, the National Education Association (NEA) in the United States coined the phrase "worthy use of leisure time" as one of the Seven Principles of Education (Colgate, 1978). In essence, the idea of capitalizing on one's leisure time became a tenet of an effective education. Greater meaning was attached to educating the whole person and to the importance of out-of-classroom educational experiences (Smith, 1991). Over time, the notion that healthy individuals are active, involved, and accomplished in activities of both mind and body became another cornerstone supporting the need for open recreation and intramural programming on campus. As the world became more technologically sophisticated, the amount of leisure time increased and the demand for recreational activities on campus continued to grow. Recreational activities were social in nature and offered opportunities both for affiliation with one's classmates or roommates and for friendly competition for bragging rights associated with pride in that group's accomplishment.

Each of these reasons for the establishment and growth of the Campus Recreation Department remains today. In addition, the extensive facilities for recreation and the breadth of such programming in today's university are drawing cards for potential students. Students and their parents are naturally drawn to those institutions with excellent facilities and programs, providing a natural link between the Campus Recreation Department and the overall mission of the university. Research indicates that student retention is favorably influenced by getting students involved in extracurricular activities such as those housed within campus recreation (Huesman, Brown, Lee, Kellogg, & Radcliffe, 2009). Finally, and perhaps most important, campus recreation programs began to flourish because of student interest. The student body's interest has grown over the years, leading to a proliferation of facilities and program offerings. In 1928, UM was the first institution to devote a building primarily to intramurals (Mueller & Reznik, 1979). Today, many campuses have complete facilities solely dedicated to recreational use.

The Formation and Evolution of National Intramural-Recreation Associations

Following World War II, while athletic and physical education groups were holding annual meetings and looking to associate with one another for a variety of purposes, recreation programmers were without such opportunities. To fill this void in the United States, Dr. William N. Wasson of Dillard University in New Orleans formed the National Intramural Association (NIA) in 1950. The mandate of the NIA was to provide an association for professionals working in college and university intramural sports programs in the United States to share ideas, develop policy, and encourage professional development. In 1975, the NIA membership voted to change its name to the current National Intramural–Recreational Sport Association (NIRSA). The membership felt NIRSA more aptly described the expanded and diversified role of recreation departments on college campuses. Such units organize and deliver programming far beyond the boundaries of intramural sports, and the scope and mission of NIRSA has expanded phenomenally to what is currently an extensive national association. The governance structure of NIRSA is described later in this chapter.

The Canadian Intramural Recreation Association (CIRA) was founded in 1977 in response to a void in Canada similar to the one in the United States. The mission of CIRA was somewhat broader than NIRSA's, extending its reach to grade schools and high schools, as well as college and university intramural and recreation programming. The ultimate goal of CIRA was to promote active living and healthy lifestyles through intramural and recreation programming within the Canadian educational community. CIRA was the only national organization promoting and supporting intramurals in Canada until April 1, 2003, when CIRA transferred its activities and resources to the Canadian Association for Health, Physical Education, Recreation, and Dance (CAHPERD). The change was prompted by a reduction in federal funding to CIRA and the goal of effectively delivering one system of physical activity programming for all schools in Canada. CAHPERD, which changed its name to Physical & Health Education Canada (PHE Canada) in 2008, now places a greater emphasis on intramurals through the development of the Intramural Recreation Program Advisory Committee and programs such as the Quality School Intramural Recreation initiative (PHE Canada, 2012).

The next section describes the governance structures of NIRSA and PHE Canada in further detail and defines how campus recreation departments are organized on college and university campuses.

GOVERNANCE

Municipal and state or provincial organizations exist as umbrella organizations with which campus recreation departments may affiliate on a local level. This section examines the two national associations to which most campus recreation professionals in the United States and Canada belong. We answer the following questions about NIRSA and CIRA: What are the missions of these organizations? How do they obtain funding? Who are their members? How are these organizations structured?

National Intramural-Recreational Sports Association

MISSION. The purpose of NIRSA has expanded greatly since it was founded in 1950. Beyond intramurals, areas of interest include aquatics, extramurals, wellness and fitness, informal recreation, instructional programs, outdoor recreation, programs for people with disabilities, special events, sport clubs, and student leadership and development. NIRSA strives to provide its members with research, teaching, presenting, and publishing opportunities as well. NIRSA is a nonprofit professional association dedicated to promoting quality recreational sports programs. The association is equally committed to providing continuing education and development for recreational sport professionals and students. NIRSA's mission statement is presented in Exhibit 7.2.

MEMBERSHIP. Today, NIRSA has an extensive reach and membership across North America, but this was not always the case. From the first organiza-

NIRSA mission statement.

exhibit **7.2**

> The mission of the National Intramural-Recreation Sports Association is to provide for the education and development of professional and student members and to foster quality recreational programs, facilities and services for diverse populations. NIRSA demonstrates its commitment to excellence by utilizing resources which promote ethical and healthy lifestyle choices.

Source: NIRSA (2012a).

tional meeting in 1950 that included 13 individuals, the association now boasts a membership of thousands of professionals and students from colleges, universities, correctional facilities, military installations, and parks and recreation departments. NIRSA initiatives and programming reach millions of recreational sport enthusiasts, including an estimated 5.5 million college students. NIRSA also reaches professionals and students in Canadian schools, colleges, and universities.

Membership is offered at the institutional, professional, and student levels, as well as the associate level for commercial organizations who provide products or services to the organization. Within each category NIRSA offers many opportunities to get involved. With its sole focus on the advancement of intramural–recreational sport programs and their professionals and students, NIRSA provides access to program standards, a code of ethics, an extensive resource library, career opportunity services, and the Sports Officials' Development Center. In addition, NIRSA's message is delivered to professionals through state and regional conferences, symposia and workshops, and the Annual National Conference and Exhibit Show. NIRSA Institutional Members represent large and small and public and private two- and four-year colleges and universities. For those with an institutional-level membership, access is provided to nationally sponsored programs and events ranging from individual and team sport events to fitness and wellness exhibitions and special publications. An example of a mission that extends across the association's mandate is the NIRSA Natural High program, an alcohol and drug awareness program, which lead to the Coalition of Higher Education Associations for Substance Abuse Prevention (CoHEASAP).

FINANCIALS. NIRSA is a nonprofit organization. However, material and financial growth led the organization to reorganize into three independent legal entities, each of which has a significant role in managing NIRSA finances.

www

Coalition of Higher Education Associations for Substance Abuse Prevention (CoHEASAP)
www.collegesubstance
abuseprevention.org/

In addition to the parent NIRSA organization, the NIRSA Foundation and the NIRSA Services Corporation were formed (NIRSA, 2012b).

NIRSA has approximately 4,000 individual and organization members. Membership fees constitute a major source of funding. The NIRSA Foundation is also a not-for-profit organization mandated to support the NIRSA mission; it receives donations to NIRSA. The NIRSA Services Corporation is the taxable, business-oriented component of NIRSA. It was established to receive revenues from advertising, sponsorship, sales of licensed goods, and sport club championships (NIRSA, 2012b).

ORGANIZATIONAL STRUCTURE. In 2010 NIRSA began a governance transition process that streamlined the number of positions on the Board of Directors (see Exhibit 7.3), and identified the board's role in visionary leadership. The board is composed of seven members, including the following elected positions: President, President Designee, President-Elect, Annual Director, and three At-Large Directors. The individuals elected to these positions hold

exhibit **7.3** Organizational chart of the NIRSA Board of Directors.

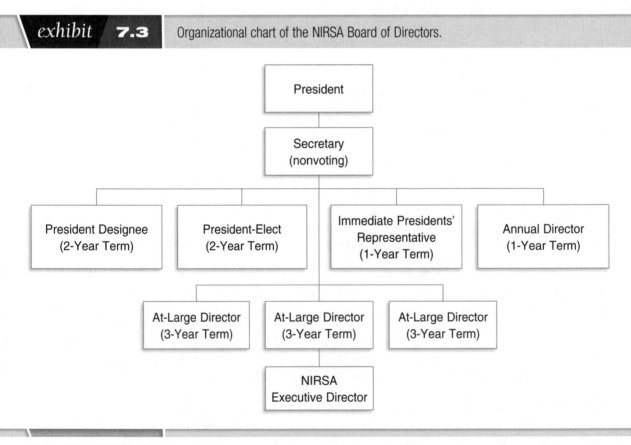

Source: NIRSA (2012b). Reprinted with permission.

one- to three-year terms, staggered to ensure continuity on the Board of Directors from year to year. The board is assisted by a nonvoting position of Secretary. The board is responsive to the members of the organization, and works in concert with the Assembly. The Assembly is a completely new element of NIRSA governance, described as a "forward-thinking think-tank" that focuses on the needs of the profession, developing new ideas, sharing knowledge, and engaging members in development opportunities. It is composed of six NIRSA members, four NIRSA professional members, three NIRSA student members, six open seats for members or non-members, and a representative of both the Past Presidents and Board of Directors.

The Executive Director (ED) of NIRSA answers to the Board of Directors and is responsible for the daily activities of the organization. The NIRSA National Center, located in Corvallis, Oregon, is further divided into six main areas of focus, with each area leader reporting to the ED. The five activity areas within the organization are (1) Professional Development and Leadership, (2) Finance and Administration, (3) Corporate Programs, (4) Communications and Marketing, and (5) National Sport Programs. Approximately 25 individuals are employed as National Center staff. The NIRSA National Center organizational chart is shown in Exhibit 7.4.

NIRSA is primarily a service organization, dedicated to continuing education for its members and the promotion of quality recreational sport programs. NIRSA provides its members with knowledge, ideas, and community for solving problems. Its prime policy role is the development of program standards for events and activities within recreation programs. Ensuring the safety of participants and quality of programming has been one focus of such policy development. Another focus has been the development of codes of ethical practices for professionals and participants within recreational sport settings.

Canadian Intramural Recreation Association (CIRA)/ Physical & Health Education Canada

As mentioned previously, in 2003, Physical & Health Education Canada (PHE Canada, formerly known as CAHPERD) assumed the activities and resources of CIRA.

MISSION. PHE Canada now promotes the mission (see Exhibit 7.5), vision, and goals statements originally articulated by CIRA. The vision is to have active intramural programs in all schools and post-secondary institutions and to ensure that children and youth are participating in daily physical activities. This vision and mission are accomplished by achieving the following goals (CIRA, 2002):

1. To decrease physical inactivity among children and youth through community programming;

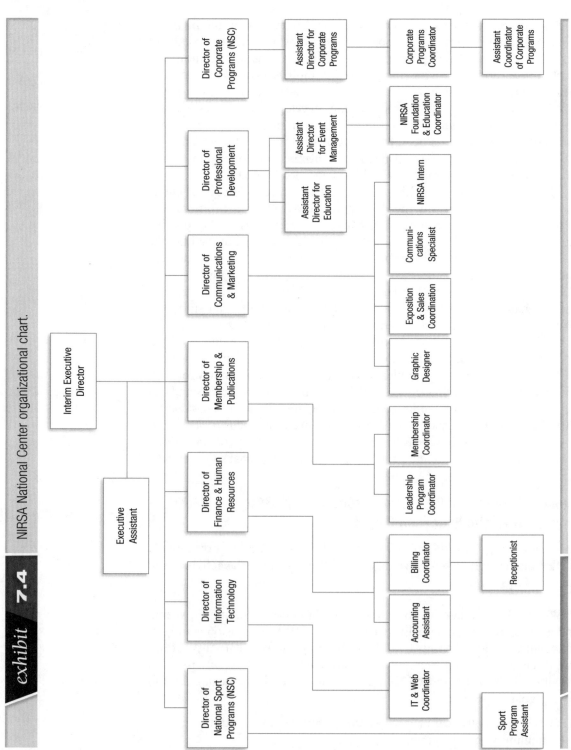

exhibit 7.4 NIRSA National Center organizational chart.

Source: NIRSA (2012b). Reprinted with permission.

Mission statement of the Canadian Intramural-Recreation Association. *exhibit*  7.5

> CIRA's mission was "to encourage, promote and develop active living, healthy lifestyles and personal growth, through intramural and recreational programs within the educational community."

Source: CIRA (2002).

2. To provide resources and leadership to enable teachers and students to lead intramural and campus recreation programs;
3. To foster a strong grassroots-delivery system through the provincial associations; and
4. To develop strategic alliances with other national and provincial like-minded associations and agencies.

To achieve its mandate, PHE Canada promotes the importance of school-based intramural programs to provide opportunities and encourage children and youth to participate in daily physical activities. The intent is to develop early life experiences of children and youth that will enable a lifelong commitment to active living and to ensure that youth are involved in all aspects of recruiting, planning, organizing, and delivering physical activity.

MEMBERSHIP. PHE Canada members that came from the former CIRA structure are primarily teachers, administrators, and students who deliver intramural and recreation programs through educational institutions. Several thousand individuals have joined the organization over the past decade from every province and territory in Canada. Many others utilize the PHE Canada resource catalog and website to acquire practical resources to implement recreational programming.

FINANCIALS. PHE Canada is a national, charitable, voluntary-sector organization advocating for quality school-based recreation and physical education. Similar to NIRSA, PHE Canada manages advertising, sponsorship, and program revenues and its growing customer base. Other sources of revenue include membership fees.

ORGANIZATIONAL STRUCTURE. PHE Canada is led by a President and governed by an Executive Council of 12 individuals, one of whom is elected from each of the 10 provinces and territories in Canada (see Exhibit 7.6). The

WWW
Physical Health Education Canada
www.phecanada.ca/

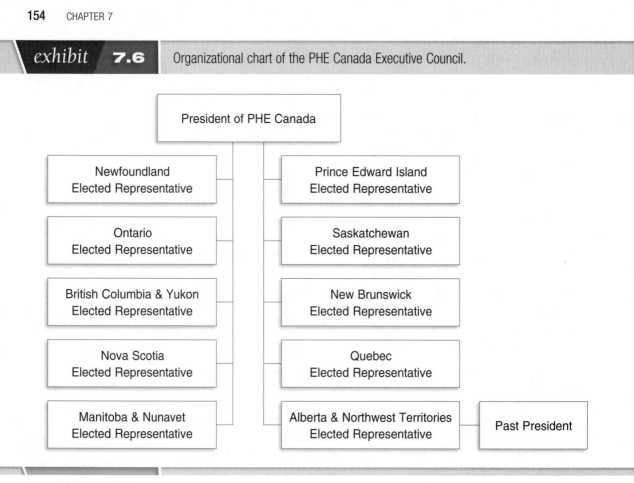

exhibit **7.6** Organizational chart of the PHE Canada Executive Council.

Source: PHE Canada (2012).

organization's National Office in Ottawa, Ontario, has 12 staff members (see Exhibit 7.7) and is organized into two major Councils, the Council of Provinces and Territories, and the Council of University Professors and Researchers. The Councils divide into five main areas of activity: (1) Executive Office, (2) Communications, (3) Programs, (4) Business Development, and (5) Finance. Each Council is represented by an elected expert to help PHE Canada set policy and direction within its respective jurisdiction of schools and professional preparation. The Quality School Intramural Recreation and Dance Education Advisory Committee comprise a number of key former CIRA members, continuing to play an advocacy and programmatic role for the promotion of intramural sport. The organizational structure of PHE Canada is presented in Exhibit 7.8.

PHE Canada does not play a large role in intramural–recreation policy development. Its main purpose is to promote and encourage active living and healthy lifestyles through intramural and recreational programming.

Organizational chart for the PHE Canada National Office.

exhibit **7.7**

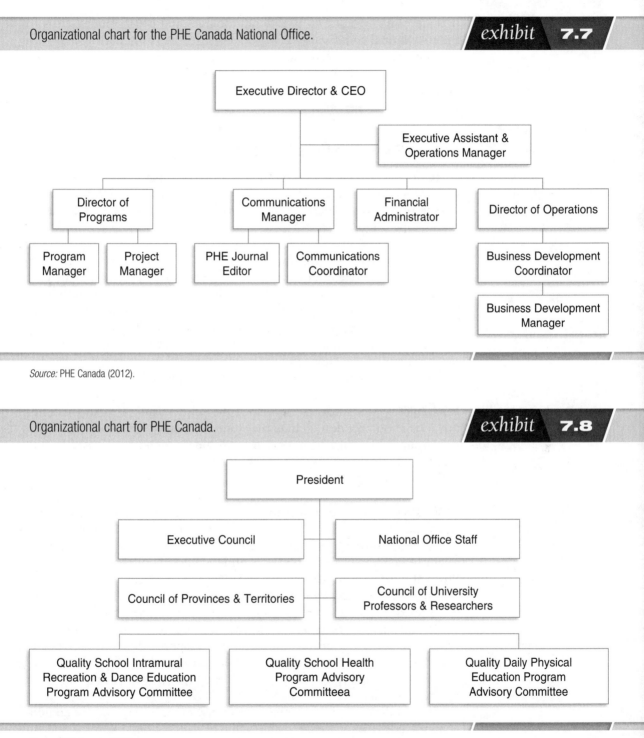

Source: PHE Canada (2012).

Organizational chart for PHE Canada.

exhibit **7.8**

Source: PHE Canada (2012).

It achieves its mandate by providing resources and programming ideas to the educational community. PHE Canada often works in partnership with Canada's federal and provincial levels of government to decrease the inactivity of children. It plays a role in advocating for healthy, active lifestyles and works to advise the appropriate levels of government in the health and education sectors regarding policy development.

Campus Recreation Department Structure

Virtually every college and university in North America has a Campus Recreation Department. The campus is viewed as a community, and the pursuit of fitness and play through sport is an important part of any community operation.

MISSION. The structure and function of the Campus Recreation Department is directly linked to the unit's mission and goal statements, which are based upon participants' and clients' goals. A typical mission statement for a Campus Recreation Department might read: "We are committed to providing the finest programs and services in order to enrich the university learning experience and to foster a lifetime appreciation of and involvement in recreational sport and wellness activities for our students, faculty, and staff." For sample mission statements, see Exhibit 7.9.

MEMBERSHIP. As mentioned previously, the constituents of a modern campus recreation program include the students, faculty, and staff. However, this group may well be broadened to include alumni, families of faculty and staff, and community members interested in recreation opportunities (Mittelstaedt et al., 2005).

FINANCIALS. The financial operations of the small versus the large Campus Recreation Department will vary. Some institutions support programming and facilities through central budgets housed in Student Affairs. Revenue might be generated through varsity athletic budgets or through academic Physical Education or Kinesiology budgets. Budgetary support ranges from full to partial funding by the institution; more commonly, university budgets provide one of several sources of the overall recreation budget. Another common source of revenue for recreation is a compulsory recreation fee charged to every university student to help support student programs and facilities. Such fees are collected in addition to tuition and other compulsory academic and nonacademic fees at the beginning of each semester or quarter. Another revenue source includes "pay for play" fees collected from the participants in a league, class, or special event. Other budget components include rentals, facility membership or daily-use fees, advertising, and other marketing initiatives. In this case, the operation is run on a break-

Example mission statements for campus recreation programs.

exhibit   **7.9**

University of Denver, Denver CO

> *"The Division of Athletics and Recreation provides athletic, recreational and entertainment opportunities that meet the needs of students, faculty, staff, alumni, and the Denver community."*

Southern Polytechnic State University, Marietta, GA

> *"The Recreational Sports program shares in the educational mission of the university by offering opportunities to experience interpersonal growth, social development, improve physical and mental health, and to develop lifetime leisure skills for a healthier lifestyle. The department organizes, administers, and promotes a broad program of competitive, recreational, and educational activities for students, faculty, and staff."*

UCLA, Los Angeles, CA

> *"Our mission is to provide high quality recreational experiences that benefit the campus community."*

WWW

University of Denver Campus Recreation
www.du.edu/live/athleticand
recreation.html

Southern Polytechnic State University Recreational Sports and Athletics
www.spsu.edu/recwellness/

University of California Los Angeles Recreation
www.recreation.ucla.edu/

Sources: University of Denver (2012), Southern Polytechnic State University (2012), UCLA (2012).

---

even basis, equating operational and program spending to the revenues generated through some combination of the sources defined above.

Other campus recreation programs are run as *profit centers*. Many institutions, regardless of size, have built multimillion-dollar facilities to service the needs of their current constituents. This proactive stance recognizes the role campus facilities can play in attracting and retaining future students, faculty, and staff. Profit centers generate revenue to offset the costs beyond those related to operations, for example, to pay a facility mortgage. Often, using the facility involves a membership fee. Students may pay through the recreation fee charged within the tuition package, and faculty and staff may be required to pay monthly membership fees. Opportunity for memberships may also be extended to alumni, family members, and community users on separate fee schedules. The proposal for building such a facility sometimes involves a student referendum for an additional building fee that might extend from as few as five years to as many as 20 years. In this case, an additional facility or building fee is charged to all students.

Some institutions look beyond their students to additional sources of revenue to build recreation facilities. An alternative model for financing the construction or renovation of facilities involves developing partnerships. In such cases, the university partners with the community, with local governments, or with the private sector to raise capital. Agreements for use and profit allocation are developed in return for building capital. The facility is run as a business with market rates charged for use. The Director of Recreation must ensure certain profit levels are maintained through memberships and sources of program revenue. Significant sources of revenues in the millions of dollars can accrue from rental payments, instructional programs, and sport camps, to name a few.

ORGANIZATIONAL STRUCTURE. The structure of the Recreation Department is also partially determined by its size. A small college may have a fairly simple organizational structure due to fewer constituents, limited facilities, smaller levels of programming, and less need for full-time staff. On the other hand, a large college will have a complex organizational structure that provides extensive levels of programming for multiple constituents through state-of-the-art facilities. Let's have a look at the administration and operation of two examples.

Small recreation programs

Consider a small, private college with 900 students and 75 faculty and staff members situated in a rural community of 5,000 people. It is possible the only constituents of the campus recreation program are students and a few faculty or staff. In this case recreation may be housed within a larger unit of Athletics and Recreation, so that the continuum of competitive and noncompetitive activity, along with the management of facilities, is combined within one department led by an individual with the title of Manager, Coordinator, or Assistant Director. Campus recreation thus coexists within a larger administrative unit responsible for varsity athletics and facilities; this alignment encourages an equitable distribution of resources (financial, physical, and human); good communication between multiple users of the same facilities; and effective, seamless delivery of the many physical activity options available to the participants. The head administrator of the overall operation, usually called the Director, is charged with maintaining some balance between the competitive and noncompetitive programming units.

In such cases, the Campus Recreation Manager may be the only full-time employee with direct responsibilities for recreational programming. She may have an assistant but often manages the area alone, with support from the Director and from employees who manage the facilities. In small programs it is easy to comprehend the large role students play in organizing and delivering the campus recreation program. Of necessity, in the beginning such programming was student run, and recreational programming today is still largely student run (Brown, 1998). Full-time university employees direct the overall program, set policy, and manage finances, but the actual development and delivery of programming is led by students.

This fact is certainly celebrated by colleges and universities, where administrators wholly applaud the concept of "for the students, by the students." These programs allow students to gain valuable management and leadership skills. Clearly, these students have their finger on the pulse of their classmates' interests when it comes to assessing programming. It is not uncommon to have 50 student leaders in both paid and volunteer positions as supervisors, officials, and event managers even within a small campus recreation program. Student leaders help govern the program as well, often by way of management teams and advisory councils that feed information to the full-time university employees. For example, student-led committees dealing with areas such as intramurals, participant conduct, special events, clubs, and officials may report through the Student Supervisors' Council to the Campus Recreation Manager. Student input and leadership is the foundation of the program. In this case, student employees and supervisors, along with the Manager of Recreation, are likely to be heavily involved in the development and implementation of policy. The Director of Athletics and Recreation and any departmental coordinating council or management team will also play a role in confirming policy. An example of the administrative structure for a small college is presented in Exhibit 7.10.

Organizational chart for a typical Campus Recreation Department for a small college.    *exhibit* **7.10**

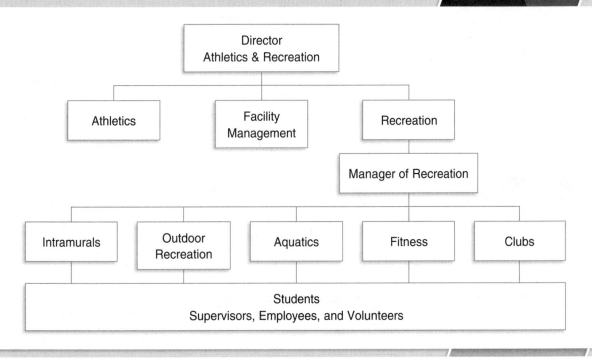

Large recreation programs

The scope of a large campus recreation program can differ significantly from that of the small college presented above. Many colleges and universities have significant student, faculty and staff, and alumni populations. Some are housed in large urban centers. In such cases, the administration and operation of the Campus Recreation Department is generally large and complex, with many full-time professional staff and several programming divisions. Consider, for example, a large public university with an enrollment of 50,000 students. The Department of Recreation may be led by a Director who is the administrative head reporting to a Vice President or Provost responsible for Student Life (see Exhibit 7.11), or it may be led by an Associate Athletic Director responsible for recreation, in which case campus recreation is once again linked to the Department of Athletics (see Exhibit 7.12).

In either case, the structure of the Campus Recreation Department is extensive and is compartmentalized into several operational and management areas based on the defined programming. Students help run the

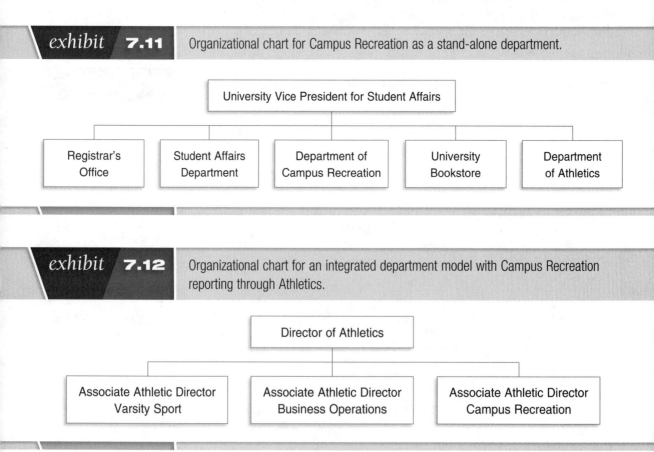

exhibit **7.11** Organizational chart for Campus Recreation as a stand-alone department.

University Vice President for Student Affairs

- Registrar's Office
- Student Affairs Department
- Department of Campus Recreation
- University Bookstore
- Department of Athletics

exhibit **7.12** Organizational chart for an integrated department model with Campus Recreation reporting through Athletics.

Director of Athletics

- Associate Athletic Director Varsity Sport
- Associate Athletic Director Business Operations
- Associate Athletic Director Campus Recreation

respective areas through positions in each of the programs areas of delivery, and a large professional staff manages the department. Associate Directors responsible for different types of programming are common, each reporting directly to the head administrator. The different programming areas depend on the campus constituents and their needs and environment. The following areas are most common: Intramural Sport, Extramural Sport, Outdoor Adventure, Sport Clubs, Fitness and Wellness Activities, Special Events, Community Programming including Sport Camps, Instructional Programming, Aquatics, Dance, Martial Arts, Family Recreation, Informal Recreation, Adapted Recreational Sports, Equipment Rentals, Facility Operations, Marketing, Technology, Business Operations, and Student Personnel. Depending on the scope of programming, each major area may operate as a separate department, with its own central office and administrative staff.

Advisory committees composed of students, faculty and staff members, and designated area (intramural sports, residence halls, fraternities and sororities) representatives provide input to a wide spectrum of programming and management issues. The deliberations of these committees contribute to policy development that might ultimately funnel to the Director of Recreational Sports, for example, a policy regarding penalties imposed on teams that are late or fail to show up for an intramural event. To erase such practices, a policy is developed to fine the offending team and impose a ban on competition for teams with further offenses. Such policy is common in intramurals today. Another level of advisory committee, perhaps called the Advisory Committee on Recreational Sports, takes on the responsibility for overall issues of program and facility equity and direction. This Advisory Committee may be led by the Director of Recreational Sport. It meets regularly and may be composed of several faculty members appointed by the College Faculty Senate, an equal number of students appointed by the Student Association(s), and a representative from central administration, perhaps appointed by the Office of the Vice President for Student Affairs. The Advisory Committee plays a role in policy development, usually considering issues of overall program magnitude, equity, finance, and public relations. An organizational chart of a complex Campus Recreation Department in a large university setting is presented in Exhibit 7.13.

PROGRAMMING IN CAMPUS RECREATION

Regardless of the size of the Campus Recreation Department or its system of funding, an important issue on every campus involves the scope of programming. When the question of scope arises, almost without exception, the one-word answer is *extensive*. Campus recreation programs certainly live up to the "something for everyone" theme, with offerings rang-

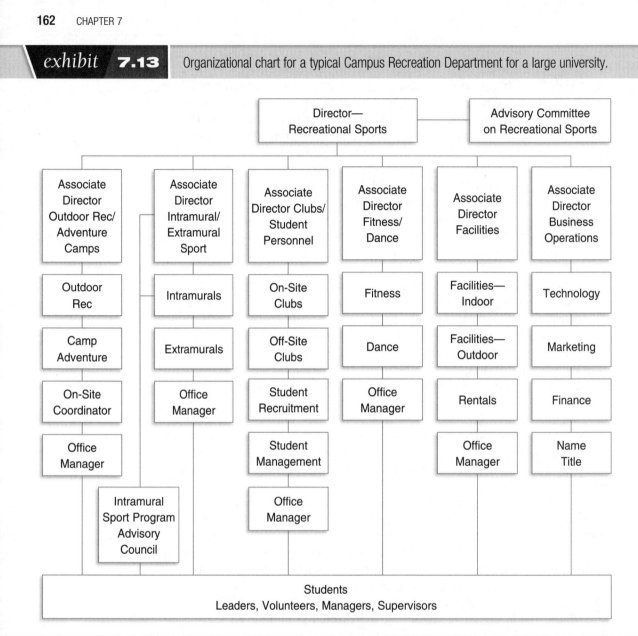

exhibit **7.13** Organizational chart for a typical Campus Recreation Department for a large university.

ing from intramural team sport leagues to instructional activities to wellness programs to events for special populations. Even small programs run by a single professional staff member with limited access to facilities can deliver extensive campus recreation programs.

Campus recreation began as intramural sport, and this area still draws strong interest today. Intramurals include not only team sports normally run in leagues but also individual sports. Intramurals encompass men-only, women-only, and coed leagues in virtually every sport of student interest.

Club sports are also popular. Clubs are student-run organizations that provide in-depth opportunities to learn and participate in a particular activity. The extensive array of possibilities ranges from archery to broomball to cycling to kayaking to ultimate Frisbee. Each club is formed, developed, governed, and administered by students. Student leadership and continuity is a key to success. Rules and regulations and administrative assistance are usually provided by the Campus Recreation Department.

Instructional activities include classes in fitness, dance, yoga, "learn to" activities, certification courses, and facility time for self-directed activities. Self-directed activities involve sport for fitness and fun, such as individual weight training or lane swimming, pickup basketball, or tennis.

In contrast to such informal activities are extramural sports, which are also gaining in popularity. *Extramural sport* refers to structured participation between groups on different campuses. For example, the intramural champion may be invited to a state or national event (such as NIRSA basketball championships or state flag football regional events), or the campus Law Society may enroll a team at the Law Student Games Festival run annually throughout Canada. The emphasis is still on fun, but competition is part of the event. Participants may engage in each of the areas mentioned above in traditional team and individual sports.

Another popular area of campus recreation programming is the pool. Aquatic activities range from self-directed lane fitness swimming to learn-to-swim to aqua-fitness programming. Aqua-fitness classes take place in the water and usually follow the same formats as regular fitness activities. Intramural inner tube water polo is also popular with participants.

When the fitness industry exploded in North America in the 1970s, demand for aerobic classes, yoga, and fitness classes soon peaked on campus, and the trend continues today. The public has become better informed of the health benefits and personal satisfaction associated with recreation and leisure activities, so campus recreation has expanded its wellness offerings with such classes as aromatherapy, reflexology, tai chi, Pilates, and power yoga. Events for individuals with disabilities (for example, wheelchair basketball) or to populations of international students (for example, a cricket festival) are also commonly offered.

Most of the activities and events described above take place indoors. The final area of campus recreation programming involves outdoor recreation and adventure activities. This includes activities in the great outdoors to take advantage of the lakes, mountains, and forest terrain of the surrounding area. Cycling, kayaking, canoeing, hiking, mountain biking, and scuba diving are popular pursuits, with classes for beginners to advanced participants. Adventure activities usually include an element of risk, such as outdoor rock climbing, an extreme triathlon, or open-water kayaking.

DALE RAMSAY, *Director of Intramural-Recreational Sports*

University of Louisville

I have been involved in campus recreation my entire 33-year professional career, all at the University of Louisville. I have served as the Director of Intramural-Recreational Sports at the University of Louisville for the past 30 years. I have also been an instructor in the Department of Health and Sports Studies for the past 30 years, teaching a class in recreational sports administration.

The recent national events concerning the abuse of children in the university setting has given campus recreation administrators cause for concern. The developments in this area demonstrate the need to thoroughly investigate the backgrounds of the people we employ to work not only with our students, but also with those minor students who participate in programs that take place in our campus facilities. Most universities conduct criminal background checks on their employees. However, many programs have volunteer positions (sports club coaches, facility workers, instructors, etc.) that also need to be subject to criminal background checks.

Many campus recreation programs make their facilities available to summer camps and various tournaments involving minor children. These events are important to institutions from a student recruitment and revenue generation standpoint. Campus recreation administrators need to work with the appropriate parties on their campus (risk management, campus police, university counsel, etc.), however, to see how their respective institutions want to handle investigating the backgrounds of non-university individuals involved with events on their campus. This area is an issue all campus recreation administrators need to address for the safety of their constituents and the minor children who participate in programs in their facilities.

Another challenge facing all campus recreation departments is to ensure that only those individuals who are eligible use our respective facilities. Technology and the development of sophisticated software has made this task easier, enabling us to identify who is a member of the university community by accessing the university database. At all campus settings, however, it is a challenge to determine who is actually eligible to use campus recreation facilities. It seems that a host of individuals claim some type of affiliation with our institutions.

At my university, our facilities exist primarily for our students, who generally pay some type of recreation fee. Other campus groups include faculty and staff, alumni, dependents, guests, community members, vendors, and visiting faculty members. At the University of Louisville we also have an arrangement with a local community college, whose students can use our facilities if they pay a fee.

Each campus has its own unique populations to deal with in determining whether or not to grant facility access. It is a constant challenge, and it is imperative that campus recreation administrators consistently monitor groups attempting to gain access to their facilities. They need to ensure they are not allowing access to ineligible groups or individuals.

Where to house the department has also been an issue for campus recreation programs. Early programs reported to HPER or athletic departments. In the early 1970s, however, there was a movement to shift many campus recreation programs to the Division of Student Affairs, which at the time was being created on many campuses. The University of Louisville Intramural Sports program, for example, reported to the Department of HPER until 1975, when it was moved to the newly created Division of Student Affairs.

One of the reasons I believe that campus recreation is a good fit in Student Affairs is that its goals are compatible with the mission of Student Affairs. Campus recreation, for example, is an excellent vehicle to improve the quality of the lives of our students. It provides students with countless learning opportunities and helps institutions create a vibrant campus life for their students. Our programs engage students and get them connected to the campus community. The earlier students get connected on campus, they are more likely to stay, to perform better academically, and to graduate. While each institution must decide the best reporting structure for its campus recreation department, Student Affairs seems to be the place where campus recreation is best aligned.

Here are five trends I anticipate for the future of campus recreation:

1. The need for campus recreation programs and services will continue to increase. Program offerings must continue to change and expand to meet the needs of a more demanding, diverse student population.

2. Universities will continue to recognize the importance of campus recreation programs and expect them to play an integral part in developing strategies for recruiting and retaining students.

3. Students will continue to place a high demand on access to campus recreation facilities. The "24-hour rec center" will continue to evolve on college campuses.

4. As demand for facility access and state-of-the-art facilities increases, universities will continue to build new student recreation centers and auxiliary recreation centers, and to renovate existing facilities to keep up with demand.

5. Increased demand for campus recreation services and programs will generate a greater need for highly qualified professionals to deliver these services.

It is easy to understand why campus recreation programmers have coined the slogans "Something for everyone" and "We do more than just play games." They clearly live up to these mottoes, providing an extensive and diverse array of recreation and leisure time activities. The sheer breadth of programming can be a "pressure point" for the Campus Recreation Director. Policy issues also require the attention of campus recreation providers, and some key policy areas are discussed next.

CURRENT POLICY AREAS

Policy is defined as the guidelines or procedures an organization follows in an effort to achieve its overall goals. Like any other department in an institution of higher education, the recreation unit must develop and update policy. The Campus Recreation Director leads the debate on issues of policy, gathering input from both full- and part-time recreation employees and participants. Some issues are impacted by policy enacted by the institution or the Athletic Department. Some of the current policy areas that impact campus recreation leaders today are discussed in this section.

Funding

The Sport Manager—perhaps any kind of manager—is always concerned with finances. What are our sources of funding? Are we maximizing our avenues of funding, and are we spending efficiently? Is the cost–benefit ratio of our programming effective? Can we justify our choices? Certainly, the campus recreation administrator is required to implement effective financial management policy.

One regularly discussed issue involves financing a broad program. How do we define what activities or events should be offered, and how do we ensure the financial support exists in the form of human and physical resources to deliver an effective program? Remember, colleges and universities are about excellence, and the delivery of excellent service and programming is a cornerstone of the Campus Recreation Department's mandate. Campus recreation leaders deal with this issue by setting policy around the viability of program offerings. Program managers conduct research to gather participants' views on the effectiveness of their programs. On an annual basis, the Director then charts hard data on participant numbers in specific activities and longitudinal participant trends. This information feeds the decision-making process by providing the leaders with quantitative information about what is of interest to participants and how they view the quality of the current offerings. Then administrators consider other relevant parameters, such as availability of funds and facilities, in their decision-making formula. The Campus Recreation Director needs to research questions such as the following:

- Do we have the facilities to support a particular endeavor?
- Are we willing to enter into a "pay for play" scheme in order to collect funds to rent extra facilities?
- How much interest must support a decision to add programming on a "pay for play" basis?
- Which activities are core support activities; that is, activities covered entirely by the campus recreation budget?
- Which events are run on a break-even basis only, requiring registration dollars and other mechanisms of funding in order to support the program?

These types of questions, plus others specific to a particular institution, will help the Campus Recreation Department set financial management policy.

Competition for Limited Facilities

Campus recreation is often in competition with other programming. The Physical Education, Athletics, and Summer Camps departments often vie for the same facility and equipment use. These competing units may even exist within the same department or faculty. When facilities are shared, leaders must develop policy that balances the needs of all areas. The Campus Recreation Director needs to take a proactive leadership role, advocating for the implementation of such boundaries. Otherwise, some of those interested in becoming active will have no opportunities. The recreation administrator needs to be armed with good information when policy is negotiated. Participant numbers, student numbers, activity interests and levels, and knowledge of user preferences are important. Setting procedures for priority status and for bumping programs is necessary to prevent interruptions to planned activities and to avoid user conflicts.

Activity Trends

Defining which activities to offer, mentioned above as an issue in funding campus recreation programs, is an important area in policy development. Interest in specific leisure and recreation activities tends to blow with the wind. Fads and trends are normal in recreation, and they shift quickly. Campus recreation leaders need to have their fingers on the pulse of shifting interests, and they can gather the information they need through three important mechanisms. First, they can administer participant and nonparticipant questionnaires to collect interests, likes, and dislikes. Second, recreation department student employees can gather informal data about interests and patterns of behavior. Finally, sport leaders can observe behaviors to learn where people are recreating, what events are popular, what events fail to draw participants, what the competition is up to, and who the competition is. Through program evaluation managers can gather information needed to make appropriate changes. This is critically important to meet the interests and needs of constituent groups, which are ever evolving and sometimes change radically. After all, the campus recreation program is nothing without participants.

Access

While having a large base of participants is important to the mission of the campus recreation program, participation, normally referred to as *participant eligibility,* is restricted. The Campus Recreation Director and his advisors are required to set eligibility policy based upon their unique environment and departmental goals. Normally, intramural and extramural sports are accessible only to the institution's currently registered students (both full- and part-time). Instructional and special-event programming may be open to faculty and staff members and their families, alumni, and community members. Other programming may have a priority listing for first-come, first-served entrance into leagues or events. To manage access, administrators of the department set policy stipulating who is eligible for a particular program. They may go so far as to create a priority listing for some activities. They may close other activities to only a certain set of the possible participant constituents. Some participants may enroll for free, while others pay fees depending on the mission of the Campus Recreation Department and of the university at large. It is important, however, that such policy is clearly communicated to participant groups and staff.

In addition to establishing participant eligibility, the Campus Recreation Department must also enforce rules limiting access to facilities and events. For example, employees must consistently check identification (ID) cards so only eligible participants enter a facility. When participants forget their ID cards, disagreements and confrontations often develop. Establishing clear policies for handling such situations helps maintain program safety and integrity.

Event Management

Recreation on today's university campus is often a huge enterprise, and consumers' expectations for excellence have kept pace with the diverse approach to programming and multimillion-dollar facilities. Students, their parents, and members of the community expect the highest quality in service and environment. To satisfy everyone's expectations, campus recreation administrators must create policy regarding event management.

Recognizing the need to develop policy may seem like common sense. However, consider the roots of the campus recreation program: "for the students, by the students." Even today, mostly student employees and student volunteers deliver recreation programs. Therefore, it is important that full-time managers of the Campus Recreation Department establish policy to define standards of event management. These may involve timelines and standards for physical setup, expectations of student managers and officials, rules for the use of logos and department letterhead, requirements concerning marketing and sponsorship, guidelines for decision making and problem solving, emergency response plans and other items related to managing risk, and media liaison and reporting of results. Of course, other issues connected to event management and requiring policy development will arise. Thus, risk management becomes particularly important to an effective and efficient Campus Recreation Department.

Risk Management

Campus Recreation Directors must be concerned with risk management (Barcelona, 2004). Of course, some risk is associated with crossing the street or playing a game of baseball. One may be run over by a speeding car or hit on the head by the baseball. Society attempts to minimize the possibility of being run over by a car by posting speed limits, building sidewalks, and setting up traffic lights and stop signs. Similarly, recreation administrators attempt to minimize risk in physical activity by requiring participants to wear protective equipment, ensuring that participants are taught proper techniques, and strictly enforcing safety rules. If the baseball player is hit in the head with a ball, hopefully her helmet will protect her. It is impossible to eliminate risk; the challenge is to manage the risk.

In other words, the recreation professional is responsible for setting up and delivering programs that reduce overt risks and communicate other levels of risks to participants. According to Miller (1998), to achieve this, policy is required to

- develop a written risk-management plan to show evidence of proactive prevention
- keep accurate and detailed records on participants and injuries that occur
- ensure that the rules of play are properly enforced and communicated
- train and certify leaders in the areas they teach and supervise
- ensure proper supervision of areas needing supervision and restrict access to some unsupervised areas
- check equipment regularly to ensure it is in good working order
- require paperwork that provides for lists of participants, identification information, and possibly health information
- develop and communicate emergency response procedures
- train event leaders in first aid and cardiopulmonary resuscitation (CPR)
- develop and implement informed consent forms and health-related questionnaires for all but the very minimal risk activities.

For example, an aerobics class should be led by a trained, certified instructor. He should have a class list, and participants should be required to complete a medical screening questionnaire such as the Physical Activity Readiness Questionnaire (PAR-Q) to identify any potential risk factors. In another activity, such as an outdoor adventure trip in white-water kayaking, medical clearance may be required, and program leaders will use waiver forms to have participants acknowledge the risks involved and to take responsibility for such risk. Waivers and informed-consent forms are commonly employed and should be a required component of the policy surrounding risk management for the Campus Recreation Department, especially where off-site travel or high-risk activities are involved.

www

PAR-Q
http://brown.edu/Athletics/
Recsports/PT%20Forms.pdf

Sport Management Resources
www.sportsmanagement
resources.com/library/
participant-waivers

Medical Issues

Pre-activity screening is important when dealing with medical conditions. However, it will not prepare employees in a recreation department for the acute medical emergencies that may result during sporting events and other physical activities. Inevitably, one player will step on another's foot while playing intramural basketball and sprain or break an ankle. The Campus Recreation Department must have set policy on procedures to help the injured participant. Having emergency supplies and equipment on-site is important, and many college recreation facilities have automated external defibrillators on site in case of cardiac incidents. Having an emergency action plan and trained supervisors who know what to do is also critically important. Some activities require collecting and keeping information on-site in the event of an emergency. The group leaders on a daylong cycling tour should have information on a participant who is allergic to insect stings, including medical insurance information and contact numbers and names. Medical information needs to be collected and collated into a manageable, perhaps laminated form that can be tucked into a sidesaddle or a fanny pack. Having on-site information and knowing what to do in the event of an emergency are critical areas for policy development and a clear responsibility of the Recreation Department in terms of employee training.

Recreational Opportunities for Individuals with Disabilities

The most critical issue with respect to recreational opportunities for students with disabilities is gaining an accurate demographic picture of who has needs and defining those needs (Frost, 1987). To achieve this, campus recreation professionals must set policy enabling the collection of important information regarding maximizing opportunity for students with disabilities. This is readily achieved through a Disabled Student Advisory Council, which sets a schedule for defining appropriate activities, defines a mechanism for publicizing activities and facility schedules, creates opportunities for training with respect to facilities and equipment, and provides ongoing leadership in the assessment of the effectiveness of the overall effort. Colleges and universities across North America must work harder to provide recreational programming designed specifically for individuals with disabilities.

SUMMARY

Recreational programming is thriving on college campuses. Universities have embraced the notion that higher education involves much more than lectures and exams and that the quality of student life is an important concern. The Campus Recreation Department helps to promote the overall goals of the institution by offering student activities that promote health, happiness, and affiliation. The diversity of programming is often extensive and usually student led. As a result of the considerable recreational scheduling on the college campus, several organizations have been established at the community, state or provincial, and national levels to promote recreation and offer recreation leaders sources of both professional development and practical resources. Two of the largest national associations are NIRSA in the United States and PHE Canada, formerly CAHPERD. Both include elected recreation officials from state or provincial associations, many of whom are campus recreation professionals.

The Campus Recreation Department can be organized as a unit with a small number of professional staff, housed within the university Athletics Department, or it can function as a stand-alone unit within the Student Affairs operation of the university, with many departments led by recreation professionals employed on a full-time basis. In either case, the organizational structure will rely on an extensive group of student employees and student volunteers who deliver a vast array of programming. Recreation professionals manage the affairs of the department by defining mission, vision, and goals; by managing facility operation and finances; and by setting and enforcing policy. Many policy areas draw the attention of the Campus Recreation Department leaders, from defining how the unit is funded and maximizing funding sources to program offerings and participant eligibility to access for people with disabilities. The Campus Recreation Department plays an extensive role in the delivery of recreational opportunities for the constituents on the modern university campus.

case STUDY

FACILITY DEVELOPMENT

As the newly hired Assistant Director of Campus Recreation at Big State University, your first assignment is to upgrade program offerings in your new facility. You have the following facilities:

- 1 gym—big enough for eight basketball courts
- 1 pool measuring 25 meters
- 1 cardiovascular room with treadmills and stationary bikes
- 1 weight room with free weights and a weight-machine system
- 2 activity rooms with 10-foot ceilings
- 4 multipurpose grass fields

Your student body enrollment of 18,000 includes many nontraditional students, and residence halls coexist with fraternities and sororities on campus.

1. What programs would you set up? What times would you schedule activities for? Leagues versus tournaments? How would you decide which activities to drop and which to add?
2. How would you go about getting funding for your programs? Whom would you ask?
3. Where would you get building and program staff? What would you include in their training program?
4. How would you ensure that your programs and facilities fairly and effectively provide for all your users?

5. Your programs must meet local and national standards. Which organizations would you join, and how would you go about ensuring that your programming reflected the best practices around the country?

CHAPTER questions

1. Using the Internet, search for the committee structure of NIRSA or the recreational component of PHE Canada. Build an organizational chart of the committees showing how they link together and where they report. How are the ideas generated and the problems solved at the committee level turned into policy? Trace and describe one example of such policy development by reading the committee meeting minutes as posted on the Web.

2. Investigate the campus recreation program at your institution. How is it structured, and how is policy developed? Who has the authority to make decisions? How is the program financed? How would you go about creating a new program activity?

3. Varsity athletics and campus recreation often compete for facilities and resources on campus. Develop an organizational structure with the best chance of downplaying this internal rivalry.

REFERENCES

Barcelona, B. (2004). Looking beyond the jockocracy. *Parks & Recreation, 39*(1), 22–29.

Brown, S. C. (1998). Campus recreation. In J. B. Parks, B. Zanger, & J. Quarterman (Eds.), *Contemporary sport management* (pp. 139–154). Champaign, IL: Human Kinetics.

CIRA. (2002). Canada's physical activity guides for children and youth. Retrieved January 3, 2002, from www.intramurals.ca/cira/overview.htm

Colgate, J. A. (1978). *Administration of intramural and recreational activities: Everyone can participate.* New York: John Wiley.

Drew University. (2012). Campus recreation services. Retrieved from http://www.drew.edu/CampusRec/

Frost, R. L. (1987). Campus recreation and the handicapped students: Attitude and opportunity. *NIRSA Journal, 11*(3), 35–36, 50.

Huesman, R., Brown, A., Lee, G., Kellogg, J., & Radcliffe, P. (2009). Gym bags and mortarboards: Is use of campus recreation facilities related to student success? *Journal of Student Affairs Research and Practice (NASPA Journals), 46*(1), 49–71.

Kane, M. J. (2007). Sociological aspects of sport. In J. B. Parks, J. Quarterman, & L. Thibault (Eds.), *Contemporary sport management* (pp. 389–413). Champaign, IL: Human Kinetics.

Langley, T. D., & Hawkins, J. D. (1999). *Administration for exercise-related professions.* Englewood, CO: Morton.

Miller, R. D. (1998). Campus recreation risk management. *NIRSA Journal, 22*(3), 23–25.

Mittelstaedt, R., Robertson, B., Russell, K., Byl, J., Temple, J., & Ogilvie, L. (2005). Unique Groups. In *Introduction to recreation and leisure.* Champaign, IL: Human Kinetics.

Mueller, P., & Reznik, W. (1979). *Intramural-recreational sports programming and administration* (5th ed.). New York: John Wiley.

NIRSA. (2012a). Mission Statement. Retrieved from http://www.nirsa.org/Content/NavigationMenu/AboutUs/MissionVision/Mission_Vision.htm

NIRSA. (2012b). About Us. Retrieved from http://www.nirsa.org/AM/Template.cfm?Section=About_Us

Ohio State Recreational Sports. (2012). Who we are: Mission. Retrieved from http://recsports.osu.edu/who-we-are.

PHE Canada. (2012). About Us. Retrieved from http://www.phecanada.ca/about-us

Smith, P. (1991). Positioning recreational sport in higher education. In R. L. Boucher & W. J. Weese (Eds.), *Management of recreational sports in higher edu-cation* (pp. 5–12). Madison, WI: WCB Brown & Benchmark.

Southern Polytechnic State University. (2007). Recreation mission statement. Retrieved from www.spsu.edu/home/sports/index.html

UCLA. (2012). Recreation department mission statement. Retrieved from www. recreation.ucla.edu/recreate/index.aspx

University of Denver. (2012). Division of Athletics and Recreation Mission Statement. Retrieved from www.denverpioneers.com/ViewArticle

University of Idaho. (2007). Campus recreation mission statement. Retrieved from www.campusrec.uidaho.edu/Mission

University of New Brunswick. (2012). URec. Retrieved from http://www.unb.ca/fredericton/urec/

Intercollegiate Athletics

Click on a college website, open a newspaper, or turn on the television and you will immediately see the interest in North American college athletics. National championship events
such as "The Final Four" are known worldwide. The spectacle of college sport will likely
continue to grow and endure the test of time, due in part to the mass media's role in
strengthening its appeal by bringing events and personalities directly into our homes. The

appeal is strongest in the United States, but colleges and universities in many countries around the world also sponsor competitive athletic opportunities for their students. In the United States and Canada, colleges and universities support extensive competitive athletic programs. This type of competition is commonly known as *intercollegiate athletics.*

The appeal of intercollegiate athletics is unquestionable and at the same time paradoxical. On one hand, the loyalty of cheering college students with painted faces, fully caught up in the excitement of events and intense rivalries, sometimes with national distinction at stake, is completely understandable. But viewed from another perspective, intercollegiate athletics is woven with problems. From the consumer viewpoint, the quality of play may not compare with professional leagues. In addition, a long history of abuses, excesses, and cheating has plagued intercollegiate athletics, challenging the very core concepts of sport in general and amateurism specifically. Ideals such as fairness, honesty, character development, competitive balance, and the dual role of the student-athlete have been questioned. In some cases the very existence of such an enterprise in connection with an educational institution has been called into question. Some of these issues, along with the huge costs of programming, have resulted in some schools dropping programs. In order to manage in times of fiscal restraint brought about by decreased resources and increased costs and to comply with Title IX legislation—the federal law that prohibits sex discrimination in education—some colleges have resorted to dropping teams. For example, in 2011 the University of Delaware dropped men's track and field and cross-country teams, a surprising move given the program celebrated its 100th anniversary that same year (Thomas, 2011a). Delaware is just one example of dozens of Division I schools who have eliminated men's teams like wrestling, gymnastics, and swimming in order to comply with Title IX (Brainard, 2006). Some institutions have also been padding women's rosters with practice players who never compete, in order to increase the proportion of women reportedly involved in intercollegiate athletics (Thomas, 2011b). Yet despite these and many other issues, consumer enthusiasm for intercollegiate athletics continues to grow as evidenced by ticket sales and television revenues (Kahn, 2006).

Growth serves as the perfect one-word descriptor of 20th-century intercollegiate athletics in the United States. Interest in supporting the local team gathered momentum to a point where now more than a thousand colleges and universities offer intercollegiate sport in the United States alone. Fueled by this momentum, the sheer magnitude of intercollegiate athletics may be one reason for its enduring and expanding appeal.

Different perspectives provide different insights into this phenomenal growth. A historian might suggest that the leadership of President Theodore Roosevelt and a group of college presidents provided the original momentum for the growth of college athletics when they intervened in college football to promote more extensive rules and safety requirements in 1905. A sociologist might identify the place of sport in American society and the feelings of personal success and hometown pride when the local college team wins (Ingham & Loy, 1993). A psychologist might point to improved psychological health with individuals identifying strongly with a local sport team (Wann, 2006). The economist might suggest that colleges and universities need the revenue generated by athletics, whether from television, recruiting students, or developing and managing the image of the institution. Other viewpoints exist, but one thing is sure: Intercollegiate athletics is a huge component of the sport industry of North America.

This chapter focuses on the many differences between the governance of organizations delivering collegiate sport in the United States (the NCAA and the National Association of Intercollegiate Athletics [NAIA]) and Canada (the CIS and the Canadian Collegiate Athletic Association [CCAA]) such as size, financial capacity, committee structures, scope of operations, sports supported, and rules and philosophy. Distinctions also exist in the governance and policy development between collegiate sport organizations in other countries around the world. Although collegiate sport exists in hundreds of countries worldwide, and athletes from these organizations represent their countries at the World University Games (Federation Internationale du Sport Universitaire [FISU] Games; see Chapter 9), their college sport programs may differ substantially from those in the United States and Canada. For instance, the British Universities and Colleges Sport (BUCS) has 157 member universities, while University Sport New Zealand (USNZ) has nine member universities. Some countries within Africa and South America may have very limited sport offerings, with emphasis on sports unknown or less popular in North America, such as footvolley (mix of football and volleyball), jujitsu, football (soccer), biribol (volleyball in a swimming pool), and running events. The big business nature of American collegiate sport fueled by considerable fan interest and television reach (and revenue) is not necessarily mirrored in other countries around the world. The organizations that manage sport and create the governance structures and policy for operations are unique to the settings, political environment, and historical events of each location. Therefore, the umbrella organizations delivering collegiate sport in countries around the world vary significantly in their size, capacity, programs, rules and regulations, and structures.

Let's turn our attention now to the governance of collegiate athletics in North America. Exactly how is it organized? How are rules made, and who decides the issues of the day? A brief look at the history and evolution of intercollegiate sport will answer those questions.

www

British Universities and
Colleges Sport (BUCS)
www.bucs.org.uk/
homepage.asp

University Sport
New Zealand (USNZ)
www.universitysport.org.nz/

HISTORY OF NORTH AMERICAN INTERCOLLEGIATE ATHLETICS

O ften the largest and most popular events are borne of the humblest beginnings, and this is exactly the case with intercollegiate athletics. The idea for athletic competition did not come from educators, nor was it a part of the curriculum. Rather, it originated with the student body.

The Beginning

College athletics began as recreational activities organized by students to meet their desire for both physical and social activities (Davenport, 1985). Although faculty members were not involved, they accepted the idea that students needed some diversions from classroom activity. It is easy to understand how college athletics developed. Two groups of students got together to play a game in the late afternoon sun; later, over dinner, the victors boasted of their success. Perhaps their classmates listened in and decided to show up for the next game to cheer on their friends. Next, for even more bragging rights, the victorious group then challenged the college in the next town. This, basically, is the story of the first intercollegiate competition, when a crew (rowing) race was organized between Harvard and Yale in 1852 (Scott, 1951).

Original Events

The next organized intercollegiate activity was baseball. The first baseball game was between Amherst College and Williams College in 1859 (Davenport, 1985). Such student-led activities gained significant interest among spectators and some notice from college faculty and administration. Administration noticed that winning athletic contests helped recruit students to campus and provide some positive attention for the college. Only 10 years later, on November 6, 1869, the first intercollegiate football game was played between Rutgers and Princeton (Davenport, 1985). Challenges for competition became more and more common. This growth was not always viewed positively, however. Administrators were concerned about the unproductive nature of athletic contests, and significant resistance was voiced against the emerging popularity of intercollegiate football.

Despite the attitude of some university administrators, tremendous interest in collegiate football was evident by the 1890s. A win-at-any-cost mentality developed, and to please the spectators in the overflowing college grandstands, players and coaches without affiliation to the college were inserted in the lineup. Street brawls became common after games. "In 1893 New York was thrown into a virtual frenzy by the annual Thanksgiving game between Yale and Princeton. Hotels were jammed. . . .

Clergymen cut short their Thanksgiving Day services in order to get off to the game in time. Clearly, football had arrived" (Rudolph, 1990, p. 375). Sports were becoming so popular on college campuses that they were likened to small business enterprises (Davenport, 1985).

Birth of College Sport Organizations

Up to this point, college athletic activities were organized and operated by students, and merely tolerated by the university administration. But it was becoming evident that athletic teams served as a unifying function of the college. Heroes emerged; public interest grew, as did the public relations opportunities. All of these factors, along with the potential for revenue generation, resulted in university administrations changing their position. College presidents and their inner circles realized successful sports teams could generate additional resources for their cash-strapped institutions, as well as draw both political favor and alumni support. College administrators, especially college faculty members, moved to take over management and control. Athletic personnel as we know them today did not exist.

On January 11, 1895, a historic meeting of faculty representatives was held in Chicago to develop eligibility and participation rules for football. This was the inaugural meeting of the Intercollegiate Conference of Faculty Representatives, forerunner to the Big Ten (Davenport, 1985). Soon thereafter, personnel in other regions of the United States also met and copied many of the rules developed at this initial meeting. Faculty exercised control over schedule development and equipment purchase. Playing rules and regulations were enforced, and some eligibility and financial restrictions were put in place.

About this same time, an alarming number of football players were seriously injured as a result of popular practices such as gang tackling and mass formations. In 1905, 18 athletes were killed and 143 seriously injured while playing collegiate football (Gerdy, 1997), prompting President Roosevelt to intervene. He called representatives from Harvard, Yale, and Princeton to two White House conferences to discuss the problems. At the request of Chancellor Henry M. MacCracken of New York University, representatives of 13 institutions met in New York City in December 1905 (NCAA, 2012a). The original intent of this meeting and a follow-up meeting later that month was to resolve issues related to football. However, the result was much more significant. More university administrators shared concerns, and as a result, 62 members founded the Intercollegiate Athletic Association of the United States (IAAUS) to oversee and regulate all college sports. The association was officially constituted on March 31, 1906.

At the same time, north of the U.S. border, Canadian colleges were experiencing growth in intercollegiate activities. In response to this growth, in the same year the IAAUS was constituted, the Canadian Interuniversity Athletic Union–Central (CIAU–Central) was formed. This association comprised faculty representatives from universities in Ontario and Quebec. Rapid growth, facility development, and the need for rules and regulations dominated CIAU–Central's initial agenda.

Evolution of College Sport Organizations

The development of the IAAUS and the CIAU–Central represented pivotal moments in the history of North American intercollegiate athletics and marked the beginning of an era in which collegiate sport instituted rules, regulations, supervision, and philosophical direction. Faculty members in physical education departments were hired to coach teams and administer programs.

In 1910, the IAAUS renamed itself the National Collegiate Athletic Association. During its initial years, the NCAA was composed only of faculty members from its affiliate institutions. It was a discussion group and rules-making body. Collegiate sports continued to grow, and more rules committees were formed. The evolution of the NCAA continued, and in 1921, the first national championship was held in track and field (NCAA, 2012a). Other sports and more championships were gradually added over the years. By 1973, the membership was divided into three legislative and competitive divisions (Divisions I, II, and III) based on institutional size. Subsequently, Division I members voted to subdivide football into Divisions I-A and I-AA. As the NCAA has grown in events and membership, a shift in power away from the collection of colleges to the centralized authority of the NCAA has taken place. Today, the NCAA is a large, powerful organization staffed by more than 320 full-time employees and delivering 38 national championships (19 for men and 19 for women) in 22 sports; its National Office is located in Indianapolis (NCAA, 2012a).

In Canada, the same period (1906–1919) saw major growth for athletics on university campuses; after World War II, conditions became relatively stable (CIS, 2012a). The CIAU–Central existed until 1955. Its main purpose was to develop common intercollegiate athletics rules and regulations. At that time regional organizations in provincial areas emerged. Eventually, the need for a truly national association became apparent, and the CIAU was reconstituted in 1961. The CIAU sustained gradual growth, moved to a central office at the National Sport Centre in Ottawa, and gained membership from all Canadian universities, a modest group of 49 institutions. In June 2001, the CIAU changed its name to Canadian Interuniversity Sport. The organization is still housed in Canada's capital city of Ottawa, and a small staff of ten employees manages 18 National Championships and special events (CIS, 2012b).

Growth of Women's Sport

In the United States, female participation in intercollegiate sport was conspicuously missing in the beginning. Little in the way of formal competition existed for women until 1971, when women physical educators established the Association for Intercollegiate Athletics for Women (AIAW). Several national championships were sponsored, and women's intercollegiate athletics gained momentum, quickly becoming an important component of college athletics. This interest prompted the NCAA to expand its structure to include programming for women just 10 years after the AIAW was established. The first NCAA programming for women occurred in 1980 when Divisions II and III took a leadership role by adding 10 national championships for women. This historic action prompted an extensive governance plan to be passed in 1981–1982, including 19 additional women's championships, along with services and representation in decision making for administrators of women's athletics.

Similarly, as women's intercollegiate sport in Canada grew and expanded, it needed organization. In 1923, the Women's Intercollegiate Athletic Union (WIAU) was established to oversee and provide programming for women's competition in Ontario, and the Ontario–Quebec Women's Intercollegiate Athletics (OQWIA) coordinated programming for female students in these regions. These two associations joined in 1971 to form the Ontario Women's Intercollegiate Athletic Association (OWIAA). Other regions gradually added women's programming as well. Much later, in 1997, the OWIAA merged with the men's Ontario University Athletics Association (OUAA) to form one association, Ontario University Athletics (OUA), to provide better services for delivering college athletics to both female and male athletes (OUA, 2012).

Historically Black Colleges and Universities

In the United States, Historically Black Colleges and Universities (HBCUs) are liberal arts institutions that were established before 1964 with the intention of serving the African American community. Those institutions with large African American student populations but founded after the *Brown v. Board of Education* ruling that outlawed racial segregation are known as "predominantly black," but not "historically black."

Today, 101 HBCUs in 19 states are divided into four categories: 41 four-year public institutions, 48 four-year private institutions, 11 two-year public institutions, and 1 two-year private institution. Over the years, HBCU graduates have gone on to make names for themselves in all spectrums of society including athletics, where some notable graduates include NFL MVP Steve McNair (Alcorn State University) and Eddie Robinson (Grambling State University), the winningest coach in college football history. HBCUs are affiliated with both the NCAA and the NAIA, but more participate in the NAIA because this organization invited them first. Examples of HBCU institutions with traditions of excellence in college athletics include Morgan State University located in Baltimore, Norfolk State University and Hampton University in Virginia, and Florida A & M.

Although the name might lead one to believe that only black student-athletes attend HBCUs, today their student populations, while predominantly black, do contain a more representative picture of society. As such, most HBCU athletic mission statements emphasize this diverse aspect to their population, such as this one from Alcorn State University:

wwww

Alcorn State Sports
www.alcornsports.com

> Alcorn State University is committed to providing a broad-based program that prepares student-athletes to succeed in their chosen field of study and to excel in their chosen sport. The mission of the Athletics Department is to provide equal opportunity for a diverse student population through competitive programs that encourage integrity, personal development, leadership, and teamwork at the highest level of academic and athletic excellence. This quest for academic excellence undergirds the University's mission of teaching, research and service through strong academics support programs for student-athletes and through the participation of all student-athletes in community service activities which lead to the development of competent, civic-minded graduates. (Alcorn State University, 2012)

However, in comparison to more "traditional" colleges and universities, HBCU athletic budgets are much lower. In 2006, Delaware State was the only black school that ranked among the top 200 (out of 331) athletic budgets in Division I (Jones, 2007). Some small schools, such as Division I-AA Southern University, rely heavily on one or two games to bring the majority of the revenue for their athletic departments, usually an annual game between two schools, or what is termed "a guarantee game," where small schools travel to face national powerhouses. While this game usually guarantees a substantial payday for the small school, it is hard to compete against more resource-rich institutions. Since the economic downturn in 2008, many HBCU institutions have cut programs, left vacant positions unfilled or eliminated them altogether, and slashed team travel budgets (Hollins, 2011).

GOVERNANCE

The growth, popularity, and subsequent reform in college sport dictated a more formal approach to managing and governing intercollegiate athletics. The NCAA is the largest and oldest organization formed for this purpose, and its history is closely intertwined with the growth of intercollegiate athletics. However, other organizations also govern intercollegiate athletics. In the United States, the NAIA is another umbrella organization of like-minded institutions, often compared in philosophical orientation to NCAA Division II schools. The National Junior College Athletic Association (NJCAA) and the National Small College Athletic Association (NSCAA) each exist to oversee the athletic programs of junior and small colleges, respectively. Finally, the National Christian College Athletic Association (NCCAA) administers intercollegiate competition for Christian schools.

Canada, with approximately one-tenth the population and a fraction of the number of universities and colleges found in the United States, has two divisions of institutions of higher education: degree-granting *universities* that offer three- and four-year undergraduate and graduate programs, and diploma-granting *colleges* that offer two- and three-year programs. (Colleges in Canada are comparable to technical schools in the United States.) Intercollegiate athletics is organized and governed by these two classifications: CIS is the organization that manages intercollegiate athletics for degree-granting universities, and the CCAA oversees intercollegiate competition for diploma-granting colleges across the nation. Following is an in-depth look at the actual structures of some of these organizations and the governance of intercollegiate athletics throughout North America.

www
National Junior College Athletic Association
www.njcaa.org

National Christian College Athletic Association
www.thenccaa.org

National Collegiate Athletic Association

The NCAA has some global recognition, thanks to television and marketing efforts. It is a voluntary association of colleges and universities, run by a President and staffed by several hundred employees. Members of the NCAA consider issues and policies affecting more than one region, thus making them national issues.

www
National Collegiate Athletic Association
www.ncaa.org

Mission

The NCAA is devoted to the expert administration of intercollegiate athletics for its membership. The core purpose of the NCAA "is to govern competition in a fair, safe, equitable and sportsmanlike manner, and to integrate intercollegiate athletics into higher education so that the educational experience of the student-athlete is paramount" (NCAA, 2012a). According to the NCAA (2012b), the goals of the organization are specific to the student-athlete: to promote college athletics, to protect the interest of the athlete by ensuring fairness and integrity, to prepare the athlete for a lifetime of leadership, and to provide funding to help accomplish these goals. The association supplies a governance structure to provide rules and establish consistent policy through which all NCAA member institutions operate. NCAA literature states eight specific purposes, as presented in Exhibit 8.1.

exhibit **8.1**   Purpose of the National Collegiate Athletic Association.

1. Programming for student-athletes and educational leadership, to include the promotion of fitness and recreational pursuits, and athletic excellence;

2. Protecting institutional control and responsibility for intercollegiate athletics, while conforming to the constitution and by-laws of the NCAA;

3. Establishing satisfactory standards of scholarship, sportsmanship, and amateurism;

4. Establishing and distributing rules of play;

5. Preserving athletic records;

6. Establishing and supervising eligibility standards for regional and national events;

7. Legislating, through by-laws and resolutions, the administration of intercollegiate athletics; and

8. Studying and researching all phases of competitive athletics in order to promote excellence.

Source: NCAA (2012b).

Membership

The NCAA comprises member institutions whose representatives retain voting privileges on setting policy and directing the future of intercollegiate athletics. Over 1,285 institutions, conferences, and organizations are members of the NCAA.

It is important to note that NCAA members are institutions, not individuals. Institutions are afforded membership by virtue of their mission in higher education, along with other membership criteria. All sizes and types of institutions are eligible for membership, as long as they are accredited by the recognized agency within their academic region, offer at least one sport for both men and women in each of the three traditional sport seasons, abide by the rules and regulations set forth by the NCAA (as certified by the CEO), and agree to cooperate fully with NCAA enforcement programs (NCAA, 2012c).

NCAA member institutions belong to one of three divisions labeled Division I, II, or III. The main criteria used for establishing an institution's divisional classification are its size, number of sports offered, financial base and sport-sponsorship minimums, focus of programming, football and basketball scheduling requirements, and availability of athletic grants-in-aid (NCAA, 2012d; Staurowsky & Abney, 2007). Division I (DI) football institutions are further subdivided into I–FBS (Football Bowl Subdivision) and I–FCS (Football Championship Subdivision): DI–FBS programs must meet minimum paid-football attendance criteria. Institutions competing in Division I in sports other than football are categorized simply as Division I. One thousand and seventy-nine active institutional members are divided fairly evenly among each division: DI has 335, DII has 302, and DIII has 442 (NCAA, 2012d).

Financials

The NCAA is a nonprofit organization, yet it is also a multimillion-dollar enterprise. Given the breadth of focus described above, it requires substantial revenue to fund an incredibly wide-ranging agenda. It is in a healthy financial situation, reporting revenues over expenses of almost $33 million in 2011. Revenues are generated from television rights, championships, royalties, investments, sales and services, and philanthropic contributions. The association's expenses include championships, special events, revenue sharing, association-wide programs, management, and the NCAA Foundation (NCAA, 2012e). At the end of 2008, the NCAA held net assets in excess of over $350 million.

Association-wide and division-specific structure

As with most other self-governing organizations, the NCAA began and existed for many years with a governance structure allotting one vote to each member institution. An annual national convention debated issues and voted on matters of policy. This organizational structure was reformed on August 1, 1997. In general, the reform provided each division greater autonomy for managing division-specific matters and gave university presidents more involvement in and control of developing legislation. For instance, in Division I the one-vote-per-institution principle was replaced with a system based on conference representation. Rather than every member voting on each issue at an annual convention, an 18-member Board of Directors is charged with managing all legislation, and one elected member from each conference votes on behalf of the conference. Members of the Board of Directors are institutional CEOs or college presidents, a move made, as mentioned above, to ensure more presidential involvement in intercollegiate athletics. Of course, the Board of Directors is not able to complete all of the Division's business.

DIVISIONAL GOVERNANCE STRUCTURE. Prior to 2008 the Division I Management Council reported to the Board of Directors. However, the Management Council was then replaced with two 31-member councils: the Leadership Council and the Legislative Council. These changes were prompted to increase efficiency and in order to provide more support to the Board of Directors. The Leadership Council is an advisory body that assists with issues of strategy and policy development. The Legislative Council, although subject to Board oversight, is now the prime legislative review body of the NCAA. Both Councils are comprised of athletic administrators and faculty athletic representatives, academics from the college faculty appointed to provide their perspective to athletic policy making.

Committees, referred to as cabinets, report to the Councils in the following areas: academic affairs; amateurism; awards, benefits, expenses and financial aid; recruiting and athletics personnel issues; championships and the administrative functions of Division I. All cabinets have 21 members, except the Championships/Sports Management Cabinet, which has 31 members. In effect, NCAA Division I is organized into three layers within its decision-making structure (see Exhibit 8.2).

Divisions II and III are structured similarly to Division I but have several important distinctions for conducting division-specific business. Each has a Board of Directors made up of institutional CEOs, but the body is called the Division Presidents Council, not a Board. The Division II Presidents Council includes 14 presidents, while the Division III Presidents Council comprises 15 presidents of institutions belonging to Division III. Both Divisions II and III also have Management Councils (with 25 and 19 members, respectively), but Division III has broadened the representation of this group by adding both institutional CEOs and student-athlete representatives to the athletic administrators and faculty athletic representatives comprising the Division I and II councils. Although Division II and III are structured in a similar way to Division I, one very important distinction remains: Legislation in both divisions is considered by the traditional one-school, one-vote method, as opposed to the conference representation used by Division I. Both Divisions

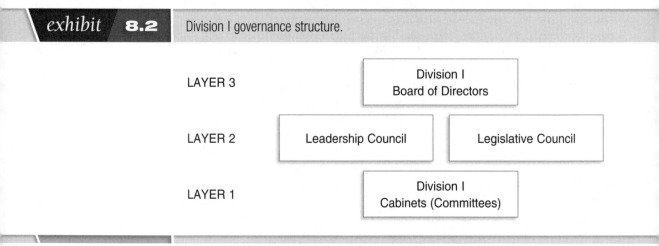

exhibit **8.2**   Division I governance structure.

LAYER 3   Division I
Board of Directors

LAYER 2   Leadership Council   Legislative Council

LAYER 1   Division I
Cabinets (Committees)

II and III have a committee structure to deal with issues specific to their business and sports.

ASSOCIATION-WIDE GOVERNANCE STRUCTURE. As you can see, the NCAA is a huge enterprise. Each division has many members and layers of committee structures for managing the business of intercollegiate sport. As with any large conglomerate, however, there is always the need to oversee association-wide issues. This coordinating function falls to the NCAA Executive Committee, comprising the 16 voting members of the Board of Directors and the Presidents Councils of the three divisions (eight from Division I–FBS, two from Division I–FCS, two from Division I, two from Division II, and two from Division III). The NCAA President and Chairs of the Division Management Councils also belong to the Executive Committee as ex officio (nonvoting) members. The Executive Committee is commissioned to ensure each division operates consistently with the overall principles, policies, and values of the NCAA.

In addition, 13 association-wide committees exist to ensure that the principles, policies, and values of the NCAA on common issues like medical and safety concerns are articulated and communicated. They include Academic Performance, Football, Men's Basketball, Women's Basketball, Athletic Certification, Infractions, Infractions Appeals, Initial Eligibility Waivers, Legislation Review and Interpretation, Process Toward Degree Waivers, Student Athlete Advisory, Student Athlete Reinstatement, and Amateurism Fact-Finding. See Exhibit 8.3 for a summary of the governance structure of the NCAA.

The NCAA has undergone much change during the last couple of decades. Major initiatives in enforcement and governance have occurred since 1981. An agenda of reform and strategy of college presidential involvement in the affairs of the organization, along with a philosophical push to put academics first in the athlete–education dyad was emphasized through changes to rules, governance structures, and institutional change. The NCAA's focus on Academic Progress Rate (APR), for example, is indicative of the action taken to improve graduation rates. Although many argue that the changes have not worked or do not go far enough, that significant changes have been made is evident given the size and complexity of the *NCAA Rule Book*. New rules have evolved governing athlete eligibility and financial aid, cost containment, recruitment, coach salaries, drug testing, championships, women's issues, and student-athlete welfare. Television has contributed to the growth and has publicized such issues as academics and amateurism, expectations put on student-athletes, growth and finance, diversity, and external interventions by government and courts of law. As the organization and its members' goals and values evolve, one area has not faded: Problems within the NCAA continue to be visible and critics are more vocal and active than ever before.

exhibit **8.3** Governance structure of the NCAA.

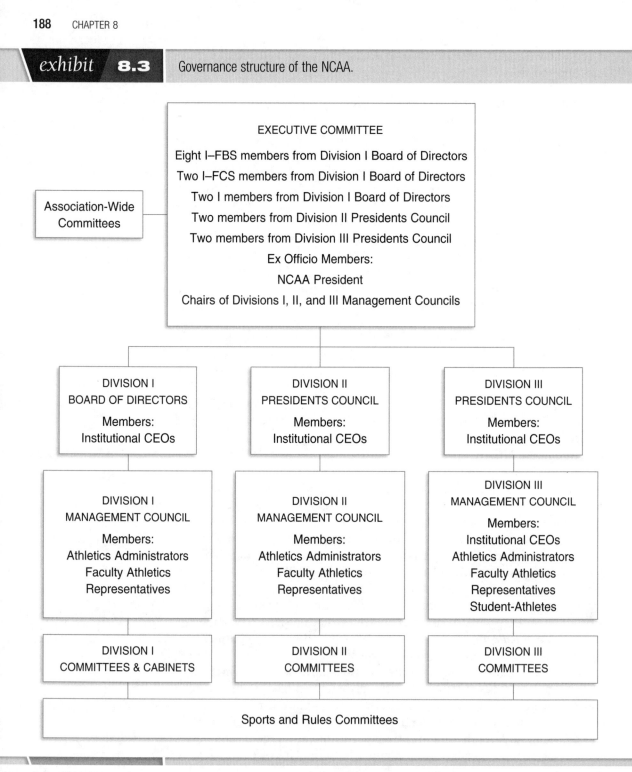

EXECUTIVE COMMITTEE

Eight I–FBS members from Division I Board of Directors

Two I–FCS members from Division I Board of Directors

Two I members from Division I Board of Directors

Two members from Division II Presidents Council

Two members from Division III Presidents Council

Ex Officio Members:

NCAA President

Chairs of Divisions I, II, and III Management Councils

Association-Wide Committees

DIVISION I BOARD OF DIRECTORS

Members:
Institutional CEOs

DIVISION II PRESIDENTS COUNCIL

Members:
Institutional CEOs

DIVISION III PRESIDENTS COUNCIL

Members:
Institutional CEOs

DIVISION I MANAGEMENT COUNCIL

Members:
Athletics Administrators
Faculty Athletics Representatives

DIVISION II MANAGEMENT COUNCIL

Members:
Athletics Administrators
Faculty Athletics Representatives

DIVISION III MANAGEMENT COUNCIL

Members:
Institutional CEOs
Athletics Administrators
Faculty Athletics Representatives
Student-Athletes

DIVISION I COMMITTEES & CABINETS

DIVISION II COMMITTEES

DIVISION III COMMITTEES

Sports and Rules Committees

National Association of Intercollegiate Athletics

The NAIA is another national association governing intercollegiate athletics in the United States. It comprises about 300 mostly small-size institutions, many of which emphasize the link between education and athletics more strongly than revenue generation. Initially formed to regulate intercollegiate basketball, the association was called the National Association of Intercollegiate Basketball (NAIB) until 1952, when the organization changed its name to the NAIA.

www

National Association of Intercollegiate Athletics
www.naia.org

Mission

NAIA institutions view athletics as "co-curricular," that is, as part of the overall educational process, something that goes hand in hand with the pursuit of academic goals. They believe involvement in athletics will enrich the student-athlete's college experience, balancing success in both the classroom and on the field of play. The NAIA National Office is the hub of organization and planning for national championships, and it defines the rules, regulations, and structures that govern member institutions. The purpose of the association is presented in Exhibit 8.4.

Fundamental to the NAIA mission is their Champions of Character initiative. The Champions of Character is a training program that attempts to instill and align the core values of integrity, respect, responsibility, sportsmanship, and servant leadership into the behaviors of athletes, coaches, and administrators. The student-athlete Champions of Character orientation program is known as Live 5. It is an interactive program that teaches student-athletes how to apply the NAIA core values to their lives in and outside sport.

www

Champions of Character
www.championsofcharacter.org/

Live 5
www.naia.org/ViewArticle.dbml?
DB_OEM_ID=27900&ATCLID=
205421991

Membership

Like the NCAA, NAIA members are institutions. NAIA membership is rather diverse, with an assorted group of institutions around the United States and a few members from Canada. The NAIA has nearly 300 member colleg-

---

Purpose of the National Association of Intercollegiate Athletics.

exhibit **8.4**

The purpose of the NAIA is to "promote education and development of students through intercollegiate athletics participation. Member institutions, although varied and diverse, share common commitment to high standards and the principle that athletics serve as an integral part of education.

Source: NAIA (2012a).

es and universities and is divided into 14 regions and 25 conferences across the United States (NAIA, 2012b). It has two categories of membership: active and associate members (NAIA, 2012c). Active members consist of four-year colleges and universities and upper-level two-year institutions in the United States or Canada that award undergraduate degrees. These institutions must be fully accredited by one of six institutional accrediting bodies from across the United States (such as the Southern Association of Colleges and Schools Commission on Colleges and the New England Association of Schools and Colleges Commission on Institutions of Higher Education), must abide by the constitution and bylaws of the NAIA, must be accepted for membership by the Council of Presidents, and must pay membership fees. Associate members are required to meet the same standards as active members except for full accreditation by one of the six accrediting bodies. These institutions must, however, be committed to the development of a fully accredited baccalaureate (undergraduate) program. Associate members are not eligible for postseason competition, nor do their institutional representatives vote on issues, serve on committees, or participate in national awards programs.

Individual institutions become members of one of the NAIA's organized regions and conferences. Issues that impact the overall association or that deal with national championships are deliberated at national meetings or in committee forums.

Financials

The NAIA is a not-for-profit association funded through membership fees, sponsorship, championship revenues, and merchandise sales. It collects fees for running national championships and other special programs and shares net revenues with its membership.

Organizational structure

The NAIA is organized to govern its business through a series of councils and committees. The association deliberately places the membership at the top of the organizational chart to emphasize the importance of each institution and its student-athletes for whom programming is organized. Responsive to the membership is the Council of Presidents. Similar to the NCAA, the NAIA relegates control and responsibility for the intercollegiate athletic program to the President or Chief Executive Officer of the institution. Each of the 14 regions within the NAIA elects one to three institutional CEOs to represent the conference membership on the Council of Presidents. The Council is composed of 38 representatives, of whom 13 are independent, at-large, or ex officio (nonvoting) members. An elected Administrative Committee, made up of a chair, three other members, and the NAIA administrative head, manages the Council. Each member of the Council holds one vote. Exhibit 8.5 illustrates the governance structure of the NAIA.

Organizational chart for the NAIA.

exhibit   **8.5**

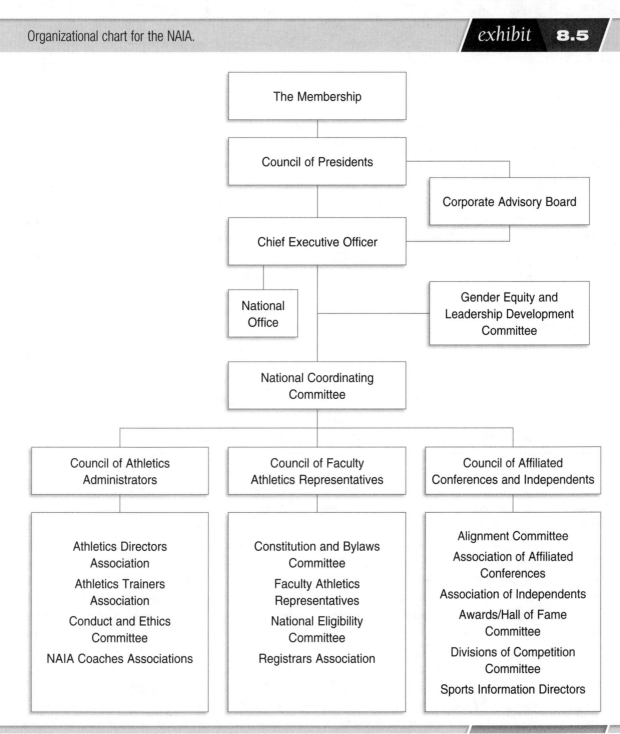

SCOTT Z. CRAWFORD, *Commissioner*

Kansas Collegiate Athletic Conference

My primary job responsibilities as Commissioner for the Kansas Collegiate Athletic Conference (KCAC) are serving as the primary spokesperson for the conference; representing the conference to the National Association of Intercollegiate Athletics (NAIA); and working with the several formal groups within the conference, which include the Board of Presidents, the Governing Council, and the various sport groups associated with the conference (for example, football, men's basketball, women's basketball, baseball, softball, and so on). Currently, the KCAC offers 19 championship sports at the varsity level.

Another of my major responsibilities is supervising the officiating for all sports. This entails hiring various coordinators who then assign and evaluate officials. This process runs concurrently for several sports; for example, it is now underway for volleyball, football, soccer, baseball, basketball, and soccer.

In my position I provide overall administrative leadership and management for the KCAC. These efforts include, but are not limited to, maintenance of the Constitution/By-Laws and overseeing all awards and certificates associated with the Conference.

The high costs associated with running intercollegiate athletic programs is relevant when discussing important policy issues. Intercollegiate athletic administrators constantly look for ways to reduce overall costs, considering items such as reductions to athletic grants-in-aid, slowing down the facility "arms race," and restructuring conferences to make travel more cost effective.

Speaking from a conference commissioner perspective, perhaps the most important policy issue is dealing with the associated costs of conference membership. Even at the small college level, the costs associated with conference membership are of major concern for the member institutions. In recent years I believe this has revealed itself clearly throughout all divisions of four-year institutions, be they NCAA Division I, II, III, or NAIA institutions.

In the NAIA world, membership is always a key focus. We deal with attrition (losing schools to NCAA Division II, a similar landscape for athletic competition and ability) and with growth (gaining as members colleges and universities dissatisfied with NCAA membership and also small colleges that are emerging from two-year community college status to become four-year institutions). I work with the NAIA leadership to find ways to differentiate ourselves from NCAA Division II with the goal of maximizing membership.

Over the past several years, I have been working both at the conference level as well as the national level to see Competitive Cheer and Competitive Dance gain credibility as varsity intercollegiate sports. Although the Quinnipiac University case and subsequent follow up from the Office of Civil Rights have determined that Cheer and Dance will not be counted toward a school's efforts to be in compliance with Title IX, I think we are on the cusp of seeing this viewpoint change.

Cheer and Dance face several challenges—including the need for sponsoring status by a true national governing body, societal perceptions of legitimacy, and a standardized competition strategy—in seeking to gain equal footing with other team sports such as volleyball and lacrosse. Over time, Cheer and Dance will need to find the right mix to develop regular season competition approaches and move away from exhibition type competition only.

My background in the academic world influences my opinions regarding how intercollegiate sports are governed. The single most positive aspect I note is how college presidents continue to exert their leadership over the world of intercollegiate sports. It is challenging to see the degree to which the highest levels of college sport are designed and managed to entertain the masses. Strong presidential leadership is needed to remind all involved parties that the college experience was designed to give students a college-level education culminating in a four-year degree, preparing them to go out into the world ready to tackle a new set of challenges.

The current governance model for the NCAA is in danger of further separation between the "haves" and the "have nots." There is continued dissatisfaction from the top-tier NCAA Division I athletic programs about having to share revenues with the lower-tier Division I institutions as well as with NCAA Division II and III schools. I wonder about the NCAA's ability to deal with these fractures.

This is a factor for the NAIA, where there is a demarcation between the top schools and conferences that use athletics differently from other small colleges within the association. In both the NCAA and NAIA, certain schools invest more in athletics as a way to entertain their campuses and communities than other schools that use athletics as an enrollment management tool to ensure there are enough students on campus to keep the doors open.

Other challenges I see on the horizon are: (1) dealing with the facility arms race extending down into the small colleges to assist with student-athlete recruitment; (2) establishing fair policies to combat inappropriate use of social media by student-athletes without stepping on their first amendment rights; and (3) resolving the "pay for play" issue currently being discussed at the top levels of intercollegiate sport.

The NAIA is further subdivided into three major administrative groups: the National Administrative Council, the National Coordinating Committee, and the Council of Faculty Athletics Administrators.

1. **NATIONAL ADMINISTRATIVE COUNCIL (NAC).** The NAC is responsible for all sport-related business. Its 34 members comprise the Chair of each of the 14 regions of the NAIA along with elected at-large members. An elected President and Vice President, chosen from among the regional chairs, and a Vice Chair govern it. The purpose of the NAC is to develop policy for national championships and postseason play, and to oversee NAIA coaches associations, along with the Conduct and Ethics Committee.

2. **NATIONAL COORDINATING COMMITTEE (NCC).** The NCC promotes the student and academic priorities clearly endorsed by the NAIA. This committee is comprised of 7 members, plus 2 staff liaison members. The NCC has a mandate for setting broad policy within the organization and hears appeals from the National Eligibility and Conduct & Ethics Committees.

3. **COUNCIL OF FACULTY ATHLETICS ADMINISTRATORS (CFAR).** This Council oversees, evaluates, and implements NAIA academic standards. It performs this role via oversight of the National Eligibility Committee and interactions with college registrars and faculty athletics representatives. CFAR members number 18 and are selected on the basis of geographic location, in which institutions are divided into East and West sections by the Mississippi River.

Committees managing specific elements of NAIA business, such as the Committee on Gender Equity, the NAIA Hall of Fame & Honors Committee, the Conduct and Ethics Committee, Constitution and Bylaws Committee, and the National Eligibility Committee, serve each of the preceding three Councils/Committees. Each group, along with the Council of Presidents, is committed to educational athletics and the true spirit of competition as described by five basic principles: (1) respect, (2) integrity, (3) responsibility, (4) servant leadership, and (5) sportsmanship (NAIA, 2012d).

Currently, the NAIA offers 23 national championships. Teams qualify for their championships through regional conferences. The NAIA sponsors a slate of 13 different sports (baseball, basketball, cross-country, football, golf, indoor track and field, outdoor track and field, soccer, softball, swimming and diving, tennis, volleyball, and wrestling), with competition scheduled for men in 12 and women in 11 sports. The organization has created two divisions for basketball for both men and women, allowing individual schools to select their level of competitive entry.

The organization is led by a CEO who manages the large NAIA National Office in Olathe, Kansas.

Canadian Interuniversity Sport

www

Canadian Interuniversity Sport
www.cis-sic.ca/splash/index

Intercollegiate competition for Canadian universities is governed by the CIS, a national association that organizes 21 Canadian National Championships, 10 for men and 11 for women.

Mission

The members of CIS believe that a university athletic program is founded on a sound educational program. The development of such individual programs, aided by and through a national forum that allows discussion of issues of common interest, is part of the mission of the CIS. The goals of the CIS are very similar to those espoused by college athletic groups in the United States: to achieve excellence through the highest possible ethical standards of equity and fair play, to encourage and coordinate competition and national championships, and to publish and disseminate information concerning interuniversity athletic activity. The CIS mission statement is presented in Exhibit 8.6.

---

exhibit **8.6**   Mission of Canadian Interuniversity Sport.

The mission of the CIS is to enrich the educational experience of the athlete through a national sport program fostering excellence through quality educational and athletic experiences, integrity and fair play, unity of purpose and respect for autonomy, trust and mutual respect, and equity and equality of experience.

Source: CIS (2012h).

Membership

Members are institutions of higher education in Canada that grant undergraduate degrees. These institutions are divided into four Regional Associations (Atlantic University Sport, Quebec Student Sports Federation, Ontario University Athletics, and Canada West), each with a minimum of eight members. With a total of 51 members, the CIS has a much smaller membership than either the NCAA or the NAIA. This number includes virtually all of the degree-granting universities in Canada. Each CIS member agrees to abide by the organization's constitution, bylaws, and rules and regulations; to pay yearly dues; to be a member in good standing of a CIS regional association; and to offer at least one intercollegiate sport for both men and women. Each institution names two delegates (one male, one female) to attend the organization's General Assembly meetings, an event normally held once a year.

Financials

The CIS is a modest enterprise with revenues of $2.5 million in 2012, a reduction of three quarters of a million dollars since 2009 (CIS, 2009, 2012c). Much of its focus is on delivering national championships and other special events in conjunction with its members. Finances are always tight, and fiscal responsibility is a major focus. The organization manages to balance its spending with revenues each year. Revenues are generated from championship guarantees, sponsorship and events, government support through Sport Canada, membership fees, publications, and investments; expenses are for championships, special events, association-wide programs, office and meeting management, and sport development (CIS, 2012c).

Organizational structure

Between General Assembly meetings, the Board of Directors governs the CIS and has "the jurisdiction to do all things necessary for carrying out the Constitutional Objectives and fulfilling the Mission Statement of Canadian Interuniversity Sport" (CIS, 2012d, p. BL6). This includes the power to manage policies and procedures, direct disputes, discipline members, and direct personnel. The Board of Directors consists of the President and President-Elect or Past-President, along with the Chair of the Finance Committee; three Vice Presidents elected by the General Assembly responsible for portfolios in Sport, Research and Development, and Marketing; Chair of the Equity and Equality Committee; Chair of the International Committee; and one person from each of the four Regional Associations. Each Regional Association names one male and one female nominee, and board members are selected for a two-year term from among the regional association members and are balanced in number of women and men. The CEO is an ex officio (nonvoting) member of the board. The Board of Directors meets at least twice a year.

The elected officers of the board comprise the Executive Committee, which is charged to act on behalf of the board between meetings. The Executive Committee is also responsible for dealing with strategic planning, budgeting, public relations, and other important items impacting the organizational effectiveness of the CIS. Its members include the President, President-Elect, Past President, Vice Presidents (Programs, Marketing, and Research and Development), Finance Committee Chair, and Chief Executive Officer (ex officio). Committees include Eligibility, Equity and Equality, Marketing, International, Discipline, Sport, Finance, and Research and Development. The committees have regional association membership and responsibility for managing specific CIS business.

The CEO and other paid employees of the organization are located in Ottawa, Ontario. Exhibit 8.7 summarizes the governance structure of the CIS.

Canadian Collegiate Athletic Association

www
Canadian Collegiate Athletic
Association (CCAA)
www.ccaa.ca

The CCAA was founded in 1974 to coordinate college sport in Canada (CCAA, 2012a). Remember, Canadian colleges are similar to technical schools in the United States.

Mission

Like the CIS, the primary objectives of the CCAA are to conduct and to promote athletic competitions for their member institutions, Canadian colleges that offer mostly two- and three-year programs. The organization is a coordinating body and thus seeks to bring together a group of administrators from a diverse set of colleges to make decisions concerning the development of college athletics in Canada. The mission statement of the CCAA is presented in Exhibit 8.8.

Membership

With 95 members, the CCAA comprises a wide variety of post-secondary institutions, including community colleges, university-colleges, and technical institutes. It is composed of five regional athletic conferences from coast to coast in Canada. Student-athletes compete for national championships in eight sports (three men's, three women's, two co-ed).

Financials

The CCAA is even smaller in scope and finances than the CIS. Revenues are generated largely from championships, sponsorship and events, and membership fees; expenses are for championships, special events, association-wide programs, and office management.

Organizational structure of CIS.

exhibit **8.7**

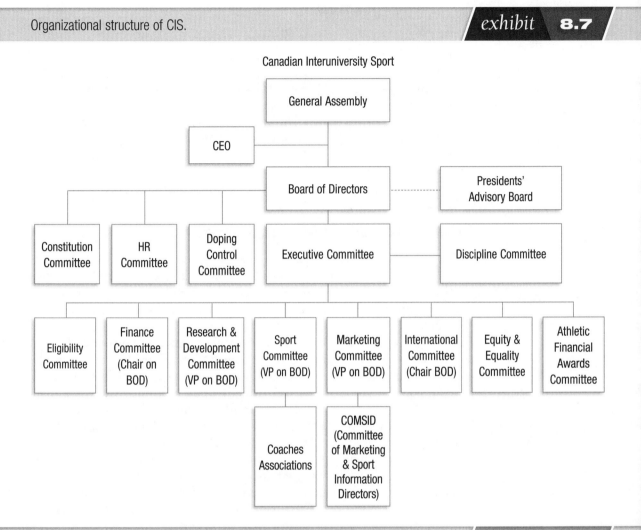

Canadian Interuniversity Sport

Source: CIS (2012f). Reprinted with permission.

Mission of the Canadian Collegiate Athletic Association.

exhibit **8.8**

The mandate of the Canadian Collegiate Athletic Association is to provide leadership, programs, and services for student-athlete development through intercollegiate sport.

Source: CCAA (2012b).

Organizational structure

The CCAA is governed by a Board of Directors comprising six elected executive positions and a representative from each conference. The executive positions include the President, Past President, and four Vice Presidents, one each for Governance, Marketing, Programs, and Finance and Administration. Leadership for the entire operation of the organization rests with five positions: CCAA Executive Director, Coordinator of Communications and Events, Finance and Administration Coordinator, Promotions and Marketing Coordinator, and an Administrative Assistant. The National Office is housed in Ottawa, Ontario.

See Exhibit 8.9 for a summary of the governance structure of the CCAA.

Individual Campus Athletics Management

The organizations discussed above operate on the national level and comprise institutional members providing competitive opportunities for their athletes and coaches. A series of rules and regulations, policies, procedures, and bylaws help regulate the competition, focusing on everything from the underlying purpose and philosophy of the competition to how events are operated. Although a great deal of regulatory power exists with the leaders of the national associations and coalitions of larger institutions, the day-to-day responsibility for the intercollegiate athletic program resides on campus in the college Athletic Department.

College athletic departments can be very large or very small, as illustrated in Exhibits 8.10 and 8.11. Larger colleges and universities employ a wide variety of sport professionals to manage, deliver, and supervise intercollegiate athletics: administrators, coaches, trainers, facility and event managers, and faculty representatives all play important roles in the intercollegiate program. Of course, all campus initiatives fall under the auspices of the President's Office. Over the years, the college or university president has had varying degrees of involvement in the athletic program. Today, direct involvement by the college president is more the rule than the exception. For example, university presidents in Ontario pushed for gender equity in athletic programming by instituting a biennial Gender-Equity Audit. Presidents in the Atlantic region refused a proposal for amalgamation of the football schedule to include another region because of costs and competitive issues.

University president

The immense popularity of intercollegiate athletics became apparent early in its history as large crowds gathered to watch games and their outcomes became front-page news. The traditional attitude of college administrators

Governance structure of the CCAA.

exhibit **8.9**

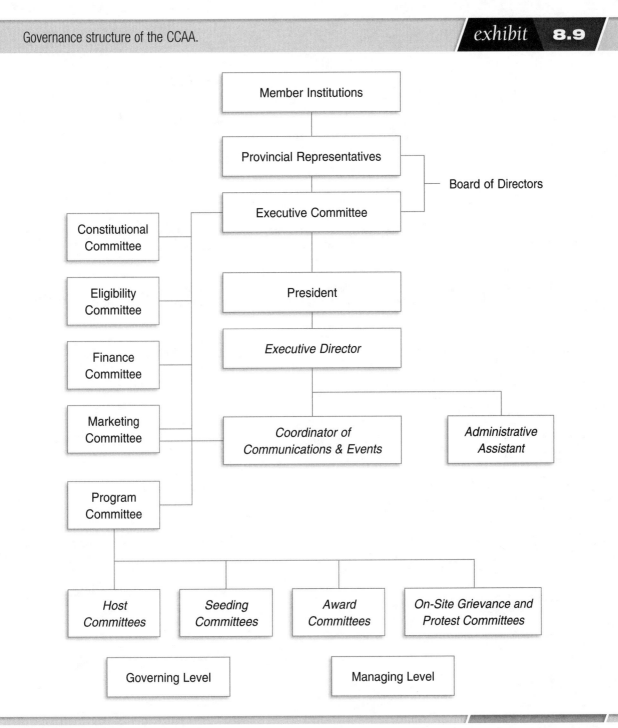

exhibit **8.10** Organizational structure for OSU's Department of Athletics.

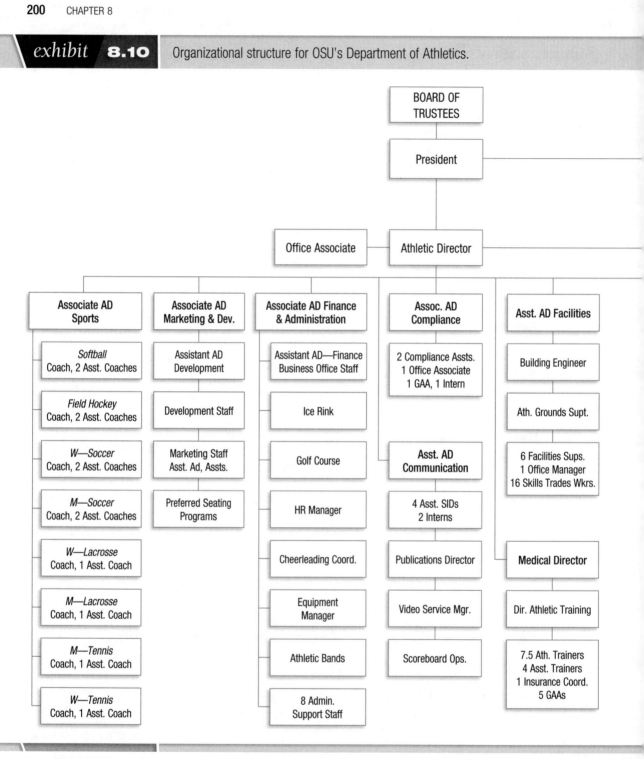

Source: The OSU Department of Athletics (2008). Reprinted with permission.

Continued.

exhibit **8.10**

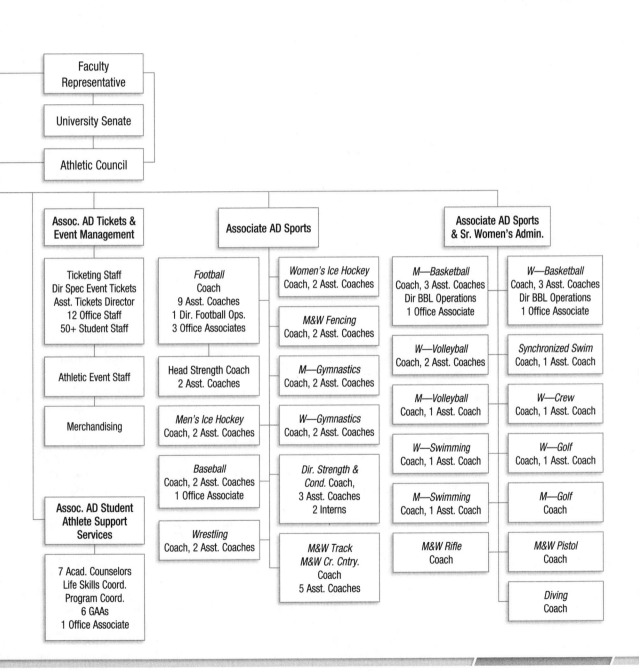

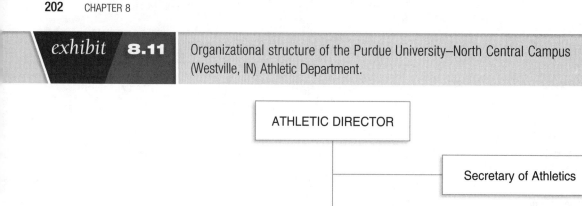

exhibit **8.11**   Organizational structure of the Purdue University–North Central Campus (Westville, IN) Athletic Department.

Source: Purdue North–Central Athletics (2008).

toward student-life initiatives has been supportive but with a hands-off approach. Historically, presidents have not meddled in Athletic Department business; instead, they hoped for positive results and no scandals. However, the proliferation of highly publicized violations and reported abuses garnered increased presidential interest in intercollegiate athletics. After nearly a decade of highly visible scandals, the Knight Foundation created a Commission on Intercollegiate Athletics (Knight Foundation Commission on Intercollegiate Athletics, 2001). The purpose of the commission was to propose an agenda of reform. One of the proposals of the Knight Commission was increased presidential control over college athletics. The fear that intercollegiate athletics had become too large, was riddled with unethical behaviors, and was separate from the academic mission of the institution led to the proposal for greater presidential and senior academic management involvement. As a result, the NCAA, for example, holds presidents accountable for member conduct and requires that they be involved in developing and managing policy through the Board of Directors and the Council of Presidents. In essence, presidential involvement is the result of negativity, corruption, and deceit. On the other hand, increased presidential involvement has also resulted from the potential institutional benefits of athletics participation, not the least of which is money. Developing an institutional image of excellence, increasing alumni involvement, and recruiting new students have always been positive goals for university presidents, but the potential for revenue generation has led to a more serious focus.

Gerdy (1997) summarizes the enhanced role of the university president in college athletics:

www
Knight Commission
www.knightcommission.org

This explosion of media attention, coupled with the growing need to market higher education to an increasingly skeptical public, suggests that presidents, and the academic community they represent, take a more active role in managing that exposure. Thus, the heretofore hands-off, keep-me-off-the-front-page approach to managing this powerful university resource no longer serves greater institutional purposes. In short, athletics' visibility and public influence must be looked upon as something not simply to be tolerated but rather harnessed and exploited for larger university gain. (p. 9)

The level of presidential involvement varies from institution to institution. Many presidents have supported the formation of an Athletic Board and a Faculty Athletics Representative to help scrutinize policy, direction, and operations of the Athletic Department and advise on athletic activities and issues.

In January 2006 the Summit on the Collegiate Athlete Experience was held, bringing together coaches, journalists, and athletes to discuss the collegiate athlete experience, substance abuse, and recruiting ethics. The results of the summit, along with NCAA statistics regarding rules violations, prompted the Knight Commission to strongly urge college presidents to support academic reform in college athletics (Knight Foundation Commission on Intercollegiate Athletics, 2007). In 2010 the Knight Commission urged three approaches to reform in intercollegiate athletics (Knight Commission, 2012):

1. Improving transparency through the reporting of assessment measures and accountability metrics.
2. Profiling and rewarding practices that make academic achievement a priority.
3. Treating college athletes as students, not as professionals.

The Athletic Board

The Athletic Board is a committee normally placed at the top of the Athletic Department hierarchy between the Director and the college President. Its purpose is to advise the Athletic Director and possibly the President and to oversee Athletic Department operations. The Athletic Board is generally composed of a large number of constituents, including faculty, students, alumni, community businesspersons, and university administrators. The group meets regularly each semester to oversee policy development and implementation and to scrutinize budgets. Since the Athletic Director is *responsible* to the university President, the Athletic Board in effect serves as part of the checks and balances on Athletic Department operations, a sounding board for the development of new initiatives, and a mechanism for control of operations. The Athletic Director is *responsive* to the Athletic Board and works in consultation with it, but usually reports directly to the university President (or indirectly via a Dean or Vice President). The Athletic Board at the University of Kentucky is a committee of the Board of Trustees, comprised of a mixed group of board members who may be community members, students, or faculty and staff. At many Canadian institutions, such as the University of Alberta, the Athletic Board is comprised solely of students. In theory, the Athletic Board wields considerable power; but in reality it may be relatively powerless, receiving general information and rubber-stamping reports that are peripheral to the major issues facing the unit and its personnel. Even so, perhaps the least powerful position associated with this group, which is sometimes actually marginalized by the Athletic Department, is the Faculty Athletics Representative (FAR).

Faculty Athletics Representative

The FAR is normally appointed by the President and is responsible for ensuring that the operation of the Athletic Department remains within the educational context of the institution. The individual appointed to this position is normally a faculty member, designated to liaise between the Athletic Department and the institution's administration. The FAR also represents the institution in affairs related to academic matters discussed at the NCAA and within the affiliated conference. The FAR addresses a variety of topics but most likely oversees policy regarding educational priorities of athletes, scheduling and time commitments, graduation rates, academic support programs, policy enforcement, and the appropriate balance between athletics and academics for an institution's student-athletes. The FAR reports to the President and works in concert with the Athletic Board and the Athletic Director.

In some cases, this reporting structure can marginalize the FAR, because members of the Athletic Department may construe his or her presence and mandate as intrusive. Since the FAR reports directly to the President, struggles over jurisdiction and perspective between the value of athletics versus the importance of education may occasionally result. Most often, however, the FAR works diligently to reduce such conflict and plays an important contributing role in delivering athletic programming in the higher education setting.

Athletic Director

The Athletic Director (AD) is the head of the Athletic Department. As the top manager, the AD is responsible for the unit and must understand the policies, activities, and actions of those working within each department. Recently, in many large athletic departments, the AD's activities have become more externally driven, with fundraising responsibilities, community and alumni relations, and capital building now a part of his or her portfolio. Ultimately, this individual is responsible for planning, organizing, leading, and evaluating both programs and personnel. Depending on the scope of these external initiatives, an Associate AD (sometimes referred to as an Athletic Coordinator) may manage the day-to-day operations of the unit. In any event, the specific responsibilities of the AD include finance, facilities, medical services, travel, event management, compliance, media, scheduling, marketing, ticket sales, public relations, personnel, communication, risk management, television, and student-athlete services. Effective ADs possess a great deal of business sense, critical-thinking and problem-solving ability, and strong communication skills. They must ensure the Athletic Department's mission coexists effectively with the mandate of higher education. Striving for excellence in two domains means conflicts will certainly arise between athletics and academics. For example, how should the AD respond when a coach develops a schedule requiring a student-athlete to be away from campus for 10 days in the middle of the semester? The games may be highly beneficial from a competitive standpoint, but taking a student out of class for this length of time might prove disastrous. The AD must balance academic and athletic goals, in this case by decreasing the length of the trip. Educational concerns must supersede athletic goals, because colleges and universities are first and foremost institutions of higher learning. Without a doubt there are ADs who lose sight of this founding principle in their quest for athletic excellence. Having the management skills to plan and organize is important, but it is perhaps more important that the leader of the Athletic Department effectively promotes the educational priorities of the institution and the personal achievement of the student-athletes. The most important role for the AD is the role of educator. This is also true for coaches, the other main constituent of the Athletic Department.

Coaches

Coaches truly are managers in that they plan, organize, lead, and evaluate their teams like small, independent organizations. You might think of the coach as the CEO of the most important component of the Athletic Department, the athletic team. A coach wears many hats in addition to being an educator. In managing and building the athletic program, she establishes liaisons with constituent groups such as student-athletes, students in general, high school recruits, the media, parents, alumni, Athletic Department administrators and colleagues, sponsors, members of the college community, and professional colleagues. Today's college coaches are skilled in a particular sport and knowledgeable generally about teaching, developing tactics and strategies, communicating, motivating athletes, and building support for their program. They represent an integral component of the structure of the college Athletic Department because they drive the main business of the organization. Coaches hold a major position of influence and authority. In their highly visible positions, they greatly affect the welfare of their student-athletes and the images of their institutions. Coaches also can have an important voice in the critical policy areas currently under review within intercollegiate athletics.

CURRENT POLICY AREAS

Many areas within intercollegiate athletics require the development of policy to ensure fairness results from common practices. Many policy areas are debated in college athletics regardless of the country of origin, division, or affiliation. The sheer numbers of individuals involved with these organizations and the issues evolving from the unique sport environment require a problem-solving, action-oriented culture. The focus on developing new policy and amending old policy helps administrators effectively manage the evolving, dynamic environment of intercollegiate athletics. Let's investigate some recurring and some new governance policy areas facing collegiate athletics today.

Eligibility

Eligibility defines who is allowed to play. In the early days of college sport, concerns arose when an individual not affiliated in any way with the college emerged as the star of the team. If collegiate athletics is about representing one's particular institution, it follows that the members of the team must also be students at the college. *Eligibility,* then, is the global term used to define the rules for entering, in-progress, and transferring student-athletes.

Initial eligibility

To be eligible to compete in intercollegiate athletics, a high school graduate must possess the required grades in a set of core courses acceptable to the college or university for entrance. Normally, meeting the entrance requirements to a college or university as a full-time student in Canada will enable the student to be an athlete. In the United States, however, the NCAA uses an external body called the NCAA Eligibility Center to process student-athlete eligibility in order to enforce common standards (NCAA, 2012f). Students register with the Eligibility Center (normally after their junior year) by submitting high school transcripts and standardized test scores (such as the Scholastic Aptitude Test [SAT] or American College Test [ACT]). The Eligibility Center then approves an application when an institution requests information about a particular student. Currently, the NCAA Divisions I and II require 16 core courses to be completed satisfactorily along with a minimum standardized test score defined

www

NCAA Initial Eligibility Center
http://web1.ncaa.org/ECWR2/
NCAA_EMS/NCAA.jsp

in conjunction with grade point average (GPA). The NCAA Division I uses a sliding scale of GPA, SAT, and ACT scores to identify minimum standards of initial eligibility. In Division II, a minimum SAT score of 820 or a sum score of 68 on the ACT is required to compete on an athletic team. The core GPA requirement is a minimum of 2.0 (NCAA, 2012f).

The NAIA (2012a) requires two of the following three items for eligibility: (1) a minimum 2.0 GPA (on a 4.0 scale), (2) graduation in the upper half of the high school graduating class, (3) a minimum score of 18 on the enhanced ACT or 860 on the SAT. Students who gain admission to a college but have scores below these NCAA or NAIA standards are ineligible to compete for their first full year of attendance (two semesters, three quarters, or the equivalent).

Academic progress

To maintain eligibility, student-athletes must take and achieve passing grades for a specific number of courses or maintain a specific GPA.

In Canada the CIS (2012e) requires that a student pass 3 full courses, 6 half courses, or 18 credit hours in order to be eligible for competition the following year. In the NAIA a freshman student must successfully complete 9 institutional credit hours in his first term of competition to be eligible for his second term of play. Thereafter, he must accumulate a minimum of 24 credit hours over 2 semesters to be eligible for competition the next year, or complete 36 credit hours of class time over 3 quarters of the years. No more than half of the 24 credit hours can be earned during the summer or noncompetition terms.

As stated earlier, the NCAA has initiated an academic reform package. In the NCAA, student-athletes must demonstrate steady progress toward graduation: they must be pursuing full-time study, be in good standing, and be making satisfactory progress toward a degree. In addition, the NCAA Division I member institutions must be accountable for the academic success of their student-athletes, and each Division I sports team receives an Academic Progress Rate score. Essentially, the APR is conceived as a metric developed to track, manage, and enforce accountability for academic achievement by NCAA athletes. One retention point is allotted to an athlete for staying in school and one eligibility point is given an athlete for being academically eligible. The points are added together for each team, divided by the number of points possible, and multiplied by one thousand, yielding the team's APR score. For example, an institution's overall APR requirement of 967 (out of 1,000) approximates a 65 percent Graduation Success Rate. Specific required team APRs are also identified, with football requiring a score of 944, men's basketball 940, and baseball 954. While teams with high APRs receive public recognition from the NCAA, teams that score below 925 can be sanctioned, for example, by receiving reductions in scholarships (NCAA, 2012g). Out of more than 6,400 NCAA teams, just over 100 were sanctioned for poor academic performance in 2011 and 15 teams (10 men's basketball, three football, one men's soccer, and one wrestling team lost postseason access in 2012–13 (NCAA, 2012g). The APR is a data-driven initiative indicative of the NCAA trend toward utilizing available data in implementing legislation reforms.

Transfer students

Rules regarding transfer students are an important aspect of intercollegiate athletics' eligibility policy. Transfers to institutions for the sole purpose of playing intercollegiate athletics are discouraged because such moves contradict the philosophy of student first, athlete second. The purpose of attending a college or a university is to get an education, earn a degree, and become a contributing member of society. To promote this philosophy, intercollegiate athletics commonly enforces a transfer rule requiring the transferring student-athlete to refrain from competition for some period of time. The NCAA transfer rule requires a student-athlete to complete one full academic year of residence (two semesters or three quarters) at a certified institution before being declared eligible to compete. The NAIA requires a 16-week residency period prior to competition after transfer from a four-year institution unless the institution from which the student-athlete transfers provides a no-objection release, in which case immediate play is allowed; it allows a transfer from a two-year institution after filing the appropriate disclosure forms. In Canada the CIS requires a student to forgo competition for one year following transfer to another institution, while the CCAA prohibits competition in the same sport during the same season but allows competition in the same sport the next season.

Eligibility is a common policy issue in intercollegiate athletics because competing institutions have always valued fairness and a balanced starting point in competition. These are achieved when the respective league-eligibility committees define benchmark standards to guide the agreed-upon concept that collegiate athletics is for full-time college students progressing toward a bona fide diploma or degree. Such eligibility requirements differentiate collegiate athletics from other avenues of amateur and professional sport.

Amateurism

Over the years, intercollegiate athletic administrators have worked hard to ensure college competition is identified as amateur as opposed to professional sport. Many will debate their success, given the requirements placed on student-athletes and the big business nature of college athletics, especially at the NCAA Division I level. According to NCAA (2012h) bylaws,

Only an amateur student-athlete is eligible for intercollegiate athletics participation in a particular sport. Member institutions' athletics programs are designed to be an integral part of the educational program. The student-athlete is considered an integral part of the student body, thus maintaining a clear line of demarcation between college athletics and professional sports. (p. 61)

In any event, student-athletes are not paid salaries for their services. Their involvement is noncontractual, and their primary purpose for attending the institution is educational. Does this ring true? Perhaps not always, and this is the specific reason amateurism is hotly debated by administrators at the institutional, regional, and national levels.

Are college athletes employees? The answer, of course, is "no" in theory and "no" in operation, at least most of the time. College athletics should reflect the tenets of amateurism without any difficulty: competition for the glory of achievement, in a voluntary environment in which no salary is paid. In most cases amateur competition is consistently portrayed in college athletics. However, the competitive nature of NCAA Division I athletics, in which both coaches and athletic administrators push to win games and balance budgets, certainly tests (if not crosses) the line between amateur and professional sport. In this case many critics have complained of a "say . . . do" gap. College athletics is said to be amateur athletics in the context of education, but the demands and the stakes suggest a more professional sport environment to some critics who maintain that colleges should pay athletes for their performance, just as professionals are compensated for the entertainment they bring.

Regardless of the debate, collegiate athletic administrators continue to embrace amateurism and have invoked rules to prohibit professionals from competition. Student-athletes are not paid to compete, but most receive athletic scholarships or grants-in-aid to help offset the costs of a college education. An "athlete turned pro" is prohibited by league policy from returning to college competition in her sport. The amateur policy of the NCAA describes many activities that result in an athlete's losing amateur status (NCAA, 2012h):

- playing for pay
- accepting a promise for pay
- signing a contract to play professionally
- prize money above actual and necessary expenses
- competing for a professional team (tryouts, practice, or competition)
- entering into a draft prior to collegiate enrollment
- entering into an agreement with an agent
- benefiting from an agent or prospective agent
- delaying initial full-time enrollment in order to compete in organized sport

Without a doubt, college administrators still believe it is important for college athletes to be students first, competing in amateur athletics as law-abiding, drug-free role models reflective of the entire student body. Policies play a role in fulfilling this mission.

Substance Abuse and Performance Enhancement

Collegiate athletic administrators are united in their opposition to performance-enhancing drugs and other forms of substance abuse by anyone involved in college athletics. Evidence of unequivocal opposition is reflected in policy statements. National and regional associations governing collegiate sport throughout North America respect the list of banned substances and methods as reported by Olympic and National and International Federations, along with the FISU, which governs the World University Games held every two years. Policies oppose the use of any banned or restricted substances or methods and the encouragement of such practices by anyone associated with college sport (coaches, administrators, athletic staff, medical practitioners, sport scientists, alumni, boosters, athletes, etc.). The opposition to doping strongly discourages participants from seeking an artificially induced advantage in competition. Student-athletes sign consent forms demonstrating their understanding of drug-testing programs and their willingness to abide by the rules. In the NCAA first-year students must sign forms indicating their willingness to comply with rules prohibiting banned substances, and, in Canada, such consent forms are a component of eligibility.

To establish doping control, policy has been invoked on two levels: education and enforcement. Educational programs have been established by the NCAA (2012i) and the CIS (2012f) and are mandatory for athletes in order to ensure awareness of the rules and the lists of banned substances and methods. Student-athletes are informed through handbooks, posters, and mandatory seminars in which a drug education video is shown and verbal explanation of doping-control policy is provided. In addition, programs of unannounced testing have been established by the leagues mentioned above, which give no notice or short notice. In Canada the doping-control program for intercollegiate athletics falls under the auspices of the Canadian Centre for Ethics in Sport, in conjunction with the CIS and the CCAA. Testing is done randomly and, in certain sports such as swimming and track and field, on the basis of finish. In the NCAA, a national drug testing program utilizes random drug testing, and a positive test for any banned substance results in loss of eligibility for one calendar year. A second positive test results in permanent loss of eligibility in all sports.

Policies, procedures, and rules regarding performance enhancement in intercollegiate sport help guide all participants (coaches, athletes, trainers, etc.) in understanding the broader issue of fairness and healthy practices. Other policy areas, such as financial aid and gender equity, help guide uni-

www

Canadian Centre for Ethics in Sport
www.cces.ca/en/home

NCAA's national drug testing program
www.ncaa.org/wps/wcm/connect/public/NCAA/Health+and+Safety/Drug+Testing/Drug+Testing+Landing+Page

versity personnel to ensure that equitable practices are maintained from one campus to the next.

Financial Aid

Providing athletes with financial aid, commonly known as an athletic scholarship, has been a source of debate within college athletics for decades. Within the NCAA, Divisions I and II have set policy providing for awarding a certain number of athletic scholarships, whereas Division III, the NAIA, and the CIS have been more restrictive in their rules. For example, NCAA Division I and II schools sponsor a certain number of athletic scholarships per sport, whereas Division III schools do not offer such awards. Canadian schools have recently begun to offer athletic scholarships but have more stringent restrictions on the value of the award and when it can be given to the athlete. In the United States the source of funding for these awards has not been the most important issue. Rather, intercollegiate leagues such as the NCAA have developed policy to ensure fair practices among institutions regarding how much financial aid can be given to a particular athlete (to ensure a distinction from paid professional athletes), to balance awards given to males and females, and to regulate when such an award can be withdrawn. Some questionable practices, such as overpaying or unjustly withdrawing an athletic scholarship, have prompted a focus on these issues.

Financial aid continues to be an area of policy debate. Specifically, the NCAA has debated the issue of whether student-athletes should be permitted to hold part-time jobs. A large proportion of the student population works part-time to offset the high costs of university tuition and living expenses. Yet, in the past, athlete eligibility rules forbade athletes to hold part-time jobs. Although the rule against part-time employment was in the students' best interests, the NCAA felt that, considering the demands of the classroom combined with the demands of athletic commitment, a change in policy was necessary. In 2003 the work rule was changed to allow employment on campus to a maximum of $2,000 (NCAA, 2003). Currently, a student-athlete is permitted to hold on- or off-campus employment for which monies do not count toward maximum financial aid allowances, provided that compensation is based solely on work performed and does not exceed the going rate for similar service (NCAA, 2012f). In addition, NCAA athletes are now permitted "pay for teaching to play," that is, using their skills as athletes to teach as music majors and fitness majors often do. This practice is restricted to the following circumstances: institutional facilities are not used, playing lessons are not provided, compensation is paid by the lesson recipient, and the student-athlete provides information about the activity to the Office of Athletics Compliance. Members of the NCAA believe this change is fair, given today's high costs of living and the belief that athletes should be treated more like the rest of the student body. The emergence and evolution of policy regarding gender equity is another good example.

Gender Equity

Virtually every administrative body governing intercollegiate athletics has a policy pertaining to gender equity. In the United States, Title IX is a component of the Education Amendments that came into law in 1972. As you may recall from Chapter 5, Title IX states that "no person in the United States shall, on the basis of sex, be excluded from participation in, be denied the benefits of, or be subjected to discrimination under any education program or activity receiving federal financial assistance" (Title IX, 2012). This law provides the impetus for committee and task force discussions and implementation for change in order to achieve equitable intercollegiate athletic programs for both men and women. The NCAA Gender-Equity Task Force delivered the following policy statement: "An athletics program can be considered gender equitable when the participants in both the men's and women's sports programs would accept as fair and equitable the overall program of the other gender. No individual should be discriminated against on the basis of gender, institutionally or nationally, in intercollegiate athletics" (NCAA, 2012j, p. 1). University Presidents and Athletic Directors determine specific compliance with Title IX on individual campuses. However, numerous lawsuits have been initiated by athletes and parents that challenge actual Title IX compliance. Title IX is also being used by males and those involved in smaller, non–revenue-producing sports to challenge practices such as alleged sex discrimination in circumstances where men's sport programs are underfunded or have been dropped. The specific duty to comply with equitable practices rests on individual campuses and must be the joint responsibility of the President, Athletic Director, and Athletic Board.

In Canada, the CIS defined its Policy for Equity and Equality in the following statement: "Canadian Interuniversity Sport accepts the principles of equity and equality and will ensure that these principles are adhered to in all its activities. . . . Equity refers to treatment that is fair and just. . . . Equality means that all persons enjoy the same status regardless of gender . . . [and] have equal conditions for realizing their full rights and potential and to benefit from the results" (CIS, 2013, p. 80.29). The CIS also defined 12 operational goals for enacting the Equity and Equality Policy. The difficulty, of course, is that the national policy might have little impact on individual campuses.

Gender equity has been a long-standing contentious issue in college athletics. The inequities are played out in many different, often systemic, ways. Participation opportunities for men have historically exceeded those for women; many sports, such as football and hockey, existed for men only. The budgets allocated to men's teams and salaries paid to coaches of men's teams are significantly higher than for women's teams. The decision makers in athletic program administration, university central administration, and coaching have dominantly been males. Many more males than females coach women's teams. These and other imbalances in gender that elevate men's sport over women's continue to create issues of inequity that must remain a focus of the reform required in collegiate athletics.

Gambling

Sports gambling is a multibillion-dollar business. Recent growth, coupled with the expansion of and media hype surrounding college sports, has resulted in a noticeable increase in gambling associated with collegiate sport. The NCAA reports a significant increase over the past decade in the number of cases it processed related to sports wagering. Concern is currently focused on the prevalence of Internet wagering, which is increasingly appealing to college-age students. Administrators and members of the NCAA are concerned about the potential for sports wagering and believe that it threatens the very existence of college sports (NCAA, 2002). For example, Ellenbogen, Jacobs, Derevensky, Gupta, and Paskus (2008) studied over 20,000 NCAA student-athletes, and reported that 62 percent of males and 43 percent of females reported gambling activities, with 13 percent of males engaged in weekly gambling. The authors suggest that

> Gambling among student athletes represents a multifaceted problem, particularly when examining sport wagering. If students incur significant losses or develop associations with other gamblers, they may be pressured to use or share information conceding collegiate games, or possibly alter their performance to influence the outcomes of games. (p. 249)

The NCAA opposes sports gambling in all its forms, legal and illegal. The zero-tolerance policy adopted by the NCAA prohibits Athletic Department staff and student-athletes from engaging in any form of gambling activities. The policy prohibits gambling on both intercollegiate and professional sports and stipulates that an individual involved in collegiate sport must not knowingly provide information to individuals involved in organized gambling, solicit a bet, accept a bet, or participate in any gambling activity through any method (NCAA, 2002).

The harshness of the policy results from the NCAA's belief that illegal sports wagering is big business, and big business attracts organized crime. The involvement of impressionable college-age students is a concern. Not only is the welfare of student-athletes jeopardized, the very integrity of sport contests can be undermined. According to the NCAA (2002), "Sports wagering demeans the competition and competitors alike by a message that is contrary to the purposes and meaning of 'sport.' Sport competition should be appreciated for the inherent benefits related to participation of student-athletes, coaches and institutions in fair contests, not the amount of money wagered on the outcome of the competition" (p. 2). The NCAA has responded aggressively to combat the problem and communicate its stance on sport wagering. A media campaign, educational meetings with Final Four participants, Web postings, liaison activities with the FBI and other law enforcement units, background checks on game officials, signatures by athletes on affidavit forms prior to some championships, public service announcements, and education programs on campuses—all are active components of the NCAA's sports-wagering education activities (NCAA, 2002).

The issue of gambling in college sport is not unique to the NCAA. The NAIA also believes gambling undermines the values of NAIA athletics and has a zero-tolerance policy for any form of sports wagering. In Canada researchers at the University of Toronto are conducting studies to assess the incidence of sports gambling and its impact on Canadian student-athletes.

Administrators and governing bodies such as the NCAA have moved quickly to set policy prohibiting any association between gambling and college athletics. Enforcing the rules is the next hurdle.

Social Media

Intercollegiate athletic departments and athletes use Facebook, Twitter, and YouTube. Many athletic departments are using social media to increase fan engagement, to interact with fans, to gain their feedback, and to build brand loyalty. Building the fan base by retaining current fans and recruiting new ones is core to using social media technologies today. However, a double standard has developed in many athletic departments related to social media use by athletes. University athletic departments have enacted policies to control and limit an athlete's use of social media, characterizing it as risky to the image and brand of the team. While athletes' social media use will likely be monitored by Athletic Department personnel for content, preventing athletes from using social media is undoubtedly a concern for their personal freedom. Policy that balances the positives and negatives of this issue is required.

Enforcement

Because intercollegiate athletic organizations are collectives of member institutions, legislation is created *by* the members of the organization *for* the members of the organization. Enforcement Services, also called Compliance, is the department that ensures that all institutions are abiding by the rules, thus maintaining the integrity of the rules and fair play among all participants. The intent of enforcement programs is to reduce violations by education, discovery, and the disbursement of appropriate penalties.

College athletic departments in both the United States and Canada are expected to monitor their rules compliance and self-report any violation. In addition, the NCAA has an Enforcement Services staff of approximately 30 specialists who work to ensure a level playing field through rules enforcement. The importance of the enforcement policy is underscored by the fact that each NCAA division has a Committee on Infractions (COI), an independent group of lawyers, law school professors, and members of the public who assess penalties for those who break the rules. Unfortunately, this arrangement is frequently perceived as inadequate by members of the NCAA because of the huge workload assumed by only 30 people. The inquiry process involves field investigations, formal correspondence of inquiry, the development of a case summary, hearings before the COI, and, if necessary, a ruling regarding the violation and penalty (NCAA, 2012i). An appeal process is also provided, and attempts are made to ensure due process is followed in any investigation.

Enforcement is not accorded as much focus in the NAIA, CIS, and CCAA, where self-reporting is virtually the sole means of policing infractions. Each organization has a committee to deal with allegations of impropriety, but none has any full-time enforcement officers. This is primarily a financial issue; these organizations do not have the resources available for full-time enforcement officers. For many sport organizations, funding is problematic, and intercollegiate athletics is no different.

Funding

It seems that every conceivable level of sport has funding woes. Children's sport programs are being dropped, professional sport is losing franchises, and recreational sport is becoming a viable option only for those who are financially well off. Funding, or lack of funding, has also become a major issue for college athletic administrators. Many are surprised that funding is included in the policy issues of intercollegiate athletics. But consider the following myths: College sports make money; competitive sports fund recreational sports; no other sports would exist without football. These statements are not accurate most of the time, but they are convenient arguments sometimes used to drive certain status quo decisions (Sperber, 2000). More accurate is that funding is a major concern in intercollegiate athletics on every level (Fizel, Gustafson, & Hadley, 1999; Zimbalist, 1999). The cost of a Division IA football program is astronomical; the revenues derived, even through television contracts, quickly vanish in the expense column. In addition, the recession of 2008 led to general reductions in university funding in both Canada and the United States.

Lenskyj (2004) identified two changes that seem to reflect athletic funding pressures: "increasing corporatization of both Canadian and American university campuses, and the attempts by university administrators to build stadium facilities by imposing higher student fees." Likewise, Keels (2004) discussed the cancellation of the football program at the historically black Central State University in Ohio due to funding shortages. To ensure the continuing viability of intercollegiate athletics, the Finance Committees of the NCAA and CIS are defining policies to help curb spending and reduce excess. This has resulted in rules defining a maximum roster size, the number of games allowed, starting dates, and scheduling efficiencies; such policy areas will continue to be an important focus for intercollegiate athletic administrators.

SUMMARY

The fall season is here! More than likely, fall conjures up thoughts of cooler weather, bright red and yellow leaves, apple picking, and college football games. For many people, the beginning of the college sports season is synonymous with the new school year. This association indicates the appeal of college athletics, not just for the participants and student body but also for the wider public who attend games and tune in to the mass media. Widespread interest in intercollegiate athletics has resulted in colleges offering a vast array of teams and developing excellent facilities for participants and spectators on campuses across North America. It has also resulted in the need for college administrators to actively supervise the intercollegiate sport enterprise, its governance, operations, and policy development. From the humble beginning of a crew race between Harvard and Yale in 1852, thousands of competitions among institutions all over the United States and Canada are played today.

To compete with other colleges and universities with similar philosophies and values, institutions become members of governing associations such as the NCAA, the NAIA, and the NJCAA in the United States, and the CIS and the CCAA in Canada. Members of these organizations meet to set policy, procedures, rules and regulations, and legislation regulating competitions, and to deal with current issues.

The policies regulating competition are debated from year to year and hinge on the current political and financial environments of the institutions involved. Eligibility seems to be a perennial concern. The preservation of amateurism is also a timeless issue. The issues of performance-enhancing drugs and the implementation of fair practices in providing gender equity have surfaced in more recent decades. Setting policy regarding gambling and enforcement are even newer issues in intercollegiate athletics, whereas financial aid and overall program funding have ignited debate from the beginning.

Intercollegiate athletics and its governance will continue to be hot topics on university campuses, and the governing structures will play an ever-increasing and important role in ensuring a safe and fair environment for competitions between colleges for participants and spectators alike.

case STUDY

AGENTS

You are the Athletic Director at Big State University. The large local newspaper, *The Elkhart Truth,* has reported that your standout player, Billy Dover, a native of Elkhart, has been receiving cash and gifts from at least one agent during the past season, and maybe even during his sophomore year. He has been seen driving around campus in a brand-new Navigator and wearing expensive-looking gold jewelry, and you know for a fact that neither he nor his family could ever have purchased these items. Your high-profile coach, John Becher, has visions of making his mark so he can coach in the NBA someday soon, and he guided the Dover-led team to the Final Four, where they lost in the semifinal game.

This afternoon, a press conference is scheduled where you will have to face members of the press and comment on the allegations.

1. If in fact Dover received these items (in obvious violation of NCAA rules), who shares responsibility here? Dover? The agent? Coach Becher? The NCAA? Who needs to be held accountable?

2. If you were a college Athletic Director at a Division I school with athletes who potentially could go pro, what sort of agent-screening system could you put in place? Who would be involved? What would be the process to help protect and educate athletes about the dangers of dealing with agents?

3. Put yourself in the shoes of the President of Big State University. Using one of the ethical decision-making models described in Chapter 4, list the steps you would take to assess the employment status and situation of Coach Becher.

CHAPTER questions

1. Compare and contrast the organizational structures of the NCAA, the NAIA, and the CIS. What is different in these three organizations, and why?

2. How might a policy help an athlete deal with the struggle of balancing requirements and expectations of academics versus athletics? Write a policy encouraging balance between both components of the term *student-athlete.*

3. Suppose you are the Athletic Director of a large Division I university with teams competing in the NCAA. It has come to your attention that the men's basketball coach has broken a series of recruiting rules

in order to attract a 7-foot center to the team. In the end the coach was unsuccessful in recruiting the athlete, but self-disclosure rules still exist in the NCAA. Using the SLEEPE Principle presented in Chapter 2, analyze the situation to help understand each of the ramifications of your decision. In the end, what will you do?

REFERENCES

Alcorn State University. (2012). Student athlete handbook: Athletic mission. Retrieved from http://www.alcorn-sports.com/documents/2011/10/6/Student_athlete_handbook.PDF?tab=student-athletehandbook

Brainard, J. (2006, October 20). James Madison U. will drop 10 sports teams, including 7 for men, to achieve gender balance. *Chronicle of Higher Education, 53*(9), 43.

CCAA. (2012a). CCAA overview. Retrieved from http://www.ccaa.ca/web/index.php/en/about-us/overview

CCAA. (2012b). Operating code. Retrieved from www.ccaa.ca/pdf/CCAAOperatingCode2006-07.pdf.

CCAA. (2012c). Organizational chart. Retrieved from www.ccaa.ca/orgchart.html.

CIS. (2009). 2009 AGM Minutes. Retrieved from http://www.universitysport.ca/e/meetings/documents/2009AGMMinutes-Final_000.pdf

CIS. (2012a). History. Retrieved from http://english.cis-sic.ca/information/about_cis/cishistory

CIS. (2012b). Programs and services. Retrieved from http://english.cis-sic.ca/information/about_cis/programs-services

CIS. (2012c). 2012 Finance Committee Report. Retrieved from http://static.psbin.com/p/f/a0r0ffvn1zn52b/2012_CIS_AGM_Report.pdf

CIS. (2012d). By-laws. P.BL9. Retrieved from http://universitysport.ca/e/pol_proc/index.cfm

CIS. (2012e). Athletes guide. Retrieved from http://english.cis-sic.ca/information/student-athlete_info/athletes_guide#eligibility

CIS. (2012f). Organizational chart. Retrieved from http://universitysport.ca/e/about/org_chart.html

CIS. (2012g). Doping and substance use. Retrieved from http://universitysport.ca/e/student/index.cfm#doping

CIS. (2012h). CIS orientation materials. Retrieved from http://www.docstoc.com/docs/125221316/THE-CIS-WEBSITE-Canadian-Interuniversity-Sport

CIS. (2013). Policy 80.80 Equity and Equality. Retrieved from http://english.cis-sic.ca/information/members_info/pdfs/pdf_bylaws_policies_procedures/12-13/14_Policy_80.50-80.100_gifting-_equality-_crisis_mgmt_2012-13.pdf

Davenport, J. (1985). From crew to commercialism—The paradox of sport in higher education. In D. Chu, J. O. Segrave, & B. J. Becker (Eds.), *Sport and higher education* (pp. 5–16). Champaign, IL: Human Kinetics.

Ellenbogen, S., Jacobs, D., Derevensky, J., Gupta, R., & Paskus, T. S. (2008). Gambling behavior among college student-athletes. *Journal of Applied Sport Psychology, 20,* 349–362.

Fizel, J., Gustafson, E., & Hadley, L. (1999). *Sports economics: Current research.* London: Praeger.

Gerdy, J. R. (1997). *The successful college athletic program—The new standard.* Phoenix, AZ: Oryx Press.

Hollins, A. (2011). Is Southern on the brink of collapse? Retrieved from http://hbcusportsonline.com/media/2011/04/southerncollapse/

Ingham, A. G., & Loy, J. W. (1993). *Sport in social development: Traditions, transitions, and transformations.* Champaign, IL: Human Kinetics.

Jones, B. (2007). *Progress, yes; but HBCUs paid a price for it.* Retrieved from http://sports.espn.go.com/espn/blackhistory2007/news/story?id=2780876.

Kahn, L. M. (2006). The economics of college sports: Cartel behavior vs. amateurism. Institute for the Study of Labor Discussion Series (IZA DP No. 2186). Retrieved from ftp://repec.iza.org/RePEc/Discussionpaper/dp2186.pdf

Keels, C. L. (2004). Funding shortages push back central state football program. *Black Issues in Higher Education, 21*(6), 12.

Knight Commission on Intercollegiate Athletics. (2007). A summit on the college athletic experience.

Retrieved from http://www.knightcommission.org/resources

Knight Commission. (2012). Students and athletes. Retrieved from http://knightcommission.org

Knight Foundation Commission on Intercollegiate Athletics. (2001). A call to action: Reconnecting college sports and higher education. Retrieved from www.ncaa.org/databases/knight_commission/2001_report

Lenskyj, H. (2004). Funding Canadian university sport facilities: The University of Toronto stadium referendum. *Journal of Sport & Social Issues, 28*(4), 379–396.

NAIA. (2012a). A guide for the college bound student athlete. Retrieved from http://www.playnaia.org/page/eligibility.php

NAIA. (2012b). About the NAIA. Retrieved from http://naia.cstv.com/member-services/about

NAIA. (2012c). Member institutions. Retrieved from http://naia.cstv.com/member-services/about/members.html

NAIA. (2012d). Councils. Retrieved from http://naia.cstv.com/member-services/legislative/Councils.html

NCAA. (2002). Gambling—Sports wagering. Retrieved from www.ncaa.org/membership /enforcement/gambling/index.html

NCAA. (2003). Pay for (teaching to) play: Fee for lesson rules afford Division I student-athletes new benefits. Retrieved from www.ncca.org/news/2003/20030609/awide/4012n04.html

NCAA. (2008a). NCAA backgrounder on academic reform. Retrieved from www2.ncaa.org/portal/academics_and_athletes/education_and_research/academic_reform/backgrounder_academic_reform.html

NCAA. (2008b). Playing rules. Retrieved from www.ncaa.org/wps/portal/legacysiteviewer?CONTENT_URL=http://www2.ncaa.org/portal/media_and_events/ncaa_publications/playing_rules.

NCAA. (2012a). NCAA history. Retrieved from www.ncaa.org/ wps/wcm/connect/public/ncaa/about+the+ncaa/who+we+are/about+the+ncaa+historyNC

NCAA. (2012b). About the NCAA: Purposes and goals. Retrieved from http://www.ncaa.org/wps/wcm/connect/public/ncaa/about+the+ncaa

NCAA. (2012c). About the NCAA: Membership. Retrieved from http://www.ncaa.org/wps/wcm/connect/public/NCAA/About+the+NCAA/Membership+NEW

NCAA. (2012d). Differences among the divisions. Retrieved, from http://www.ncaa.org/wps/wcm/connect/public/ncaa/about+the+ncaa/who+we+are/differences+among+the+divisions/division+i/about+division+i

NCAA. (2012e). NCAA budget. Retrieved from http://www.ncaa.org/wps/wcm/connect/6d3874004e51aadc96e0d622cf56f2f3/2010-11+Condensed+Budget.pdf?MOD=AJPERES&CACHEID=6d3874004e51aadc96e0d622cf56f2f3

NCAA. (2012f). 2012–13 guide for the college-bound student-athlete. Retrieved from http://www.ncaa-publications.com/productdownloads/CBSA.pdf

NCAA. (2012g). Most Division I teams deliver top grades. Retrieved from http://www.ncaa.org/wps/wcm/connect/public/NCAA/Resources/Latest+News/2012/June/Most+Division+I+teams+deliver+top+grades

NCAA. (2012h). Bylaw, Article 12 Amateurism. Retrieved from http://www.ncaapublications.com/productdownloads/D112.pdf

NCAA. (2012i). Enforcement. Retrieved from http://www.ncaa.org/wps/wcm/connect/public/ncaa/enforcement/index.html

NCAA. (2012j). Gender equity 2004-2010. Retrieved from http://www.ncaapublications.com/product-downloads/GEQS10.pdf

OSU Department of Athletics. (2008). Athletic Department Directory. Retrieved April 1, 2008, from www.ohiostatebuckeyes.com/ ViewArticle.dbml?DB_OEM_ID=17300&KEY=& ATCLID=925292.

OUA. (2012). The history of Ontario University Athletics. Retrieved from http://oua.ca/about/about.

Purdue North-Central Athletics. (2008). Our staff. Retrieved April 1, 2008, from www.pnc.edu/athletics/staff.html

Rudolph, F. (1990). *The American college and university: A history.* Athens: University of Georgia Press.

Scott, H. A. (1951). *Competitive sports in schools and colleges.* New York: Harper and Brothers.

Sperber, M. (2000). *Beer and circus: How big-time college sports is crippling undergraduate education.* New York: Holt.

Staurowsky, E. J., & Abney, R. (2007). Intercollegiate athletics. In J. B. Parks, B. R. K. Zanger, & J. Quarterman (Eds.), *Contemporary sport management* (3d ed., pp. 67–96). Champaign, IL: Human Kinetics.

Thomas, K. (2011a, May 2). Gender games. Colleges cut men's programs to satisfy Title IX. *New York Times*. Retrieved from http://www.nytimes.com/2011/05/02/sports/02gender.html?_r=1

Thomas, K. (2011b, April 26). Gender games. Colleges teams, relying on deception, undermine Title IX. *New York Times*. Retrieved from http://www.nytimes.com/2011/04/26/sports/26titleix.html?pagewanted=all

Title IX. (2012). Title IX and Sex Discrimination. Retrieved from http://www2.ed.gov/about/offices/list/ocr/docs/tix_dis.html

U.S. Department of Education. (2012). White House initiative on historically black colleges and universities. Retrieved from http://www2.ed.gov/about/inits/list/whhbcu/edlite-index.htmlWann, D.L. (2006).

Wann, D. L. (2006). Examining the potential causal relationship between sport team identification and psychological well-being. *Journal of Sport Behavior, 29*(1), 79–95.

Zimbalist, A. S. (1999). *Unpaid professionals: Commercialism and conflict in big-time college sports*. Princeton, NJ: Princeton University Press.

The Major Games
in Amateur Sport

Think of amateur sport as a highway. The highway is a stretch of road spanning informal, recreational opportunities (such as pickup basketball and Sunday afternoon touch football) to elite, multi-event competitions (such as World Championships and the Olympic Games). Lanes are open for participants, coaches, officials, and spectators. Participants can easily enter and exit the highway as their interests and abilities dictate. Events are organized all along the highway, filling specific needs for competition for all age groups and ability levels of the athletes. Along the road amateur sport evolves from recreation into elite competition. Such events exist for a variety of age groups at the local, national, and international levels. For example, teams compete for National Championships. Athletes are selected to represent their country on national teams competing in the World Championships, World University Games (also called the FISU Games), and Pan American Games. Such competitions lead to the pinnacle event staged every four years—the Olympic and the Paralympic Games. The purpose of this chapter is to investigate the governance structures of the organizations delivering the major games in elite amateur athletics. Given the scope and the importance of the Olympic and Paralympic Games, the organization and governance of the Olympics and the Paralympics will be discussed in separate chapters.

How did other major games come to exist, and how are they organized and governed? This chapter approaches these questions in two ways. First, we discuss the governance of different organizations that provide athletes for major games. Second, we present several major games to illustrate the governance structures of the actual events. Let's look briefly at the evolution and history of the major games of amateur sport.

HISTORY OF THE MAJOR GAMES

Major advances in technology and urbanization led historians to describe the 19th century as "the age of progress" (Riess, 1995). Sport progressed at a phenomenal rate as well: "[T]he international foundation was truly laid for the gigantic proportions of sport today" (Glassford & Redmond, 1988, p. 140). Inventions such as the railroad (1830), the motorcar (1885), the camera (1826), the electric lamp (1881), and the radio (1901) were among the profound technological changes contributing to the evolution of sport (Glassford & Redmond, 1988).

Urbanization was also a major factor in the growth of the sport industry. The city became the site of huge stadiums and other facilities and the focal point for crowds of participants and spectators. Tournaments, festivals, and special events became more commonplace as both leisure time and general affluence increased (Kidd, 1999). Technology, especially that related to easing long-distance transportation, provided the opportunity for both national and international competition. Before long, governments focused on the idea of sport as an alternative to war, in which political ideologies and national strength could be displayed by winning international sporting competitions (Riordan & Kruger, 1999).

The advancement of political ideology through sport likely occurred around the time Baron Pierre de Coubertin revived the ancient Olympic

Games in the late 19th century. Baron de Coubertin's dream was that sport could be used to increase goodwill among nations of the world. He reinstated Olympic competition when, in 1894, officials from 12 countries endorsed a modern cycle of Olympic Games (Glassford & Redmond, 1988).

Baron de Coubertin's Olympic Games were not entirely original. Games in England's Cotswolds and the Highland Games of Scotland were staged in the 19th century. But the concept of major games and festivals spread quickly. The Far Eastern Championship Games were organized in 1913 as regional games after the rebirth of the modern Olympics. Teams from China, Japan, the Philippines, Thailand, and Malaysia participated (Glassford & Redmond, 1988). Similar games were established in Central America, and teams from Puerto Rico, Cuba, Mexico, and other Latin American countries participated. The first British Empire Games (later renamed the Commonwealth Games) took place in Hamilton, Canada, in 1930. Other countries organized regional games such as State Games and National Championships. In addition, international competitions such as the Asian Games, the Pan American Games, the Goodwill Games, and other special group events developed. For instance, the International Student Games were first held in 1924 (renamed the Universiade in 1959), and in 1960 the first Paralympic Games were held for individuals with physical disabilities. Today, games exist for every age group in virtually every sport. The World Little League Baseball Championships, the America's Cup yachting competition, World Championships for speed skating, and the World Deaf Games are examples of major amateur sporting events that dominate today's sporting calendar. Who organizes these events, and how are they operated? Next, we investigate the organizations and governance structures of several major games in amateur sport.

GOVERNANCE

The governance of amateur sport differs in countries around the world. Government focus on policy involving amateur sport via nonprofit and voluntary organizations became more prominent in the latter half of the 20th century (Statistics Canada, 2005). Even so, the degree to which a government is involved in sport policy differs depending on a nation's social, cultural, and political perspectives. In the United States, sport is intensely popular and a cause for national unity. However, American public policy has historically claimed (some say rhetorically) that sport is independent of government (Chalip & Johnson, 1996). In Canada the promotion of national unity and identity are central themes in government involvement in sport-policy development. In both nations, some level of government involvement helps shape the policies governing the athletes representing their nations at the major games of amateur athletics.

Governing Structures for Amateur Sport in North America

Three branches of government exist in the United States: The legislative branch is responsible for policy making; the executive branch implements laws and public policies; and the judicial branch interprets the law. Each branch plays an important role in policy development, along with state and local governments. In fact, many state and local governments are influenced by national policies. The policy developed at each level of government has implications for amateur sport. At the national level, laws specific to sport have been enacted; for example, the Amateur Sports Act of 1978 promotes, coordinates, and sets national goals for amateur sport in the United States through the development of national governing bodies (United States Amateur Sports Act, 1978). Another example is the Stevens Amendment of 1998, which changed the Amateur Sports Act so that it became known as the Ted Stevens Olympic and Amateur Sports Act; the new law strengthened athletes' rights, provided procedures for dispute resolution, and incorporated the Paralympics into the Act by updating provisions for disabled athletes (U.S. Senate Committee on Commerce, Science, and Transportation, 1998). Policies affecting sport might also result from the application of laws not written specifically for sport, such as the Americans with Disabilities Act of 1990, established to prevent discrimination on the basis of disability, or through federal government agencies such as the President's Council on Physical Fitness and Sport, which sets policy on issues related to physical fitness and sport (Americans with Disabilities Act, 1990; Chalip & Johnson, 1996).

State and national organizations exist in order to provide rules, regulations, promotion, and competition for specific sports. In the next sections three examples of state and national organizations are presented. First, the Amateur Athletic Union (AAU) is described. It is one of the largest multisport organizations in the United States, incorporating both state and national offices with the mandate to promote and develop amateur opportunities in a variety of sports. Second, Sport Canada is discussed. In Canada, the federal government oversees the development of amateur sport through Sport Canada, a department helping to set policy and provide leadership for Canadian national teams. Finally, USA Basketball is presented. This is an example of a national sport organization that organizes basketball in the United States by operating in conjunction with 16 affiliate associations. How are these groups organized and how is policy developed?

The Amateur Athletic Union

The AAU is a multisport organization dedicated to promoting and developing amateur sport and physical fitness programs. It was founded in 1888 to establish standards for amateur sport participation (AAU, 2012). In the early days, the AAU represented all amateur sports at International Federation meetings and was responsible for organizing national teams to represent the United States at international competitions, including the Olympic Games. As mentioned earlier, in 1978 the U.S. Senate and the U.S. House of Representatives enacted the Amateur Sports Act, the purpose of which was to coordinate amateur sport throughout the United States. This was done, in part, by establishing individual organizations for the purpose of developing specific sports. The Amateur Sports Act had a profound effect on the mandate of the AAU and caused the organization to refocus its purpose away from representing U.S. teams internationally and toward the development and provision of sports programs for a wider spectrum of participants (AAU, 2012). At this point the AAU introduced the "sports for all, forever" philosophy. Today, the AAU offers a broad spectrum of activities, from baton twirling to flag football and pretty much everything in between.

MISSION. The AAU promotes and delivers amateur sport widely within the United States. It is a network of local chapters that provides programs for children, men, and women in a large number of activities. The breadth of its mandate is illustrated by the inclusiveness of its programming. The mission statement of the AAU is presented in Exhibit 9.1.

MEMBERSHIP. Athletes, coaches, volunteers, and officials make up the membership of the AAU. The organization has thousands of members (500,000 participants and 50,000 volunteers) and offers programming for both youth and adult participants.

FINANCIALS. The AAU is a nonprofit organization funded through membership dues and donations. Yearly member dues are modest: Any youth can belong for only $12, and the Added Benefits Membership option (which allows participation in nonsanctioned events) is only an additional $14. Dues for coaches and adults are only slightly higher. Sponsorships and partnerships are solicited, such as the alliance made between the AAU and Walt Disney World in 1996, which precipitated the relocation of the AAU

www

Amateur Athletic Union
www.aausports.org

Mission of the Amateur Athletic Union.

exhibit **9.1**

> The mission of the AAU is "to offer amateur sports programs through a volunteer base for all people to have the physical, mental, and moral development of amateur athletes and to promote good sportsmanship and good citizenship.

Source: AAU (2012).

www

ESPN Wide World of Sports Complex
http://espnwwos.disney.
go.com/complex/

National Office to Orlando, Florida. Each year more than 40 AAU national events are held at the ESPN Wide World of Sports Complex near the Disney Resorts in Florida.

ORGANIZATIONAL STRUCTURE. Fifty-six district offices for associations make up the AAU, each representing either a state (for example, Oklahoma) or a region (for example, New England) of the United States. The AAU is managed by a small Executive Committee, which comprises a group of officers elected by the Congress: the President, First and Second Vice President, Secretary, and Treasurer. Each officer is elected for a four-year term. The Congress is the primary actor for the business of the AAU and is composed of district representatives elected at either the local, National Sport Committee, or National Officers levels. The Congress consists of approximately 600 members. The Congress constitutes a 36-member Board of Directors, consisting of designated members and those elected to act on AAU business between meetings of the Congress. National Sport Committees responsible for a particular sport define and direct policy related to that sport. The entire operation is managed by full-time staff members led by the Executive Director. In addition, a host of committees deal with AAU activities such as Finance, Insurance, Youth Sport, Adult Sport, and Law and Legislation. Policy is developed through committees, analyzed and voted on by the Executive Committee, and then voted upon by the Board of Directors at annual national meetings. Much of the policy discussion involves the development of rules, regulations, and hosting guidelines for events. Exhibit 9.2 depicts the organizational structure of the AAU Board of Directors.

Sport Canada

www

Sport Canada
www.pch.gc.ca/progs/sc

Sport Canada is a branch within the Department of Canadian Heritage of the Canadian federal government. It is responsible for elite sport programming and sport policy development and is dedicated to valuing and strengthening the Canadian sport experience. Sport Canada is guided by the following strategic directions (Sport Canada, 2007):

1. strengthening sport leadership
2. providing strategic support for high performance programming
3. promoting technically sound sport development
4. enhancing opportunities for sport participation
5. maximizing the benefits of hosting
6. promoting linguistic duality in the Canadian sport system
7. strengthening the ethical foundation of sport
8. expanding the body of knowledge about sport
9. strengthening sport Canada program and policy evaluation
10. harmonizing the Canadian sport system.

Organizational structure of the AAU.

exhibit **9.2**

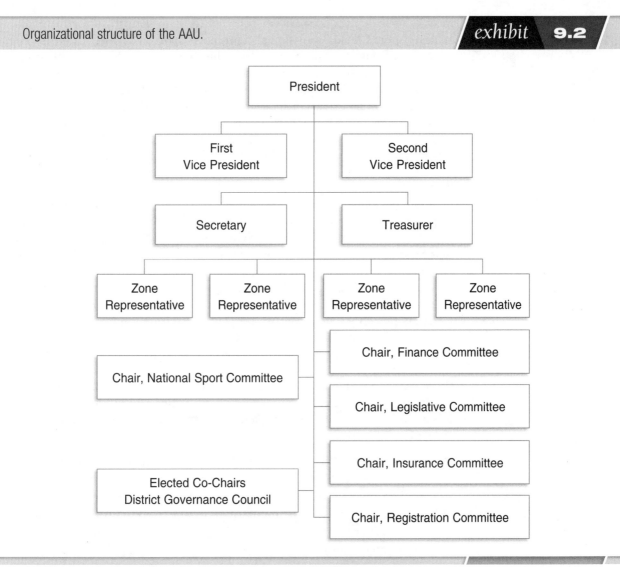

Source: AAU (2012).

Recently identified priority areas include sport community capacity, long-term athlete development, the Canada Games, performance management metrics, and enhancing sport participation and an integrated Canadian sport system (Sport Canada, 2012a).

MISSION. The mission of Sport Canada is to promote sport opportunities for all Canadians. The organization coordinates and encourages excellence among Canadian athletes on the world stage and works with a variety of partners, including national sport organizations, coaches, and other levels of government to provide the necessary environment for high-performance athletes to achieve. Sport Canada's mission also promotes sport as a source of pleasure, personal satisfaction, and a means of achieving good health. Each of these pursuits is captured in the Canadian Sport Policy, a document that originally defined the goals for sport to achieve in Canada by 2012 (Canadian Sport Policy, 2002). These goals include enhancing participation, excellence, capacity, and interaction of members of the sport community. This policy is now under revision in order to provide direction for the next decade in Canadian sport. The mission statement of Sport Canada is presented in Exhibit 9.3.

MEMBERSHIP. Sport Canada is an umbrella organization that supports the mandate of high-performance sport. As such, it does not have a membership like national or state sport organizations have, but instead is comprised of civil servants of the Canadian federal government. It is important to note that Sport Canada is separate and distinct from Canadian National Sport Organizations (NSOs) and the Canadian Olympic Committee (COC). The NSOs are linked to Sport Canada because they provide some degree of funding in return for compliance with policy and directives as set by Sport Canada. The COC, however, is completely separate from Sport Canada. While consultation and an open chain of communication are encouraged by both organizations, no formal relationship or reporting structure exists.

FINANCIALS. Sport Canada receives its funding from the Canadian federal government. It then establishes funding priorities and guidelines for the Canadian sport system. Sport Canada finances the following programs (Sport Canada, 2012b):

1. Athlete Assistance Program—living and training allowances for athletes
2. Sport Support Program—national team funding; development of coaches and officials; increasing Canadian's sport participation
3. Sport Hosting Program—financial assistance for the hosting of international events (World Championships, World Cups, Qualification Tournaments) in Canada.

exhibit **9.3**	Mission of Sport Canada.

Sport Canada supports the achievement of high performance excellence and the development of the Canadian sport system to strengthen the unique contribution that sport makes to Canadian identity, culture and society.

Source: Sport Canada (2013).

ORGANIZATIONAL STRUCTURE. Sport Canada is led by a Director General who reports through a Deputy Minister to the Minister of State for Sport. The organization is subdivided into five areas: Policy and Planning, Sport Support, Sport Excellence, Major Games and Hosting, and Business Operations. The areas of sport policy and sport programs are further subdivided to deal with specific areas of focus, for instance, national sport policy. Within this unit, policy is set regarding eligible forms of funding for athletes, NSO requirements regarding gender and language equity, and intergovernmental strategy and communication. A variety of program managers and sport consultants handle the duties within each subunit of Sport Canada. The organizational structure of Sport Canada is presented in Exhibit 9.4.

Organizational structure for the Department of Canadian Heritage, Sport Canada Branch. *exhibit*  **9.4**

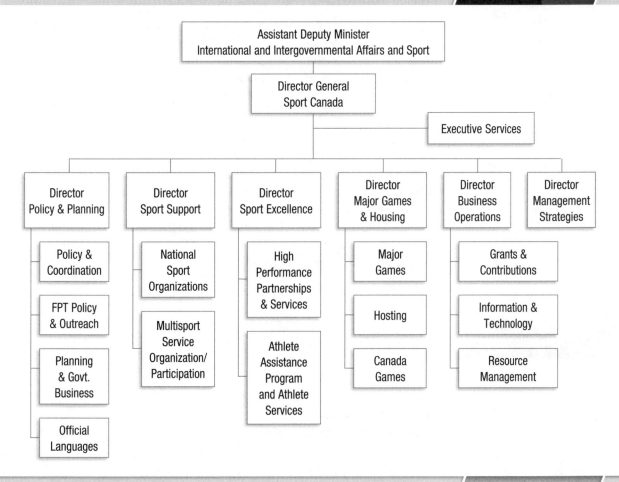

Source: Sport Canada (2012c).

National Sport Governing Bodies

Within each country, one national-level sport organization generally is recognized as the regulatory body for a particular sport. Sometimes these are governmental units, and other times they are freestanding sport organizations. These organizations have names like USA Baseball, Judo Canada, or Scottish Cycling. Depending on the nation, these organizations are called national governing bodies or national sport organizations. To illustrate the governance structure, USA Basketball is an excellent example.

USA Basketball

USA Basketball is the NGB for basketball in the United States. As such, its employees oversee the development of the game of basketball from the grass roots through the elite levels.

MISSION. USA Basketball is the international U.S. representative to the USOC, and acts as the FIBA member in the United States (USA Basketball, 2012). FIBA is the international governing body for basketball. USA Basketball is responsible for selecting, training, and fielding national teams to compete in international FIBA competitions and in the Olympic Games. The association is also responsible for the development, promotion, and coordination of basketball in the United States. The mission statement of USA Basketball is presented in Exhibit 9.5.

MEMBERSHIP. There are five membership types at USA Basketball: professional, collegiate, scholastic, youth, and associate. Professional membership includes those organizations delivering a national, professional competitive basketball program, such as the NBA and WNBA. Collegiate membership includes national sport organizations delivering basketball in university, college, and collegiate-level programs, like the NCAA and NAIA. The scholastic membership category involves national organizations in school sport, like the National Federation of State High School Associations. Youth membership

---

exhibit **9.5**   Mission statement of USA Basketball.

> The purpose of this Association is to act as the national governing body for the sport of basketball in the United States, and in such connection, to be recognized as such by the USOC and to act as the FIBA member in the U.S.

Source: USA Basketball (2012).

currently includes only the Amateur Athletic Association, a community-based non-scholastic and non-collegiate sport organization that delivers national basketball programs for youth. Finally, associate memberships include other organizations that conduct significant basketball programs in the United States. Examples of associate members include Athletes in Action, National Basketball Players Association, USA Deaf Sports Federation, and United States Armed Forces. Members are non-voting, except that they have the right to elect or select certain members of the Board of Directors.

FINANCIALS. USA Basketball is a nonprofit organization. Although member organizations pay annual dues, the majority of funding is derived from revenues associated with corporate partnerships and sponsorships, television, sales of apparel and souvenirs, hosting rights, and Olympic revenue sharing.

ORGANIZATIONAL STRUCTURE. USA Basketball members meet at an Annual Assembly of the association. In addition to the memberships defined above, active athletes are eligible for 20 percent of the total Board of Directors voting power and are elected to the Assembly. The USA Basketball Assembly is required to receive reports from the President on past and future activities, receive a Nominating Committee Report, and hold elections. The Assembly has no rule-making, budgetary, legislative, or other authority, but rather acts in an advisory capacity to the Board of Directors.

USA Basketball is governed by a Board of Directors. The Board is led by the President, and the immediate Past President holds a position. The majority of the board consists of elected members from three categories of directors whose votes each count as two votes: professional (3), collegiate (3), and athlete (2). One scholastic director is appointed by the National Federation of High Schools, and this vote counts as one vote. The organizational membership directors also have a vote that counts as one. The membership directors include one elected person from each of the following organizations: Continental Basketball Association, NBA, National Basketball Development League, WNBA, NCAA, NJCAA, NAIA, NFHS, and AAU. The board meets at least annually and has primary responsibility for developing policy and approving actions regarding the competitive basketball programs of the association (USA Basketball, 2012). The Board of Directors provides leadership for the organization's Executive Director/CEO and professional staff. The Board of Directors includes 11 members, led by an elected Chair, and includes appointed NBA, NCAA, NFHS, Players Associations, athlete representatives, and at-large members. The past USA Basketball President is an ex-officio member of the Board. Policy is defined by the Board and the Executive Committee and via committee work. Standing committees of the association include Constitution and Bylaws, Disabled, Finance, Membership, Officials, and committees defined by the board for specific basketball programs and events. The organizational structure of USA Basketball is presented in Exhibit 9.6.

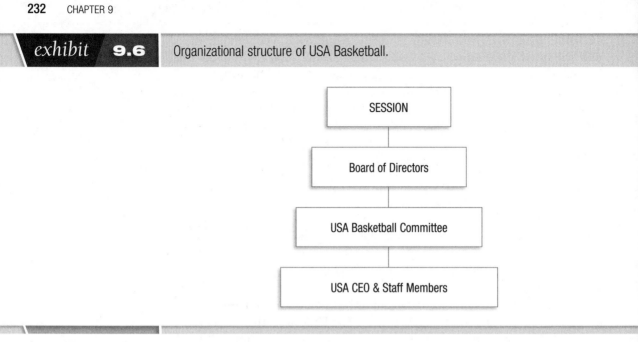

exhibit 9.6 Organizational structure of USA Basketball.

SESSION

Board of Directors

USA Basketball Committee

USA CEO & Staff Members

Source: USA Basketball (2012).

The organizations discussed above are all involved in organizing athletic competitions for elite-level athletes or sending elite athletes to major competitions. State and provincial organizations feed into NGBs and NSOs, respectively. NSOs are aided by other organizations such as the AAU, Sport Canada, the national coaches associations, and the NCAA via their roles in training elite athletes, coaches, and officials. One component of their collective missions is to enhance the ability of athletes to perform on the world stage at international competitions and major games. Next, we investigate the governance structures of some of the major games of amateur athletics.

Organizations That Manage Major Games in Amateur Sport

www

Fédération Internationale de
Basketball Amateur
www.fiba.com

Fédération Internationale de
Football Association
www.fifa.com

Major games are national or international events run as single-sport or multisport championships. International world championships are common to many sports, for example, the FIBA World Basketball Championships and the FIFA Soccer World Cup. Also common are major international multisport games for which participation is restricted by eligibility criteria (such as country of origin, age group, or disability). This includes the Pan American Games, Commonwealth Games, World University Games, World Games for the Deaf, and Special Olympics World Games. How are these major games organized? The next sections will address these multisport competitions.

Pan American Games

The Pan American Games are a celebration of sport, competition, and international friendship for nations of the Americas in the Western Hemisphere (Rio 2007 Pan American Games, 2007). The Games have run on a strict quadrennial cycle since the first competition in 1951, typically scheduled for the summer in the year preceding the Olympic Games (Pan American Games Summer, 2012).

MISSION. The Pan American Games are first and foremost an international multisport competition. However, since the event's inception the organizers have sought a broader purpose. Along with sporting competition, the Pan American Games are about friendship, life, culture, and the strength of human spirit (Pan American Games '99, 2012). They are also a celebration of the Americas' community and of each country's dedication to their fellow nations making up the Americas. The motto of the Pan American Sports Organization (PASO) incorporates Spanish, Portuguese, English, and French: "America, Espirito, Sport, Fraternite," which translates loosely as "The American spirit of friendship through sports" (Pan American Games Summer, 2012). The mission statement of the Pan Am Games is presented in Exhibit 9.7.

MEMBERSHIP. Athletes from countries in the Americas are eligible to compete in the Pan American Games. This includes North, Central, and South America, as well as Caribbean nations. More than 2,500 athletes from 22 nations competed at the first Pan Am Games in 1951 (Pan American Games Summer, 2012). Currently, 41 nations belong to PASO, divided as follows: 3 North American members, 19 Caribbean members, 7 Central American members, and 12 South American members.

FINANCIALS. The Pan American Games are a huge undertaking, third in scope after the Olympic Games and World University Games (Pan American Games '99, 2012). Depending upon the extent of facility development

www

Pan American Games
http://espn.go.com/espnw/
pan-am-games/

Mission statement of the Pan American Games.

exhibit **9.7**

The Pan American Games bring together athletes from the countries of the Americas in a festival of sport and international friendship. The games are held every four years in the year preceding the Olympic Games.

Source: XIV Pan American Games (2002).

required, the budget for the games can be in the millions or even billions of dollars. The majority of the expenses include building or upgrading facilities, organizing the games and festivals, housing the competitors, and hosting dignitaries. While competing nations are responsible for their own travel costs, the host committee covers on-site expenses. A fee is guaranteed to PASO for the hosting rights, and additional revenues are generated from television, sales, sponsorships and advertising, and entry fees. For example, Toronto, Canada, is hosting the Pan American Games in 2015. Projecting for inflation, the overall budget for these games is estimated to be approximately C$1.4 billion in 2014. The budget is split almost equally between operating funds and capital development budgets for facility construction. In the case of Toronto, the Athlete's Village is part of a billion-dollar initiative to accelerate the development of the city's downtown waterfront.

ORGANIZATIONAL STRUCTURE. PASO governs the games, awards the hosting rights, and sets the policy and direction for the competition. PASO headquarters is located in Mexico City and is presided over by a President and an Executive Council. Each host country then establishes its own organizing committee. Normally, the organizing committee comprises the President, Executive Vice President, Secretary, Treasurer, Second Vice President, Sports Commissioner, and an extensive number of Organizing Committee members who are assigned portfolios and committees (XIV Pan American Games, 2002). An example of the host organizing committee structure for the XV Pan American Games in Rio de Janeiro, Brazil, which attracted over 5,600 athletes in 34 sports, is presented in Exhibit 9.8. The 2007 Games

exhibit **9.8** Organizational structure of the 2003 Pan Am Games.

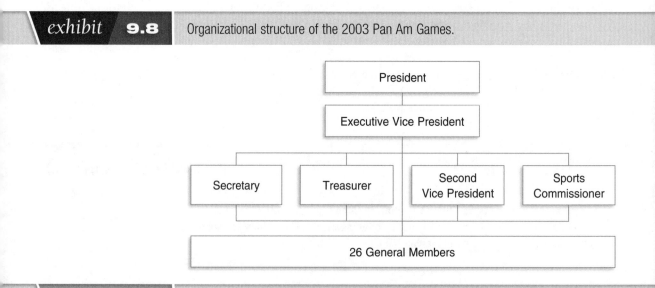

Source: XIV Pan American Games (2002).

in Brazil were the first in which the Parapan American Games for disabled athletes were held in conjunction with the events for able-bodied athletes, a practice that quickly became the standard.

Commonwealth Games

The Commonwealth Games are a multisport competition bringing together countries from around the world that are united by history, as opposed to geography (as in the Pan American Games). The Commonwealth Games involve competition among countries that once belonged to the British Empire (see Exhibit 9.9) and for nations and territories that subsequently

www

Commonwealth Games
www.thecgf.com

Competing countries of the 2010 Commonwealth Games.

exhibit **9.9**

AFRICA				
Botswana	Kenya	Mozambique	Sierra Leone	Uganda
Cameroon	Lesotho	Namibia	South Africa	Zambia
The Gambia	Malawi	Nigeria	Swaziland	Zimbabwe
Ghana	Mauritius	Seychelles	Tanzania	

AMERICAS				
Belize	Canada	Guyana		
Bermuda	Falkland Islands	St. Helena		

OCEANIA				
Australia	Kiribati	Niue	Samoa	Tuvalu
Cook Islands	Nauru	Norfolk Islands	Solomon Islands	Vanuatu
Fiji	New Zealand	Papua New Guinea	Tongo	

CARIBBEAN				
Anguilla	Barbados	Grenada	St. Kitts	Trinidad and Tobago
Antigua	Cayman Islands	Jamaica	St. Lucia	Turks and Caicos Isles
Bahamas	Dominica	Montserrat	St. Vincent	Virgin Islands

EUROPE				
Cyprus	Gibraltar	Isle of Man	Malta	Scotland
England	Guernsey	Jersey	Northern Ireland	Wales

ASIA				
Bangladesh	India	Maldives	Singapore	
Brunei	Malaysia	Pakistan	Sri Lanka	

Source: Commonwealth Games Federation (2012).

joined the British Commonwealth after the empire (Dheensaw, 1994). The countries comprising the Commonwealth share a history and acceptance of a common past. The Commonwealth Games continue to bring athletes and spectators of these nations together every four years for a significant festival of sport.

MISSION. The mission of the Commonwealth Games is to host a world-class multisport event for peoples of Commonwealth nations. The idea of a friendly festival of competition, held on a four-year cycle, is part of their mission statement, presented in Exhibit 9.10.

MEMBERSHIP. Athletes from 71 nations worldwide compete in a variety of individual and team sports at the Commonwealth Games. These nations and territories are located in parts of Africa, the Americas, Asia, Caribbean, Europe, and Oceania. Some countries are eligible to compete in both the Pan American and Commonwealth Games, including Canada and many Caribbean countries.

FINANCIALS. The economics of the Commonwealth Games are very similar to the Pan American Games. Revenues are generated through television, sponsorship and advertising, and ticket and merchandise sales. Perhaps more importantly, the games play an economic role and create a legacy for the hosting community; one of the first host committees to embrace this approach was Manchester, England, in 2002. Part of Manchester's platform for hosting was based on the economic impact to be gained for the region. The organizing committee stated: "The games will play a crucial role in the continued physical, economic and social regeneration of Manchester, but will also bring regional economic benefits and provide a boost to national claims to host future international sporting events" (Manchester Commonwealth Games, 2002, n.p.). The 2006 Commonwealth Games were also

exhibit **9.10**   Mission statement of the Commonwealth Games.

Our vision is to promote a unique, friendly, world class Games and to develop sport for the benefit of the people, the nations, and the territories of the Commonwealth, and thereby strengthen the Commonwealth. Every four years the Games celebrate the shared values, traditions, and language of the Commonwealth.

Source: Commonwealth Games Federation (2012).

successful in creating a financial legacy for the City of Melbourne, Australia (Tucker, 2006). Surplus revenue of $26 million was reinvested into the city's and region of Victoria's sport programs: $6.8 million to sport development, $5.85 million to community programs, and $13.25 million to develop community facilities (Government of Victoria, 2012). The 2014 Commonwealth Games being hosted by Glasgow, Scotland, is also focusing on legacy, sustainability, accessibility, and the environment.

ORGANIZATIONAL STRUCTURE. The Commonwealth Games Federation (CGF) is the umbrella organization responsible for regulating the competition. It is led by a President and two Vice Presidents, along with an Executive Board. The Executive Board is composed of a Vice Patron (nonvoting); six elected Regional Vice Presidents (representing Africa, America, Asia, Caribbean, Europe, Oceania, and Australia, but not the host region); honorary positions of Secretary, Treasurer, Legal Advisor, and Medical Advisor; an Athlete's Representative (it is stipulated that the athlete representative must have participated at the previous two Commonwealth Games); a member representing the host region; a group of Officers co-opted by the Executive Board to meet gender equity requirements; and a nonvoting CEO (CGF, 2012). The Executive Board and Officers help to set policy enacted by a CGF professional staff led by the CEO.

As with the Pan American Games, the local hosting community develops an organizing committee to deliver the competition. This group forms to bid for the event and, if successful, operates for several years prior to staging the Commonwealth Games. The committee then dissolves in the year after the games, when final financial and operational reports are completed.

World University Games

The World University Games (also called the Universiade) is a sporting and cultural festival held every two years for university-level athletes and governed by FISU (FISU, 2012a).

WWW

World University Games
www.fisu.net

MISSION. Founded in 1949, FISU is responsible for supervising the summer and the winter Universiades, as well as World University Championships in select sports. Universiades bring university-level student-athletes from around the world to different countries to compete in both compulsory (sports contested at each Universiade) and optional sports (as chosen by the host country) (FISU, 2012b). For example, the 2013 FISU Summer Games were in Kazan, Russia. The theme for the Universiade is "U or the World," implying the infinite value of a human being, illustrated by uniqueness, depth, power, and potential. The Kazan FISU Games include competition in the 12 compulsory sports: athletics (track and field), basketball, fencing, football (soccer), gymnastics (rhythmic and artistic), judo, swimming, diving, water polo, table tennis, tennis, and volleyball; and 14 (the largest number in history) optional sports: badminton, beach volleyball, boxing, belt wrestling, chess, canoe sprint, field hockey, rugby 7-aside, sambo, sport shooting, synchronized swimming, rowing, weightlifting, and wrestling (2013 Summer Universiade, 2012). The mission statement of the 2013 Summer Games in Kazan is presented in Exhibit 9.11.

MEMBERSHIP. FISU comprises 163 National University Sports Federations (FISU, 2012b). One of these is the United States Collegiate Sports Council, which is composed of representatives of the various administrators and support staff of the NCAA, NAIA, and their member institutions. The CIS is the federation that represents Canada at FISU. National university sports federations gain membership by paying fees and providing proof of eligibility. The Universiades are open to all student-athletes between the ages of 17 and 28 who are eligible to compete in university sport at home and who have not been out of school for more than a year (FISU, 2012b).

FINANCIALS. FISU is funded through marketing activities, television revenue, organizing and entry fees, and subscriptions (FISU, 2012b). The Universiade is run as a multisport festival, bid for by a host country, and run as a business. Revenues are generated in manner similar to the Pan American and the Commonwealth Games, with government funding, corporate sponsorship, television-rights fees, entry fees, and sales making up the largest components of the budget. Summer World University Games are second in size to the Olympic Games, involving as many as 174 nations (in Daegu, Korea, in 2003) and 10,622 participants (in Shenzhen, China, in 2011) (FISU, 2012b). Size alone often dictates the need to develop new facilities to stage the FISU Games.

exhibit **9.11**   Mission of the 27th World University Summer Games in Kazan, Russia.

> The mission of the Kazan 2013 Summer Universiade is to gather young athletes from all over the world in the city of unique multiethnic heritage. To continue Russian sport traditions, to become a launch pad for future generations of athletes. To make the life of Kazan citizens more diverse, interesting and convenient. To give Kazan citizens of all ages a possibility to play any kind of sport they like, to live a healthy life. To make a major contribution to the creation of Russia's positive image in the world.

Source: 2013 Summer Universiade (2012).

ORGANIZATIONAL STRUCTURE. FISU is composed of a General Assembly in which each of the 141 member nations is represented. The General Assembly elects an Executive Committee to act on its behalf between meetings of the Assembly. The Executive Committee of FISU is composed of 27 positions and most members are elected for four-year terms. It is led by the President and comprises a Senior Vice President, four Vice Presidents, a Secretary-General, a Treasurer, and the Senior Assessor. This committee meets twice per year and periodically at the call of the President, and is the main policy-making group within FISU. In addition, the host city for the Universiade names an Organizing Committee to plan and manage the staging of the World University Games.

World Games for the Deaf: The Deaflympics

The first International Games for the Deaf (renamed World Games for the Deaf in 1969) were held in 1924 in Paris, France (Carbin, 1996). Just prior to the inaugural games, a group of Deaf European men organized the International Committee of Silent Sports, abbreviated CISS. Today, CISS refers to the International Committee of Sports for the Deaf (CISS, 2007). This organization oversees the World Games for the Deaf (known as the *Deaf-lympics*) and the Deaf World Championships.

The Deaflympics
www.deaflympics.com

MISSION. The motto of the International Committee of Sports of the Deaf (ICSD) is "Equal Through Sports." The organization brings deaf athletes together to compete in a range of athletic events, offering them the opportunity to celebrate their achievements and uniqueness as deaf athletes. The ICSD mission statement is presented in Exhibit 9.12. It stresses the value of competition, equality through sports, and adhering to the ideas of the Olympic Games (ICSD, 2012).

MEMBERSHIP. The CISS has four membership categories: full and associate members, regional confederations, and honorary life members. Full members are national associations and have voting privileges and participate

---

Mission of the International Committee of Sports of the Deaf.

exhibit **9.12**

The mission of CISS is to celebrate the spirit of Deaf Sports where deaf athletes come together as members of a cultural and linguistic minority to strive to reach the pinnacle of competition.

Source: CISS (2007).

at the Congress, the governing body of the ICSD. National associations are admitted to the Congress upon review of the report of the Legal Committee, which investigates each applicant's constitution, documents of incorporation, financial reports, and qualifications for membership. Only one national association per country may be admitted as a full member of the ICSD. Currently, the organization has 104 national deaf sports federations as members from around the world. Members pay annual fees and contribute their services to the organization.

FINANCIALS. The ICSD is funded through annual membership fees and levies, along with contributions, donations, sponsorships, and government grants (ICSD, 2012). Local communities bid for the hosting rights of the World Games or sport-specific world championships and raise dollars in support of the event through government funding, corporate sponsorship, sales, and other marketing initiatives.

ORGANIZATIONAL STRUCTURE. Each member has a vote at the Congress. Between congresses, an Executive Committee has the power to deal with the business of the association. The Executive Committee is composed of the President, the Vice President of World Sports, the Vice President of World Youth Sports, two at-large members, and the President of each regional confederation (nonvoting). In a similar fashion to other World Games, the Deaflympics are awarded to a city on the basis of a bid to host the event. An organizing committee, convened to carry out the event, includes a President; Vice President; Secretary; Treasurer; and Chairs for Facilities, Marketing, Sport Operations, Transportation, Special Events, and Media Relations.

Special Olympics World Games

www
Special Olympics World Games
www.specialolympics.org

Most people are familiar with Special Olympics. Perhaps you have volunteered at local- or state-level events. But did you know that Special Olympics also holds a major international event? The Special Olympics World Games is a multisport festival held every four years for individuals with all levels of cognitive and developmental disabilities. The Special Olympics and the Paralympics are two separate organizations recognized by the IOC. The Special Olympics provides sport opportunities for individuals with cognitive and developmental disabilities, while the Paralympics provides sports opportunities for elite athletes with physical disabilities. The Special Olympics World Games take place the year before the Olympic Games, while the Paralympic Games are conducted immediately following the Olympics (2007 Special Olympics World Games, 2007).

MISSION. The mission of the Special Olympics World Games includes providing an exceptional sporting experience for participants with disabilities from around the world. The motto of the Special Olympics World Games (2011) in Greece in 2011 was "I'm in," which organizers chose because it

> delivers a dynamic message, which refers to the value of participation. It inspires, gives incentive and impulse to all of us, volunteers, athletes, guests, as well as the general public in order to endorse the values of the Special Olympics Movement. At the same time, the motto invites us all to embrace these really unique games that constitute the biggest international humanitarian event, hosted by our country in the year 2011. The motto is in perfect harmony with the Hellenic philosophy and culture, as we Greeks, as a nation, always get together for a greater common cause.

The mission statement of the organizers of the Special Olympics World Games is presented in Exhibit 9.13.

MEMBERSHIP. The Special Olympics World Games have participants rather than members. The 2011 Games in Athens showcased the athletic skills, courage, and dignity of thousands of athletes with cognitive and developmental disabilities from around the world. Approximately 7,000 athletes, 2,500 coaches, 25,000 volunteers, 3,500 event officials, and thousands of families, journalists, and spectators attended the games (2011 Special Olympics World Games, 2011). The athletes' oath for the Games was "Let me win, but if I cannot win, let me be brave in the attempt."

FINANCIALS. The host committee of the 2003 Games in Ireland estimated the Special Olympics World Games would cost $34 million (US$32 million at that time) outright and a further $23 million (US$21 million) for

---

Mission of the Special Olympic World Games Organizing Committee.   *exhibit* **9.13**

The organizing committee strives to

- ensure the athletes will be the centre of the Games.
- stage a truly global and quality event that will allow all athletes to compete and participate at a fair and challenging level and where all athletes will have a reasonable opportunity to succeed.
- promote the Games in such a way that everyone will feel they have contributed and that they belong.
- encourage family participation.
- showcase the cultural heritage of Ireland and Europe.
- ensure that everyone involved approaches the event with a sense of enthusiasm, dignity and respect.

Source: 2003 Special Olympics World Games (2002, p.1).

AMY SIMMONS, *Volunteer Director*

Special Olympics New Jersey

As the Volunteer Director at Special Olympics New Jersey, my major responsibilities include volunteer recruitment, management, orientation/training, and onsite event execution, including registration and management of volunteers for all statewide and sectional-level sports events. This includes both Class A volunteers (coaches, chaperones, unified partners, individuals with direct supervisory responsibilities for athletes) and Class B volunteers (day-of-event volunteers). It important for all volunteers to understand the mission of Special Olympics, with emphasis on the delivery of quality sports training and athletic competition for children and adults with intellectual disabilities.

Special Olympics New Jersey is a statewide organization that engages volunteers on the local, county, sectional, and state levels. While there is a formal process for Class A volunteers, background checks still prove to be an imperfect means to screen volunteers and cannot identify a person who may commit a first-time offense. A large percentage of the athletes we serve require supervision by volunteers during events as well as on overnight stays. The responsibility to ensure the health and safety of athletes under volunteer supervision is paramount to my responsibilities and fundamental to the integrity of local selection and screening of these individuals who are so critical to the delivery of our program.

Speaking only in regard to the volunteer aspect of Special Olympics New Jersey, we are working on an ongoing basis to ensure all Class A volunteers are registered, screened, and properly certified in compliance with the Special Olympics U.S. Volunteer Screening Policy. Because of the large number of volunteers in the state (both Class A and Class B), it is imperative a standard registration process is in place. The difficulty lies in clearly distinguishing what constitutes a Class A and Class B volunteer. Just as the line between the two definitions of volunteers is established, additional volunteer needs

are developed and created that may fall in a gray area between the two defined types of volunteers.

Special Olympics New Jersey governance structure includes the Board of Directors and Senior Management followed by Departments (Program, Development, Law Enforcement Torch Run, Communication, and Administration), Area Directors, and Athlete Congress. Each division of this structure has a distinct purpose, all guided by and mindful of the Special Olympics New Jersey Mission Statement.

One positive aspect of the structure is our Athlete Congress, which includes Special Olympics New Jersey athletes who are selected to represent the Special Olympics athletes from our state. The athletes of the Athlete Congress are empowered to voice their opinons and recommend a course of action about various facets of the competition and training programs. Every other year, Athlete Congress meets at the New Jersey State House to vote on recommendations for changes to the Special Olympics program. They then create action plans that have passed and submit them to Special Olympics New Jersey staff and Board of Directors.

Another positive element of our structure includes the Area Directors. Special Olympics New Jersey is divided into 13 areas based on county. Each of these areas consists of an Area Director, the majority of whom have been involved in Special Olympics New Jersey for an extended period of time, many as a parent of an athlete or a coach. The Area Directors run local events and are instrumental in our grassroots programming. They manage the training programs in their area and serve as facilitators for relaying information between the area programs and the state office.

A negative, as with many organizations, is an occasional inconsistent form of communication between the divisions of the governance structure. Even as technology and the number of social media outlets advance, one missed email or incorrect event date can create new challenges to overcome. However, as the importance of communication grows, whether it be event information to the public or internal information within the staff, we are always working to ensure all parties involved are fully informed.

We continually strive to increase the number of opportunities available for our athletes to train and compete as well as the resources available to the families of Special Olympics New Jersey. One challenge we face now and as we move into the future is getting into the school districts and encouraging them to implement inclusive physical education and sport in their curriculums. The Get Into Our Game program focuses on breaking down barriers and providing opportunities for Special Olympics athletes and teammates to participate as a unified program through sport. Though this is not a new Special Olympics New Jersey policy, we renew our efforts in working with the school districts, hoping to help them amend their policies to make more opportunities available to those with special needs.

in-kind products and services. Adjusting for inflation, those costs would be 8 percent higher in 2013. To deliver the event, sponsorship and corporate partnerships were needed, along with revenue from sales and municipal support. For 2003 the Bank of Ireland was the premier partner for the Games and over $15.23 million (US$14 million) was raised in sponsorship one year out from the games (2003 Special Olympics World Games, 2002). Beyond corporate sponsorship, fundraising was initiated through programs such as Support an Athlete, Golf Challenge, Race Day, and a Gala Ball.

ORGANIZATIONAL STRUCTURE. The Special Olympics World Games are managed by a Games Organizing Committee (GOC). The GOC is led by a Chair and is composed of a fairly large number of high-profile community members who act as Directors. The 2003 Ireland GOC had 23 Directors, and the 2007 Games in Shanghai and the 2011 Games in Athens maintained a large organizational structure and over 20 Directors. The GOCs are incorporated as a company under the name of the Games being organized. The GOC's Board of Directors includes highly experienced individuals from a variety of public and private sector backgrounds. These volunteers, led by a CEO, oversee the activities of paid staff. For the 2011 Athens Games, committees such as Security, Quality Management, Transportation, Information Technology, Competitions, Volunteers, among many others, were employed. The 2013 Special Olympic Winter World Games were hosted in PyeongChang, Republic of Korea, and the 2015 Special Olympic Summer Games will be held in Los Angeles.

CURRENT POLICY AREAS

Hosting major games as described above is a significant undertaking. Each event requires considerable organizational efforts, large financial support, and thousands of workers, both paid and volunteer. The organizing committee may plan for three or four years to ensure a safe and effective competition. Some issues organizers will surely deal with are internal to the particular event, such as fundraising and security. Many others are externally imposed, often by the governing international federation and include issues such as doping control and the influences of the media. Other concerns stem from our global society and involve the world's perspective on global conflict, political involvement in sport, and the very definition of *amateurism*. Each of these issues involves current policy areas.

Sport and International Politics

The association between sport and politics, and the subsequent political maneuvering that might occur through major games, is a policy area of interest to event participants and organizers. Recent issues of the international politics of sport include the advance of political ideologies such as democracy versus communism; capitalism and international relations; religion, gender, and disability sport; and sport and terrorism (Levermore & Budd, 2004). Sport has traditionally been used for nation building. It symbolizes the values of success, "of our ways compared to your ways," "of our people over your people." Sport illustrates power, wealth, business might, and general superiority. It has even been used as a show of moral authority and political legitimization (Allison, 2005; Houlihan, 1994).

Political factors have influenced the location of game sites. For instance, international federations have chosen host sites on the basis of generating economic support and facilitating legacy to an underdeveloped part of the world. Boycotting tactics—a nation refusing to send athletes and teams to an event in protest over another country's domestic or foreign policy—have been used as a form of political maneuvering. In this case national policy might directly influence sport policy, and a nation may decide the extent to which sport will be used on the world stage to further other national objectives. The degree to which sport is used to enhance a national political agenda directly affects the political maneuvering associated with major games. Another factor might include the involvement of business and the commercialization of sporting events. Today, the long-term involvement of businesses in sport might actually weaken the ability of a government to manipulate and exploit sport as a means for promoting a diplomatic agenda, as the international sport agenda becomes more and more dominated by big business as opposed to state politics (Allison, 2005).

Marketing and Fundraising

Fundraising and marketing have become increasingly important to hosting major games in amateur athletics (Amis, 2005). While several levels of a government might commit to contributing some financial support, such an offering is seen as a component of a larger financial landscape. Therefore, since hosting requires significant resources, particularly when new facilities are required, developing the financial backing to deliver the event is critical for success.

The importance of marketing for a major amateur athletic event is a given (Maguire, 2005). While significant positive results can accrue from attracting donor funds and marketing the event (even to the extent that one without the other may well be impossible), other issues arise from marketing and fundraising practices. Members of organizing committees are debating methods of increasing the value of television and sponsorship packages. Increased commercialization of amateur sport results in a shift of power and control toward sponsors. Struggles develop as a result of exclusive sponsorship categories. For example, water and isotonic drinks are obviously an important sponsorship category associated with major games. When exclusive sponsorship rights are awarded to one company, the extent of the sponsorship agreement might become a source of problems. Does the sponsorship agreement extend to all other products associated with the company? This becomes an issue because today's multinational conglomerates produce a vast array of products. A balance between the sponsor's needs and the best interests of the games is required. Without fundraising, sponsorship, and marketing, the very existence of major games could be jeopardized, given the significant requirement for operating revenues.

Today's global economy drives both cost and value. On the one hand the hosting of most major games runs in the millions of dollars or euros. The value of selling certain properties associated with major games, such as title sponsorship or television rights, slides on a scale depending on the location and economic factors. Organizers are constantly concerned with keeping costs down and value up. While costs can remain fairly neutral once established, the values of the properties of major games are more difficult to pinpoint. These values depend on many factors, and they change as a result of economic and political factors. For instance, how does the value of television rights for hosting the Pan American Games differ between a host site in North America versus South America? Many factors, such as the number of potential television carriers, the size of target markets, the time of year, competition with other established events, and the ability of the host to attract other corporate partners affect the value of the television package. Of course, the organizing committee enacts policies to drive the value of the contract as high as possible. These policies might suggest the importance of publicity to increase the television audience, scheduling games and events at the best time of day to ensure the highest possible television numbers, and so on.

Broadcasting and sponsorship revenues come with an associated cost. When outside groups buy services or properties, conflict may arise over how the event is run. Policies to define rights and privileges associated with each partnership are critical to successfully hosting major games. For instance, the organizing committee must define a specific television policy that establishes explicit guidelines for how the event will be scheduled, with game-day timelines determined in advance. The policy will also suggest how changes to the timelines can be made, naming the groups or individuals who must be consulted.

Exclusivity is a term used for selling sponsorships that involves dividing the event into sponsorship categories and allowing for each category to be sold only one time, thereby providing one sponsor with "exclusive rights" without competition for its product. For instance, selling soft drink sponsorship exclusively to Pepsi would preclude any sponsorship with Coca-Cola or any other soft drink company. It may be difficult to decide which categories of sponsorship should be sold exclusively. Often, the sponsorship policy defines exactly which sales categories will be sold with exclusivity. Preferably, the marketing and sales personnel of the organizing committee will carefully define and communicate this practice to sponsors in advance, thereby lessening the potential for conflict between sponsors and enhancing the sponsors' interest in being associated with the event.

Amateur athletic organizers rely heavily on marketing and sponsorship to deliver an event of the magnitude of FISU or Commonwealth Games. The comments made by Slack (1998) still apply: "in no previous time period have we seen the type of growth in the commercialization of sport that we have seen in the last two decades. Today, sport is big business and big businesses are heavily involved in sport" (p. 1). Such reliance, however, is of concern to event organizers. In a best-case scenario, a major games could run as an entity by itself. Given this is not the case, international federations and major games organizing committees set policy to encourage revenue generation beyond corporate sponsorship and advertising. For example, the Finance Committee of a major games would define sources of funding in order to manage the event. Those sources will be as diverse as possible in order to decrease the threat of reliance on any one funding category. Government funding, television rights, categories of exclusive and nonexclusive sponsors and corporate partners, pure advertising, ticket sales, merchandising, entry fees—all are sought by organizing committees to diversify revenue sources, prevent running an overall deficit, and deflect undue influence and/or control of the games by outside groups.

Global Conflict, Terrorism, and Security

Global conflict and the war on terrorism seem to be constant issues on the world agenda. War, conflict, terrorism, political maneuvering, and alliance building are issues for virtually every government. Terrorism is defined as a politically motivated form of violence, usually employed to overthrow governments (Toohey, 2008). Terrorism, especially since the September 11, 2001, attacks on the United States, continue to have world leaders and the rest of the world on alert.

The changes to daily life associated with a world on alert are manifested in many ways. Citizenship, travel, security, privacy, and global politics each take on heightened meaning. The impact on event management is particularly important. Imagine being the Director of Security for a large international event in this environment. Your task is to ensure the safety of 5,000 competitors from 145 countries and the 400,000 people who will gather to enjoy the competition and related cultural events. This is a monumental task and the focus of extensive debate and policy development. Unfortunately, the issue is not brand new. The tragic hostage crisis in the Olympic Village during the Munich Olympic Games of 1972 resulted in the deaths of 11 Israeli athletes and coaches, 5 Palestinian terrorists, and 1 German police officer. Major games bring global representatives and world media attention. In 1996, Atlanta hosted the Olympic Summer Games and was the site of a terrorist bombing that tragically killed two and injured 111 people. The potential for terrorist action at major games is of real and continued concern for Games organizers.

Enacting policy regarding safety at major athletic games involves the collaboration of several levels of administration. Security and law enforcement personnel from local and governmental offices provide the foundation. Sport federations might provide expertise on past experience that proves valuable for future actions. The organizing committee ensures the coordination of all agencies and the implementation of the policy. Other levels within the government of the host country help with coordination. The governments of competing countries may offer assistance and will undoubtedly require assurances of readiness. In the end the policy will define parameters for safe and secure travel, admittance, contact, and conduct of participants, spectators, and affiliates of the major games.

The successful bid by Glasgow, Scotland, to host the 2014 Commonwealth Games identifies security as a main planning theme. Historical evidence of managing security, having the capacity and systems in place to coordinate huge numbers of visitors and venues, and experience in command and control are a consistent requirement of major games hosting. At this event, as with Pan American Games, World University Games, and other events and championships, security is of paramount concern, and significant resources, planning, and collaboration with local and national law enforcement are required.

www
Glasgow Bid for the 2014 Commonwealth Games
www.glasgow2014.com

Performance Enhancement

The use of drugs to enhance performance and influence the outcomes of athletic contests is termed *doping*. Worldwide, sport agencies and federations view doping as cheating and prohibit the use of performance-enhancing drugs. Athletic competition is about pitting the natural athleticism and skills of an individual or group against another. Fairness requires each individual or group to compete within a common set of parameters. Performance-enhancing drugs are considered detours around the rigors of training and preparation. As such, doping is considered artificial and is thus banned as a means of achieving a competitive edge. In addition, many doping practices are dangerous and in direct opposition to the concept of "healthy mind, healthy body" that is the benefit of sport and physical activity. To combat the issue of doping in sports, national associations such as the United States Anti-Doping Association (USADA) and the Canadian Centre for Ethics in Sport (CCES) have been organized to work in conjunction with the World Anti-Doping Agency (WADA). Policy on doping in sport has been defined in order to

- protect those who play fair
- deter those who might cheat
- apply common sanctions for doping infractions
- provide detailed procedures for establishing a breach in the rules (CCES, 2012).

All major games, international federations, and the Olympic Movement have provided a unified approach to setting policy that outlines banned substances and practices and outlaws anyone contributing to doping in sport. WADA provides for this required unified approach to developing doping-control policy, referred to as the World Anti Doping Code (WADA, 2012). Testing procedures, penalties, laboratory analyses, results management, protests and appeals, and reinstatement procedures are basic elements of doping-control policy. The ultimate goal of the policy is to create anti-doping rules, set mandatory international standards for banned substances and testing procedures, and model best practices. The issue is defined as a current policy area because it remains a dynamic issue. The use of banned substances and subsequent reports of positive tests remain a common occurrence at major games such as the Commonwealth Games and Pan American Games. Testing and strict anti-doping procedures are enacted at all major games by organizing committees. However, the will to win and the stakes for winning on the world stage help promulgate a win-at-any-cost attitude, which results in the development of new performance-enhancing techniques and substances. Thus, policy makers at all national and international levels continue to focus on this issue to curb such behaviors.

SUMMARY

The major games of amateur sport have a rich and diverse history. The Olympic Games are still the world's largest and most prestigious sport festival, but between Olympics many other events are organized and attended by nations worldwide. Major games are organized mostly for amateur competitors, and NGBs and NSOs help initiate and manage the competitors selected to represent their nation. In the United States, the AAU plays a major role in developing and organizing competitive athletics. State and national governing bodies oversee national-level competition and send representatives to international games. In Canada, provincial and national sport organizations have the same governance role, and Sport Canada sets policy and provides funding for teams to compete at world championships.

Major international games include the Pan American Games, the Commonwealth Games, the FISU Games, and the World Games for the Deaf. Such events require extensive planning and organizing and are major financial undertakings. Organizing committees spend years preparing and managing many policy areas in an effort to ensure a safe, effective sporting competition. Current policy issues include the very definition of *amateurism*, political maneuvering, funding, security and issues of global conflict, mass media influences, and doping control. The stakes are high for participants and organizers, given the enormity of the overall profile, size, and financial commitment involved in major games.

case STUDY

MAJOR GAMES IN AMATEUR SPORT

You work for your local area sports commission. You are putting together your strategic plans for the next 10 years and have decided to put in a bid for the Commonwealth Games. You are located in a major metropolitan area with a population of approximately two million residents. Your city has a large university with excellent sport facilities and a college with good outdoor facilities. Your community also has one AAA minor league baseball team; considerable other sports facilities, both private and public; and extensive park areas that could serve as potential venues.

Using the bids created by the communities of Gold Coast, Australia, and Hambantota, Sri Lanka, for the 2018 Commonwealth Games that are presented on the Bids for the 2018 Commonwealth Games website for assistance, answer the following questions:

www

Bids for the 2018 Commonwealth Games
www.thecgf.com/games/bid.asp

1. Make a list identifying each area of information that will be required, forming an outline of the sections of the bid document.

2. With which governing bodies (local, national, international) will you need to communicate?

3. Exactly which sports will be on the games program, and what is your plan for selecting the venues you would like to use for each sport?

4. Whom will you work with to ensure the security of athletes, coaches, and fans?

5. What local community groups will you actively pursue to assist with your bid, and what will their specific roles be?

CHAPTER questions

1. Choose any two of the major games presented in this chapter. Using the Internet, compare the content of their constitution and bylaws. How are they different or similar?

2. How do major games market their product and entice sponsors? Using the websites of any three major games, review the fundraising practices of the organizing committee. Given the four strategic management practices (presented in Chapter 3), used by sport managers to maximize their potential, assess the degree to which the organizing committees maximize their revenue-generating potential.

3. What is WADA, and why does it exist? Explain WADA's goal. What role do major games organizers play in helping WADA achieve its mission?

REFERENCES

AAU. (2012). About AAU. Retrieved from http://aau sports.org/AboutAAU.aspx

Allison, L. (2005). The curious role of the USA in world sport. In L. Allison (Ed.), *The global politics of sport—the role of global institutions in sport* (pp. 101–117). London: Routledge.

Americans With Disabilities Act. (1990). ADA of 1990. Retrieved from www.ada.gov/pubs/ada.htm

Amis, J. (2005). Global sport sponsorship. In B. Mullin, S. Hardy, and W. Sutton (Eds.), *Sport marketing*. Champaign, IL: Human Kinetics.

Canadian Sport Policy. (2002). The Canadian sport policy. Retrieved from www. sport.mb.ca/Canadian_Sport_Policy.pdf

Carbin, C. F. (1996). *Deaf heritage in Canada: A distinctive, diverse and enduring culture*. Toronto: McGraw-Hill Ryerson.

CCES. (2012). About CCES. Retrieved from www.cces. ca/en/antidoping/cadp/wadp

CGF. (2012). About the Commonwealth Games. Retrieved from www.thecgf.com/about/constitution.pdf

Chalip, L., & Johnson, A. (1996). Sport policy in the United States. In L. Chalip, A. Johnson, & L. Stachura (Eds.), *National sport policies: An international handbook* (pp. 404–430). Westport, CT: Greenwood Press.

CISS. (2007). International Committee of Sports for the Deaf. Retrieved from www. deaflympics.com

Dheensaw, C. (1994). *The Commonwealth Games*. Victoria, BC: Orca.

FISU. (2012a). FISU history. Retrieved from www.fisu. net/en/FISU-today-517.html

FISU. (2012b). FISU today. Retrieved from http: //www. fisu.net/en/FISU-today—517.html

XIV Pan American Games. (2002). XIV Pan American Games. Retrieved from www.santodomingo2003. org.do/ingles/paginas/comite/Ecomiteorganizador. html

Glassford, R. G., & Redmond, G. (1988). Physical education and sport in modern times. In E. F. Zeigler (Ed.), *History of physical education and sport* (pp. 103–171). Champaign, IL: Stipes.

Government of Victoria. (2012). Commonwealth Games Legacy. Retrieved from http://www.dpcd.vic.gov.au/sport/major-events/commonwealth-games/commonwealth-games-legacy

Houlihan, B. (1994). *Sport and international politics*. London: Harvester Wheatsheaf.

ICSD. (2012). About Us. Retrieved from http://www.deaflympics.com/about/index.asp?ID=1107

Kidd, B. (1999). *The struggle for Canadian sport*. Toronto: University of Toronto Press.

Levermore, R., & Budd, A. (2004). *Sport & international relations: An emerging relationship*. London: Routledge.

Maguire, J. (2005). *Power and global sport: Zone of prestige, emulation, and resistance*. New York: Routledge.

Manchester Commonwealth Games. (2002). Background to the Manchester 2002 Games. Retrieved from www.commonwealthgames.com/The_Games

Pan American Games '99. (2002). Pan American Games '99—Winnipeg, Manitoba, Canada. Retrieved from www.americascanada.org/eventpanam/menu-e.asp

Pan American Games Summer. (2012). A history of the Pan American Games. Retrieved from www.aafla.org/8saa/PanAm/pan_am_history.htm

Riess, S. A. (1995). *Sport in industrial America 1850–1920*. Wheeling, IL: Harlan Davidson.

Rio 2007 Pan American Games. (2007). XV Pan American Games Rio 2007. Retrieved May 11, 2007, from www.rio2007.org.br/pan2007/ingles/ indexing.asp

Riordan, J., & Kruger, A. (1999). *The international politics of sport in the 20th century*. New York: Routledge.

Slack, T. (1998). Studying the commercialisation of sport: The need for critical analysis. *Sociology of Sport Online, 1*(1). Retrieved October 30, 2002, from www.physed.otago.ac.nz/sosol/v1i1/v1i1a6.htm

Sport Canada. (2007). Sport Canada strategic directions. Retrieved from www.pch. gc.ca/progs/sc/mission/index_e.cfm

Sport Canada. (2012a). Action 2007–2012. Retrieved from http://www.pch.gc.ca/pgm/sc/pol/actn07-12/booklet-eng.pdf

Sport Canada. (2012b). Sport Canada organization chart. Retrieved from www.pch.gc.ca/pgm/sc/mssn/org_sprt2_eng.cfm

Sport Canada. (2012c). Sport Canada funding programs. Retrieved from www.pch.gc.ca/eng/1267375779921/126841349485/

Sport Canada. (2013). Sport Canada mission. Retrieved from www.pch.gc.ca/ pgm/sc/mss/index-eng.cfm

Statistics Canada. (2005). Cornerstones of community: Highlights of the national survey of nonprofit and voluntary organizations. Retrieved from http://library.imaginecanada.ca/files/nonprofitscan/en/nsnvo/nsnvo_report_english.pdf

Ted Stevens Olympic and Amateur Sports Act. (1998). 36 U.S.C. sec. 220501 et seq. of the United States Code.

Toohey, C. (2008). Terrorism, sport and public policy in the risk society. *Sport in Society: Cultures, Commerce, Media, Politics, 11*, 429–442.

Tucker, S. (2006, April 8). Rewards for a city that lifted its game. *Financial Times*, p. 16.

2003 Special Olympics World Games. (2002). Games organizing committee board members. Retrieved www.2003specialolympics.com/en/?page=goc_boa_01

2007 Special Olympics World Games. (2007). 2007 Special Olympics World Summer Games. Retrieved from www.2007specialolympics.org/world_games/2007_world_summer_games/default.html

2011 Special Olympics World Games. (2011). World Summer Games Athens 2011. Retrieved from http://www.specialolympicsee.eu/uploadedFiles/specialolympicseurasia/Press_Room/2011%20WSG%20Official%20Brochure.pdf

2013 Summer Universiade. (2012). Kazan, Russia. Retrieved from http://www.fisu.net/en/Kazan-2013-SU-2306.html

United States Amateur Sports Act. (1978). United States Amateur Sports Act. Retrieved from www.whitewaterslalom.org/rules/asa-1978.html

U.S. Senate Committee on Commerce, Science, and Transportation. (1998). Committee clears legislation, nominations. Retrieved June 16, 2003, from www.senate.gov/~commerce/press/105-278.htm

USA Basketball. (2012). USA basketball today. Retrieved from http://www.usabasketball.com/about/inside.html

WADA. (2012). World anti-doping code. Retrieved from www.wada-ama.org/en/World-Anti-Doping-Program/Sports-and-Anti-Doping-Organizations/The-Code/

Olympic Sport

Imagine what it must be like to strive to be the best in the world in your chosen sport: the years of preparation, the excitement of the competitions, the media attention, the applause of fans, the travel, the agony of defeat, and the thrill of victory. Now imagine the feelings of competing at the Olympic Games, often described by athletes as the adventure of a lifetime. Without doubt, the Olympics are the most significant sporting competition in the world, scheduled every four years for both summer and winter events. Athletes at virtually every level dream of one day competing for their nation on the world stage in the Olympic Games. Winning an Olympic Gold Medal holds tremendous meaning worldwide. Not only does it signify world supremacy for the athlete(s) involved, Olympic Gold means instant recognition, fame, financial success, nation building, and legitimization of political ideologies. Olympic Gold Medals are symbolic of success throughout the society the winner represents. No wonder the Olympic Games are held in such high regard and taken so seriously by nations around the world.

Citius, Altius, Fortius ("Faster, Higher, Stronger") is the motto of the modern Olympic Games. The Summer and Winter Olympics alternate every two years so that four years (a *quadrennial*) passes in a full cycle. A global audience of nearly 4.8 billion people watched some portion of the 2012 London Summer Games worldwide, and the Vancouver 2010 Games enjoyed the most extensive coverage ever produced for the Winter Olympics, reaching a record potential audience of 3.8 billion people, with 235 broadcasters and television stations providing coverage in 220 countries and territories of the world (IOC, 2012a). The incredible global reach of the Olympic Games makes them more than just a sporting event. They are a media extravaganza, a cultural festival, an international political stage, an economic colossus, and a location for developing friendships. Everyone strives for excellence, from the competing athletes to the host city. The Olympic Games are a showcase, and "Faster, Higher, Stronger" is the very essence of everything associated with the Olympic Games. This chapter looks at the history of the Games, their organization and governance, and the policy issues currently confronting organizers.

HISTORY OF THE OLYMPIC GAMES

The history of the Olympic Games can be divided into two distinct time frames. The games originated in Ancient Greece, were discontinued for at least fifteen hundred years, and then were reinstituted in the late 19th century. In the early Olympic Games, the ancient Greeks competed for the glory of their gods. Much later in history, in the so-called modern era of the games, the ancient festival was reintroduced and evolved into the event we know today.

The Ancient Olympic Games

Early Greek civilizations loved athletics and assimilated strength and vigor with rhythm, beauty, and music in their style of games and pursuits (Howell & Howell, 1988). The Greeks participated in contests and athletic events like chariot racing, boxing, wrestling, footraces, discus throwing, and archery. The first Olympic Games were held in 776 BCE and were celebrated again every four years until their abolition by the Roman Emperor Theodosius in 393 CE (Howell & Howell, 1988). The four years between games were called an *Olympiad,* a system upon which time was calculated in ancient Greek history (The Ancient Olympics, 2004). Specific events changed over the centuries, but footraces, the pentathlon, boxing, and various types of chariot races were common. The ancient Olympic Games were restricted to Greek men. It was not until the modern Olympic era that women were included (either as competitors or as spectators) and that people of different nations were allowed to compete.

The Modern Era of the Olympic Games

From 1859 until the actual revival of the Olympic Games in 1896, the idea of reinstituting the festival of the Olympiad was discussed by both Greek nationalist Evagelis Zappas and Englishman William Brooks (1896 Athens, Greece, 2007). Baron Pierre de Coubertin of Paris visited with Brooks and is the individual now credited with successfully launching the modern Olympic Games. Baron de Coubertin believed strongly in the healthy mind–healthy body connection (de Coubertin, 2000). He envisioned amateur athletes from all around the world competing in a festival of sports similar to those of ancient Greece. In 1894, the Baron presided over a congress held at the Sorbonne in Paris. Representatives from 13 countries attended the meeting, and another 21 wrote to support the concept of reviving the Olympic Games (Tyler & Soar, 1980). The assembled nations unanimously supported the revival of the Greek Olympic festival, to be held every four years, and to which every nation would be invited to send representatives. The modern Olympic Games were reborn in 1896 and were held in Athens, Greece. Two hundred and forty-one athletes (all men) from 13 nations participated in nine sports in the first modern Olympiad (IOC, 2007a).

Many traditions taken for granted in the Olympic Games today were born during the early modern Olympics, including the opening ceremony and the parade of nations into a stadium; the medal ceremonies and the flag raising of the Gold Medal–winning athlete; the housing of participants in an Olympic Village at the site of the games; and beginning and ending the Games with the lighting and the extinguishing of the Olympic flame, brought to the site from the ancient site in Olympia, Greece. Quickly, the Olympic Games became a world focus, and today young men and women come from all over the world to compete in various sports for the glory of representing their nation (Tyler & Soar, 1980). Since the revitalization of the modern Games, the Olympics have grown in size and complexity, requiring an increasingly sophisticated international governance structure. Exactly how are the Olympics governed, and how is an Olympic Games planned, organized, and managed?

GOVERNANCE

Mention "the Olympic Games" and competition, ceremony, and colors of the world come to mind, along with memories of spectacle and stories of unimaginable achievements. But from a sport management perspective, what makes these Games happen? In fact, an enormous amount of planning and coordination is required, in addition to volumes of policy that set standards for what and how things are done. Three main levels of organizational influence direct the Olympic Games as we know them. First, the Olympics are organized through the jurisdiction of the International Olympic Committee (IOC), led by its President, the Session (an annual General Assembly or Annual Meeting), and the Executive Board (similar to an Executive Committee). Bids to host the Olympic Games are made by National Olympic Committees (NOC) from interested countries. Once a bid has been awarded to a particular country, the responsibility for organizing an Olympics falls upon the Organizing Committee for the Olympic Games (OCOG). Each, in turn, contributes significantly to the staging of the Olympic Games.

International Olympic Committee

www

International Olympic Committee

www.olympic.org

The IOC, founded on June 23, 1894, is a group of officials governing Olympic organization and policy. The members are elected at the Session from the worldwide sport community. The headquarters of the IOC is located in Lausanne, Switzerland, and the committee is a nonprofit organization independent of any government or nation. Having an NOC does not guarantee that a country will be eligible to have an IOC representative. However, an effort is made to ensure that IOC membership represents geographical regions of the world. In addition, while countries that have hosted Olympic competitions are eligible to have two IOC members, some other countries choose not to fill their IOC seat, and they are not required to do so. Some countries have more than two IOC members because those additional members head an International Sports Federation (ISF) for one of the sports on the program of the Olympic Games. Keep in mind that all IOC members are elected to their positions and serve as representatives to the IOC to promote Olympism. They may not necessarily reside in the country for which they are a delegate to the IOC.

MISSION. The roles of IOC members are specific: First, they are expected to serve the Olympic Movement (that is, to promote the tenets of Olympism) by helping to organize and govern policy relative to the staging of the Olympic Games. They are also expected to further the cause and understanding of all things associated with the Olympic Movement in their respective countries. IOC members are not representatives of their *nation* to the IOC. Rather, they are representatives of the *IOC* to their nations. They are expected to care first and foremost about what's best for the Olympics and work only on furthering the Olympic Movement. Overall, the IOC's "fundamental task is to supervise the regular celebrations of the Olympic Games, and toward that end, it promotes the 'development of those physical and moral qualities which are the basis of sport' and of propagating the 'Olympic ideal' so as to create 'international goodwill'" (Senn, 1999, p. 7). The IOC (2012b) defines its mission as follows:

> The International Olympic Committee is the supreme authority of the Olympic Movement. Acting as a catalyst for collaboration between all parties of the Olympic family, from the National Olympic Committees (NOCs), the International Sports Federations (IFs), the athletes, the Organising Committees for the Olympic Games (OCOGs), to the TOP partners, broadcast partners and United Nations agencies, the International Olympic Committee (IOC) shepherds success through a wide range of programmes and projects. On this basis it ensures the regular celebration of the Olympic Games, supports all affiliated member organisations of the Olympic Movement and strongly encourages, by appropriate means, the promotion of the Olympic values.

The goals of the IOC are presented in Exhibit 10.1.

Goals of the International Olympic Committee.

exhibit **10.1**

The goal of the Olympic Movement is to contribute to building a peaceful and better world by educating youth through sport practiced without discrimination of any kind and in the Olympic spirit, which requires mutual understanding with a spirit of friendship, solidarity, and fair play. The essential missions of the Olympic include

- Choice of the host city
- Organization of the Olympic Games
- Equality in sport
- Promotion of women in sport
- Protection of athletes
- Human development assistance
- The Olympic Truce

Source: IOC (2012b).

MEMBERSHIP. Historically, IOC members were elected by the other members of the committee, a practice that labeled the committee as elitist, incestuous, and existing for the gratification of its members. In the beginning, the committee was an extended group of friends and business associates of the original members, mostly from the upper class of society. Following the corruption allegations associated with the 2002 Salt Lake City Winter Olympic Games bid, the IOC changed some of its procedures. For instance, the IOC is now composed of a maximum of 115 members (IOC, 2007b). Members of the IOC are allowed to serve until age 70 (lowered from 75), although some choose to retire earlier. Positions are still elected by the members of the General Assembly, but a breakdown of the 115 positions was changed as follows: 70 are reserved for individual members, 15 are active Olympic athletes elected by their peers at the Olympic Games, 15 members come from IFs, and 15 from NOCs. Restrictions limit the numbers of a particular group being from the same country or Federation.

www
IOC Marketing Fact File
www.olympic.org/Documents/
fact_file_2010.pdf

FINANCIALS. The IOC generates extensive revenues through its ownership of the rights to the Olympic Games and associated marks and terminology. These include the Olympic symbol, consisting of the five interlocking Olympic rings, and the Olympic motto, anthem, flag, and the Olympic flame and torch. Permission to use these symbols is granted to the host organizing committee, and NOCs are permitted to use the rings in developing their own national Olympic symbol. (In the United States, a special statute requires the USOC's consent to all commercial uses of Olympic-related marks and terminology.) Countries hoping to host the Olympics guarantee a percentage of the money they will raise to the IOC in return for the rights to host. The size of the IOC's share became an issue after the 1984 Summer Olympics in Los Angeles. These games generated a surplus of $225 million. The IOC was unsuccessful in getting a share of the revenue, but it intensified its resolve to get a fair share of Olympic revenues in the future. The committee accepted the decree of then-President Samaranch, who said, "Sport without money is impossible today" (*Korea Herald*, 1986). The IOC resolved to increase its revenue share from hosting rights and acted to establish its own sources of income through marketing the Olympic symbols, with amazing success (Senn, 1999). According to the IOC Marketing Fact File (2010, n.p.):

> The Olympic Movement generates revenues through five major programs, including Broadcasting, TOP [The Olympic Partner] Sponsorship Program, Domestic Sponsorship, Ticketing, and Licensing. The IOC manages broadcast partnerships and the TOP worldwide sponsorship programme. The OCOGs manage domestic sponsorship, ticketing and licensing programmes within the host country, under the direction of the IOC.

The total revenue for the 2005–2008 quadrennium was US$5.45 billion, an increase of $1.25 billion over the Beijing Olympiad (IOC Marketing Fact File, 2010).

ORGANIZATIONAL STRUCTURE. Three components are central to IOC governance and the development of policy: the Session, the Executive Board, and the Office of the President.

1. *The Session.* The Session, comparable to a General Assembly, is a general meeting of all IOC members. The purpose of the Session is to adopt or modify policy relating to the Olympic Charter. The Olympic Charter includes the purpose and description of the ideals of Olympic participation, along with the rules and regulations for Olympic events, membership in and recognition by the IOC (IOC, 2007c; USOC, 2007). The Olympic Charter provides the framework for governing the organization and operation of the Olympic Movement and stipulates conditions for hosting the Olympic Games. Elections for accepting new IOC members are also held during the Session. Meetings are held annually unless unusual circumstances dictate the calling of a special meeting.

2. *The Executive Board.* The Executive Board is a smaller subset of the Session and is responsible for the management and overall direction of the IOC between meetings of the Session. It was first conceived by Baron de Coubertin in order to share the responsibility for directing the IOC and to prepare for an orderly succession of leadership (Senn, 1999). Executive Board membership (Exhibit 10.2) includes 15 positions: the President, 4 Vice Presidents, and 10 additional members elected by the Session. Each Executive Board member's term of office is a minimum of four years, with

Executive Board of the IOC.

exhibit **10.2**

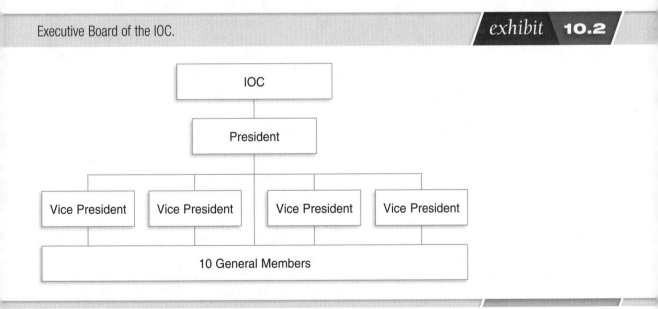

Source: IOC (2007b).

the exception of the President, who is elected to an eight-year term. The board meets regularly, at the call of the President or at the request of a majority of its members. The Executive Board of the IOC has the following specific responsibilities (Schaffer & Smith, 2000; Senn, 1999; Thoma & Chalip, 1996):

- ensures that the Olympic Charter is observed and promoted
- administers the IOC and appoints the Director General, who oversees the daily business affairs of the IOC
- manages IOC finances and financial reporting
- formulates bylaw or rule changes for implementation by the General Assembly
- approves the organizational chart of the IOC
- makes recommendations for elections
- establishes the agenda for all IOC meetings
- enacts all regulations for the proper organization of the Olympic Games
- maintains the records of the IOC

3. *The Office of the President.* The President of the IOC is elected from members of the Session. It is a critical position with power and responsibility for directing the general course of the IOC. The President is the official spokesperson of the IOC and presides over the Executive Board. It is the President's role to convene the Executive Board and lead the business of the IOC. The term of office is initially eight years, and the incumbent President may be reelected for one subsequent four-year term. In the modern era, the Olympic Games has had only eight Presidents (see Exhibit 10.3).

The officers of the IOC do not actually organize the Olympic Games. Rather, the IOC works with the groups responsible for Olympic sport and hosting activities within individual nations, NOCs, and OCOGs.

National Olympic Committees (NOCs)

NOCs control operations and policy relative to the Olympics for a particular country, as well as the delegation sent to represent a nation at the Olympic Games. With rare exceptions, only athletes certified by an NOC are permitted to compete at the Olympics. The NOC is required to check participant eligibility rules as defined by Olympic, ISF, and NOC policies. NOCs have been described as "the basic building blocks in the structure of the Olympic Games" (Senn, 1999, p. 11).

If a nation is interested in hosting an Olympic Games, the NOC is responsible for choosing one city to go forward to the IOC for consideration. The NOC selects that city no later than nine years in advance of

exhibit **10.3**

Presidents of the IOC.

President	Country of Origin	Years of Service
Dimitrius Vikelas	Greece	1894–1896
Pierre de Coubertin	France	1896–1925
Henri Baillet-Latour	Belgium	1925–1942
J. Sigfrid Edstrom	Sweden	1942–1946 (acting) 1946–1952
Avery Brundage	United States	1952–1972
Lord Killanin	Ireland	1972–1980
Juan Antonio Samaranch	Spain	1980–2001
Jacques Rogge	Belgium	2001–2013

Source: USOC (2011).

the Games. For example, in 2006 the USOC chose the city of Chicago as a potential host for the 2016 Summer Olympic Games. The NOC makes this choice nine years in advance because the IOC makes its final selection seven years in advance of the Games.

The USOC (founded in 1894) and the COC (founded in 1907) represent Olympic interests within the United States and Canada, respectively.

United States Olympic Committee (USOC)

The USOC governs, manages, promotes, and liaises within and outside the United States for all activities of the Olympic, Paralympic, and Pan American Games. As mentioned in Chapter 9, in 1978 the U.S. Congress passed the Amateur Sports Act, which was amended in 1998 and is now called the Ted Stevens Olympic and Amateur Sports Act. The amended law includes activities associated with the Paralympic Games and addresses athletes' rights and other matters. The law specifically mandates the USOC to govern all American activities for the three major Games. The USOC is the self-professed "premier sports organization" in the United States. It is composed of a group of individuals and organizations whose common goals are athletic excellence and achievement on the world stage and promoting nation building through the achievement of athletes.

The year 2003 represented a historic time for the USOC. In 2002, the USOC's President was forced to resign because of misstatements on her

www
United States Olympic Committee
www.teamusa.org

resume. In 2003, the organization was confronted with allegations of violations of its Code of Ethics by its CEO, and infighting between the CEO and the President of the organization. The good name of the USOC was tarnished, and the image of the association was at an all-time low. The U.S. Congress even voiced concern: Three Senators requested an independent commission be appointed to investigate the practices of the organization and recommend change. In addition, the USOC appointed a Governance and Ethics Task Force to recommend a course of action for changing the practices, mandate, and expectations of the USOC. The sizes of the Board of Directors and Executive Committee were particularly criticized, along with the breadth of the USOC's all-encompassing mandate, which extends very broadly beyond training athletes, building facilities, and designing equipment.

The independent commission and the USOC Governance and Ethics Task Force focused their recommendations on these three major issues (USOC, 2003):

1. narrowing the USOC mandate to focus on training athletes for national and international competition related to the Olympic and Paralympic Games
2. ensuring ethical, responsible, and transparent business and financial practices
3. creating a workable governance structure that better defines the responsibility of volunteers and professional staff and that reduces and changes the numbers and constituents involved in decision making.

They recommended that (1) the mission, goals, and objectives of the organization be focused to ensure that the ideals of the Olympics be preserved and reflected in practice and conduct; (2) the governance structure of the USOC be clearly redefined concerning responsibilities, authority, and accountability; (3) the overall governance structure of the USOC be streamlined and downsized; and (4) that ethical policy and compliance with ethical policy be instituted (USOC, 2003).

MISSION. The USOC mission connects to the themes and the meanings of the Olympics as outlined by the IOC. The mission statement speaks to the ideals of Olympism, the promotion of ethical conduct, and peace between nations achieved through sport competitions. The USOC hopes to drive national unity and pride within the United States through the accomplishments of U.S. athletes in competition with their peers from other countries. The USOC mission statement is presented in Exhibit 10.4.

MEMBERSHIP. The USOC has an extensive membership of 78 member organizations divided into seven categories. These categories include Olympic sport organizations, Pan American sport organizations, community-based multisport organizations, affiliated sport organizations, education-based

Preserve and promote the Olympic ideal as an effective, positive role model that inspires all Americans; and to lead the world's best Olympic organization in enabling United States athletes to sustain the highest levels of competitive excellence, and through their achievements be a source of inspiration for the Olympic ideal. There is no single sporting event that is more captivating and unifying than the Olympic Games. The accomplishments of United States athletes engender great national pride. The character they exhibit in their pursuit of athletic excellence provides vivid testimony to the nobility of the human spirit.

Source: USOC (2010).

multisport organizations, and the armed forces (USOC, 2004). The entire membership of the USOC is presented in Exhibit 10.5.

FINANCIALS. In the past 20 years the USOC's budget for the four-year span between Olympic Games has grown from $13 million to $491.5 million (USOC, 2002). The organization is continually ranked among the top 100 nonprofit organizations in the United States. In 2010 the USOC declared total revenues of $251 million, with expenses of $191 million (USOC, 2012). Funding comes from several sources. The USOC owns the rights to all Olympic symbols within the United States and generates considerable revenue from sales of Olympic products. It also has extensive reach in the corporate world, with a corporate partnership and advertising program contributing high yearly revenues. In addition, the USOC established a trust fund after the successful Los Angeles Olympics in 1984 as an endowment for Olympic sports. The trust fund is called the United States Olympic Foundation and operates as a separate not-for-profit corporation. Although the initial endowment of $111 million must remain intact according to the terms of the trust, it generates an annual grant that has varied by year between 5 percent and 10 percent (or just under $9 million) to the USOC for the promotion of Olympic-related sports in the United States (IOC, 2007a).

ORGANIZATIONAL STRUCTURE. The USOC employs almost 500 staff members and relies heavily on the expertise of its volunteer leadership (USOC, 2005). Volunteers involved with the USOC include some of the most influential leaders in both sport and business from around the United States.

exhibit 10.5 Member organizations of the United States Olympic Committee.

Olympic Sport Organizations (39)

National Archery Association	United States Rowing Association
USA Badminton	United States Sailing Association
USA Baseball	USA Shooting
USA Basketball	U.S. Ski and Snowboarding Association
U.S. Biathlon Association	U.S. Soccer Federation
U.S. Bobsled and Skeleton Association	Amateur Softball Association
USA Boxing	U.S. Speedskating
USA Canoe and Kayak	USA Swimming
USA Curling	U.S. Synchronized Swimming, Inc.
USA Cycling, Inc.	USA Table Tennis
United States Diving, Inc.	USA Taekwondo Union
USA Equestrian	U.S. Team Handball Federation
U.S. Fencing Association	U.S. Tennis Association
U.S. Field Hockey Association	USA Track & Field
U.S. Figure Skating Association	USA Triathlon
USA Gymnastics/Trampoline/Tumbling	USA Volleyball
USA Hockey, Inc.	United States Water Polo
USA Judo	USA Weightlifting
USA Luge Association	USA Wrestling
USA Modern Pentathlon Association	

Pan American Sport Organizations (6)

USA Bowling	USA Roller Sports
United States of America National Karate-Do Federation, Inc.	U.S. Squash Racquets Association
United States Racquetball Association	USA Water Ski

Affiliated Sport Organizations (5)

Underwater Society of America	USA Rugby
United States Amateur Ballroom Dancers Association	United States Sport Acrobatics Federation
U.S. Orienteering Federation	

Continued.

exhibit **10.5**

Community-Based Multi Sport Organizations (20)

Amateur Athletic Union

American Alliance for Health, Physical Education, Recreation, and Dance

American Legion

Boy Scouts of America

Boys and Girls Clubs of America

Catholic Youth Organization

Disabled Sports USA

Dwarf Athletic Association of America

Jewish Community Centers Association

National Association of Police Athletic Leagues, Inc.

National Congress of State Games

National Disability Sports Alliance

National Senior Games Association

Native American Sports Alliance

Special Olympics International

U.S. Association for Blind Athletes

USA Deaf Sports Federation

Wheelchair Sports USA

YMCA of the USA

YWCA of the USA

Education-Based Multisport Organizations (4)

National Association of Intercollegiate Athletics (NAIA)

National Collegiate Athletic Association (NCAA)

National Federation of State High School Associations (NFSHSA)

National Junior College Athletic Associations (NJCAA)

Armed Forces (4)

U.S. Air Force

U.S. Army

U.S. Marine Corps

U.S. Navy

Source: USOC (2012).

The organization is structured such that an appointed group of officers form the Board of Directors and various other committees, which provide direction to the staff, who implement policy (see Exhibit 10.6).

Officers. The most important leaders of the USOC are the Chair (an elected volunteer) and the CEO (a paid employee). Both fulfill leadership roles in establishing USOC policy and are the principal spokespersons for the organization. The CEO is also responsible for day-to-day operations, strategic policy initiatives and directions, and management of the professional staff (USOC, 2006).

exhibit **10.6**   Organizational structure of the USOC.

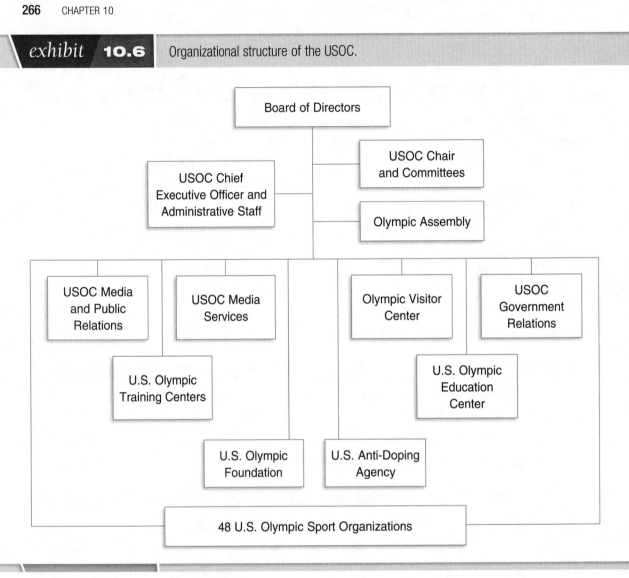

Source: USOC (2012).

Board of Directors. The task force investigating USOC reform began working on a new leadership structure for the organization in February 2003. The organization was viewed as being too large and overly bureaucratic. To overcome these issues, the Task Force recommended that the Board of Directors be reduced in size (from 125 members to 11, which has since been amended to 15), the numbers of standing committees be reduced, the Executive Committee be eliminated from the governance structure, delineation of roles and responsibilities be enacted, and an Olympic Assembly be created. Like many other sport organizations, a two-tiered governance structure is used to manage USOC affairs. The Board of Directors has the ultimate authority and responsibility for the business, policy development, election of officers, and activities of the USOC. The Board has the authority to amend the constitution and bylaws of the USOC, admit and terminate members, and receive and review reports from committees and members. The Board of Directors meets four times each year. (See Exhibit 10.7 for a list of the 2013 Board of Directors, included to show their diverse backgrounds.)

Olympic Assembly. The Olympic Assembly is held once per year, and is an event for which all constituent groups of the USOC gather to discuss the achievements of the organization and communicate to the Board of Directors. According to the USOC (2006) Bylaws, the Olympic Assembly has the following purpose:

> The Board, in conjunction with the CEO, shall provide information to the members of the Olympic Assembly on the affairs of the corporation, which shall include information on the performance of the organization,

WWW

USOC Board of Directors
www.teamusa.org/About-the-USOC/Organization/Board-of-Directors.aspx

WWW

USOC Bylaws
http://assets.teamusa.org/assets/documents/attached_file/filename1/50638/2011_Bylaws_Approved_9.24.11.pdf

Membership of the 2013 USOC Board of Directors, reflecting diverse backgrounds. *exhibit* **10.7**

Name	Position	Distinguished Background
Larry Probst	Chairman, IOC member	Chairman, Electronic Arts
Anita DeFrantz	Director, IOC member	Olympian, President of Kids in Sports
James Easton	Director, IOC member	Olympian, Chairman of Easton Sports, Inc.
Angela Ruggiero	Director, IOC member	Olympian, entrepreneur
Robert Bach	Director	Business executive, Microsoft
James Benson	Director	Business executive, Financial Services
Bob Bowlsby	Director	College Athletic Director
Ursula Burns	Director	CEO, Xerox Corp.
John Hendricks	Director	Founder of the Discovery Channel
Nina Kemppel	Director	Olympian, entrepreneur
Jair Lynch	Director	Olympian, entrepreneur
Susanne Lyons	Director	Business executive
Mary McCagg	Director	Olympian, business executive
Dave Ogrean	Director	Executive Director, USA Hockey
Bill Marloft	Director	VP, International Ski Federation

the financial performance and well being of the corporation, preparations for the Olympic, Pan American, and Paralympic Games, achievement of the corporation's mission, and actions taken, results achieved, and programs being implemented by the corporation. At the Olympic Assembly the members of the Olympic Assembly will have an opportunity to provide information and to communicate with the Board and the CEO concerning the performance, policies and other matters related to the corporation. Such input shall be advisory in nature and shall not be deemed to direct the Board or the CEO to take or not take any particular action. The Olympic Assembly shall not conduct or perform any governance functions. (pp. 19–20)

Other committees. Four additional committees deal with specific USOC areas of importance, interest, and concern; these are the (1) Audit, (2) Compensation, (3) Ethics, and (4) Nominating and Governance committees. The Athletes' Advisory Council and the NGB Council are also important USOC committees.

Canadian Olympic Committee

WWW

Canadian Olympic Committee
www.olympic.ca

The COC is responsible for Canada's involvement in the Olympic movement. It is a private, not-for-profit corporation managing Canada's participation in the Olympic, Paralympic, and Pan American Games, promoting Olympic values within Canada, and selecting and supporting Canadian cities' bidding to host Olympic or Pan American Games.

MISSION. The COC's mission statement (see Exhibit 10.8) proclaims developing and advancing sport and the Olympic Movement for all Canadians (COC, 2007). This mission to promote, organize, develop, and manage the ideals of Olympic participation within Canada is extended to include a vision for sport in Canada. The stated vision is intended as an impetus for the COC and the rest of the Canadian sport community to improve the high-performance system of sport for the country. The plan provides steps designed to make Canada a world leader in sport, which includes grassroots sport development, identifying and training athletes and coaches,

exhibit **10.8**   Mission of the Canadian Olympic Committee.

> To lead the achievement of the Canadian Olympic Team's podium success and to advance the Olympic values in Canada.

Source: COC (2011).

coordinating between constituents of the sport system, providing funds for the monitoring of success, developing and applying sport research, developing facilities, and hosting world events. For further information regarding the COC's performance indicators and vision, see www.olympic.ca.

MEMBERSHIP AND ORGANIZATIONAL STRUCTURE. The COC uses a two-tiered system of governance. A large Session and smaller Board of Directors manage and develop policy and direction for the COC, and this policy is implemented through a full-time paid staff. The board is led by a President and Executive Committee elected by Board members, and comprises 12 elected members. The Session consists of the following representatives (COC, 2013):

- 60 Olympic and Pan American Canadian Sport Federation representatives
- 12 COC members at large
- 1 Olympic or Pan American Games Coaches representative
- 2 individuals affiliated with sport
- all IOC members in Canada.

The Executive Committee is composed of 16 members, including elected officers and at least two athlete members of the board. The organizational structure of the COC is presented in Exhibit 10.9.

NOCs, like the USOC and the COC, are the rights-holders to the Olympics within their respective countries. They play a role in endorsing and assisting a city that wishes to bid for the Olympic Games, but they do not actually act to host the Olympic Games. Rather, they turn over the duties of planning and managing the hosting of the Olympic Games to an organizing committee specifically created for that purpose.

FINANCIALS. In 2010, the COC's consolidated revenues were C$39.372 million. These moneys were derived, in part, from the following sources (COC, 2012):

- partner and marketing revenues (C$27.159 million)
- investment income (C$6.506 million)
- grants and donations (C$1.317 million)

In contrast, COC expenses involve grants and scholarships to athletes and coaches, National Sport Federation (NSF) and Games Mission costs (60%); marketing and business operation outlay (31%); athlete and community relations (5%); governance (2%); advocacy and partner relations (2%); and communications (1%) (COC, 2006). The COC also operates a legacy trust from the 1988 Calgary Winter Olympic Games that provided original capital of C$53,152,000. The fund, called the Canadian Olympic Family Fund, was worth C$100 million on December 31, 2005, of which

exhibit **10.9**   Organizational structure of the COC.

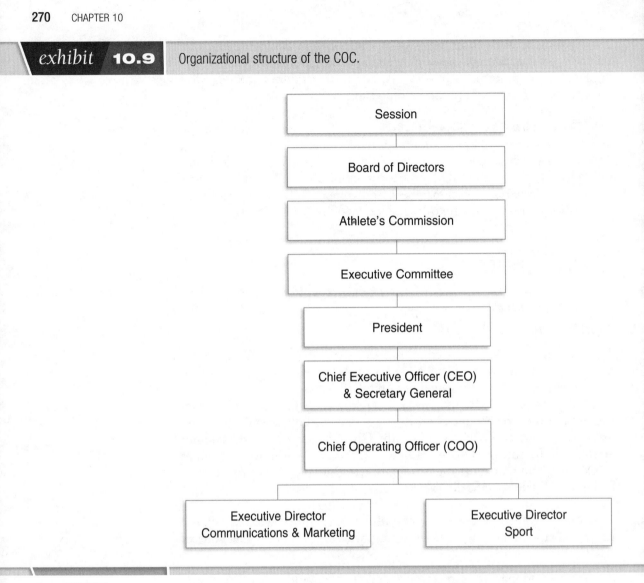

Source: COC (2011).

C\$71 million is protected as investment capital under the direction of the fund managers. Revenues over investments are available to help finance COC programs.

Organizing Committees for the Olympic Games

OCOGs are another vital component of the Olympic structure. An OCOG is formed within a community after it has successfully won the bid to host the Olympic Games. The work for the OCOG begins many years (perhaps

10 to 14) in advance of the actual Olympic event. The predecessor to this committee prepares the bid and plans for all aspects of hosting. With the support of the host country's NOC, the bid is submitted to the IOC and judged on many criteria. If the bid is unsuccessful, the bid committee finalizes its affairs and dissolves. The bid committee that is awarded the hosting rights becomes an OCOG and continues and intensifies planning. Some examples of successful OCOG bids were the Vancouver–Whistler (Canada) Organizing Committee (VANOC), which organized the 2010 Winter Games, and the London Organizing Committee for the Olympic Games (LOCOG), which organized the 2012 Summer Games.

Given that the summer and winter Olympic Games occur in a different location each four years, OCOGs are developed to manage one event at a time. As mentioned in the discussion on NOCs, bids for hosting the Olympic Games are made well in advance of the event to allow for facility development and proper event planning. Developing a bid is a process that takes years from idea to plan to concept. The IOC awards the Games to a host city seven years in advance of the Games (Senn, 1999). Although the bid is presented to the IOC by a city interested in hosting, the OCOG must demonstrate the support of various levels of government and the NOC. The process is so competitive that few cities receive the IOC's support after their first application. Once the application to bid is supported, the OCOG will move into action to prepare for the Games and will stay active for about a year after the event to finalize all financial accounting and final reports. In total, members of the OCOG are likely to be involved in some stage of bidding, planning, executing, or reporting for 10 to 12 years. At any given time, four OCOGs (two for the Winter Games and two for the Summer Games) are in some stage of this process. Many OCOG employees come from the host city, while some sport and event managers travel the world with the Olympic Games, moving from position to position as specialists in some capacity with the organizing committees.

MISSION. The mission of an OCOG clearly reflects the ideals of the Olympic movement: to be the best, to host the best, to show the world the best Olympic Games ever. When the President of the IOC speaks at the Olympic closing ceremonies, the local organizers listen carefully. They want to hear something to the effect of "This was the best Olympic Games ever," which is the goal of every OCOG. An example mission statement of the Torino, Italy, OCOG is presented in Exhibit 10.10.

MEMBERSHIP AND ORGANIZATIONAL STRUCTURE. OCOG members include both paid professional staff and volunteers. The OCOG is usually led by a volunteer President and Board of Directors, and a staff CEO. The OCOG is then subdivided into areas of responsibility such as finance, facility development,

WWW

Vancouver–Whistler
Organizing Committee
www.vancouver2010.com

London Organizing Committee
for the Olympic Games
www.london2012.com

| *exhibit* **10.10** | Example mission of an Olympic Games Organizing Committee—Torino, Italy, 2006 |

TOROC, which is the official acronym used to identify the Organising Committee of the XX Olympic Winter Games in Torino, is a no-profit private foundation established to organize the sports events and the opening and closing ceremonies, to manage the Olympic villages, which will provide hospitality to athletes and technical staff, and to deal with matters related to the Media Villages, the Main Press Centre and the International Broadcasting Centre for television and radio services. The Committee will co-ordinate transportation and medical services, set up the temporary structures needed for athletes and spectators, plan and promote the cultural program, organize accommodation and transportation for athletes, sports staff, the media and all other personnel involved in the event. Finally, the Committee will be responsible for drawing up a marketing programme with the co-operation of the IOC and CONI.

Source: Torino 2006: XX Olympic Winter Games (2003).

sports, technical liaison, marketing and sponsorship, volunteers, security, ticket sales, merchandising, television, doping control, and so forth.

Each of the governing structures presented above plays a role in setting or enforcing policy for the Olympic Games. The IOC is charged with this mandate, and the NOCs and OCOGs help enact it. Policy is often under scrutiny, depending upon the prevailing issues of the day. For example, the 1999 scandal associated with IOC members accepting bribes from the Salt Lake City Organizing Committee resulted in a focus on procedures for choosing the host city. The presence of doping, as illustrated by positive drug tests at virtually every recent Olympic Games, continues to focus attention on testing procedures. The threat of terrorism has resulted in heightened security measures and the scrutiny of security procedures. These and other current policy issues are discussed next.

FINANCIALS. The Olympic Games are run like a business. The goal is to have surplus funds available after the Games in order to leave a legacy for the next host city and country. An inordinate amount of money goes into hosting, and it is raised through government grants and funding, television rights, corporate sponsorship and advertising, licensing and sale of merchandise, ticket sales, and other marketing and special event functions. For example, VANOC's budget for the 2010 Winter Olympic Games was just over C$2 billion (VANOC, 2006).

CURRENT POLICY AREAS

Baron Pierre de Coubertin envisioned the modern Olympics as the focus of the world spotlight, and he purposely kept the four-year time span between games so the spotlight would continue to burn bright long into the future. Given the continued interest and prestige of the Games today, de Coubertin and his collaborators would be well pleased. Every so often during the interlude between Olympics the media focuses on an issue related to international sport and ultimately the Olympic Games. These areas of intense interest and speculation are a good starting point for discussing current Olympic policy issues.

Choosing a Host City

Imagine this: the President of the IOC moves toward the microphone, paper in hand, to announce the successful bid for hosting the next Summer Olympic Games. You and other members of the Organizing Committee sit in the audience of the capacity-crowd press conference, thinking back over the last seven years of work spent on the bid: hundreds of meetings; millions of dollars or euros raised and a good sum spent; victory upon victory in convincing citizens, city workers, and government officials of the value of bringing the Olympics home; visits by Olympic and IOC members; a massive enterprise coordinated. Yet, you still have not won the bid to host the Olympic Games. The President of the IOC announces, "And the winner is . . . ."

At the press conference to award the bid to host the Olympic Games, the stakes are huge because of the time and money invested as well as the potential for gain in achieving the bid. It is a city's chance to gain the world spotlight.

Given this situation, it is easy to understand why the IOC procedures for awarding the bid to host are considered an important area for policy development. The policy must stipulate exactly how the decision will be made, what criteria will be used, and what the timeline will be. In this case, a policy provides a framework for the bidding committee. What is important to the IOC in terms of staging the Olympics? Who will make the decision, and when will the decision be made? How can we position our bid to be held in the best possible regard by members of the IOC? The IOC has established a set of themes to guide this process. Consider the example of the U.S. bid for the 2012 Summer Olympic Games presented in Exhibit 10.11. The selection criteria themes upon which Olympic bids are judged have a dual purpose. They define the content of the bid and also provide a framework for members of the IOC who will vote on the bids. Policy to guide IOC voting members in deciding the successful bid has long been a topic of discussion that has come under intense criticism. Rumors of IOC members accepting bribes of money, trips, gifts, and promises had been

exhibit   **10.11** Example of timelines and selection criteria in the U.S. bid to host the 2012 Summer Olympic Games.

Timelines

December 15, 2000	Deadline to submit bid to USOC by interested cities
December 15, 2000–February 28, 2001	USOC staff reviews bids
March 1, 2001	Bids sent back to cities for clarification / changes
June 1, 2001	Deadline for resubmission of bids to USOC
June 1, 2001–September 30, 2001	USOC site visits
October 26, 2001	USOC Board of Directors selects finalist cities
April 8, 2002	Bid additions due to USOC
June 28–29, 2002	Washington, DC site visit
June 30–July 1, 2002	New York City site visit
July 12–13, 2002	Houston site visit
July 14–15, 2002	San Francisco site visit
August 27, 2002	USOC to short-list to two candidate cities
October 1, 2002	Bid cities executive summary due to USOC
November 2, 2002	USOC Board of Directors selects U.S. candidate city (New York City)
March, 2003	USOC nominates U.S. candidate city to IOC
September, 2005	IOC selects host for the 2012 Olympic Games

Selection Criteria Themes

18 Required Themes From the IOC: National, Regional & Bid City Characteristics, Legal Aspects, Customs & Immigration Formalities, Environmental Protection, Meteorological and Environmental Conditions, Security, Medical and Health Services, Official Program of the XXXth Olympiad, General Sports Organization, Sports, Olympism and Culture, Olympic Village, Accommodation, Transportation, Technology, Media, Finance, Marketing, Guarantees

Additional Themes From the USOC: Sport Event Experience, Sports Infrastructure, Olympic Village, Finance, Paralympic Games, OCOG Governance/Ethics, International Strategies

Fifty-four per cent of the scoring is according to International Olympic Committee guidelines for host city candidates, fifteen per cent will relate to financial and budget stability and 31 per cent judges USOC partnership opportunities, Paralympics planning and the ability to win a vote before the IOC.

Highlights of Nominated Bid

New York City, U.S.A.

Proposed Budget: $3.2 billion

Dates: July 27–August 12, 2012

Highlights: Melting pot of America welcomes the world; business/media centre; tourist area.

Challenges: traffic congestion; security issues; massive construction projects

Source: New York City 2012 Summer Olympic Games Bid (2003).

debated for years, but the December 1998 scandal that erupted as a result of alleged bribes associated with the 2002 Salt Lake City Olympic bid resulted in a thorough scrutiny and revision of the policy that mandates the conduct of IOC members. In the past, the IOC did not condone IOC Bid Selection Committee members accepting gifts, but it also did little to monitor the policy. In effect, it produced a scenario where it appeared that the votes of IOC members had to be secured through bribes in order to win the bid. Organizing committees spent considerable time, money, and thought on planning how to best influence members of the IOC. However, the public outcry resulting from the Salt Lake City corruption allegations resulted in the IOC sanctioning those involved. Investigators discovered that the Salt Lake City Bid Committee paid hundreds of thousands of dollars in cash, gifts, travel, and medical aid to IOC members. In the end, four IOC violators resigned, six were expelled, and 10 received official warnings by the IOC President (IOC, 2002). The IOC Vice President at the time, Canadian Richard Pound, was tasked with investigating the bribery scandal and developing policies to "modernize" IOC procedures. The following changes were implemented in 1999 as a result of his investigation (IOC, 2002):

- Specific procedures for electing the candidate cities for 2006 onwards were amended.
- Visits by IOC members to candidate cities were abolished.
- An IOC Ethics Commission was created.
- IOC General Assembly (Sessions) were opened to the media for the first time.
- Financial transparency was mandated through publication of sources of revenue and expenditures.

In addition to the changes implemented in 1999, the election procedure has been revised to consist of three phases:

1. the *Applicant City phase,* which includes applicant cities completing a comprehensive questionnaire about their bid intentions regarding motivation to host, venues, transportation, etc.;

2. the *Candidature phase,* in which five candidate cities respond to a new 250-page questionnaire covering topics like media operations, marketing, athlete's village, financial management, etc., followed by a comprehensive evaluation of the bid by the IOC Evaluations Commission over four days of on-site visit; and

3. the *Selection phase,* during which reports are created outlining strengths, weaknesses, and recommendations regarding bids, and IOC members vote at a General Assembly meeting by secret ballot. In the first round of voting, if no city receives a majority of votes, the city receiving the fewest votes is dropped from the ballot, and subsequent rounds of voting continue until a winner is identified. (IOC, 2007d)

I am the Director of High Performance for USA Taekwondo. As the Director of High Performance, I am responsible for all athlete and coach development programs in the United States for the sport of taekwondo. This spans from grassroots coaching education programs to working with Olympic-level athletes as they prepare to win medals at the Olympic Games. Our main goal is to achieve sustained international competitive excellence.

I believe the most important policy issue facing Olympic sport today is Safe-Sport. Safe-Sport in the Olympic movement is defined as creating a healthy, supportive environment for all sport participants. Safe Sport is a difficult challenge with extreme legal and public perception ramifications. Each National Governing Body (NGB) is responsible for the safety of its membership. Furthermore, each NGB can be perceived to be responsible for non-members who participate in its sport through other governing bodies or private businesses. It can be very costly to operate effective programs and provide the necessary resources to members and participants of the sport. This is especially challenging to a smaller NGB that may not be able to hire its own legal team or provide a hotline for reporting misconduct. Also, as a relatively new challenge, most of the policies created to combat misconduct are being created from scratch, leaving lots of room for making mistakes.

It is our duty as the National Governing Body for Taekwondo, however, to educate and provide training and resources to those who participate in our respective sports with the goal of recognizing and responding to misconduct. Misconduct can include sexual abuse, emotional or physical abuse, or bullying or hazing. This complex issue requires educating and training coaches, athletes, parents, volunteers, and staff. It is also necessary for the NGB to implement policies and procedures to limit the risks within its sport. These can include mandatory background checks, mandatory training and education, establishing rules and boundaries for teams and events, and implementing procedures for responding to abuse.

Other important policy issues include the globalization of sport in regards to coaching conflicts of interest, medical procedures, and rules. The medical procedures and rules are particularly important in a sport like taekwondo where athletes are vulnerable to head injuries, including problems such as second impact syndrome, a serious condition that results from a second concussion before the effects of the first concussion have subsided.

As the Director of High Performance for USA Taekwondo I am responsible for our athletes' health and safety at domestic and international competitions. I have worked hard to improve our policies and procedures concerning medical practices. For example, in the international rules of taekwondo, athletes who get knocked out are required to sit out competition for 30 days. Domestically, our rules have been made stricter, requiring athletes to sit out for 90 days. We have also altered the international competition rules for our younger and less skilled athletes. We implemented "Junior Safety Rules" for those athletes under the age of 14 and all color belts. The domestic rules do not allow these age groups and skill levels to kick to the head using force. Athletes can kick to the head but they must use controlled light touches to avoid being penalized.

We have also raised the level of medical coverage for our teams traveling internationally. Any medical personnel who travel with our teams must complete a two-week program at the Olympic Training Center. We provide international medical insurance for all team members and staff traveling internationally. This coverage even allows for helicopter evacuation in case of emergency. The policies regarding international travel are very important and have helped me feel more comfortable about my position of responsibility. As I have experienced, even with proper personnel and proper medical insurance, medical injuries such as a broken leg can turn into a big problem when you are traveling in a less developed country. Having good policies in place prior to traveling certainly helps to minimize the challenges.

Most NGBs have primarily constituency-based governance systems. This can be both positive and negative. It can be positive because members of the Board of Directors bring sport-specific knowledge. It can also be negative as it often leads to very passionate directors who can sometimes be more self-serving than organization-serving. Having passionate directors can lead to misjudgments or decisions that are not always in the best interest of the organization. Constituency-based governance systems can also be negative because they do not guarantee ethnic or skill diversity on the Board.

One positive change occurring in the Olympic Movement is the shift toward directors who are independent versus constituency-voted. These independent board members usually bring less sport specific knowledge but have good connections to business world. This situation can lead to potential sponsorships and offer access to best business practices and cutting-edge ideas.

A few additional challenges or threats to the future of Olympic sports should be mentioned. These include physical education classes being removed from the public school system and how future tax laws may change the status of charitable donations. The United States is currently the only country in the world that does not use government funding to help support its Olympic team. Most NGBs rely heavily on charitable donations in order to operate. A change in government policy regarding charitable donations could be a significant threat to the future of Olympic sport in the United States.

Corporate Sponsorship

Financing an Olympic Games may be the biggest issue facing an OCOG (Sleeman, 1992). "With the sheer size and complexity of today's Olympic Games, it is evident that if there were no sponsors, there would be no Games according to the IOC" (VISA, 2007). Some countries rely on their government for funding, others get funding from public sources such as lottery returns, and many will raise money privately through corporate sponsorship. The United States and Australia relied heavily on revenues raised from corporate partnerships for hosting the 2002 Salt Lake City Winter Games and the 2000 Sydney Summer Games, respectively.

Sponsorship is a complicated area. The stakes are high because of the potential for revenue generation. The issue is complicated because of the need to define exactly who owns the rights to the various Olympic symbols. Three layers of organizations have an interest or a right to sponsorship associated with the Olympics: the IOC, the NOC, and the OCOG.

Therefore, the IOC has a written policy to define who has the right to market and sell which sponsorships. Beyond outlining who has the right to which properties, Olympic sponsorship policy is intended to set guidelines for the practices of the different levels of governance. For example, are title sponsorships allowed? Could the Olympic Games be called the Coke Olympics? Obviously, the practice is not allowed by the IOC. However, defining the limits of acceptance regarding sponsors is a hot topic for debate.

The IOC regularly debates the issue of commercialization of the Olympics. From the beginning, organizers have worked to keep the Games from becoming overly commercial to ensure that the advertising at and around Olympic venues is tasteful and discreet. The issue, of course, is power. What happens if a sponsor contributing millions of dollars requests an action or accommodation? As former IOC President Samaranch told the press in Atlanta, "This commercialization must not run the games; the games must be run by the IOC" (Senn, 1999, p. 258). Concern over commercialization and a carnival atmosphere with too many sponsors was discussed after the Atlanta Olympics because of the extensive number of sponsors involved. In taking action to combat this problem, the IOC updated its sponsorship policies by adding a clause giving them veto power over sponsors' marketing plans. The IOC also required a financial guarantee from the government of the host city in order to balance funding and eliminate Olympic reliance on commercial sponsorship (Senn, 1999). But according to then-IOC Vice President Richard Pound, the increasing commercialism of the Olympics was inevitable: "You can't have organized sports without corporate involvement" (Palmer, 2001).

Television Rights

Of all the sponsorship, advertising, and marketing opportunities available at the Olympics, no property for potential revenue generation is larger than television. In the aftermath of the 1984 Los Angeles Olympics, when huge profits were realized from hosting, the IOC began intense scrutiny of its own funding portfolio. It focused first on hosting guarantees and revenue-sharing methods and second on the revenues to be generated from selling television broadcast rights. The IOC decided to retain the right to negotiate television contracts and to share the revenues among the IOC, NOCs, OGOCs, and ISFs. For example, in December 1996 the IOC sold the American television rights to the Summer Games of 2004 and 2008 and the Winter Games of 2006 for $2.3 billion (Senn, 1999), an unprecedented action, given that host sites for some of those games had not yet been awarded. The policy issue regarding television rights involves ownership and value. The IOC has acted to retain the rights of negotiation and dispersal of television revenues. Its purpose included control, consistency, and ensuring value. By setting policy ensuring central control of this important negotiation, the IOC has ensured the potential for developing consistent, long-term contracts of the highest possible value. Of course, OGOCs would prefer to hold the rights themselves, and they can be expected to push for further debate on this issue. In addition, in the United States, the USOC takes the position, and the IOC recognizes, that the Ted Stevens Olympic and Amateur Sports Act grants it certain rights to participate in and to share in the proceeds of the U.S. television-rights broadcast negotiations.

New Olympic Sports

The size of the Olympic festival has been a topic of recent debate. The masses of visitors and spectators at the Sydney 2000 Olympics resulted in further scrutiny and policy development by the IOC, and the concern is revisited with each Olympic hosting. The issue of the number of competitors and sports has been added to the debate. Of course, many ISFs lobby intensely to be included in the Olympics. How many sports should the Olympics include? How many competitors are too many? How can the IOC balance the interest in Olympic competition and its mandate to provide opportunities for nations all around the world (203 NOCs), with the management issues that arise from competitions that are simply too large? Should every nation be permitted to send Olympic participants in all sports, even though the individuals may not meet world standards?

The IOC has developed policy to define exactly which sports will compete in the Olympics and how to add new sports. Currently there are 35 Summer and Winter Games sports with nearly 400 events (The Olympic Movement, 2007). Within the Olympic Charter, policy is written to define the following:

- Olympic sports (for example, only sports practiced by men in 75 countries and on four continents, and by women in 40 countries and three continents may be included in the Olympic program)
- disciplines (different events within sports)
- events (competitions resulting in medals)
- criteria for admitting each sport.

Often, the IOC will name an addition to the sport program at a particular Olympics in accordance with the wishes of the OCOG. As you might imagine, a significant amount of lobbying occurs in an attempt to have a sport recognized for Olympic competition. Policy is required to define the criteria, procedure, and timing of decisions relative to the sports program of an Olympic Games. A recent debate involved whether to drop baseball and softball from the Olympic program and to add rugby and golf. The discussions revolved around spectator interest, worldwide participation in these sports, and the number of competitors in the Games. In another example, snowboarding was added to the Winter Olympic Games program to attract young viewers and thereby boost television ratings and sponsorship revenues. Defining which sports will be offered at Olympic Games is the responsibility of the Olympic Programme Commission. This committee is charged with reviewing and analyzing the program of sports and defining the permissible number of athletes in each Olympic sport. It is also responsible for developing recommendations on the principles and structure of the Olympic program. Members of the commission vote on adding or removing sports from the program; traditionally it took a simple major-

www

Olympic Programme Commission
www.olympic.org/olympic-programme-commission

ity of votes (50% plus 1) to add a sport and two-thirds of the votes (67%) to remove one. In July 2007 this voting procedure was changed so that a simple majority of votes is now required to add or remove sports from the Olympic program. The maximum number of sports to be offered is set at 28, with 25 being the purview of the IOC and up to three others that may be added by the host organizing committee. The Olympic Programme Commission makes recommendations to the IOC Executive Board and presents reports to the IOC Session.

Image

For more than a century, members of the Olympic Movement have been concerned with image. Significant effort has been put forth to ensure that the Olympic Games are perceived to be outside the realms of government interference, beyond partisanship and corruption, and a contribution to improving conditions in the world. Caring for the image of the Olympic Movement is in concert with other tenets of Olympism. The Olympics involve excellence; being and doing your best; demonstrating strong ethical and moral behavior; building up, never breaking down; and giving, as opposed to just taking. The Olympics are proposed as a festival of nations, with sporting competition as its mainstay, but also including cultural events and other ways of promoting world peace.

The IOC has taken great pains to maintain its image of excellence. Policy exists within the Olympic Charter illustrating an Olympic mandate far beyond a sporting competition. In building this Olympic image, the IOC has spoken out in favor of world peace; improved living conditions in poorer parts of the world; environmental renewal and care; cultural, ethnic, religious, and racial tolerance; economic growth and legacy for underdeveloped areas; and overall social responsibility for balancing resources between the haves and the have-nots in the world. The IOC wants the public to associate the Olympics with the image of a caring, contributing, concerned partner working toward a better world.

Some might argue the degree to which the IOC has succeeded in achieving these goals. Regardless, striving to create such an image has motivated the IOC to act in recent years. The corruption allegations and subsequent findings of the commission against members of the IOC Bid Selection Committee resulted in expelling members from the IOC. Increasing the number of active Olympic athletes elected to the IOC and changing policy relative to IOC vacancies and terms of office are also the results of outside criticism. In fact, the IOC had gained the reputation of being a closed shop, devoid of women and out-of-touch with the real world. Then IOC President Samaranch acted to increase the number of women on the committee (somewhat successfully) and to open the activities of the IOC by promoting financial transparency through public reports and by opening meetings to the press. Each of these actions reflect the IOC's commitment to promote the image of all things Olympic.

Politics at the Olympic Games

The originators of the Olympic Games sought to avert governmental interference by forming the IOC as a group independent of the funding requirements, politics, and power of a particular nation's government. In reality, however, it has been impossible to keep politics out of the Olympics. The IOC is a very political organization in which alliances are regularly formed to enact some vision or goal. Even more so, political involvement in the Olympic Games occurs as a result of the gains possible for a national government and its ruling ideology. The Olympic Games have a huge following of people around the world, and governments naturally try to exploit the Games for their own purpose. In this way, the Olympics provide an avenue to unite people, to develop a national consciousness, and to provide ammunition to suggest that "our ways" are better than "your ways." Governments have used sport to send political messages to another country by sending a team to compete prior to an Olympics; for example, when the U.S. table tennis team went to China in the early 1970s, it signaled a renewed interest in discussing foreign policy between the two nations. There are many other examples of political motives driving decisions associated with athletic competitions. However, none is more profound than a nation boycotting an Olympic Games.

In the context of the Olympics, *boycott* refers to a nation's (or nations') refusing to attend a particular Games to protest some action or policy. Several boycotts have taken place over the years: the U.S.-led boycott of the 1980 Moscow Olympics over the Soviet invasion of Afghanistan, and the subsequent retaliatory boycott of the Los Angeles Games by the Soviet Union and other Eastern Bloc nations in 1984; the African nations' boycott of the 1976 Montreal Olympics after the New Zealand rugby team toured apartheid South Africa; and the boycott of the 1956 Melbourne Olympics over the Soviet Union's invasion of Hungary and the United States' involvement in the Suez crisis (Schaffer & Smith, 2000). During these and other boycotts the Games went on without the athletes of the boycotting nations. Without a doubt, political statements were made, fewer athletes competed, and some individuals won medals they may not otherwise have won.

Debate regarding the usefulness of boycotts continues. Today, protesting at Olympic-related events offers great visibility and impact, given the speed and global nature of media coverage. For example, the whole world witnessed protests during the Olympic torch global relay prior to the 2008 Beijing Summer Olympic Games. Rights groups and citizens in countries within Europe and around the world (United States, Australia, and Canada) used these rallies to protest China's policies in Tibet, which many view as repressive and in violation of basic human rights. The protests caused political leaders such as the President of the European Union to reconsider their nations' involvement in the Games, and the notion of a boycott was discussed, particularly in regard to political leaders attending the Opening Ceremonies.

The political ramifications of the Olympic Games are most cerainly an issue for policy definition, whether the political issues are related to the internal workings of the IOC or external to the governments of the participating nations. Each group will set policies to manage their own interests and perspectives. Perhaps organizing committees and their sponsors engage in political maneuvering. Or perhaps all parties are worried about the dangers of terrorist violence, the embarrassment of positive tests for performance-enhancing drugs, legal injunctions over team membership, or the authority of ISFs. One thing is for sure: Policies to deal with issues of power and politics in the Olympics will be necessary into the foreseeable future. As Senn (1999) put it, "Those who refuse to recognize the politics of the Games put themselves at the mercy of the people and organizations who actively participate in the political competition" (p. 296).

SUMMARY

The Olympic Games are the pinnacle of world sporting events. Even professional athletes dream of winning an Olympic Gold Medal. Participating at an Olympics is described as an experience of a lifetime, and athletic careers are routinely described in terms of Olympic Medals won and number of Games attended.

All things Olympic are governed by the IOC, an elected group of Olympic enthusiasts charged with overseeing Olympic events and promoting the Olympic Charter. Policies of the Olympic Charter are developed by IOC committees and approved by the Session of the IOC, which meets at least once per year.

caseSTUDY

OLYMPIC SPORTS

You are lucky enough to be involved with putting together the Olympic bid for the Summer Olympic Games in 2024. You have a choice of the following cities: Boston, Central Florida, Dallas, Edmonton, Los Angeles, Seattle, St. Louis, Windsor, and Winnipeg.

For your choice of cities, you have been asked to help assemble the bid documents for 6 of the 18 required IOC bid themes.

1. Choose a city.
2. Choose any 6 of the 18 themes presented in Exhibit 10.11 that are required components of the Olympic bid.
3. For your choice of city, explain as thoroughly as possible what information will go into the sections you are writing. You may need to do some Internet research to learn more about the specific city.
4. What procedures might you implement to ensure that all procedures and actions detailed in the bid document meet the highest legal and ethical standards?

CHAPTER questions

1. Compile a chart that depicts the levels of all organizations involved in delivering Olympic sport. Because the IOC has supreme authority, put it at the top of the chart and work down to state or provincial sport organizations.
2. Does television have a positive or negative effect on the Olympic Games? Make a list of both positive and negative effects before making your final decision.
3. How do sports become Olympic events? Review the list of current Olympic sports. Are they popular and interesting? Are there any sports that might be replaced? If so, which ones, and what would replace them? What rationale would you provide the IOC for adding or dropping a sport?
4. Consider the costs of hosting an Olympic Games. Using a search engine such as Google Research, compare the predicted costs of hosting identified in London's 2012 bid to actual costs involved in hosting. If there was a change in predicted versus actual costs, where did it come from?

REFERENCES

Ancient Olympics, The. (2004). Frequently asked questions about the ancient Olympic Games. Retrieved from www.perseus.tufts.edu/edu/Olympics/faq11.html.

COC. (2006). Annual Report 2005. Retrieved from www.olympic.ca/EN/organization/publications/publications/.shtml

COC. (2007). Role of COC. Retrieved from www.olympic.ca/EN/organization/aboutus/.shtml

COC. (2011). Canadian Olympic Committee governance structure. Retrieved from www.olympic.ca/EN/organization/governance/index.shtml

COC. (2012). Canadian Olympic Committee annual report 2010. Retrieved from www.olympic.ca/wp-content/uploads/2012/07/COC-2010-AR-110420-FINAL.pdf

COC. (2013). Canadian Olympic Committee governance. Retrieved from www.olympic.ca/canadian-olympic-committee/governance

de Coubertin, P. (2000). *Olympism: Selected writings.* Ed., Norbert Muller. Lausanne: IOC.

1896 Athens, Greece. (2007). The Olympic Games. Retrieved from www. cartage.org.lb/en/themes/Sports/olympicgames/1896/athens.htm.

Howell, M. L., & Howell, R. (1988). Physical activities and sport in early societies. In E. F. Zeigler (Ed.), *History of physical education and sport* (pp. 1–56). Champaign, IL: Stipes.

IOC. (2002). Evolution of its structure. Retrieved from www.olympic.org/uk/organisation/ioc/organisation/index_uk.asp

IOC. (2007a). Athens 1896. Retrieved from www.olympic.org/uk/games/past/index_uk.asp?OLGT=1&OLGY=1896

IOC. (2007b). Organization. Retrieved from www.olympic.org/uk/organization/index_uk.asp.

IOC. (2007c). Organization. Retrieved from www.olympic.org/uk/organization/missions/ charter_uk.asp.

IOC. (2007d). Choice of the host city. Retrieved from www.olympic.org/uk/organization/missions/cities_uk.asp.

IOC. (2012a). IOC Broadcasting. Retrieved from http://www.olympic.org/Documents/IOC_Marketing/Broadcasting

IOC. (2012b). IOC Mission. Retrieved from htt://www.olympic.org/about-IOC-institution?tab=mission

IOC Marketing Fact File. (2010). Olympic marketing revenue generation. Retrieved from http://www.olympic.org/Documents/IOC_Marketing/IOC_Marketing_Fact_File_2010%20r.pdf

Korea Herald. (1986, May 24). In A. E. Senn (1999). *Power, politics, and the Olympic Games.* Champaign, IL: Human Kinetics.

New York City 2012 Summer Olympic Games Bid. (2003). Bid city profile and games sheet—New York, U.S.A. Retrieved from www.gamesbids.com/english/bids/usa.shtml

The Olympic Movement. (2007). Sports. Retrieved from www.olympic.org/uk/sports/index_uk.asp

Palmer, S. (2001). Executive says thrill of games trumps scandal. *Eugene Register-Guard.* Retrieved from www.warsawcenter.com/news_2001_0322.html

Schaffer, K., & Smith, S. (2000). *The Olympics at the millennium.* London: Rutgers Press.

Senn, A. E. (1999). *Power, politics, and the Olympic Games.* Champaign, IL: Human Kinetics.

Sleeman, R. (1992). What price Sydney 2000? *Inside Sport, 1*(10), 14–16, 19–20, 115.

Thoma, J. E., & Chalip, L. (1996). *Sport governance in the global community.* Morgantown, WV: Fitness Information Technology.

Torino 2006. (2003). XX Olympic Winter Games, 10–26 February, 2006: Mission. Retrieved June 23, 2003, from www.Torino2006.it/eng/toroc_ 1.html

Tyler, M., & Soar, P. (1980). *The history of the Olympics.* London: Marshall Cavendish.

USOC. (2002). United States Olympic Committee. Retrieved from www.usoc.org

USOC. (2003). Board of directors meeting. April 12–13, 2003. Retrieved from www.olympic-usa.org/about_us/document.htm

USOC. (2004). Olympic link directory. Retrieved from www.usoc.org/12181_ 36427.htm

USOC. (2005). 2005 Annual report. Retrieved from www.usoc.org/12699.htm.

USOC. (2006). USOC bylaws. Retrieved from www.usolympicteam.com/12699.htm

USOC. (2007). United States Olympic Committee. Retrieved from www.usoc.org.

USOC. (2010). Mission statement. Retrieved from www.teamusa.org/About-the-USOC.aspx

USOC. (2011). IOC presidents. Retrieved from www.history1900s.about.com/fadsfashion/a/ioupresidents.htm

USOC. (2012). Financials. Retrieved from http://assets.teamusa.org/assets/documents/attached_file/filename1/50638/2011_Bylaws_Approved_9.24.11.pdf

USOC Directory. (2013). Organization. Retrieved from www.teamusa.org/About-the-USOC/Organization.aspx

VANOC. (2006). VANOC business plan and games budget. Retrieved from www. vancouver2010.com/en/OrganizingCommittee/AboutOrganizing Committee/BusinessPlanGames Budget

VISA. (2007). VISA Olympic partnership. Retrieved from http://sponsorships.visa.com/olympic/corporate_sponsorship.jsp

Paralympic Sport

When we hear the word *athlete,* certain images come to mind. We envision people who are strong and fast, can throw or run great distances, shoot three pointers, or ski downhill at incredible speed. When we read about athletes running the 100 meters in just under 11 seconds, high jumping more than 6 feet (1.97 meters), or lifting 600 pounds (272 kilograms), we know they most certainly are elite athletes. All these *are* accomplishments of elite athletes—elite athletes with physical disabilities who competed in the Paralympic Games, an event that draws thousands of elite athletes with disabilities from more than 140 nations every four years and that enjoys millions of corporate sponsorship dollars and worldwide media coverage. Who are these athletes, and what are the Paralympic Games?

DEFINING DISABILITY SPORT

The term *disability sport* may bring to mind the image of a Special Olympian. However, that is not the only form of sport for individuals with disabilities. DePauw and Gavron (2005) define *disability sport* as "sport designed for or specifically practiced by athletes with disabilities" (p. 8). For the purposes of this chapter, the focus will be on highly competitive, international, elite-level disability sport, specifically, the Paralympic Games.

PARALYMPIC ATHLETES

The Paralympic Games showcase elite-level athletes with disabilities. Incorporating the same ideology as the Olympic Games in celebrating the accomplishments of elite international athletes, the Paralympic Games are scheduled approximately two weeks later than the Olympic Games in the same cities and venues, and are staged by the same organizing committee. When a host city is awarded the Olympic Games, the Paralympic Games are an obligatory part of the host city bid process.

The motto of the Paralympic Games is "Spirit in Motion." This motto represents the vision of the International Paralympic Committee (IPC), which is "to enable Paralympic athletes to achieve sporting excellence and excite the world." The sports on the official Paralympic Games Programme are presented in Exhibit 11.1. Not all disability types are eligible to compete in the Paralympic Games. The athletes who compete in the Paralympic Games have a range of disabilities, including visual impairments, cerebral palsy, amputations, spinal cord injuries, and on a very limited basis, athletes with intellectual disabilities. Note that athletes with hearing impairments do not compete in the Paralympic Games; they compete in separate World Games and other competitions for the deaf, including the Deaflympics. Athletes with cognitive disabilities such as Down syndrome also do not compete in the Paralympic Games. The Special Olympics were established to provide opportunities for people with cognitive and developmental disabilities. The mission of Special Olympics includes skill development and social interaction, not the development of international elite-level athletes.

Current sports on the official Paralympic Programme.

exhibit **11.1**

Paralympic Games Programme for Sochi 2014 Winter Games		
Alpine Skiing	Cross-Country Skiing	Wheelchair Curling
Biathlon	Ice Sledge Hockey	

Paralympic Games Programme for Rio de Janeiro 2016 Summer Games		
Archery	Judo	Table Tennis
Athletics	Para-Canoe	Volleyball (Sitting)
Boccia	Para-Triathalon	Wheelchair Basketball
Cycling	Powerlifting	Wheelchair Fencing
Equestrian	Rowing	Wheelchair Rugby
Football 5-a-Side	Sailing	Wheelchair Tennis
Football 7-a-Side	Shooting	
Goalball	Swimming	

HISTORY OF THE PARALYMPIC GAMES

S port for people with disabilities existed for many years before the founding of the Paralympic Games and began to grow after World War II, when sport was used to rehabilitate the many injured military and civilian persons. In 1944, Sir Ludwig Guttmann opened the Spinal Injuries Center at Stoke Mandeville Hospital in England and incorporated sport as an integral part of the rehabilitation process (IPC, n.d.b). On July 28, 1948, the first Stoke Mandeville Wheelchair Games were held. The date was significant because it corresponded to the Opening Ceremonies for the Summer Olympic Games in London that same day. Disability sport expanded beyond athletes who used wheelchairs, the International Sport Organization for the Disabled (ISOD) was formed in 1964. The ISOD brought together athletes with disabilities such as visual impairments, cerebral palsy, and amputees. Additional sport organizations for people with disabilities formed as well, such as the Cerebral Palsy International Sport and Recreation Association (CPISRA) and the International Blind Sports Association (IBSA), organized in 1978 and 1980, respectively. To help these and other sport organizations for athletes with disabilities coordinate their activities, the IPC was founded in 1989 in Düsseldorf, Germany. The IPC remains today the only multidisability international sport organization in the world recognized by the IOC (IPC, n.d.a).

The Summer Paralympic Games began with the 1952 Summer Games at Stoke Mandeville, the first international games for athletes with disabilities. The first Winter Paralympic Games were held in 1976 in Sweden. The first Paralympic Games under the direct management of the IPC were the Winter Paralympic Games in Lillehammer in 1994. Exhibit 11.2 lists the dates of the Paralympic Summer and Winter Games, the numbers of athletes and nations participating, and additional information. As the statistics show, the Paralympic Games are showing steady growth in the number of both athletes and nation members participating. The 2008 Paralympic Summer Games in Beijing, China, had 3,951 athletes from 146 nations, and 4,237 athletes from 164 countries competed at the London 2012 Paralympic Games.

---

exhibit **11.2**   Overview of Paralympic Games.

Summer Games Overview

Year	Location	Disabilities Included	Number of Countries	Number of Athletes	Shared Venue with Olympics	Highlights
2016	Rio, Brazil	Spinal injury Amputee Visual impairment Cerebral palsy Les Autres Intellectual disability	TBC	4,200		Para-Canoe and Para-Triathlon added as sports bringing total number to 22
2012	London, Great Britain	Spinal injury Amputee Visual impairment Cerebral palsy Les Autres Intellectual disability	160	4,200	Yes	After an absence of 12 years intellectually disabled athletes competed in Athletics, Swimming and Table Tennis
2008	China	Spinal injury Amputee Visual impairment Cerebral palsy Les Autres	146	3,951	Yes	Rowing added as sport Cumulated TV audience of 3.8 billion
2004	Athens, Greece	Spinal injury Amputee Visual impairment Cerebral palsy Les Autres	136	3,806	Yes	Football 5-a-side added Record media attendance

Continued.

exhibit   11.2

Year	Location	Disabilities Included	Number of Countries	Number of Athletes	Shared Venue with Olympics	Highlights
2000	Sydney, Australia	Spinal injury Amputee Visual impairment Cerebral palsy Les Autres Intellectual disability	122	3,843	Yes	Sailing and wheelchair rugby added Record ticket sales
1996	Atlanta, USA	Spinal injury Amputee Visual impairment Cerebral palsy Les Autres Intellectual disability	103	3,195	Yes	Equestrian added Track cycling added First worldwide corporate sponsorship
1992	Barcelona, Spain	Spinal injury Amputee Visual impairment Cerebral palsy Les Autres	82	3,021	Yes	Event benchmark in organizational excellence
1988	Seoul, Korea	Spinal injury Amputee Visual impairment Cerebral palsy Les Autres	61	3,013	Yes	Judo, wheelchair tennis added Cooperation between Olympic and Paralympic Organizing Committees
1984	Stoke Mandeville, UK, & New York, USA	Spinal injury Amputee Visual impairment Cerebral palsy Les Autres	41 (UK) 45 (USA)	1,100 (UK) 1,800 (USA)	No	Football 7-a-side and Boccia added Road cycling added Demonstration event at Olympic Games in L.A.: Wheelchair racing
1980	Arnhem, Netherlands	Spinal injury Amputee Visual impairment Cerebral palsy Les Autres	42	1,973	No	Sitting volleyball added Events for athletes with cerebral palsy included
1976	Toronto, Canada	Spinal injury Amputee Visual impairment Les Autres	38	1,657	No	First use of specialized racing wheelchairs Volleyball (standing), goalball, and shooting added

(continued)

exhibit **11.2** Continued.

Year	Location	Disabilities Included	Number of Countries	Number of Athletes	Shared Venue with Olympics	Highlights
1972	Heidelberg, Germany	Spinal injury	43	984	No	First quadriplegic competition added; Demonstration events for athletes with a visual impairment
1968	Tel Aviv, Israel	Spinal injury	29	750	No	Lawn bowling added
1964	Tokyo, Japan	Spinal injury	21	357	Yes	Weightlifting added
1960	Rome, Italy	Spinal injury	23	400	Yes	First games for athletes with a disability held in same venue as Olympic games
1952	Stoke Mandeville, UK	Spinal injury	2	130	No	First international games for athletes with a disability

Winter Games Overview

Year	Location	Disabilities Included	Number of Countries	Number of Athletes	Shared Venue with Olympics	Highlights
2018	Pyeong Chang, Korea	Spinal injury, Amputee, Visual impairment, Cerebral palsy, Les Autres				
2014	Sochi, Russia	Spinal injury, Amputee, Visual impairment, Cerebral palsy, Les Autres				
2010	Vancouver, Canada	Spinal injury, Amputee, Visual impairment, Cerebral palsy, Les Autres	44	502	Yes	Record high Winter Paralympic Games ticket sales
2006	Torino, Italy	Spinal injury, Amputee, Visual impairment, Cerebral palsy, Les Autres	39	477	Yes	Wheelchair curling added

Continued.

exhibit **11.2**

Year	Location	Disabilities Included	Number of Countries	Number of Athletes	Shared Venue with Olympics	Highlights
2002	Salt Lake City, USA	Spinal injury Amputee Visual impairment Cerebral palsy Les Autres	36	416	Yes	Number of tickets on sale had to be augmented due to high demand
1998	Nagano, Japan	Spinal injury Amputee Visual impairment Cerebral palsy Les Autres	32	571	Yes	Demonstrated rising media and public interest in Paralympic winter sport
1994	Lillehammer, Norway	Spinal injury Amputee Visual impairment Cerebral palsy Les Autres	31	492	Yes	Ice sledge hockey added
1992	Tignes-Albertville, France	Spinal injury Amputee Visual impairment Cerebral palsy Les Autres	24	475	Yes	Biathlon added Demonstration events: Alpine and cross-country skiing for athletes with an intellectual disability
1988	Innsbruck, Austria	Spinal injury Amputee Visual impairment Cerebral palsy Les Autres	22	397	No	Sit-ski events introduced in the sports of Alpine and Nordic skiing
1984	Innsbruck, Austria	Spinal injury Amputee Visual impairment Cerebral palsy Les Autres	21	457	No	Demonstration event at Olympics in Sarajevo: Giant slalom
1980	Geilo, Norway	Spinal injury Amputee Visual impairment Cerebral palsy Les Autres	18	350	No	Demonstration event: Downhill sledge racing
1976	Örnsköldsvik, Sweden	Visual impairment Amputee	17	250+	No	Demonstration event: Sledge racing

Source: IPC (n.d.f).

GOVERNANCE

Just as with the Olympic Movement, the Paralympic Movement and the Paralympic Games fit into a complex set of governance structures. A number of governing bodies are involved with Paralympic Sport, including the IPC, National Paralympic Committees (NPCs), and international federations (IFs).

International Paralympic Committee (IPC)

www
International Paralympic
Committee
www.paralympic.org

The IPC, the supreme authority of the Paralympic Movement, is the international representative organization of elite sports for athletes with disabilities. The IPC organizes, supervises, and coordinates the Paralympic Games and other multidisability competitions at the elite sports level, of which the most important are the regional and world championships.

VISION/MISSION. The IPC has a vision statement and a mission statement. (See Exhibits 11.3 and 11.4.) The vision statement for the IPC contains an overall picture of IPC philosophy (IPC, n.d.a). Its mission statement is more detailed, including statements that could also be seen as goals for the organization. This mission statement is longer than mission statements for some sport organizations, but it provides a detailed picture of what the IPC does and strives for.

www
CPISRA
www.cpisra.org

IBSA
www.ibsa.es

INAS-FID
www.inas.org/

IWAS
www.iwasf.com/iwasf/

MEMBERSHIP. The members of the IPC include the International Organizations of Sport for the Disabled (IOSDs), the NPCs, the IPSFs, and regional/continental Paralympic organizations.

The IOSD organizations are as follows:

CPISRA   Cerebral Palsy International Sport and Recreation Association

IBSA   International Blind Sport Federation

INAS-FID   International Association for Sport for Para-Athletes with an Intellectual Disability

IWAS   International Wheelchair and Amputee Sports Federation

www
Asian Paralympic Committee
www.asianparalympic.org

European Paralympic
Committee
www.europaralympic.org

Oceania Paralympic Committee
www.oceaniaparalympic.org/

In addition to these international sport organizations, NPCs or National Contact Agencies from different nations are also full members of the IPC. Currently, approximately 170 NPCs are members of the IPC. Four regional organizations (the African Paralympic Committee, the African Sports Confederation for the Disabled [ASCOD], the European Paralympic Committee [EPC], and the Oceania Paralympic Committee) and two regional committees—the Americas Paralympic Committee and the Asian Paralympic Committee—are also members. These full members have voting rights at the IPC's General Assembly. In addition to the above-mentioned full members,

Vision statement of the IPC.

exhibit **11.3**

The Vision	To Enable Paralympic Athletes to Achieve Sporting Excellence and Inspire and Excite the World.
Enable	Creating conditions for athlete empowerment
Paralympic Athletes	Sporting excellence is the goal of a sports centered organization
Inspire & Excite	Touch the heart of all people for a more equitable society

Source: IPC (n.d.a).

Mission statement of the IPC.

exhibit **11.4**

- To guarantee and supervise the organization of successful Paralympic Games
- To ensure the growth and strength of the Paralympic Movement through the development of National Paralympic Committees in all countries and the support to the activities of all IPC member organizations
- To promote and contribute to the development of sport opportunities and competitions, from initiation to elite level, for Paralympic athletes as the foundation of elite Paralympic sport
- To develop opportunities for female athletes and athletes with a severe disability in sport at all levels and in all structures
- To support and encourage educational, cultural, research and scientific activities that contribute to the development and promotion of the Paralympic Movement
- To seek the continuous global promotion and media coverage of the Paralympic Movement, its vision of inspiration and excitement through sport, its ideals and activities
- To promote the self-governance of each Paralympic sport either as an integral part of the international sport movement for able-bodied athletes, or as an independent sport organization, whilst at all times safeguarding and preserving its own identity
- To ensure that in sport practiced within the Paralympic Movement the spirit of fair play prevails, violence is banned, the health risk of the athletes is managed and fundamental ethical principles are upheld
- To contribute to the creation of a drug-free sport environment for all Paralympic athletes in conjunction with the World Anti-Doping Agency (WADA)
- To promote Paralympic sport without discrimination for political, religious, economic, disability, gender, sexual orientation, or race reasons
- To ensure the means necessary to support the future growth of the Paralympic Movement

Source: IPC (2011b).

the IPSFs have voting and speaking rights at the IPC's General Assembly. Besides being the supreme authority for the supervision and organization of the Paralympic Games, the IPC also fulfills an important role as the international federation for several sports.

FINANCIALS. Approximately 50 percent of IPC funding comes from the Paralympic Games revenues (IPC, n.d.g). "The IPC grants all the related marketing rights to the local Games Organizing Committees in exchange for a fixed rights fee" (IPC, n.d.g, para. 1). Income used by organizing committees to operate the Games themselves is derived from a combination of government support, Olympic support, and sponsorship deals. Currently, the IPC has four worldwide partners: VISA, Otto Bock, Atos Origin, and Samsung. In addition, Allianz SE is an international sponsor (IPC, n.d.e). Other companies sign on to be sponsors of a specific Games, for example, British Airways and Sainsbury's during the 2012 Summer Games in London.

ORGANIZATIONAL STRUCTURE. The structure of the IPC consists of the General Assembly, the Governing Board, Management Team, and a number of Standing Committees. Exhibit 11.5 illustrates the general structure of the IPC.

The General Assembly is the governance body for the IPC and its highest authority. The General Assembly is the biannual assembly of the IPC members and decides on any matters relevant to the IPC (IPC, n.d.c). Members of the General Assembly meet at least once every two years to discuss and vote on policy matters of concern to the Paralympic Games. At the General Assembly, each full member has one vote. The 14-person Governing Board members include a President, Vice President, 10 Members-at-Large, one Athlete Representative and one CEO ex-officio member.

The Governing Board is primarily responsible for the implementation of policies and directions set by the General Assembly. Additionally, the Governing Board provides recommendations on membership to the General Assembly, including motions received from members. It is also responsible for approving budgets and auditing accounts, IPC Rules and Regulations, membership of IPC Committees and the Paralympic Games (IPC, n.d.c).

The IPC Management Team "consists of the professional staff working under the direction of the CEO" (IPC, n.d.c, para. 2). These are the paid sport managers who work at IPC Headquarters. The headquarters for the IPC has been located in Bonn, Germany, since 1999. Approximately 50 paid Executive Staff members work at the headquarters, including the COO, who oversees numerous departments including Sports; Development; Administration, Finances, Human Resources, and IT; Fundraising and Sponsorship; Marketing and Commercials; Media and Communications; Medical and Scientific; Membership Relations and Services; and Paralympic Games (IPC, n.d.c).

General structure of the IPC.

exhibit **11.5**

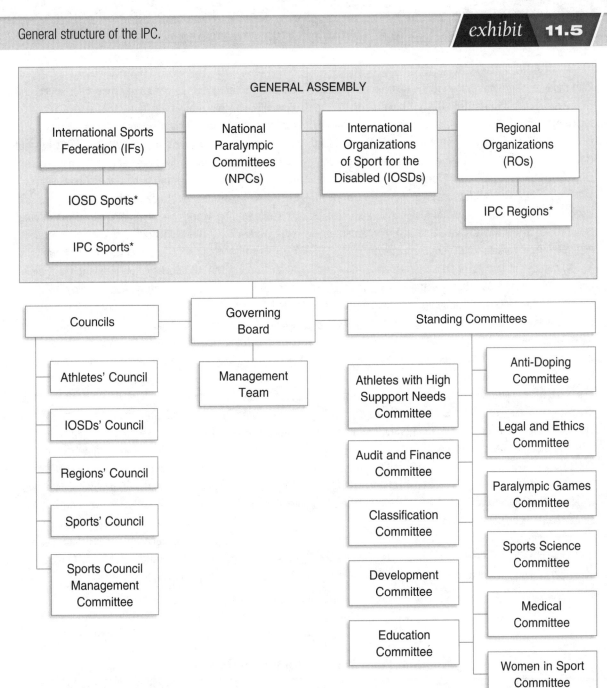

GENERAL ASSEMBLY

International Sports Federation (IFs)

National Paralympic Committees (NPCs)

International Organizations of Sport for the Disabled (IOSDs)

Regional Organizations (ROs)

IOSD Sports*

IPC Sports*

IPC Regions*

Councils

Governing Board

Standing Committees

Athletes' Council

Management Team

Athletes with High Suppport Needs Committee

Anti-Doping Committee

IOSDs' Council

Audit and Finance Committee

Legal and Ethics Committee

Regions' Council

Classification Committee

Paralympic Games Committee

Sports' Council

Sports Science Committee

Development Committee

Sports Council Management Committee

Medical Committee

Education Committee

Women in Sport Committee

*Speaking and Voting Rights

Source: IPC (n.d.a).

portraits+perspectives

DAVID LEGG, *President/Chairperson of the Board*

Canadian Paralympic Committee

I am the President/Chairperson of the Board for the Canadian Paralympic Committee (CPC). I have been on the board of directors since 1999. In addition, I represent the CPC on the Toronto 2015 Pan Parapan American Games Governing Board. Finally, I am a member of the Leadership Team for Canadian Sport for Life, which is responsible for long-term athlete development. My area of speciality is with athletes with a disability. I also have a background in the sport of wheelchair rugby, as an official and former assistant national team coach.

A number of important policy issues face the Paralympic Movement today, but one that comes to mind is brand infringement. The Paralympic brand has to date been relatively weak, and in the past any recognition or association was perceived as positive. Today, perhaps as a result of the Games being held in Canada in 2010 and the explosion of interest from 2012, this is no longer the case. We have a stronger brand and need to protect it in the same manner and with the same vigor as the Olympic brand. We also need to be wary of brand infringement from the Olympic brand itself. I believe the Olympic Movement now recognizes the value and benefit of the Paralympic brand, and future associations and cooperation need to be established from positions of strength versus simply being happy to get attention.

One ongoing governance issue I deal with relates to responsibilities for the developing athlete. The history and evolution of sport for persons with disabilities are complex and interwoven, incorporating medicine, sport, and disability-specific groups. Ensuring that a person with a disability has opportunities to enter the sport system is crucial for our movement and to date this effort has not been consistently managed or led across Canada in every sport. I am optimistic we are getting there, however.

Any organizational structure choice offers pros and cons. In an ideal world, I believe governance within what was traditionally the able-bodied (AB) sport system is best. But that would be in an ideal world, which we rarely encounter. The AB sport system needs to want inclusion and have the capacity to manage it; even then, we need the persistence of others to constantly push the evolution. I sometimes wonder if we followed the wrong path regarding inclusion in the sport system, just as Block (1999) questioned the manner in which children with disabilities were included in the school system.

As the brand and movement become more established, both opportunities and challenges arise. There might be a willingness to consider "going it alone," breaking away from what some have argued is a natural evolution toward the able-bodied system. The growth of our brand could also result in the AB system seeing value (economically, socially, and so on) in working together more closely. I feel the latter course is more likely, and that within the next two decades we will see a greater merging of the Olympic and Paralympic Movements, Games, and sport development systems.

Block, M.E. (1999). Did we jump on the wrong bandwagon? Making general physical education placement work. *Palaestra*, 15(3).

National Paralympic Committees (NPCs)

Every nation participating in the Paralympic Games must have an NPC or, if an NPC has not yet been established, a National Contact Agency. In terms of sport governance, "NPCs undertake the coordination within the respective country or territory and are responsible for relations and communications with the IPC" (IPC, 2011b, Rights and Obligations of IPC Members section).

In the United States, the USOC acts as the NPC and is constitutionally obligated to do so by the Amateur Sports Act. This is very unusual, as most nations have a separate NPC. For example, in Canada the Canadian Paralympic Committee is responsible for the Paralympic Movement, Australia has the Australian Paralympic Committee, and Greece has the Hellenic Paralympic Committee. In 2002, the USOC established U.S. Paralympics, a division of the USOC, to manage Paralympic sport. The mission statement of U.S. Paralympics reads as follows: "U.S. Paralympics, a division of the U.S. Olympic Committee, is dedicated to becoming the world leader in the Paralympic sports movement, and promoting excellence in the lives of persons with physical disabilities" (USOC, 2012a, para. 1).

U.S. Paralympics and the appropriate national governing body (NGB) help prepare and select the athletes who will represent the United States at the Paralympic Games. It also works with local organizations to promote sport programs for children who have disabilities, spreading Olympic ideals to the next generation (USOC, 2012a).

International Federations

The IPC officially recognizes 13 international federations as the sole representatives of Paralympic Sports. IFs are responsible for technical jurisdiction and guidance over the competition and training venues of their respective sports during the Paralympic Games. They have voting and speaking rights at the IPC General Assembly. In addition, as of 2010, the IPC itself acts as the international federation for nine sports.

CURRENT POLICY AREAS

Like any major international sport entity, the Paralympic Movement faces a wide variety of issues for which it must formulate policies. Because of the Movement's global nature, many of these policy issues are complex and many have strong ethical components (Hums, 2006). To illustrate some of these issues, the six strategic goals presented in Exhibit 11.6 from the 2011–2014 IPC Strategic Plan will serve as a starting point for this section (IPC, 2010). This Strategic Plan illustrates how a sport governing body identifies and addresses important issues. Selected strategic priorities for each of the six goals clearly outline the most important current issues facing the Paralympic Movement today.

Although some of these goals represent issues mainly directed inward to the organization, forces external to the IPC also raise important questions for sport managers in the Paralympic Movement. Many of these

WWW

Canadian Paralympic Committee
www.paralympic.ca

Australian Paralympic Committee
www.paralympic.org.au

Hellenic Paralympic Committee
www.paralympic.org/npc/greece

U.S. Paralympics
www.usparalympics.com

exhibit **11.6** | Strategic Goals of the IPC.

STRATEGIC GOAL #1: Paralympic Games: Ensure a Successful Paralympic Games for All Participants. Included in this goal are several strategic priorities:

- Extending the IPC's contractual relationship with the IOC.
- Maximizing media coverage before, during, and after the Paralympic Games.
- Defining legacy benchmarks of the Games.
- Offering an attractive program for elite athletes with disabilities based on solid qualification standards and classification systems.

STRATEGIC GOAL #2: Athlete Development: Promote Opportunities to Engage and Grow Paralympic Sport. To do this, the IPC strives to:

- Develop leadership, management, and governances skills in NPC and IF employees and volunteers.
- Develop pathway programs to boost athlete participation from the grassroots to the elite levels.
- Ensure that sports are practiced in ways that promote safety, fair play, and sound ethics.

STRATEGIC GOAL #3: Paralympic Brand: Build Greater Understanding and Use of the Paralympic Brand.

- Develop clear strategies, best practices, and policies for using the Paralympic brand at sport events.
- Make greater use of athlete profiles and their roles as ambassadors.
- Examine commonalities and distinctions from the Olympic brand.

STRATEGIC GOAL #4: Funding. Ensure Appropriate Funding and Identify Revenue Opportunities. In these difficult economic times, creating a sufficient revenue stream is of the essence.

- Ensure the market value of the Paralympic brand is understood.
- Identify and develop marketable properties.
- Develop business plans with clear revenue streams from a variety of sources.
- Reduce constraints on the IPC's ability to grow revenues associated with the Paralympic Games.

Continued.

exhibit **11.6**

STRATEGIC GOAL #5: Organizational Capability: Enhance Efficient Structures to Increase the Ability to Deliver. This strategic goal relates particularly to governance.

■ Maintain and develop organizational, legal, and financial frameworks and procedures for the IPC.

■ Define and maintain the appropriate levels of volunteers and staff in order to deliver corporate and strategic plans.

■ Further develop adequate management systems, tools, and content.

STRATEGIC GOAL #6: Strategic Partnerships: Leverage Partnerships to Build Synergies and Broaden the Reach. Today's global marketplace is all about building effective partnerships.

■ Actively seek to develop new partnerships that can grow and stabilize the IPC's funding and global recognition.

■ Strengthen the relationship and understanding with the IOC for a deeper sporting partnership.

■ Encourage and assist the membership to actively deepen and manage partnerships.

■ Further develop partnerships throughout a diverse group of organizations.

Source: IPC (2010).

result in ethical dilemmas as well (Hums, 2006, 2007). One of these external forces is attitudes toward people with disabilities. As the IPC attempts to develop more competitions for athletes with significant disabilities, some of those in the media or sponsors may not consider these competitors to be athletes, making it difficult for the IPC to be more inclusive. Another external factor is the economy. Companies with limited sponsorship budgets may decide that sponsoring athletes with disabilities is not essential to their business plans. Thus, the IPC may have fewer resources and will need to make decisions on how to distribute its limited resources fairly.

Changing Technologies

Advances in technology have an impact on sport every day, whether through introduction of a new golf club, lighter football shoes, or improved athletic turf. The impact of technology is felt deeply in the Paralympic Games, as prosthetics and wheelchairs become lighter and stronger and athletes become faster. Oscar Pistorius, a double-amputee runner from South Africa, rose to international recognition in his pursuit of qualifying for the Olympic Games, rather than the Paralympic Games, as a sprinter. Ultimately, he was chosen to represent Team South Africa in both the individual 400m and also the 4x400m relay team, making him the first amputee Olympic track and field athlete. His quest was not without controversy, however; some people questioned whether or not his prosthetic devices gave him an unfair advantage, and scientists weighed in with studies supporting both sides. In an interesting twist, when defeated in the 2012 Paralympic Games by sprinter Alan Fonteles Cardosa Oliveira from Brazil in the 200m, Pistorius himself claimed to have been at a disadvantage because of the length of the blades used by his competitor, although he later retracted his comments. Although in early 2013 Pistorius's legal troubles garnered negative publicity for him, his presence on the Olympic and Paralympic stages did bring needed attention to sport for individuals with disabilities.

How technology affects sport presents larger questions for sport managers. Just because new equipment can be manufactured that improves performance, does that mean the equipment should be allowed in competition? For example, just because a company can manufacture a golf ball that can fly 500 meters does not necessarily mean golf governing bodies must sanction the ball for use in competition. In making such decisions, sport governing bodies need to assess three factors: (1) safety, (2) ability of people to access or acquire the equipment, and (3) fairness. First and foremost, sport equipment must be safe for the athletes using the equipment and for the other athletes competing in the same game or event. Second, governing bodies must assess whether the cost of the new equipment is excessive, thereby eliminating the possibility for athletes, particularly those from developing countries, to acquire it. Finally, there is the basic question of fairness. Does using certain equipment provide one athlete an unfair advantage over the competition?

Sport and Human Rights

The United Nations General Assembly recently adopted the Treaty on the Rights of Persons with Disabilities. Article 30.5 of this Treaty pertains to sport and physical activity. In addition, in 2004 the International Paralympic Committee Governing Board approved a position statement on sport and human rights (see Exhibit 11.7). The notion of sport and human rights extends beyond the competition of the Paralympic Games:

> Not everyone can qualify for the Paralympic Games, but people with disabilities can still be part of the Paralympic Movement at the grass roots level. We need to inform people the Movement is broader than the 10-day competition

IPC Position Statement on Human Rights.

exhibit **11.7**

1. The Paralympic Vision of IPC is "To Enable Paralympic Athletes to Achieve Sporting Excellence and Inspire and Excite the World."

2. The IPC believes all individuals should enjoy equal access and opportunities for leisure, recreation and sporting activities, and such rights be granted and guarded by the legal and administrative systems of the responsible governments and communities.

3. The IPC firmly believes in the unlimited athletic potential of persons with a disability, and thereby embraces the sporting achievements of Paralympic athletes. Equal opportunities for sporting development, participation, training, and recognition of achievement should be provided for persons with disabilities in all schools, sports clubs and venues, sports organizations and communities.

4. The IPC believes in sport as a vehicle to promote peace, which will result in the preservation of human dignity and equality for all.

The IPC shall promote the above philosophy and actualize its policy through the Paralympic Games and all other sporting activities, and through its Membership and work with countries, regions, sports, and groups representing persons with disability.

Source: IPC (2011b).

we call the Paralympic Games. Any person with a disability should be able to be a part of the Paralympic Movement. The overall Paralympic Movement is more about sport for all, similar to the notion of Olympism. (Hums, 2007)

As of 2013, 127 countries had ratified the UN Convention. Now the question is how these countries will blend the Convention into their laws regarding people with disabilities (United Nations, n.d.). Increasingly, scholars, activists, and sport management professionals are including the notion of sport and human rights into their programs of action.

Integration of Athletes with Disabilities into Able-Bodied Sport

This complex policy area is one in which the solutions are evolving differently in different parts of the world. The extent to which athletes with disabilities have been integrated into able-bodied sport can be measured by the following organizational components: (1) governance, (2) media and information distribution, (3) management, (4) funding and sponsorship, (5) awareness and education, (6) events and programs, (7) awards and recognition, (8) philosophy, and (9) advocacy (Hums, Legg, & Wolff, 2003; Hums, Moorman, & Wolff, 2009; Wolff, 2000). Each of these components can be examined as presented in Exhibit 11.8.

exhibit   **11.8**   Nine organizational component models for analyzing the integration of athletes with disabilities.

1. *Governance:* Examine how organizational policies and procedures deal with athletes with disabilities.
2. *Media and information:* Look at representation of athletes with disabilities in organizational publications or media guides.
3. *Management:* Examine the number of persons with disabilities working in management positions or sitting on governing boards.
4. *Funding and sponsorship:* Determine from the budget how much money raised by the organization is going to support athletes with disabilities.
5. *Awareness and education:* Consider how informed and knowledgeable people within the organization are about disability sport.
6. *Events and programs:* Determine the number of competitive opportunities the organization provides for athletes with disabilities.
7. *Awards and recognitions:* Evaluate how the organization publicly recognizes the accomplishments of its athletes with disabilities.
8. *Philosophy:* Review the organization's mission statement and determine how athletes with disabilities are reflected in it.
9. *Advocacy:* Determine whether a sport organization is actively promoting sport for people with disabilities via special programming.

How can these components relate to policy development within a sport organization? For media and information distribution, sport organizations can make sure athletes with disabilities are presented on a consistent basis in printed materials or press releases. Under management, sport organizations could establish hiring procedures creating opportunities for people with disabilities to be represented in the pool of candidates for open management positions. Under events and programs, sport organizations could establish participation categories for athletes with disabilities, just as there are categories of participation for men and women. For funding, sport organizations could establish funding opportunities specifically for athletes with disabilities so when organizational representatives meet with potential donors, disability sport is part of the conversation. These examples show how criteria for inclusion can influence organizational policy making, and they also provide a solid framework for assessing the status of athletes and people with disabilities within sport organizations.

Organizations that embrace diversity are acting as socially responsible partners within society. Including athletes with disabilities into the management structure of sport organizations increases the size of the networks involved and allows for more voices at the table.

The Wounded Warriors

Given the reality of war and conflict around the world, a growing number of wounded soldiers and civilians are seeking ways to reclaim their lives as best they can. One way people feel more fully alive after having been injured is through sport and physical activity. One program that supports wounded servicemen and servicewomen is the U.S. Olympic Committee Paralympic Military & Veteran Programs. The programs "provide post-rehabilitation support and mentoring to American servicemen and women who've sustained physical injuries such as traumatic brain injury, spinal cord injury, amputation, visual impairment/blindness and stroke. Veterans are introduced to adaptive sport techniques and opportunities through clinics and camps and are also connected with ongoing Paralympic sport programs in their hometowns" (USOC, 2012c, para. 1).

At the 2012 London Paralympic Games, Team USA featured 20 military athletes as U.S. Paralympic Team members (USOC, 2012c). It is interesting to see how the Paralympic Movement has come full circle. The first Stoke-Mandeville games were held to help wounded World War II veterans, and today we see the benefits of sport for wounded veterans from the wars and occupations in Iraq and Afghanistan. The spirit of those first games lives on today.

WWW

U.S. Olympic Committee (USOC) Paralympic Military & Veteran Programs
www.teamusa.org/
US-Paralympics/Military.aspx

SUMMARY

The Paralympic Games motto is "Spirit in Motion." The Games are an ever-growing, international, multidisability, multisport competition. Attracting thousands of athletes from numerous nations, the Games showcase the best elite athletes with disabilities. As a sport property, the Games are gaining the interest of corporations eager to connect with millions of consumers around the world. The governing structure of the Paralympic Games parallels that of the Olympic Games in many ways; both are large multisport international events. Just as women and racial and ethnic minorities have contributed to diversifying the sport industry, so too are people with disabilities making an impact. This large part of the sport industry is often overlooked in spite of its size and importance, and sport managers are advised to keep an eye on the growth and development in this area.

The Paralympic Games, as a growing competition, must deal with evolving policy issues and refocused strategic goals. The question of inclusion of athletes with disabilities into able-bodied sport will continue to be an ongoing debate, and Oscar Pistorius's Olympic Games debut brought this discussion to the forefront. As the Games grow, pressure will increase to maximize corporate sponsorship opportunities. It is an exciting time for the Paralympic Games, given their future growth potential.

caseSTUDY

SPORT FOR INDIVIDUALS WITH DISABILITIES

You are working with USA Hockey, the NGB for ice hockey in the United States. Recently, the USOC has asked you to consider the inclusion of the Paralympic men's ice sledge hockey team into USA Hockey. At the 2010 Vancouver Paralympic Games, the U.S. men's team brought home the Gold Medal. Playing before sold-out audiences in the Thunderbird Arena, the team's performance was widely applauded.

The ultimate goal after making this assessment is to integrate the activities of the Paralympic sledge hockey team within USA Hockey. What types of events or activities for the Paralympic sledge hockey team could USA Hockey sponsor? What types of publicity could it provide? In other words, what are some concrete strategies USA Hockey could use to help sledge hockey grow and prosper? How should you go about starting your task?

1. The best place to start is to use the nine-component model designed by Hums, Legg, and Wolff, 2003; Hums, Moorman, and Wolff, 2009; and Wolff (2000) and presented in Exhibit 11.8. Using each component, show how USA Hockey could incorporate the ice sledge hockey team into its organization.

2. Think of other sport organizations that could assist you in your tasks, such as the NHL, Hockey Canada, or any other sport organization that could potentially be working with hockey players with disabilities.

3. Some people would argue that athletes with disabilities should retain a separate identity from able-bodied athletes and compete only with other athletes with disabilities. Do you agree or disagree, and why? What benefits do disability sport and athletes with disabilities offer to able-bodied sport organizations?

CHAPTER questions

1. The IPC is considering expanding the Summer and Winter Games by one sport each. Which sports would you choose to add, and why?

2. The U.S. Paralympic men's soccer team is playing a series of exhibition matches against the Brazilian Paralympic men's soccer team. Your college or university has been awarded one of the matches. Develop a series of marketing strategies to promote the event. What community groups and sponsors will you want to involve?

3. What are some specific strategies the IPC could use to increase sport participation by athletes with disabilities who live in developing nations?

4. Oscar Pistorius, a double amputee runner from South Africa, was selected to compete at the 2012 London Olympic Games. What are your thoughts on Paralympic athletes competing in the Olympic Games? What effect could competing in the Olympic Games possibly have on the Paralympic Games, where they also compete? Where do you weigh in on the ongoing debate about the perceived "advantage" of a runner using prosthetic legs?

REFERENCES

DePauw, K., & Gavron, S. (2005). *Disability and sport* (2d ed.). Champaign, IL: Human Kinetics.

Hums, M. A. (2006, July). Ethical issues facing the Paralympic Movement. Paper presented at the International Olympic Academy Educator's Session, Olympia, Greece.

Hums, M. A. (2007). Ethical issues of changing classification systems. *Proceedings of the II Conferencia Internacional sobre Deporte Adaptado,* Malaga, Spain.

Hums, M. A., Legg, D., & Wolff, E. A. (2003, June). Examining opportunities for athletes with disabilities within the International Olympic Committee. Paper presented at the Annual Conference of the North American Society for Sport Management, Ithaca, NY.

Hums, M. A., Moorman, A. M., & Wolff, E. A. (2009). Emerging disability rights in sport: Sport as a human right for persons with disabilities and the 2006 Convention on the Rights of Persons with Disabilities. *Cambrian Law Review, 40,* 36–48.

IPC. (n.d.a). About us. Retrieved from http://www.paralympic.org/TheIPC/HWA/AboutUs

IPC. (n.d.b). History of the Movement. Retrieved from http://www.paralympic.org/TheIPC/HWA/HistoryoftheMovement

IPC. (n.d.c). IPC management team. Retrieved from http://www.paralympic.org/TheIPC/HWA/ManagementTeam

IPC. (n.d.d). IPC operational structure. Retrieved from http://www.paralympic.org/TheIPC/HWA/Operational Structure

IPC. (n.d.e). Partnerships. Retrieved from http://www.paralympic.org/TheIPC/HWD/Partnerships

IPC. (n.d.f). Summer Games overview. Retrieved from http://www.paralympic.org/ParalympicGames/SummerOverview

IPC. (n.d.g). The IPC: How we do it. Retrieved from http://www.paralympic.org/TheIPC/HWD/Funding

IPC. (2010). *International Paralympic Committee strategic plan 2011-2014.* Bonn, Germany: Author.

IPC. (2011a). Annual report 2010. Retrieved from http://www.paralympic.org/sites/default/files/document/120118144049350_IPC_AnnualReport_2010_final_web.pdf

IPC. (2011b). Handbook. Retrieved from http://www.paralympic.org/TheIPC/HWA/Handbook

United Nations. (n.d.). Latest developments. Retrieved from http://www.un.org/disabilities/latest.asp?id=169

USOC. (2012a). About us. Retrieved from http://usparalympics.org/resources/about-us

USOC. (2012b). Military. Retrieved from http://www.teamusa.org/US-Paralympics/Military.aspx

USOC. (2012c). Military athletes. Retrieved from http://www.teamusa.org/US-Paralympics/Military/Military-Athletes.aspx

Wolff, E. A. (2000). Inclusion and integration of soccer opportunities for players with disabilities within the United States Soccer Federation: Strategies and recommendations. Senior Honors Thesis, Brown University.

Professional Sport
Leagues in North America

Many people dream of hitting a home run in the bottom of the ninth inning to win the World Series, making the game-winning shot at the buzzer in the NBA Finals, throwing a touchdown pass to a wide-open receiver in the Super Bowl, or scoring the game-winning goal in the final game of the Stanley Cup. In North America we have grown up watching these exciting moments live on TV or seeing the highlights on ESPN, TSN, or online. All these spectacular plays belong to the most visible of all our sport industry segments—professional sport. Yet most of us have warning track power at best, shoot the occasional air ball, are unable to throw a true spiral, and cannot even skate backward. The odds against making it as a professional athlete in the Big Four—MLB, the NBA, the NFL, and the NHL—are astronomical, but these athletes' games would not happen and their exploits would remain relatively unknown if not for the sport managers, "The People Who Make the Games Happen" (Robinson, Hums, Crow, & Phillips, 2001). Without these individuals, there would be no season tickets for sale, no sponsorships available, no games broadcast on TV, no T-shirts emblazoned with logos, no team Facebook pages to like, and no new high-tech stadiums to visit.

Professional sport in North America takes many forms. We think first of the Big Four. Professional sport also takes place in other forms: tours or organized series, such as we see in professional golf with the PGA, LPGA, and the Champions Tour; or in motor sports with the Sprint Cup Series and the Camping World Truck Series, both from the National Association of Stock Car Auto Racing (NASCAR). These tours and series will be addressed in Chapter 13. Other professional leagues exist as well, including the WNBA and MLS, and we should not overlook the current popularity of UFC—Ultimate Fighting Championship. There are also minor league sports, particularly baseball, hockey, and basketball. Other sports also have professional competition, such as the Professional Bull Riders (PBR), Professional Bowlers Association (PBA), and Bass Anglers Sportsman Society (B.A.S.S.). (Some of you will want to know about professional wrestling, like World Wrestling Entertainment, but that is a topic for another class.)

How are these professional sports organized? Who are the people delivering the product to the public? Who are the power players and groups governing these sports? This chapter focuses on the governance structures of professional sport leagues in North America. The authors recognize there are a wide variety of these leagues in North America, but the main focus of the chapter is on the traditional Big Four. Chapter 13 addresses the governance of individual sports, and Chapter 14 explains the governance structures of professional sport outside of North America.

HISTORY AND DEVELOPMENT OF PROFESSIONAL SPORT

While a comprehensive history of the development of professional sport in North America is beyond the scope of this book, it is important to note key dates for certain events in the histories of each of the Big Four; for example, when the leagues took the form they have today. It is also important to note governance issues, such as when rival leagues formed to compete with existing leagues.

Major League Baseball (MLB)

MLB has the longest history of any professional sport in North America. The first professional club, the Cincinnati Red Stockings, was founded in 1869. The first professional sports league was baseball's National League, established in 1876, followed by the American League in 1901. The signing of the National Agreement between the National League and the American League in 1903 established much of the basic governance structure for MLB (Scully, 1989). Early on, the players formed a number of rival leagues such as the Players' League and the Federal League. Players objected to management's strict rules, such as the reserve system that "reserved" a player to his club and prohibited other clubs from negotiating with him, thus controlling players' salaries. While these leagues presented brief challenges to professional baseball's structure, all eventually failed (Abrams, 1998). MLB has not had a serious competitor since 1915 (Wise & Meyer, 1997). As you will discover, this long-standing unchallenged status is quite different from the history of the other Big Four leagues.

Major League Baseball
www.mlb.com

Currently, MLB has 30 teams. The American League has 15 (five in the East, five in the Central, and five in the West Division). The National League has 15 (five in the East, five in the Central, and five in the West Division).

National Football League (NFL)

The first professional football league, the American Professional Football Association, was established in 1920. It changed its name to the National Football League in 1922 (NFL, 2011). The NFL has experienced a long history of rival leagues, dating all the way back to its first inter-league battle in 1926 with the American Football League (AFL) (Quirk & Fort, 1992). Different forms of the AFL emerged and challenged the NFL, and finally in 1966 the leagues signed an agreement establishing an inter-league championship, and full amalgamation began in 1970. This event marked the first time that TV income played a critical role in the survival of a rival league, because the AFL had an existing TV contract that by 1969 gave each team approximately $900,000 (Quirk & Fort, 1992). Since then, the NFL has been challenged by the World Football League (WFL) in 1974–1975, the United States Football League (USFL) in 1983–1985, and the Xtreme Football League (XFL) in 2001.

National Football League
www.nfl.com

Currently, the NFL has 32 teams with two conferences, the American Football Conference (AFC) and the National Football Conference (NFC). The AFC North, AFC South, AFC East, and AFC West each have four teams, as do the NFC North, NFC South, NFC East, and NFC West.

National Basketball Association (NBA)

The first professional basketball league was established in 1924 as the American Basketball League. It disbanded in 1947, and another league emerged,

National Basketball Association
www.nba.com

the Basketball Association of America (BAA) (Quirk & Fort, 1992). At the same time a league called the National Basketball League (NBL) was also in existence. By 1949 the BAA absorbed the remaining NBL teams, and the organization renamed itself the National Basketball Association (NBA, 2012b). In 1967, the rival American Basketball Association formed, which had sufficient financial backing and talent to pose a threat to the NBA. In 1976, however, an agreement was reached between the two leagues, resulting in four franchises from the ABA—Denver, Indiana, New York, and San Antonio—moving to the NBA (Quirk & Fort, 1992). No rival leagues have attempted to compete with the NBA since then.

Currently, the NBA has 30 teams in two conferences. The Eastern Conference has five teams each in the Atlantic, Central, and Southeast Divisions. The Western Conference has five teams each in the Northwest, Pacific, and Southwest Divisions.

National Hockey League (NHL)

www

National Hockey League
www.nhl.com

The NHL started in 1917 with four teams located in Canada—Toronto, Ottawa, and two teams in Montreal. The league expanded to the United States in 1924 (Quirk & Fort, 1992). The NHL faced its biggest challenge from rival leagues from the World Hockey Association (WHA), a league that began in 1972. The WHA attempted to establish itself in medium-size Canadian markets without NHL franchises as well as in major United States cities in direct competition with existing NHL teams. After a seven-year war with the NHL, four remaining franchises—Winnipeg, Quebec, Edmonton, and Hartford—moved to the NHL in 1979 (Quirk & Fort, 1992).

Currently, the NHL has 30 teams in two conferences. The Eastern Conference has five teams each in the Northeast, Southeast, and Atlantic Divisions. The Western Conference has five teams each in the Central, Northwest, and Pacific Divisions.

GOVERNANCE

Each professional sport league has various levels of governance structures. The governance structures exist at the league level and the front-office level. The league level includes the league offices and the Office of the Commissioner, which constitute the structures on the management side of professional sport. The players' side is governed by Players Associations. Although the governance structures of the various leagues are not identical, they share common components. According to Gladden and Sutton (2011), these components are:

1. a league Commissioner
2. a Board of Governors or a committee composed of team owners

3. a central administrative unit that negotiates contracts and agreements on behalf of the league and assumes responsibility for scheduling, licensing, record keeping, financial management, discipline and fines, revenue sharing payments, marketing and promotional activities, developing and managing special events, and other functions such as coordinating publicity and advertising on behalf of the teams as a whole. (p. 125)

In addition to these components, governance issues are also dealt with at the team level. We will briefly examine each of these components.

Commissioner's Office

Major professional sports leagues are led by a Commissioner. The first Commissioner in professional sport was Kenesaw Mountain Landis, who became Major League Baseball Commissioner in 1921 (Abrams, 1998). As Commissioner, he ruled with an iron fist, basing his decisions on his interpretation of what was in the game's best interest. Although the original concept of a Commissioner's role was modeled on Landis, commissioners in different sports did not follow his lead completely (Masteralexis, 2012). Some would argue, however, that NFL Commissioner Roger Goodell "has acted with more power than any other Commissioner in U.S. sports history" (McCann, 2012).

The Office of the Commissioner is typically created and defined within a league's constitution and bylaws. According to Wise and Meyer (1997), the Commissioner's

> jurisdiction, authority, and duties are principally derived from the league constitution and/or by-laws adopted by the league members, or a special contract among them, although some powers flow from and/or are limited by collective bargaining agreements. . . . Under these documents they are granted a broad and often extensive array of powers over players, management, teams, owners, and others connected with their league or organization. (p. 150)

The Commissioner is in some ways an employee of the owners, because the owners have the power to hire and terminate him or her. However, in other ways the Commissioner is the owners' boss, having disciplinary power over them (Wong, 2002).

The role of the Commissioner in professional sport has evolved over time, but some of the basic powers of the office have remained throughout the years in different sports. In general, the discretionary powers of the Commissioner include (Yasser, McGurdy, Goplerud, & Weston, 2003):

- approval of player contracts
- resolution of disputes between players and clubs
- resolution of disputes between clubs
- resolution of disputes between players or clubs and the league

- disciplinary matters involving owners, clubs, players, and other personnel
- rule-making authority (p. 381)

Wise and Meyer (1997) further explain these powers by stating that "in addition to specific authority in particular situations, the constitution, by-laws or some other agreement generally contain a 'best interest in the league and/or sport' clause, the wording varying by sport, under which the Commissioner . . . has wide authority to act" (p. 150).

As Wharton (2011) notes, however, "the scope of the commissioner's power—as it has developed over the years—varies from sport to sport. The NHL does not have a 'best interests' clause as baseball does, a league spokesman said. The NFL and NBA do" (para. 12). The Professional Baseball Agreement (MLB, 2008) contains the following language:

> Sec. 2. The functions of the Commissioner shall include:
>
> (b) To investigate, either upon complaint or upon the Commissioner's own initiative, any act, transaction or practice charged, alleged or suspected to be not in the best interests of the national game of Baseball, with authority to summon persons and to order the production of documents, and, in case of refusal to appear or produce, to impose and enforce penalties as are hereinafter provided . . . (a) a reprimand; (b) deprivation of a Major League Club of representation in Major League Meetings; (c) suspension or removal of any owner, officer or employee of a Major League Club; (d) temporary or permanent ineligibility of a player; (e) a fine, not to exceed $2,000,000 in the case of a Major League Club, not to exceed $500,000 in the case of an owner, officer or employee, and in an amount consistent with the then-current Basic Agreement with the Major League Baseball Players Association, in the case of a player. (pp. 1–2)

Commissioners' actions often go unnoticed by the public, as they are handled internal to the league. However, some notable exceptions include MLB Commissioner Bart Giamatti's banning Pete Rose from baseball for life for gambling, NFL Commissioner Roger Goodell's actions against the New Orleans Saints in the "Bounty Gate" case, and NBA Commissioner David Stern's veto of a trade involving player Chris Paul and the Los Angeles Lakers. The Commissioner's Office exercises its regulatory power in professional sports leagues through decisions concerning fines, suspensions, and disciplinary actions. Some regulatory power also rests at the league level and with the Players Associations.

Board of Governors or Owners Committee

Despite a wide range of powers, the Commissioner is not necessarily the final decision maker in issues involving governance of professional sport leagues. Although the Commissioner is very influential, the owners still have the ultimate say in policy development (Robinson, Lizandra, & Vail, 2001b). We have all read about the annual league owners' meetings, where policies, rules, and business decisions concerning league operations are addressed. Each league has a committee structure made up of owners who ultimately make decisions on matters concerning franchise relocation, league expansion or contraction, playing facility issues, collective bargaining rules and rule changes, and revenue sharing (Sharp, Moorman, & Claussen, 2010). This committee also represents management in labor negotiations with players (Robinson et al., 2001b). At this level policy making often takes place, within the frameworks of each league's constitution and bylaws. In professional sport this level is where the power lies on the management side. As we will see shortly, the players' side has a governance structure as well. Although policy making occurs at this level, daily league operations occur at another league-wide governance level. Each league has a league office employing paid sport managers to handle these tasks.

Central Administrative Unit—League Office

As mentioned earlier, this governance level deals with league-wide operations. A unique aspect of professional sport, as opposed to other businesses, is that the teams must simultaneously compete and cooperate (Mullin, Hardy, & Sutton, 2007). League offices schedule games, hire and train officials, discipline players, market and license logoed merchandise, and negotiate broadcast contracts (Sharp et al., 2010). League offices are usually organized by function, with a range of different departments. For example, in addition to the Commissioner and President or CEO, the MLB League Office includes the following departments: Baseball Operations, Security/ Investigations, Communications/Public Relations, Merchandising/Licensing, Television/Production/Programming, Special Events, Broadcasting, Marketing/Advertising/Sales, Community Relations, General Administration, International, Information Technology/Internet/E-Commerce, and On Field (MLB, 2012). The NBA League Office includes the following departments: Commissioner's Office, Basketball Operations, Broadcast Operations, Communications, Community and Player Programs, Creative Services, Events and Attractions, Facilities and Administration, Finance, Global Business Development, Human Resources, Information Technology, Interactive Services, International Media Distribution, League Operations, Legal, Marketing, NBA Development League, Referee Operations, Security, Strategic Development, Team Marketing and Operations, and WNBA (NBA, 2011).

Individual Team Level

The day-to-day operations of a professional sports franchise take place on the individual team level. The two major groups that are responsible for daily operations—the owners and the front-office staff—are discussed in the following sections.

Owners

What drives the people who own major professional sport franchises? Today's ownership is driven largely by revenue generation (Masteralexis, 2012) and today's owners are multibillionaires, many of whom are members of the Forbes 400 richest individuals in the nation. Some of the more recognizable team owners are Microsoft's Paul Allen (Portland Trailblazers and Seattle Seahawks), former NBA superstar Michael Jordan (Charlotte Bobcats), music mogul Jay-Z (Brooklyn Nets), and entrepreneur Mark Cuban (Dallas Mavericks). What motivates a person with money to purchase a professional sports franchise? Reasons include the excitement of being involved in professional sport and the publicity and spotlight that accompany owning a team, especially a winning team. But do not be fooled—these individuals did not accumulate wealth without keeping a sharp eye on the bottom line. According to Quirk and Fort (1999), "As important as winning is to them, it might well be a matter of ego and personal pride that they manage to do this while pocketing a good profit at the same time" (p. 97). Owners also know that in the long run, few franchises have ever been sold for less than their purchase price, basically ensuring future long-term capital gains.

While some owners, such as Cuban, want to be closely involved with the daily operations of their franchises, for the most part the owners leave those daily chores to the people who work in the front offices. The owners' place in the policy-making process lies mainly at the league level, as discussed earlier. Some owners may impose policies on their front-office staff and players, but that is not necessarily the norm. For example, Steven Bisciotti, owner of the NFL's Baltimore Ravens, refused to silence Brendon Ayanbadejo in his support for same-sex marriage in Maryland, despite being asked to do so by a state legislator.

Front-office staff

The front office is the place where the day-to-day operational and business decisions are made for the individual professional sports franchise. Similar to league offices, the front office staff is usually departmentalized by function. In Major League Baseball, a typical front office is divided into two main areas: Business Operations and Baseball Operations. For example, on the Business Operations side the front-office staff of the Atlanta Braves includes an Executive VP, Business Operations; Executive VP, Sales and Marketing; Senior VP and General Counsel; Accounting; Administrative Services; Guest Services; Human Resources; Information Technology; Merchandising; Museum; Special Events; and Properties. The Baseball Operations side includes the Major League Staff (manager and coaches), Medical and Training, Player Development, Grounds Crew, and Scouting (Atlanta Braves, 2012).

A typical NBA front office has departments such as Basketball Operations, Sports Media Relations, Marketing, Operations, Finance, Corporate Partnerships, Ticket Operations and Strategic Planning, Human Resources, Player Personnel, Player Programs, and General Counsel (Miami Heat, 2012). As you can see, front-office staffs across the Big Four are similar in composition.

The entities and governance levels described so far in this chapter all deal with the management side of professional sport. However, governance structures also exist on the players' side of professional sport. These organizations, the players' unions, are commonly referred to as *Players Associations.*

Players Associations

Each of the Big Four professional leagues has what is known as a Players Association. These Players Associations, or PAs as they are sometimes called, are the players' unions. Professional baseball has the longest history of labor organization of all the professional sports. A player named John Montgomery Ward led the earliest unionization efforts; he founded the first players' union in 1885 and the Players League in 1890 (Abrams, 1998). Baseball players saw themselves as skilled tradespeople, similar to those workers who filled the factories of that era. Professional baseball witnessed these and other failed attempts at unionization until the Major League Baseball Players Association (MLBPA) was established in 1953. In 1966, former United Steelworkers employee Marvin Miller became its first Executive Director (Korr, 1991). Miller negotiated the players' first collective bargaining agreement in 1968 (MLBPA, 2012b). The National Hockey League Players Association (NHLPA) began in 1967 when player representatives from the original six clubs met, adopted a constitution, and elected a president (NHLPA, 2011). In 1954, NBA All Star Bob Cousy began organizing the players, ultimately forming the National Basketball Players Association (NBPA) (NBPA, n.d.a). The NFL players' efforts were first organized in 1956, when a group of NFL players authorized a man named Creighton Miller and the newly formed National Football League Players Association (NFLPA) to represent them (NFLPA, 2011b).

wwww

Major League Baseball
Players Association
www.mlbplayers.com

National Hockey League
Players Association
www.nhlpa.com

National Basketball Players
Association
www.nbpa.com

National Football League
Players Association
www.nflplayers.com

MISSION STATEMENTS. Each PA has its own mission statement. The mission statement of the NBPA is presented in Exhibit 12.1. This mission statement clarifies that the number-one priority of any PA is its members—the players—and protecting their rights.

PAs share the common goals of representing players in matters related to wages, hours, working conditions, and players' rights. They help players with any type of dispute or problem they may have with management. They

exhibit **12.1** Mission statement of the NBPA.

> To ensure that the rights of NBA players are protected and that every conceivable measure is taken to assist players in maximizing their opportunities and achieving their goals, both on and off the court.

Source: NBPA (n.d.a).

also deal with insurance benefits, retirement, and charitable opportunities, just as non-sport labor unions do. The NFLPA, for example, is a member of the American Federation of Labor–Congress of Industrial Organizations (AFL-CIO), a major non-sport union representing workers from a variety of industries.

MEMBERSHIP. The membership of any PA may include more than just active players. MLBPA membership includes all players, managers, coaches, and trainers holding a signed contract with MLB (MLBPA, 2012a).

FINANCIALS. PAs rely on two primary sources of revenues. The first is individual membership dues. For example, in the MLBPA in 2012, the players' dues were set at $60 per day during the season (MLBPA, 2012a). The second revenue source is each association's licensing division. For example, National Football League Players Incorporated, which is known as NFL PLAYERS, is the for-profit licensing, marketing, sponsorship, and content development subsidiary of the NFL Players Association (NFLPA, 2011c). Created in 1994, its mission is "taking the helmets off" the players and marketing them as personalities as well as professional athletes.

ORGANIZATIONAL STRUCTURE. PAs share relatively common governance structures, with Player Representatives, an Executive Board, and an Executive Committee. However, ultimate power rests with the players themselves. Every year each team elects, by secret ballot, a Player Representative (called a "Player Rep") and an Alternate Player Representative to serve on a Board of Player Representatives (for the NFL) or on an Executive Board (for MLB and the NHL). Player Reps generally serve one-year terms and act as liaisons between the union and the team members. According to the NFLPA, the Player Reps serve the following roles:

- assist in the implementation of the Collective Bargaining Agreement;
- exercise direct responsibility for new memberships and for the execution of check-off authorizations by members and non-members;

- receive and provide information concerning the processing of grievances;
- cooperate with the officers and staff of the NFLPA in the promotion and operation of the NFLPA programs;
- attend, unless physically incapacitated, all meetings of the Board of Representatives, and all NFLPA conventions;
- appoint and coordinate the operation of the Team Council which will assist him in performing his duties;
- advance the policies and interests of the NFLPA;
- perform such duties as may be from time to time directed by the Board; and
- facilitate communication between members and the NFLPA. (NFLPA, 2007, p. 9)

The Player Reps also come together to form the governance structure at the Board level. In the NFL the Board of Player Reps is responsible for the following tasks:

- enactment of policies governing the affairs of the NFLPA;
- provision for the location and maintenance of a principal and any regional offices;
- election of an Executive Director who shall be an ex officio member of all committees;
- appointment of the representatives of the NFLPA to boards, commissions and other organizations;
- the general conduct of collective bargaining and the ratification of the Collective Bargaining Agreement;
- the establishment and specification of the duties of standing and temporary committees;
- approval of the annual budget of the NFLPA;
- establishment of the annual membership dues;
- establishment of trusts for disabled, needy or deceased players or former players; and
- adoption and administration of a system of regulation of player agents. (NFLPA, 2007, p. 15)

These Boards of Player Reps select the members of an Executive Committee. For the NBPA the Executive Committee consists of nine players, and for the NHLPA the Executive Committee consists of seven players, one of whom holds the title of President.

PAs also employ full-time sport managers to staff their offices. The staff members of the MLBPA have titles such as Executive Director, Chief Administrative Officer, General Counsel, Chief Financial Officer, Contract Administrator, Director of Player Relations, Category Director of

Interactive Media, Category Director of Retail Development and Apparel, and Director of Players Trust (MLBPA, 2012c). The NBPA is divided into departments including the Executive Director's Office, Legal, Finance, Security and Agent Administration, Special Events and Sponsorships, Communications, Player Programs, Career Development, Player Benefits and Concierge Services, and WNBPA Operations (NBPA, n.d.b). Currently, the offices for the MLBPA, NBPA, and NFLPA are located in New York City, while the offices for the NHLPA are housed in Toronto.

CURRENT POLICY AREAS

As with any segment of the sport industry, professional sport has a myriad of policy areas to discuss. Among these are labor issues (particularly salary caps), use of social media, drug use, criminal activity by players, misconduct by players and coaches, and increasing the hiring of racial and ethnic minorities into management positions.

Labor Issues

As long as labor and management coexist in professional sport, labor issues will remain. Players have a deep-seated distrust of management, dating back to the days when management established the reserve system in professional baseball and kept the system secret among themselves (Abrams, 2000). Strikes and lockouts are common disruptions to sports fans. During the 1994 MLB strike, then-Acting Commissioner Bud Selig went so far as to cancel the World Series. The NHL shut down operations for its entire 2004 season when the players were locked out. The 2011–2012 NBA season opened on Christmas Day, with teams playing an abbreviated regular season schedule of 66 games. The NFL narrowly averted a shutdown of the 2011–2012 season as well. Players and owners are in constant struggles over revenue sharing, salary caps, salaries, pensions, and benefits.

One particular policy issue affecting all of the Big Four is the salary cap. A salary cap, or luxury tax, is established as part of the collective bargaining process and undergoes many iterations through the process (Zimbalist, 2003). According to the NBPA Collective Bargaining Agreement (NBPA, 2009), a salary cap is defined as "the maximum allowable Team Salary for each Team for a Salary Cap year, subject to the rules and exceptions set forth in this Agreement" (p. 11). In the NFLPA Collective Bargaining Agreement (NFLPA, 2011a), a salary cap is defined as "the absolute maximum amount of Salary that each Club may pay or be obligated to pay or provide to Players or Player Affiliates, or may pay or be obligated to pay to third parties at the request of and for the benefit of Players or Player Affiliates, at any time during a particular League Year, in

www

NBPA Collective Bargaining
Agreement
www.nbpa.com/cba.php

NFLPA Collective Bargaining
Agreement
https://www.nflplayers.com/
Articles/CBA-News/2011-
Collective-Bargaining-
Agreement/

accordance with the rules set forth" (pp. 3–4). In other words, a salary cap sets a limit on the amount a team can designate for its total team payroll.

For example, the NFL salary cap has grown from $34.6 million in its initial year of 1994 to $52.4 million in 1998, to $71.1 million in 2002, to $102.5 million in 2006, to $120.6 million in 2012, and with expectations of significant growth for the 2014 season (Duberstein, 2002b; NFL, 2012; Weisman, 2006). Although teams may slightly exceed the cap, it is still considered a "hard cap." For example, in 2000 the NFL salary cap limit was $62.2 million, but average club salary expenditures were $68.3 million (Duberstein, 2002a). In 2006 the cap was $85.5 million, but the average team was approximately $1.3 million over that (Horrow, 2006). In 2011 the cap was slightly over $120 million with seven teams having total payrolls above that mark (Maxwell, 2011).

In terms of the other Big Four professional leagues, the NBA cap was set at $53.135 million for the 2006–2007 season, an increase of $3.6 million from the previous year (Ford, 2006), and in 2012, the NBA cap was set at $58 million (NBA, 2012a). The NBA salary cap has specified built-in exceptions, including exceptions for veteran free agents, disabled players, rookies, and assigned players (Coon, 2013). This acts as a "soft cap." For the NHL, salary cap was set for $44 million in the 2006–2007 season (Burnside, 2006), and in 2011 there was a lower limit of $48.3 million, an adjusted midpoint of $56.3 million, and an upper limit of $64.3 million (NHL, 2011). MLB does not have a salary cap, but instead imposes a luxury tax on owners whose payroll exceeds a certain amount. In the latest collective bargaining agreement, "thresholds for luxury tax on team payrolls [were] set at $148 million for 2007, $155 million for 2008, $162 million in 2009, $170 million in 2010 and $178 million in 2011. Tax rates on [the] amount over threshold remain at 22.5 percent for first time over threshold, 30 percent for second time over threshold, 40 percent for third or subsequent time over threshold" (Associated Press, 2006). For the 2012 season, the threshold is $178 million (Kraslow, 2012). A luxury tax, while not a hard cap, can act as a disincentive to clubs to spend on player salaries (Erdes, 2002).

With spending reaching astronomical proportions in professional sport, discussions of salaries and salary caps will continue. Owners favor the caps, and players vehemently oppose them, because they serve as a method to limit their salaries. Salary caps are not as simple as they may appear; many interpretations and options are available. For example, the section in the NBPA Collective Bargaining Agreement related to the salary cap is 64 pages long. This topic will continue to be an ongoing battlefield even as players become millionaires and owners become billionaires.

Because of the monetary amounts involved in this industry, sometimes it is difficult to see issues of fairness. When fans see billionaire owners battling millionaire athletes, it can be difficult to realize that labor-management disputes still come down to issues of fairness in the workplace. Just because the workplace is a professional sports arena, fundamental rights in the workplace cannot be ignored.

Drug Policies

Reports of professional athletes using performance-enhancing substances, including illegal drugs, are everyday occurrences. To help ensure that athletic competitions are as fair as possible, sport organizations construct drug policies. Each of the Big Four has developed extensive drug policies. The policies enacted at this level are notably different from the ones at, say, the high school level. In professional sport, everyone is an adult. Also, one could argue these professional athletes are role models to others, especially children and young athletes.

MLB was at the forefront of this debate in 2005 when its current and former stars took the stand in Congressional hearings about use of steroids. Player icons such as Mark Maguire, Sammy Sosa, Rafael Palmiero, Curt Schilling, and Barry Bonds, as well as MLB executives, faced public scrutiny in these televised hearings. Neither the players nor the league emerged from these hearings unscathed. MLB again became the focus in 2007 with the release of the Mitchell Report, an 18-month, independent investigation headed by Senator George Mitchell into use of performance-enhancing substances in professional baseball. The 409-page report included 86 names, ranging from utility players to superstars, and painted a picture of a game stained during what is sure to be known as "the steroid era" (ESPN, 2007). To strengthen the joint drug prevention and treatment program, the report recommended that the program should

www

Mitchell Report
http://mlb.mlb.com/mlb/
news/mitchell/index.jsp

1. be independent
2. be transparent
3. perform adequate year-round unannounced drug testing
4. be flexible enough to employ best practices as they develop
5. continue to respect the legitimate rights of players
6. have adequate funding. (Mitchell, 2007, p. iv)

When developing these policies, professional sport organizations must be mindful of numerous legal considerations. Because professional athletes are employees and members of unions (PAs), leagues must be aware of the fact that drug testing is a condition of employment, and therefore any alteration to a drug-testing policy is a mandatory subject of bargaining between the players and the league (Wong, 2002). The NFLPA Collective Bargaining Agreement section titled Substance Abuse contains the following statement (NFLPA, 2011a):

> The parties agree that substance abuse and the use of anabolic steroids
> are unacceptable within the NFL, and that it is the responsibilities of the

parties to deter and detect substance abuse and steroid use and to offer programs of intervention, rehabilitation, and support to players who have substance abuse problems. (pp. 173–174)

Some main points of difference among the four leagues' testing policies are as follows:

- MLB players are tested twice a season, once during the first week of spring training and a second time randomly during the season.
- In the NBA and NHL, not all players are subject to mandatory drug tests. NBA players can be randomly tested up to four times per year, while NHL players can be tested no more than twice (Lemire, 2008).
- The NFL tests all players at the start of training camp for drugs like marijuana and cocaine. During the season, ten players per team are randomly tested each week.

In addition to outlining testing procedures, professional sport leagues' drug policies typically contain information about the administration of the program, discipline, and lists of prohibited substances. For example, the NFL Drug Policy states (NFLPA, 2010):

The illegal use of drugs and the abuse of prescription drugs, over-the-counter drugs, and alcohol (hereinafter referred to as "substances of abuse") is prohibited for players in the National Football League (NFL). . . . Substance abuse can lead to on-the-field injuries, to alienation of the fans, to diminished job performance, and to personal hardship. The deaths of several NFL players have demonstrated the potentially tragic consequences of substance abuse. NFL players should not by their conduct suggest that substance abuse is either acceptable or safe. . . . The primary purpose of this policy is to assist players who misuse substances of abuse, but players who do not comply with the requirements of the Policy will be subject to discipline. An important principle of this Policy is that a player will be held responsible for whatever goes into his body. (pp. 1–2)

The NFL Drug Policy also includes the following sections (NFLPA, 2010):

- administration
- confidentiality
- testing for substances of abuse
- entrance into the intervention stages
- intervention stages
- notice
- discipline for violations of law related to substances of abuse other than alcohol
- discipline for alcohol-related violations of the law or abuse of alcohol
- imposition of fines and penalties
- appeal rights

For comparison, the NBA Anti-Drug Program, as contained in the NBPA Collective Bargaining Agreement, consists of the following sections (NBPA, 2009):

- definitions
- administration
- confidentiality
- testing
- reasonable cause testing or hearing
- random testing
- drugs of abuse program
- marijuana program
- steroids, performance-enhancing drugs, and masking agents program
- noncompliance with treatment
- dismissal and disqualification
- reinstatement
- exclusivity of the program
- additional bases for testing additional prohibited substances

In 2005, MLB instituted a new drug-testing policy. The increased number of home runs coupled with allegations of rampant steroid use by players prompted this policy. The policy includes the following:

> The first positive test will result in a suspension of up to ten days. The second positive test will result in a suspension of thirty days. The third positive test will result in a suspension of sixty days. The fourth positive test will result in a suspension of one full year. Finally, the fifth positive test will result in a penalty at the discretion of the Commissioner of Major League Baseball. Players will be tested at least once per year, with a chance that several players can be tested numerous times per year. (Baseball Almanac, 2012, para. 3)

In the 2009 season, four MLB players were suspended for violating the policy, two players were suspended in 2010, and two in 2011 (Baseball Almanac, 2012). These suspensions were all related to steroid use. In 2012, a notable suspension of Melky Cabrera cost him the chance to be on the field when his team, the San Francisco Giants, won the World Series.

Questions still remain as to whether MLB has done enough to rid itself of the shadow cast over it, particularly during the 2007 home-run record chase by Barry Bonds, which was surrounded by controversy and allegations about Bonds's use of steroids. Certainly other sport organizations use much stricter codes, such as the Anti-Doping Code of the World Anti-Doping Agency (WADA). The use of performance enhancers can create an uneven playing field. Use of banned performance enhancers taints the essence of sport and fair play for fans and athletes alike.

Use of Social Media in Professional Sport

The use of social media in sport by athletes, coaches, and front office staff has exploded in the past few years. From Facebook to Twitter to Pinterest to the next form of social media, fans and the media cannot get enough information about their favorite teams or athletes. How are teams using social media to engage fans? According to Greenhalgh and Greenwell (2012), six distinct categories of tweets exist: interactivity, diversion, information sharing, content, fanship, and promotional. For example, the Cleveland Indians, dubbed one of MLB's and pro sports most Twitter-friendly teams, opened the first social media-only space in professional sport in their home stadium, Progressive Field (Olensky, 2012). As another example, the Boston Celtics launched a Facebook application called 3-Point Play, which fans have received enthusiastically (Stringer, 2012).

Athletes are also jumping on the social media bandwagon. Hambrick, Simmons, Greenhalgh, and Greenwell (2010) examined Twitter usage by 101 professional athletes from NBA/WNBA, MLB/Minor League Baseball (MiLB), NFL, NHL, MLS, golf, auto racing, and other sports. The athletes used the social networking site primarily to interact with other Twitter users (34% of the time) and discuss non-sports topics (28%), while using the site less frequently to talk about sports (15%) and promote their sponsors or endorse products (5%). With such a small percentage of time devoted to promoting their sponsors, more opportunities exist for athletes to use Twitter for promotional purposes as part of their sponsor/endorsement contracts.

Of course, the downside to social media is the lack of control by the front office. Interactivity gives athletes the chance to connect with their fans, but the open nature of Twitter can cause problems, such as athletes revealing too much about themselves or their teams. Players may wish to express their opinions and air out their grievance against their teammates, coaching staff, opponents, and the league itself. Hence, sport organizations have established policies that provide some parameters for social media use. Here is a synopsis of the social media policies for the Big Four (Ortiz, 2011, paras. 6, 10, 12, 14):

> **Major League Baseball:** Social media policy governs social media use by MLB personnel, but the policy does not include players. Players must abide by rules regarding use of electronic equipment in the clubhouse and on the field. Those rules stipulate that players, uniformed personnel and clubhouse staff cannot use cell phones or other devices on the bench, in the bullpen or on the field after batting practice has started. Cell phone use in the clubhouse is prohibited 30 minutes before game time. These rules are in effect until the end of the game, after which players can tweet and Facebook away.

National Basketball Association: Use of cell phones and other electronic devices is banned during games. This period is defined as 45 minutes before tipoff until after media obligations have been completed. Players can use social media during pregame media access.

National Football League: Players, coaches and operations staff cannot use social media less than 90 minutes before kickoff. Social media use can resume after traditional media interviews conclude. Updates to player accounts (by the player or anyone else) are prohibited.

National Hockey League: The most recent sports body to adopt a social media policy, the NHL has a policy similar to the NBA's and NFL's stance. Players cannot use social media from two hours before faceoff until media interviews are completed. The policy also makes clear that players are as responsible for statements made in social media as in traditional media.

The fact is that social media is here to stay. Teams and athletes need to recognize the potential public relations and monetary values of utilizing social media to expand and engage their fan base as well as the drawbacks involved with its use.

Criminal Activity by Players

Unfortunately, professional athletes' names are linked to run-ins with the law almost daily. The stories of current and former NFL players Michael Vick, Plaxico Burress, Justin Blackmun, and Ray Lewis and former NBA player Jayson Williams are all too familiar to sports fans in North America. The six months following Super Bowl XVLI in 2012 saw 27 different arrests of NFL players (Farrar, 2012).

Dealing with off-the-field incidents is difficult from the league perspective. First, the incidents are widely covered in the media. Second, taking punitive action may give the appearance of guilt even if the legal system has not yet passed judgment on an accused athlete. Third, if a team or league controls information about an incident, it is often accused of covering up information. Finally, the issue of how the PA will react to punishing players for off-the-field incidents remains. In 1997, the NFL introduced a new violent-crime policy to deter criminal behavior by its players (Wong, 2002). The Conduct Policy for NFL Players includes this statement (ESPN, 2013):

www
Conduct Policy for NFL Players
http://images.nflplayers.com/
mediaResources/files/PDFs/
General/2010%20Personal
%20Conduct%20Policy.pdf

All persons associated with the NFL are required to avoid "conduct detrimental to the integrity of and public confidence in the National Football League." . . . For many years, it has been well understood that rules promoting lawful, ethical, and responsible conduct serve the interests of the League, its players, and fans. Illegal or irresponsible conduct does more than simply tarnish the offender. It puts innocent people at risk, sullies the reputations of others involved in the game, and undermines public respect and support for the NFL. (para. 1–2)

The policy further defines *prohibited conduct* as including, but not limited to, violent or criminal activity such as crimes involving use or threat of physical violence, use of a deadly weapon in committing a crime, domestic violence, and sex offenses, as well as involvement in hate crimes. Players charged with criminal activity must undergo immediate clinical evaluation and counseling, if necessary. Players convicted of criminal activity are subject to discipline as determined by the Commissioner, including possible fines and suspensions (NFLPA, 2010). Players always have the right to appeal any sanctions.

In 2007, Roger Goodell faced serious issues in his early time as NFL Commissioner. He responded quickly and forcefully when dealing with both Michael Vick and Pacman Jones, whose brushes with the law placed the NFL in a poor light for the public. The message was clear—the good name and brand value of the NFL are essential for league success—and players acting inappropriately will be punished.

Responding to allegations of player misconduct is a delicate area for sport managers, and one where the SLEEPE Principle is very important in deciding on a course of action, because the decisions have social, legal, ethical, economic, and political ramifications. Athletes are role models, and criminal activities, like issues involving drugs and violence, reflect negatively on the players or the leagues. Thus, codes of conduct are necessary.

Player and Coach Misconduct

The NFL faced a significant on-the-field scandal with the "Bounty Gate" allegations and punishment of the New Orleans Saints. Everyone recognizes football is a violent contact sport, but in the eyes of many, players on the New Orleans Saints crossed the line. According to the Sporting News (2012, para. 2), "The program included 'bounty' payments for 'knock-outs' and 'cart-offs,' plays on which an opposing player was forced to leave the game. At times, the bounties even targeted specific players by name." Goodell stepped in and handed out punishments and suspensions not only to players, but to the front office as well. "[Head Coach Sean] Payton (one season), general manager Mickey Loomis (eight games) and assistant head coach Joe Vitt (six games) were punished for not doing enough to stop the bounty system after repeated NFL warnings. The Saints also were fined $500,000 and stripped of 2012 and 2013 second-round draft choices" (Marvez, 2012, para. 25). Despite early efforts by the players involved to appeal, Goodell stood strong and upheld the suspensions, much to the chagrin of the NFLPA (Yahoo! Sports, 2012). It is important to note how the Commissioner chose to sanction not just players, but also the coaching staff and the front office. This should serve as a signal to sport managers that they are ethically responsible for the actions of their employees. The days of owners actually sanctioning this type of player misconduct may be nearing an end.

Actions by coaches that affect the integrity of the game have also been in the news. The New England Patriots were at the center of a storm over stealing signals from other teams, resulting in monetary fines and loss of draft picks. MLB's Toronto Blue Jays, the Cleveland Indians, and the Philadelphia Phillies have also been accused of stealing signs and tipping batters off about pitches. Former Miami Marlins manager Ozzie Guillion angered many in the team's community with statements about Fidel Castro, prompting team ownership to suspend him for five games. These types of activities negatively impact the integrity of each sport. Of course, no one is naïve enough to believe coaches will not do everything possible to help their teams win. However, it is up to the sport managers in each organization to set the tone for ethical behavior from the top down.

Policies on Increasing Diversity in Front Offices

Sports previously played predominantly by white athletes are now diversified, and we see players from different racial and ethnic groups and numerous international players. These changes have been noticeable on the field, but off the field, in positions with power over the governance of professional sport, we have not, unfortunately, seen enough progress.

The Racial and Gender Report Card, published by the Institute for Diversity and Ethics in Sport in the DeVos Sport Business Management Program at the University of Central Florida, serves as a barometer to measure representation of women and racial and ethnic minorities in management positions in sport. The institute assigns grades to each sport organization as a barometer of how the organization is doing in terms of diversity. Because 24 percent of the U.S. population is made up of people of color, organizations with people of color holding 24 percent of managerial positions received an A grade. Organizations received a B if the percentage was 12 percent, a C for 9 percent, D for 6 percent, and an F for 5 percent or less. For gender, an organization received an A if 40 percent of employees were women, a B for 32 percent, a C for 27 percent, a D for 22 percent, and an F for less than 22 percent (Lapchick, 2011). As shown in Exhibit 12.2, front offices have become more diverse over the past few years. Check the website in the margin for updates to the Racial and Gender Report Cards for various sport leagues.

How have professional leagues responded to this issue, and what is being done to attempt to achieve diversity in front-office personnel and others in management positions? MLB Commissioner Bud Selig issued a memo in 1999 ordering teams to consider minority candidates in five positions: General Manager, Assistant General Manager, Field Manager, Directors of Player Development, and Directors of Scouting. In the memo Selig wrote, "If a club has an opening in any of these positions, the club must notify me personally. In addition, your list of candidates must be provided to me.

www
Institute for Diversity and Ethics in Sport
http://www.tidesport.org/

exhibit **12.2**

2010 Racial and Gender Report Card grades.

	Combined Grade	Race Grade	Gender Grade
NBA	A	A+	A–
NFL	B	A	C
MLB	B+	A	B–
MLS	B+	A	B–
WNBA	A	A+	A
College Sport	B	B	B

Source: Lapchick (2011). Reprinted with permission.

I expect the list to include minority candidates whom you and your staff have identified. I will provide assistance to you if you cannot identify candidates on your own" (Bodley, 2002, p. 11C). Since this initiative began, the number of minority managers grew to six in 2011 with 29 percent of all MLB coaches being minorities (Lapchick, 2011).

MLB also has a number of other diversity initiatives. First is MLB's Diverse Business Partners Program. This program has resulted in millions of dollars being spent with minority- and women-owned businesses who are suppliers for MLB and for individual teams. MLB also has established a number of urban youth initiatives, including Reviving Baseball in the Inner Cities (RBI), MLB's Urban Youth Academy, Breaking Barriers in Sports and in Life, and the Baseball Tomorrow Fund (Lapchick, 2011).

The NFL has also developed a policy addressing the issue of diversity. In the NFL's policy, announced in December 2002, owners agreed to seriously interview at least one minority candidate for each coaching vacancy. The policy, known as the Rooney Rule, was developed by a committee initially headed by Pittsburgh Steelers' owner Dan Rooney, following a report on minority hiring issued by a group led by attorney Cyrus Mehri (CBSSports.com, 2003). During the 2002–2003 season, NFL teams averaged two minority coaches but later that rose to six. The rule has its flaws, but proponents feel it has been effective (Scrom, 2011). Time will tell whether these initiatives are taken seriously and result in any significant changes in the makeup of front-office staffs.

Another largely overlooked group when examining diversity in sport management is people with disabilities. Data on people with disabilities as sport managers has not yet been gathered. Approximately 54 million peo-

WWW

Diverse Business Partners Program
http://mlb.mlb.com/mlb/official_info/dbp/about.jsp

RBI
http://mlb.mlb.com/mlb/official_info/community/rbi.jsp

Urban Youth Academy
http://mlb.mlb.com/mlb/official_info/community/urban_youth.jsp

Breaking Barriers Program in Sports and Life
http://mlb.mlb.com/mlb/official_info/community/bb.jsp

Baseball Tomorrow Fund
http://mlbplayers.mlb.com/mlb/official_info/community/btf.jsp

ple in the United States have a disability—approximately 19 percent of the population (United States Census Bureau, 2010)—many of whom participate or have a great interest in sport. The time has come to have a look at how to foster inclusion by people with disabilities on the management side of professional sport.

As stated in the previous chapter, increasingly diversified sport organizations allow for more voices to be heard and for continued growth. As mentioned in the chapter on ethics, sport reflects society. With society as a whole becoming more diverse, so must the sport industry embrace this diversity, not just on the player level but on the management level as well.

SUMMARY

Professional sport in North America takes many forms. Most prominent are the Big Four—MLB, the NBA, the NFL, and the NHL. These major sport organizations have different governance levels, including Commissioners, league offices, and individual franchise levels on the management side, and PAs on the players' side. The policy issues facing managers in the professional sport industry segment are numerous and include areas such as drug policies, social media use, player and coach misconduct, and labor-related issues such as salary caps and luxury taxes. These areas become more complex when athletes belong to a players' union, so both sides must be cognizant of their respective Collective Bargaining Agreements when developing policy and deciding on governance issues.

caseSTUDY

NORTH AMERICAN PROFESSIONAL SPORT

You have probably heard or read about the Mitchell Report mentioned in this chapter, which exposed the use of performance-enhancing substances in MLB. Obviously, some successful professional athletes will choose to use these substances as a way to gain an advantage over their competition. The use of performance-enhancing substances presents a number of governance-related questions and issues. Assume the role of an MLB team owner and consider the following questions:

1. Should professional sports leagues adopt the more stringent rules and regulations set forth by WADA? What are the pros and cons to doing so?

2. What should happen to the records set by players during the so-called "steroid era"? Should they be nullified, marked with an asterisk, or left as they are?

3. As the recommendations of the Mitchell Report are discussed, how will the relationship between management and labor (MLBPA) play out?

4. Most people agree that athletes are role models and many young athletes look up to them. Should athletes be role models? Do athletes have an ethical obligation to be role models?

CHAPTER questions

1. Which of the Big Four do you consider to be the model example of a professional sport league? Why?

2. You have been hired to work in the Marketing Department of an NHL franchise. In your position, how will you interact with the various governance levels in the NHL, both directly and indirectly?

3. Who are the Commissioners of each of the Big Four, and what are their employment backgrounds? Which do you consider to be the most powerful, and why? If you could write a letter to one Commissioner and give that Commissioner five suggestions to improve that league's operation, which league would you choose, and what suggestions would you offer?

REFERENCES

Abrams, R. I. (1998). *Legal bases: Baseball and the law.* Philadelphia: Temple University Press.

Abrams, R. I. (2000). *The money pitch: Baseball free agency and salary arbitration.* Philadelphia: Temple University Press.

Associated Press. (2006, October 25). MLB players, owners announce five-year labor deal. Retrieved from http://sports.espn.go.com/mlb/news/story?id=2637615

Atlanta Braves. (2012). Atlanta Braves executive offices. Retrieved from http://atlanta.braves.mlb.com/team/front_office.jsp?c_id=atl

Baseball Almanac. (2012). Steroid suspensions. Retrieved from http://www.baseball-almanac.com/legendary/steroids_baseball.shtml

Bodley, H. (2002, November 15). Major leagues take big step forward then step back in minority manager hires. *USA Today,* p. 11C.

Burnside, S. (2006, December 5). With happy cap news, board set to settle schedule. Retrieved from http://sports.espn.go.com/nhl/columns/story?columnist=burnside_scott&id=2686411

CBSSports.com. (2003, January 23). Cochran: NFL can do better in hiring minorities. Retrieved from http://www.cbssports.com/nfl/story/6143804

Coon, L. (2013). NBA salary cap facts. Retrieved from http://www.cbafaq.com/salarycap.htm#Q25

Duberstein, M. J. (2002a). It happens every February: Media misperceptions of the current NFL system. New York: NFLPA Research Department[mah1].

Duberstein, M. J. (2002b). NFL economics primer. New York: NFLPA Research Department.

Erdes, G. (2002, August 31). Baseball strike averted. *Boston Globe*, p. E1.

ESPN. (2007). Mitchell report: Baseball slow to react to players steroid use. Retrieved from http://sports.espn.go.com/mlb/news/story?id=3153509

ESPN. (2013). NFL personal conduct policy. Retrieved from http://espn.go.com/blog/nflnation/post/_/id/21598/nfl-personal-conduct-policy

Farrar, D. (2012, July 20). Kenny Britt's DUI arrest and some interesting NFL crime facts. Retrieved from http://sports.yahoo.com/blogs/nfl-shutdown-corner/kenny-britt-dui-arrest-interesting-nfl-crime-facts-160048314—nfl.html

Ford, C. (2006). Salary cap for 2006–2007 set at $53.135 million. Retrieved from http://sports.espn.go.com/nba/news/story?id=2516704

Gladden, J., & Sutton, W. A. (2011). Professional sport. In P. M. Pedersen, J. B. Parks, J. Quarterman, & L. Thibault (Eds.), *Contemporary sport management* (4th ed., pp. 122–141). Champaign, IL: Human Kinetics.

Greenhalgh, G., & Greenwell, T. C. (2012, June). What did they say? Content analysis of professional team tweets. Presented at the 2012 annual conference of the North American Society for Sport Management, Seattle, WA.

Hambrick, M. E., Simmons, J. M., Greenhalgh, G. P., & Greenwell, T. C. (2010). Understanding professional athletes' use of Twitter: A content analysis of athlete tweets. *International Journal of Sport Communication, 3*, 454–471.

Horrow, R. (2006, January 20). Heading to Super Bowl XL: NFL business issues. Retrieved from http://cbs.sportsline.com/general/story/9177560

Korr, C. (1991). *Marvin Miller and the new unionism in sports*. Urbana, IL: University of Illinois Press.

Kraslow, D. (2012). Why certain MLB teams can afford star players and others cannot. *Northwestern Business Review*. Retrieved from http://northwesternbusinessreview.org/mlbpayroll/

Lapchick, R. (2011, April 21). *The 2011 racial and gender report card: Major League Baseball*. Orlando, FL: Institute for Diversity and Ethics in Sport, University of Central Florida.

Lemire, J. (2008, March 11). The screening process: A guide to testing policies, from pros to high school. *Sport Illustrated*. Retrieved from http://sportsillustrated.cnn.com/2008/magazine/03/11/steroid.testingpolicies/index.html

Marvez, M. (2012, May 3). NFL suspends four players in New Orleans Saints bounty scandal. Retrieved from http://msn.foxsports.com/nfl/story/jonathan-vilma-scott-fujita-anthony-hargrove-will-smith-suspended-in-new-orleans-saints-bounty-scandal-050212

Masteralexis, L. P. (2012). Professional sport. In L. P. Masteralexis, C. A. Barr, & M. A. Hums (Eds.), *Principles and practice of sport management* (4th ed., pp. 221–249). Sudbury, MA: Jones & Bartlett.

Maxwell, J. (2011, July 26). Some NFL salary cap math. Retrieved from http://www.gazettenet.com/blog/everything-else/some-nfl-salary-cap-math

McCann, M. (2012, May 17). Why *Vilma v. Goodell* is so much more than a defamation lawsuit. *Sports Illustrated*. Retrieved from http://sportsillustrated.cnn.com/2012/writers/michael_mccann/05/17/vilma.goodell.suit/index.html

Miami Heat. (2012). Contact directory list. Retrieved from http://www.nba.com/heat/contact/directory_list.html

Mitchell, G. J. (2007, December 13). Report to the Commissioner of Baseball of an independent investigation into the illegal use of steroids and other performance enhancing substances by players in Major League Baseball. Retrieved from http://files.mlb.com/mitchrpt.pdf

MLB. (2008). *Major League Constitution*. New York: Author.

MLB. (2012). Career opportunities. Retrieved from http://mlb.mlb.com/careers/opportunities.jsp?c_id=mlb

MLBPA. (2012a). Frequently asked questions. Retrieved from http://mlbplayers.mlb.com/pa/info/faq.jsp#membership

MLBPA. (2012b). History of the Major League Baseball Players Association. Retrieved from http://mlbplayers.mlb.com/pa/info/history.jsp

MLBPA. (2012c). MLBPA contact information. Retrieved from http://mlb.mlb.com/pa/info/contact.jsp

Mullin, B. J., Hardy, S., & Sutton, W. A. (2007). *Sport marketing* (3rd ed.). Champaign, IL: Human Kinetics.

NBA. (2011). League office career opportunities. Retrieved from http://careers.peopleclick.com/careerscp/client_nba/external/search.do

NBA. (2012a). NBA Board of Governors ratify 10 year CBA. Retrieved from http://www.nba.com/2011/news/12/08/labor-deal-reached/index.html

NBA. (2012b). Season review: 1949–50. Retrieved from http://www.nba.com/history/seasonreviews/1949-50/index.html

NBPA. (n.d.a). About the NBPA. Retrieved from http://www.nbpa.org/about-us

NBPA. (n.d.b). Departments. Retrieved from http://www.nbpa.org/departments

NBPA. (2009). *2005 NBPA Collective bargaining agreement.* New York: Author.

NFL. (2011). NFL chronology of professional football. Retrieved from http://static.nfl.com/static/content/public/image/history/pdfs/History/Chronology_2011.pdf

NFL. (2012). NFLPA reportedly expects "significant growth" for 2014 cap. Retrieved from http://www.nfl.com/news/story/09000d5d827db3d3/article/nflpa-reportedly-expects-significant-growth-for-2014-cap

NFLPA. (2007). NFL Players Association constitution. Retrieved from https://images.nflplayers.com/mediaResources/images/oldImages/fck/NFLPA%20Constitution%20-%20March%202007.pdf

NFLPA. (2010). *National Football League policy and program for substances of abuse.* New York: Author.

NFLPA. (2011a). *Collective bargaining agreement.* New York: Author.

NFLPA. (2011b). History. Retrieved from https://www.nflplayers.com/About-us/History/

NFLPA. (2011c). Sponsors—licensees. Retrieved from https://www.nflplayers.com/about-us/Sponsors—Licensees/

NHL. (2011). Salary cap set for 2011-12. Retrieved from http://www.nhl.com/ice/news.htm?id=566916

NHLPA. (2011). About the NHLPA. Retrieved from http://www.nhlpa.com/about-us

Olensky, S., (2012, April 21). Cleveland Indians offer social media suite. Retrieved from http://espn.go.com/blog/playbook/fandom/post/_/id/133/cleveland-indians-offer-social-media-suite

Ortiz, M. B. (2011, September 27). Guide to league social media policies. Retrieved from http://espn.go.com/espn/page2/story/_/id/7026246/examining-sports-leagues-social-media-policies-offenders

Quirk, J., & Fort, R. (1992). *Pay dirt: The business of professional team sports.* Princeton, NJ: Princeton University Press.

Quirk, J., & Fort, R. (1999). *Hard ball: The abuse of power in pro team sports.* Princeton, NJ: Princeton University Press.

Robinson, M. J., Hums, M. A., Crow, B., & Phillips, D. (2001). *Profiles of sport management professionals: The people who make the games happen.* Gaithersburg, MD: Aspen.

Robinson, M. J., Lizandra, M., & Vail, S. (2001b). Sport governance. In B. L. Parkhouse (Ed.), *The management of sport: Its foundation and application* (3d ed., pp. 237–269). Boston: McGraw-Hill.

Scrom, P. L. (2011). Expansion of the Rooney Rule; The NFL shaping state legislation. Retrieved from http://thelejer.wordpress.com/2011/03/18/expansion-of-the-rooney-rule-the-nfl-shaping-state-legislation/

Scully, G. W. (1989). *The business of Major League Baseball.* Chicago, IL: University of Chicago Press.

Sharp, L. A., Moorman, A. M., & Claussen, C. L. (2010). *Sport law: A managerial approach* (2d ed.). Scottsdale, AZ: Holcomb Hathaway.

Sporting News. (2012). NFL statement on Saints 'bounty-gate' punishment. Retrieved from http://aol.sportingnews.com/nfl/story/2012-03-21/new-orleans-saints-sean-payton-gregg-williams-suspended

Stringer, P. (2012, Feb. 27). Moving beyond like: How one team monetized Facebook base. Retrieved from http://www.sportsbusinessdaily.com/Journal/Issues/2012/02/27/Opinion/Peter-Stringer.aspx

United States Census Bureau. (2010). Profile America facts and features: 20th anniversary of the Americans with Disabilities Act. Retrieved from http://www.census.gov/newsroom/releases/archives/facts_for_features_special_editions/cb10-ff13.html

Weisman, L. (2006, July 7). Expect NFL salary cap to keep going through the roof. Retrieved October 5, 2007, from www.usatoday.com/sports/football/nfl/2006-07-07-salary-report_x.htm.

Wharton, D. (2011). Commissioners walk a fine line. *Los Angeles Times.* Retrieved from http://articles.latimes.com/2011/may/15/sports/la-sp-0515-commissioner-power-20110515

Wise, A. N., & Meyer, B. S. (1997). *International sports law and business* (Vol. 1). The Hague, The Netherlands: Kluwer Law International.

Wong, G. M. (2002). *Essentials of sport law* (3rd ed.). Westport, CT: Praeger.

Yahoo! Sports. (2012,). Goodell upholds player suspensions in Saints' bountygate. Retrieved from http://sports.yahoo.com/news/goodell-upholds-player-suspensions-saints-203010955—nfl.html

Yasser, R., McCurdy, J., Goplerud, P., & Weston, M. A. (2003). *Sports law: Cases and materials* (5th ed.). Cincinnati, OH: Anderson Publishing.

Zimbalist, A. (2003). *May the best team win: Baseball economics and public policy*. Washington, DC: Brookings Institute.

Professional Individual Sports

This chapter contributed by Marion E. Hambrick and Sun J. Kang

The previous chapter focused on the governance of North American professional team sports. As mentioned in that chapter, not all professional sports are team sports. Individual sports also have a professional component. The governance of these sports competitions differs from the governance of professional team sports and leagues. For example, individual sports such as professional golf and automobile racing require athletes to complete extensive qualifying requirements before they can compete in select events. Other individual sports such as professional tennis place a heightened focus on grassroots development, similar to National Governing Bodies in the Olympic Movement. Overall, individual sport organizations develop and focus their rules and structures based on individual athletes' needs rather than on a team.

Each year in the United States alone, an estimated 21 million people play golf and over 13 million people play tennis (National Sporting Goods Association, 2012). These numbers reflect participation on the recreational level, but as we all know, professionals compete internationally in organized pro tours in both sports. Governing bodies such as the U.S. Golf Association and the U.S. Tennis Association play integral roles in the governance and growth of these sports. Another highly successful professional sport is automobile racing, particularly NASCAR. Speedways dot the countryside, ranging from small town tracks like the Salem Speedway in Salem, Indiana, or Dixie Speedway in Woodstock, Georgia, to superspeedways like Talledega in Alabama or Daytona in Florida, which accommodate over 100,000 spectators.

Although there are many differences between these professional sports and professional leagues and teams, one aspect remains the same—the need for governing structures to establish rules, regulations, and policies. This chapter examines golf, tennis, and automobile racing and each sport's history, governance structure, and current policy issues.

PROFESSIONAL GOLF

Four major organizations are involved in the governance of golf: the United States Golf Association (USGA), the Professional Golfers' Association of America (PGA), the PGA TOUR, and the Ladies Professional Golf Association (LPGA). Although all four work closely together, they have different purposes (see Exhibit 13.1). The USGA oversees the regulation and rules of golf and equipment standards. The PGA and LPGA serve professional golfers, and the PGA TOUR organizes national tour events.

USGA

History

www
United States Golf Association
(USGA)
www.usga.org/default.aspx

The USGA, formally known as the Amateur Golf Association of the United States, is a nonprofit organization established in 1894 as the central body of golf in the United States.

Professional golf organization responsibilities in the United States.

exhibit   **13.1**

USGA

Establishes Rules of Golf

Determines equipment standards

Sets handicap and course rating systems

Sponsors turf management research

Operates 13 national championships

PGA

Focuses on professional instruction and golf management

Operates 4 major championships:

- Ryder Cup
- PGA Championship
- PGA Grand Slam of Golf
- Senior PGA Championship

Sponsors a juniors golf program

PGA TOUR

Focuses on professional play

Hosts 47 events for 3 tours:

- PGA TOUR
- Champions Tour
- Nationwide Tour

LPGA

LPGA Teaching and Club Professionals (T&CP)

- Focuses on female golf instruction

LPGA Tour

- Focuses on female professional play
- Operates 30 tournaments

Operates the Symetra Tour with 16 events

Sponsors a juniors golf program

Governance

MISSION. The USGA is dedicated to serving those who share "a love and respect for golf" and strives "to preserve its past, foster its future, and champion its best interests for everyone who enjoys the game" (USGA, 2012c). The USGA oversees the Rules of Golf (revised every four years), ensures golf equipment complies with current rules, manages the Course Handicap and Course Rating Systems, and offers research-based turf management expertise (USGA, 2012a). Currently, the organization also hosts 13 national championships, including three open championships (U.S. Open, U.S. Women's Open, and U.S. Senior Open) and 10 amateur championships each year.

At the international level, the Royal and Ancient Golf Club of St. Andrews was founded in Scotland in 1754 to serve the United Kingdom and other countries. Until recently, this organization oversaw all the golfers and tours around the world except those in the United States. In 2004, a major reorganization took place that formed a separate entity called the R&A, which is independent from the Royal and Ancient Golf Club of St. Andrews, to take over joint administration of the rules of golf with the USGA. The R&A is responsible for administering the rules of golf for over 30 million golfers in 128 countries in Europe, Africa, Asia-Pacific, and the Americas, while the R&A and USGA jointly develop and issue the rules of golf for the United States and Mexico. Additionally, the R&A organizes the Open Championship (British Open) as well as other amateur and junior events sanctioned by golf governing bodies around the world.

www

R&A
www.randa.org

MEMBERSHIP. As of 2012 the USGA listed membership as over 700,000, with 9,000 member clubs. USGA membership is open to both amateur and professional golfers—in essence, to anyone interested in playing golf. Golf clubs, public and private, can also be members of the USGA. In fact, USGA member club representatives control over 10,600 golf courses nationwide, and more than 680 golf clubs hold qualifying rounds for USGA or state golf championships. Finally, USGA membership includes approximately 130 men's and women's state and regional golf associations that provide services to millions of golfers across the United States (USGA, 2012b).

FINANCIALS. The USGA's main sources of revenue are generated from championships and broadcast rights. In 2011 the USGA received over $99 million from the U.S. Open, the U.S. Women's Open, the U.S. Senior Open, 10 national amateur championships, team championships, and international matches (USGA, 2012d). The 2012 prize fund was $8 million for the U.S. Open, $3.25 million for the U.S. Women's Open, and $2.6 million for the U.S. Senior Open (USGA, 2012e). Additional revenues come from USGA membership fees, corporate sponsorships, merchandise licensing, green section services (turf grass management), and equipment testing. From the revenues generated, the USGA spends a large portion of its earnings supporting grassroots level development programs such as The First Tee, LPGA–USGA Girls Golf, and Hook A Kid on Golf. The USGA also provides financial support for the Special Olympics, which hosts the Special Olympics Golf National Invitational Tournament annually (USGA, 2012g).

ORGANIZATIONAL STRUCTURE. The leadership of the USGA is organized as shown in Exhibit 13.2.

PGA of America and PGA TOUR

History

The PGA of America was founded in 1916 in New York City with 35 charter members. These golf professionals and amateurs believed the formation of a golf association would improve golf equipment sales. The inaugural PGA Championship was held from October 10 through October 14 that same year at Siwanoy Country Club in Bronxville, New York, and the organizers awarded the winning trophy and $2,580 in prize earnings to James M. Barnes, who defeated Jock Huthinson 1-up in match play. In 1917 the USGA extended privileges to the PGA, and allowed the organization to choose host golf club Whitemarsh Valley Country Club in Pennsylvania for the U.S. Open (PGA, 2012a). With the continuous support of professional golfers, the PGA published the first issue of the *Professional Golfer of America* in 1920. The close relationship between

---

Organization of the USGA leadership.   *exhibit* **13.2**

EXECUTIVE COMMITTEE

A 15-member volunteer group serves as the Association's executive policy-making board.

SENIOR LEADERSHIP TEAM

The senior management team directs and oversees the Association's day-to-day operations.

REGIONAL AFFAIRS TEAM

A nationwide network of professionals serves as "key liaisons between the Association and State and Regional Golf Associations."

Source: USGA (2012f).

the PGA and the USGA flourished when the USGA adopted the PGA's suggestion to host the U.S. Open annually in June. They also worked together in adopting the new steel iron club technology, and the USGA legalized the PGA line of irons in 1926. The two organizations still maintain this relationship today as PGA and PGA TOUR golfers compete under the rules and guidelines established by the USGA (PGA, 2012a).

As an individual sport, professional golf is divided into two distinct organizations: the PGA and the PGA TOUR. The PGA serves male and female professional instructors, players, and local clubs, while the PGA TOUR is the tournament division organizing men's professional golf tours in North America. In 1968 the PGA TOUR separated from the PGA to operate the Tournament Players Division. Although the separation was considered risky at the time, it seemed inevitable due to the two distinct groups of professional golfers involved in the sport (PGA, 2012a). One group of golf professionals includes players who compete regularly on national tours (e.g., Bubba Watson, USA; Rory McIlroy, Ireland; K. J. Choi, Korea; Luke Donald, England), while the second group represents professional golfers operating or teaching golf at local country clubs and golf facilities. The separation became necessary to better serve golf professionals with different needs. For example, players on national tours are trained toward perfecting the game of golf and mastering the skills necessary to win tour events. In comparison, teaching professionals are trained to help amateur golfers learn and better understand the fundamentals and mechanics of the golf swing and other elements of the game. Some golf professionals are also trained to operate, maintain, and design golf courses.

Since making this distinction, the PGA and the PGA Tour organize and operate separate major tournaments. The PGA operates four major golf championships: the Ryder Cup, the PGA Championship, the PGA Grand Slam of Golf, and the Senior PGA Championship (PGA, 2012a), and the PGA Tour hosts 47 annual events for three tours: the PGA Tour for qualified professionals, the Champions Tour for players 50 and over, and the Nationwide Tour for professionals who have not qualified for the Tour card or are not on the PGA TOUR (PGA TOUR, 2012d). An athlete who demonstrates top performance in the Nationwide Tour may compete in the PGA TOUR the following year. In fact, Phil Mickelson and Tiger Woods competed in the Nationwide Tour prior to joining the PGA TOUR. When players turn 50, they are eligible to compete in either the PGA TOUR or the Champions Tour. Details of the tour qualifications are discussed in the membership section.

Governance

MISSION. The mission of the PGA "is to promote the enjoyment and involvement in the game of golf and to contribute to its growth by providing services to golf professionals and the golf industry" (PGA Links, 2012),

www

Professional Golfers' Association of America (PGA)
www.pga.com/home

PGA TOUR
www.pgatour.com

while the PGA TOUR's mission is to "expand domestically and internationally to substantially increase player financial benefits while maintaining its commitment to the integrity of the game. The PGA TOUR events are also committed to generating revenue for charitable causes in their communities" (PGA TOUR, 2012a). As stated earlier, the PGA and PGA TOUR both serve professional golfers with distinctively different purposes. The PGA provides services and support for teaching professionals, while the PGA TOUR only serves professional athletes who play for the national tours.

MEMBERSHIP. The PGA is currently comprised of 27,000 qualified men and women professionals teaching and managing the game of golf in its 41 PGA sections (PGA, 2012a). The PGA of America membership license features 31 different categories depending on the type of qualification each professional has earned as shown in Exhibit 13.3 (PGA, 2012b).

Conversely, PGA TOUR membership is exclusive to professional golfers who have earned a PGA TOUR card by finishing in the top 25 of the PGA Qualifying Tournament (Q-School), finishing in the top 25 on the Nationwide money list for a year, or winning three Nationwide Tour tournaments in a season. Players receiving exemptions to the above qualifications include former major champions, former multiple tournament winners, and those listed in the top 50 in lifetime career earnings or listed numbers 126 to 150 on the money list the previous year. To participate in the qualifying tournament as an amateur, players must have a handicap index of two or under (Ross, 2010).

FINANCIALS. The PGA organizes and operates four major championships, which represent the organization's main source of revenue. In 2011 the PGA generated over $86 million from these championships, which included revenues from spectator ticket sales, PGA merchandise sales, and sponsorships (see Exhibit 13.4). Spectator attendance is limited at each tournament based on each golf course's capacity, yet 27,000 spectators visited the PGA Championship each day during the tournament in 2012. An estimated economic impact of $92 million resulted from direct visitor spending and $75 million from 154 hours of media coverage during the event (Iacobelli, 2011). The PGA also has negotiated sponsorship revenues. Additional revenues derive from business development, member dues, golf course operations, and other investments (PGA, 2012c).

Similar to the PGA of America, the PGA TOUR generates revenues from tournament operations, sponsorships, licenses, merchandise sales, membership dues, and network media rights deals. The PGA TOUR signed a $491.7 million media rights deal with CBS and NBC, an agreement that will end in 2012, and an exclusive 15-year cable television agreement (Ourand, 2011). Sponsorship revenues come from major corporate partners, and the organization has negotiated merchandise license contracts with many major golf

exhibit 13.3　PGA of America member classifications.

Member Classification	Apprentice Classification	Description
A-1	B-1	Head Professional at a PGA Recognized Golf Course
A-2	B-2	Head Professional at a PGA Recognized Golf Range
A-3	Not Applicable	Exempt PGA TOUR, Champions Tour, Nationwide Tour, LPGA Tour and Futures Tour players
A-4	B-4	Director of Golf at PGA Recognized Golf Facilities
A-5	Not Applicable	Past Presidents of the Association
A-6	B-6	Golf Instructor at a PGA Recognized Facility
A-7	B-7	Head Professional at a PGA Recognized Facility Under Construction
A-8	B-8	Assistant Golf Professional at a PGA Recognized Facility
A-9	B-9	Employed in Professional Positions in Management, Development, Ownership Operation and/or Financing of Facilities
A-10	B-10	Golf Clinician
A-11	B-11	Golf Administrator
A-12	B-12	College or University Golf Coach
A-13	B-13	General Manager
A-14	B-14	Director of Instruction at a PGA Recognized Facility
A-15	B-15	Ownership or Management of a Retail Golf Facility
A-16	B-16	Golf Course Architect
A-17	B-17	Golf Course Superintendent
A-18	B-18	Golf Media
A-19	B-19	Golf Manufacturer Management
A-20	B-20	Golf Manufacturer Sales Representative
A-21	B-21	Tournament Coordinator/Director for Organizations, Businesses or Associations
A-22	B-22	Rules Official
A-23	B-23	Club Fitting/Club Repair
A-24	Not Applicable	Employed within the golf industry and not eligible for another Active classification
HM	Not Applicable	Honorary Member
IN	Not Applicable	Not eligible for classification as Active, Life Member or Retired Member
LM/LMM	Not Applicable	Not eligible for classification as Active Member and who have held a minimum of 20 years in an Active Classification (whether continuous or not)
LMA/LMMA	Not Applicable	Not eligible for classification as Active Member and who have held a minimum of 20 years in an Active Classification (whether continuous or not)
MP	Not Applicable	Master Professional
RM	Not Applicable	Members who are fully retired (cannot be working in either a golf or non-golf position) and who have achieved a combined 65 years of age and Active membership and who are not eligible for Life Member
F	Not Applicable	Failure to meet the requirements of the Professional Development Program

Source: PGA (2012b).

The PGA of America Statement of Activities.

exhibit **13.4**

THE PROFESSIONAL GOLFERS' ASSOCIATION OF AMERICA
COMBINED Statements OF ACTIVITIES (000s OMITTED)

	Revenue	2011 Expense	Increase (Decrease)	Revenue	2010 Expense	Increase (Decrease)
Revenue-Producing Activities:						
Championships	$86,571	$53,453	$33,118	$70,359	45,661	24,698
Business development	8,263	3,113	5,150	7,293	2,881	4,412
Member dues	2,414	568	1,846	2,392	663	1,729
Golf course operations	15,521	20,898	(5,377)	18,250	20,702	(2,452)
Investment income, designated funds	24,693	534	24,159	13,011	642	12,369
Investment income, other	126	-	126	139	-	139
Total revenue producing activities	137,588	78,566		111,444	70,549	
Unrestricted net assets available for support			59,022			40,895
General and Administrative Costs:						
Corporate services	-	9,752	(9,752)	-	9,052	(9,052)
Income tax benefit	18,385	-	18,385	4	-	4
Board, officers, past presidents	-	1,610	(1,610)	-	1,170	(1,170)
Total general and administrative costs	18,385	11,362		4	10,222	
	155,973	89,928		111,448	80,771	
Unrestricted net assets available for program support			66,045			30,677
Program Activities:						
Golf 2.0	-	840	(840)	-	-	-
Education	8,542	8,584	(42)	7,554	7,366	188
Research and information services	5	1,062	(1,057)	6	872	(866)
Awards	-	559	(559)	-	480	(480)
Member benefits	10,770	9,093	1,677	11,213	9,641	1,572
Membership program administration	3,158	3,467	(309)	1,191	1,559	(368)
Membership meetings	-	2,085	(2,085)	-	1,633	(1,633)
Member communications	148	1,480	(1,332)	183	1,421	(1,238)
Employment services	50	2,427	(2,377)	82	2,396	(2,314)
Public awareness	128	8,939	(8,811)	155	7,406	(7,251)
Section affairs	936	7,715	(6,779)	1,048	7,656	(6,608)
Club professional tournaments	3,455	4,204	(749)	3,460	4,684	(1,224)
Growth of game	1,742	5,039	(3,297)	5,820	8,361	(2,541)
Total program activities	28,934	55,494		30,712	53,475	
	$184,907	$145,422		$142,160	$134,246	
Increase in unrestricted net assets			$39,485			$7,914

Source: PGALinks.com (2012).

brands (PGA TOUR, 2012c). PGA TOUR expenses take the form of prize money, salary and benefits, and tournament operations. The organization paid $280 million to the players in 2011 (Mell, 2011). As a major part of its mission, PGA TOUR events have donated more than $1.1 billion to help over 2,000 charities and countless individuals (McCormick, 2012).

ORGANIZATIONAL STRUCTURE. The PGA's national office Board of Directors is elected by the organization's Board Members. The members serve a minimum of one year as an officer, and become eligible for re-election and re-appointment after their first term. The national office also has a President, Vice President, Secretary, Honorary President, and 17 Directors who establish association policies. The Directors include representatives from each of the PGA's 14 districts, two independent directors, and a member of the PGA TOUR. Each section of the PGA in the United States also elects its own board members to serve members nationwide (PGA, 2012e). The CEO of the PGA in 2013 was Peter Bevacqua (PGA, 2012d).

The PGA TOUR is a tax-exempt membership organization with three Executive Officers. Timothy W. Finchem has served as the PGA TOUR Commissioner since June 1994, and his responsibilities include expanding and strengthening the PGA TOUR's position within the sport. Just as with many other sports, the Commissioner can directly influence and decide on player suspensions, policies, and regulations. However, PGA TOUR officials abide by the USGA's Rules of Golf during their decision making. The Commissioner and Board Members also can request the review and modification of USGA rules. Two co–Chief Operating Officers report to the Commissioner and are responsible for financial strategies and operations, legal affairs, business development, marketing, retail licensing, broadcasting and television rights, and international federation tours (PGA TOUR, 2012b).

LPGA

History

To meet the needs of female golfers, the Ladies Professional Golf Association (LPGA) was founded in 1950 by 14 pioneering women seeking to create a full professional tour. Over the years, the LPGA has developed 14 U.S. tournaments featuring players from 29 different countries. Similar to the PGA and the PGA TOUR, in 1959 the LPGA established the LPGA Teaching division, called the LPGA Teaching and Club Professionals (LPGA T&CP), and the LPGA Tour to serve two types of golf professionals. In 1980 the LPGA also created Duramed Futures Tour (currently known as the Symetra Tour) to assist players at the developmental level. The creation of the event proved successful; more than 500 players have moved on to the LPGA Tour over the years (LPGA, n.d.a). To strengthen the grassroots development of women's golf, the LPGA Foundation in 1991 started to support junior golf programs. The LPGA and USGA also jointly created the LPGA–USGA Girls to increase their grassroots developmental program. The LPGA has earned the distinction of being "one of the longest-running women's professional sports associations in the world" (LPGA, n.d.a).

Governance

MISSION. The LPGA's mission is "to be a leader in the world of sports and to promote economic empowerment for our members. We will also serve as role models on and off the course" (LPGA, n.d.a). Its vision is "to inspire, empower, educate and entertain by showcasing the best golf professionals in the world—the members of the LPGA" (LPGA, n.d.a). Separate from the PGA and PGA TOUR, the LPGA specifically focuses on serving all professional female golfers around the world, including teaching professionals and professional athletes on tour. The LPGA, PGA, and PGA TOUR have different missions and visions, yet the three organizations strive to improve the game of golf and increase the numbers of individuals watching and playing the sport.

MEMBERSHIP. The LPGA represents the ultimate governing body for female golf professionals. For female tour professionals, the organization administers an annual qualifying school (Q-School) and operates the Symetra Tour, providing privileges for top finishers to join the LPGA Tour the following year.

For teaching and club professional (T&CP) members, the qualification and certification process is similar to PGA members. One major difference between the LPGA and PGA is the type of licenses available to their respective members. Whereas the PGA provides 31 different membership categories, the LPGA only provides two membership types (class A and B) for teaching and operation. Female professionals who wish to obtain specialty licenses, for example as a college or university golf coach or golf course superintendent, must achieve certification through the PGA. In 2012 the LPGA served approximately 460 tour professional members and 1,400 LPGA T&CP members (LPGA, n.d.a).

FINANCIALS. Similar to the PGA and PGA TOUR, the LPGA generates revenues from sponsorships, golf facility management, licenses, merchandise sales, membership dues, tournament operations, and network media rights deals. The prize money for 2012 increased to $48 million, adding $6.6 million from the prior year (Pucin, 2012). The LPGA also receives sponsorship revenues from numerous major marketing partners (LPGA, n.d.b).

ORGANIZATIONAL STRUCTURE. As a non-profit organization, the LPGA is under the guidance of Commissioner Michael Whan. The LPGA executive team also contains a Chief Financial Officer, Chief Marketing Officer, and General Counsel. The Board of Directors is composed of six independent directors, including the LPGA Player Directors (Player Executive Committee) and the National President of the LPGA Teaching and Club Professionals (LPGA, n.d.a). Similar to the PGA TOUR, LPGA officials make decisions on player eligibility, suspension, and disqualification while adhering to the USGA golf rules. However, the LPGA is only affiliated with the Legends Tour for female professionals aged 45 and older (LPGA, n.d.a).

Current Policy Areas

The professional golf industry faces potential challenges and growth opportunities in several key areas: changing rules for college players, retaining corporate sponsors, and attracting younger audiences.

Changing rules for college players

In 2012 the PGA TOUR introduced a new rule whereby college players who qualify will play in the Nationwide Tour unless they receive sponsor exemptions and win enough to play in the PGA TOUR. Traditionally, college players had two options to play in PGA TOUR events. First, they could enter the events with sponsor exemptions and earn enough prize money to earn a tour card. Tiger Woods and Phil Mickelson took this route—earning a tour card and skipping the Q-School (discussed next), and this option still remains. Second, players could earn a tour card by becoming a top-25 player in the Q-School. This second option is where the new rule takes effect. PGA TOUR officials decided that all the players who qualify through the Q-School would compete in the Nationwide Tour instead of the PGA TOUR. Corporate sponsors responded to the change, saying they will no longer award the same lucrative endorsement contracts to college players as they did in the past. Differences in television and spectator exposure between the Nationwide Tour and PGA TOURs dictate lower contract values for Nationwide players, who receive around $50,000 for product endorsements versus upwards of $250,000 for PGA TOUR players. The rule change took effect in 2013, and college players and sponsors are awaiting its short- and long-term effects on when players decide to leave school for tournament play and how sponsors will compensate them for their decisions and endorsement potential (Mullen & Smith, 2012).

The financial implications of the rule change are significant, as collegiate golfers may incur significant expenses to reach this level of play. Receiving sizable product endorsements would help offset some of their earlier expenses. Prior to joining the collegiate ranks, young golfers may pay as much as $70,000 to attend golf academies and receive specialized instruction. They may also participate in junior tournaments, which can cost $5,000 with travel. As college coaches move toward scouting at such events, players view these expenses as necessary investments to attract the attention of collegiate coaches and earn scholarships (Schupak, 2012).

Retaining corporate sponsors

The professional golf industry faced numerous challenges when Tiger Woods took a break from golf from late 2009 to early 2010. Attendance at PGA TOUR events decreased by 20 percent, and corporate sponsorships proved harder to attract and retain (Futterman & Blackmon, 2010). Although Woods's absence likely affected the PGA TOUR's popularity during that time, Finchem, Commissioner of the PGA TOUR, attributed declining sponsorships to other factors such as "the battered economy, a general decline in sponsorships across all sports, and the bankruptcy filings of GM, Chrysler LLC, and Stanford Group Co., all major golf backers" (Futterman & Blackmon, 2010). After Woods's return and an improvement in the economy, the industry has since regained its momentum. The PGA TOUR has identified new corporate sponsors and received renewed commitments from current sponsors, both of which represent important revenue sources. For example, FedEx is the PGA TOUR's title sponsor, paying an estimated $30 to $35 million annually for that privilege. The company renewed its sponsorship contract through 2017, citing new opportunities to reach more international golf fans (Smith, 2012). Tour organizers must ensure corporate sponsor satisfaction to continue future revenue streams.

Attracting younger audiences

Professional golf traditionally has appealed to older adults. Yet industry leaders recognize the need to expand beyond the core fan base and attract younger viewers, who may develop a lifelong appreciation for the sport (Starr, 2012). PGA TOUR events such as the Masters now provide interactive websites and mobile applications for spectators. Beginning in 2010 the Masters tournament took an innovative approach by offering a live webcast, interactive leaderboard, video of the entire course, video highlights, overview of the pairings, and player information on the official website and mobile application. These features provided spectators with additional information and content. For example, the interactive leaderboard gave users a choice between the traditional view of plus and minus overall score and a player's hole-by-hole score, simply by pressing the player's name. This function also provided player biographies, highlights, and live video during the Masters week. Furthermore, the Masters' official Facebook page (over 280,000 likes for the event) and players on Twitter (providing event updates to their millions of followers) helped promote the event. The combined effort to promote the event through the interactive website, mobile apps, and social media attract-

WWW

Masters Tournament
Facebook page
www.facebook.com/Masters.
Tournament

ed a larger fan base, including spectators from younger demographic groups (Starr, 2012). The PGA TOUR's charitable arm also offers special events catering to young adults as a way to introduce potential fans to the sport.

Other industry organizations also recognize the importance of attracting younger fans. Golf club manufacturer Callaway partnered with singer and actor Justin Timberlake in its advertising efforts, hoping to appeal to a more youthful audience (Starr, 2012). Focusing on younger players along with attracting and retaining corporate sponsors may help the professional golf industry extend its reach and create a positive long-term industry outlook.

UNITED STATES TENNIS ASSOCIATION (USTA)

History

The United States Tennis Association began in 1881 as the United States National Lawn Tennis Association (USNLTA), and later shortened its name to the United States Lawn Tennis Association (USLTA) in 1920 and finally to the USTA in 1975 (USTA, 2008). The governing body's original goals were to provide standardized playing rules while growing the sport. The organization and its sanctioned events evolved quickly as the doors opened to international players in 1886 and to women in 1889. Other changes over time included the Mixed Doubles Championships in 1892, the National Clay Court Championships in 1910, and the U.S. Open in 1968 (USTA, 2008). Women received greater recognition in the 1970s with the USTA's sanctioning of the Virginia Slims Women's tour and offering equal prize money to female and male competitors at the U.S. Open (USTA, 2008). The governing body also sought to attract new adult and junior players by offering more activities at local parks and recreational facilities and introducing new programs such as the National Junior Tennis League in 1969 and Senior League Tennis in 1991. USTA membership grew to 250,000 in 1984 and doubled to 500,000 by 1993 (USTA, 2008). Capitalizing on the sport's increasing popularity, the governing body opened the $285 million Billie Jean King National Tennis Center (NTC) in New York City's Flushing Meadows Corona Park in 1995 (USTA, 2008).

Today, the USTA serves as the governing body for tennis in the United States, and promotes tennis from the grassroots to the professional levels with three divisions: Community Tennis, Player Development, and Professional Tennis (USTA, 2012a). The Community Tennis division emphasizes the USTA's national grassroots efforts. Programs in this division include the USTA League, which offers tennis opportunities for 330,000 adult members, and the USTA Jr. Team Tennis, which serves 100,000 children and young adults participating in tournaments and other activities (USTA, 2012c). The Player Development division provides coaching services and facilities for the nation's best junior players (ages 18 and younger) to fill the pipeline of top tennis performers from the United States (USTA, 2012c). Finally, the Professional Tennis division arguably represents the most visible part of the USTA, as it hosts the U.S. Open and other tennis tournaments leading up to the Grand Slam tournaments (the Australian Open, the French Open, Wimbledon, and the U.S. Open). This arm of the USTA also assists in forming teams for the Olympic and Paralympic Games as well as the Davis Cup and Fed Cup, the premier international tennis team events for men and women, respectively. USTA leaders believe the division helps attract new players to the sport, as professional tennis increases fan exposure through television viewing and event attendance (USTA, 2012c).

Governance

MISSION. The USTA mission statement reads, "To promote and develop the growth of tennis" (USTA, 2012a). Additionally, the Player Development division mission statement is "To develop world-class American players through a clearly defined training structure and competitive pathway as well as through the implementation of a comprehensive coaching philosophy and structure" (USTA, 2012c). The governing body strives to increase the number and diversity of people watching and participating in the sport from the grassroots to the professional levels and uses numerous financial resources to help achieve its mission.

MEMBERSHIP. As stated above, membership fees represent an important revenue source for the USTA, and the association received $21 million in related revenues in 2011 (USTA, 2012). The governing body offers a variety of memberships for individuals and organizations. Individuals can take advantage of adult, junior, and family memberships, while organizations can obtain community tennis association, club, school, park and recreation department, or other USTA memberships (USTA, 2012e). The governing body takes pride in its memberships and programs, noting that it used revenues from membership dues and other sources to invest in community outreach activities such as improving public tennis courts and providing scholarships and athletic equipment to those in need. Individual members receive access to tournaments and leagues, and organization members receive benefits, such as resources to conduct community tennis development workshops and host USTA sanctioned tournaments (USTA, 2012b).

FINANCIALS. In 2011 the USTA generated $296 million, a 6 percent increase from the previous year, with the U.S. Open representing the USTA's primary revenue source (USTA, 2012f). Held in Queens, New York, the annual Grand Slam event takes place in late summer and attracts top players from around the world. Spectator numbers rival the Indianapolis 500 with over 700,000 people attending each year (Hoy, 2008) and many more watching at home and online (Kaplan, 2010). The USTA earned $226 million for the 2011 event, or 76 percent of the organization's total annual revenues (USTA, 2012f). Approximately half of the U.S. Open revenues derive from media and sponsorship rights, as the USTA has negotiated television contracts with CBS, ESPN, and the Tennis Channel (Kaplan, 2010) and retains sponsorship deals with major corporations (Vasquez, 2010). Most of the governing body's remaining revenues come from membership fees, USA team events, and Tour events, and the revenues help offset organizational expenses. In 2011 the USTA spent almost $94 million on the U.S. Open. Other large cost categories included $79 million for the Community Tennis division, $24 million for USA Team and Tour events, and $19 million for administrative and support services (USTA, 2012). See Exhibit 13.5.

exhibit **13.5**   USTA revenues and expenses.

	2011 (in thousands)	2010 (in thousands)
Operating Revenues:		
US Open	$ 226,006	$ 216,501
USA team events	4,741	1,946
Tour events	21,890	18,603
Membership	21,002	21,057
Advanced media	3,726	3,140
NTC tennis facility programs (other than US Open)	3,658	3,543
Community tennis sponsorships	2,990	3,380
Investment return reported in operations	5,900	5,500
Barter received	5,735	5,593
Other	432	1,187
Total Operating Revenues	$ 296,080	$ 280,450
Operating Expenses:		
US Open:		
Direct expenses	$ 68,548	$ 63,450
Depreciation and interest expense	25,208	24,526
USA team events	4,632	4,343
Tour events (including depreciation)	19,205	18,007
Membership	11,798	12,095
Advanced media	2,975	2,952
NTC tennis facility programs (including depreciation and interest)	11,904	12,161
Community tennis:		
Direct Section funding	42,956	42,245
Other community tennis programs	36,168	33,749
Player development	16,533	15,560
Pro circuit and officials	6,767	6,627
Barter used	5,735	5,593
Other program services	6,098	6,912
Total Program Services	$ 258,527	$ 248,220
Administrative and supporting services (incl. depreciation and taxes)	19,129	19,766
Total Operating Expenses	$ 277,656	$ 267,986
Excess of Operating Revenues over Operating Expenses	$ 18,424	$ 12,464

Source: USTA (2012f).

ORGANIZATIONAL STRUCTURE. This nonprofit organization boasts a base membership of 750,000 located in 17 regions around the United States and is run by a mixture of volunteer Executive Board Members, paid full-time staff, and other volunteers (USTA, 2012a). Gordon Smith serves as the USTA's Executive Director and Chief Operating Officer, and other executive leaders at the national headquarters in White Plains, New York, include the Chief Financial Officer, Chief Marketing Officer, Chief Administrative Officer and Legal Counsel, Chief Information Officer, and Chief Medical Officer (USTA, 2012d). The USTA has three divisions: Community Tennis, Player Development, and Professional Tennis (see Exhibit 13.6), which also have leadership teams to manage their various initiatives and programs. Additionally, each regional section has its own association, and 50 state associations operate alongside the regional sections and the national headquarters. Whether regional, district, or state, the associations are nonprofit organizations run separately with their own boards of directors and staff members. The associations receive support from the Community Tennis Associations, which help the associations provide programs and initiatives to their respective members (USTA, 2012a).

At the international level, the International Tennis Federation (ITF) is the governing body for the sport. It regulates the game and controls major international events, including the Davis Cup and Fed Cup. The ITF has over 200 national tennis organizations as affiliates. Globally, the families of ITF include the Confederation Africaine de Tennis (CAT), Asian Tennis Federation (ATF), Central American & Caribbean Tennis Confederation (COTECC), Confederación Sudamericana de Tenis (COSAT), Oceania Tennis Federation (OTF), and Tennis Canada. As opposed to the United States, other countries around the world belong to their country's tennis associa-

WWW

International Tennis Federation (ITF)
www.itftennis.com/home.aspx

Confederation Africaine de Tennis (CAT)
www.cattennis.com

Asian Tennis Federation (ATF)
www.asiantennis.com

Central American & Caribbean Tennis Confederation (COTECC)
www.cotecc.org.sv/contenido/index.html

Confederación Sudamericana de Tenis (COSAT)
www.cosat.org

Oceania Tennis Federation (OTF)
www.oceaniatennis.com

Tennis Canada
www.tenniscanada.com

Tennis Europe
www.tenniseurope.org

Divisions of the USTA.

exhibit **13.6**

USTA		
Community Tennis Division Focuses on grassroots efforts through the USTA League and USTA Jr. Team Tennis	**Player Development Division** Provides coaching services and facilities for the best junior players	**Professional Tennis Division** Focuses on professional play by hosting the U.S. Open and other tournaments leading to the Grand Slam tournaments

Source: USTA (2012a).

tion as well as the regional tennis federations. Tennis Europe comprises 49 European member nations, making it the largest regional association of the ITF. Similar to USTA, Tennis Europe organizes events that are independent from the ITF and executes tasks delegated by the ITF.

Current Policy Areas

Despite its successes, professional tennis has faced challenging policy issues. Executive Director Gordon Smith of the USTA outlined several initiatives that address some of the challenges facing the organization, including making improvements to the U.S. Open, attracting more participants to the sport, and increasing the professional talent pool (Kaplan, 2011). In addition, gambling has been an issue in the sport at the international level.

Improving the U.S. Open

The U.S. Open takes place in Arthur Ashe Stadium, located at the Billie Jean King National Tennis Center (NTC) in Queens, New York. The stadium was constructed in 1997 for $254 million, and features 90 suites and state-of-the-art amenities (Crouse, 2011). Yet in recent years, the stadium—the largest tennis facility in the world—and the USTA have come under fire, because the stadium does not have a roof. Rain delays have become an annual occurrence at the U.S. Open, much to the exasperation of players, fans, and media organizations alike (Crouse, 2011). The weather challenges led the USTA to consider adding a roof to the stadium, but costs were projected to reach $100 to $300 million (Zinser, 2011). As a nonprofit organization, the USTA questioned whether such an expense represented a worthy investment in light of other organizational goals, which focused on grassroots expansion and player development (Crouse, 2011). Ultimately, the USTA decided to invest $500 million in the NTC for renovations and upgrades, but the investment would not include a new roof for Arthur Ashe Stadium (Russo, 2012).

Attracting younger audiences

As is the case for the golf associations, the USTA faces the challenge of getting young people involved in the sport at an early age to ensure its continued popularity and growth. At the grassroots level, the USTA has introduced the 10 and Under Tennis program to spur interest in the sport among a younger audience. With this program, children use smaller rackets with foam or low-compression balls and play on smaller courts with lower nets. The changes were introduced after tennis analysts observed the challenges children face when playing on regulation courts with adult-sized equipment. Oversized nets and racquets might cause younger players to quickly become discouraged and lose interest in the sport. Smaller-sized equipment and courts allow them to experience more success sooner and potentially sustain their participation through childhood and beyond. The USTA believes strongly in the movement and has spent millions of dollars for thousands of 10 and Under Tennis courts nationwide (Miller, 2012).

Moreover, tennis players have a strong presence on Twitter and Facebook, facilitating interaction with younger fans. Among the top athletes on Facebook, tennis players dominated the top 20 athletes category: Roger Federer placed 9th, followed by Rafael Nadal in 10th, and Maria Sharapova placing 13th ("Top Athletes on Facebook," 2012). There are 151 professional tennis players on Twitter, and star player Rafael Nadal has close to three million followers. The athletes' efforts to leverage these direct communication channels with fans not only build strong bonds with the individual athletes, but also a stronger connection to the sport (Hambrick, Simmons, Greenhalgh, & Greenwell, 2010). The grassroots development plan for the USTA and the strong presence of role model athletes on social media may help to overcome some of the challenges faced by the USTA.

Developing a professional talent pool

In addition to a heightened focus on young players, tennis analysts have stressed the need for more professional player development, commenting on the dearth of top players from the United States at such Grand Slam events as the Australian Open (Miller, 2012) and the French Open (Monson, 2012). While the 10 and Under Tennis initiative and other programs may help, a stronger demand for players ready to compete professionally continues. Despite its popularity in other countries, tennis has lost its cachet in the United States, where sports fans often choose to play and watch other sports (Monson, 2012). Expenses represent another challenge, as it costs an estimated $20,000 to $100,000 to develop a top junior player into a skilled professional through enrollment at tennis training centers and academies coupled with steady participation in tennis tournaments around the country (Monson, 2012). The USTA uses junior programs to identify potential talent, with the hopes of placing them into intensive training early and instilling the devotion and skills necessary to succeed at the highest levels (Monson, 2012). Ensuring the sport's popularity at the grassroots and professional levels represents critical components to the USTA, and will likely represent continued focus areas for years to come.

Gambling

Professional tennis has grappled with a global cheating issue. Most notably, in 2007 five Italian professional tennis players received suspensions from the Association of Tennis Professionals (ATP) for either gambling on or purposefully influencing the outcome of their tennis matches. The players sued the ATP, asserting that they represented only a few of the many players involved in gambling schemes. The Tennis Integrity Unit was formed in 2008 to monitor the sport more closely and prevent future gambling activities (Tuohy, 2011).

NASCAR

History

The National Association for Stock Car Auto Racing is the sanctioning body for North American stock-car automobile racing and is the largest such organization in the United States. NASCAR began in 1948 when Bill France, Sr., along with race car drivers, racetrack owners, and racing enthusiasts, met in Daytona Beach, Florida, to form a new racing series (Homestead Miami Speedway, 2013). The sport's popularity had increased rapidly through the 1930s and 1940s, and France and others wanted to develop an organized structure to capitalize on surging interest in the sport. During their 1948 meeting, the group settled on an organizational structure and declared France the organization's first Chief Executive Officer (Clarke, 2008). The first race sanctioned by NASCAR took place on February 15, 1948, and a Cup Series was introduced for the 1949 season. Changes occurred quickly in the 1950s and 1960s as more drivers gravitated to the sport. New racetracks emerged to accommodate the rising demand. The tracks were built not just in the South, where a large portion of the organization's fans resided, but farther north in Michigan, Delaware, and Pennsylvania as the fan base spread (Homestead Miami Speedway, 2013). The 1970s ushered in additional changes, as Bill France, Sr., relinquished the helm to his son, Bill France, Jr., who led the organization until 2003. In 1971, tobacco company R.J. Reynolds became the title sponsor of NASCAR's premier racing series, and the name changed from the Grand National Series to the Winston Cup Series (Clarke, 2008). A strong corporate presence continued into the 1980s and 1990s, and NASCAR witnessed a significant increase in corporate sponsorships and advertising, as other companies followed suit and initiated sponsorships with racetracks and drivers. In 2003 NASCAR moved from long-time title sponsor R.J. Reynolds to a sponsorship with the telecommunications industry's Nextel Corporation. When Nextel and Sprint merged, the Nextel Cup became the Sprint Cup (Clarke, 2008).

Beyond corporate sponsorships, NASCAR has also experienced an expanded television presence. The organization entered a television partnership with FOX, NBC, and TNT in the 1990s, and the contract proved a boon for all parties, as television viewership continued to grow, particularly for the Daytona 500, whose viewership increased by 48 percent from 1993 to 2002. Racetrack owners reported a corresponding growth in attendance, as their facilities often hold from 100,000 to 200,000 fans—rivaling attendance at the National Football League's annual Super Bowl (Amato, Peters, & Shao, 2005). Fans flocked to races, and attendance grew by 80 percent from 1993 to 1998. A large portion of the growth was attributed to the Sprint Cup Series, which witnessed a 57 percent increase during the same time period. The organization also created an online presence, introducing NASCAR.com in 1995, to reach fans before, during, and after the events (Homestead Miami Speedway, 2013).

Governance

MISSION. Headquartered in Daytona Beach, Florida, NASCAR serves as the sanctioning body for the Sprint Cup Series as well as the Nationwide Series, Camping World Truck Series, and other smaller series such as NASCAR K&N Pro Series, Whelen Modified Tour, Whelen Southern Modified Tour, Whelen All-American Series, Canadian Tire Series, and Mexico Series at racetracks across the United States, Canada, and Mexico (NASCAR, 2012a). The Sprint Cup Series is undoubtedly NASCAR's most popular, but the organization also promotes other regional and local events. For example, the Whelen All-American Series represents a training ground for local drivers aspiring to one day compete at the sport's highest levels, and drivers can win local track, state, and national titles for their performances. Other series such as the Canadian Tire Series and Mexico Series help develop talent at tracks across North America. As drivers improve on the local and regional circuits, they may seek greater opportunities with the Camping World Truck Series, Nationwide Series, and eventually the Sprint Cup Series (NASCAR, 2012a).

The organization's mission statement reads, "NASCAR is committed to ensuring that our sport better reflects America's composition. Our mission is to engage females and people of diverse ethnic and racial backgrounds in all facets of the NASCAR industry" (NASCAR, 2012a). To accomplish this mission, NASCAR has created several diversity initiatives, including the Drive for Diversity and Diversity Internship Program to attract more diverse drivers and employees to the organization (NASCAR, 2012c).

MEMBERSHIP. As a privately owned, family-run organization, NASCAR tries to consistently provide a family-oriented sports product, and this goal has helped the company grow from a regional diversion into an international sports giant (Clarke, 2008). Part of NASCAR's success derives from consistency through strict management controls. The governing body establishes guidelines for its owners, drivers, and support personnel both on and off the racetrack, and NASCAR members agree to abide by them. Any disagreements regarding the rules are reviewed and resolved in house, using the published NASCAR Rule Book as the ultimate authority. The rules include details about membership. NASCAR drivers must pay membership fees, the amount of which is not disclosed by NASCAR, to the racing organization in exchange for participation in NASCAR-sanctioned events (Clarke, 2008).

FINANCIALS. NASCAR generates more than $3 billion annually, and racetrack revenues along with corporate sponsorships, television broadcast rights, and licensed merchandise fuel the organization's revenue growth (Schorn, 2009). NASCAR fans represent a highly brand-loyal group, eager to watch races and purchase related products, and the organization receives significant revenues through its television contracts. In 1999 the sanctioning body negotiated a $2.4 billion agreement with FOX, F/X, NBC, and TNT, and nearly doubled the amount to $4.5 billion in its 2005 contracts with ABC, ESPN, FOX, SPEED, and TNT (Hinton, 2005). In late 2012, NASCAR revealed its contract extension with Fox Sports Media Group. Fox will continue broadcasting the Daytona 500 and a portion of the season's races through 2022; the media organization paid $2.4 billion for the media rights (NASCAR, 2012d). Television revenues will likely continue their upward trajectory with the next round of negotiations, as NBC expects to bid when negotiations begin again in 2014 (Mickle & Ourand, 2012a).

Coupled with media rights, sponsorships represent an important revenue source. Research indicates that 70 percent of NASCAR fans would purchase products from corporations sponsoring drivers and races, and 40 percent said they would switch brands if a competing company became a sponsor (Amato et al., 2005). Corporate sponsors recognize the value of associating with NASCAR, and the organization has reaped the benefits of this ongoing interest, including $750 million for a ten-year contract with title sponsor Nextel/Sprint (Clarke, 2008). Race car owners and drivers also benefit from sponsorship agreements. Primary sponsors dictate the car's logos and color schemes, and Sprint Cup drivers receive $12 to $15 million, although this is down substantially from the $25 to $30 million seen during the early 2000s (NASCAR, 2012b).

Drivers also receive purse earnings, depending on where they finish in each race. Sprint Cup events such as the Daytona 500 and All-Star Race pay over $1 million to the winner, while other races may pay as little as $200,000. Earnings, endorsements, and sponsorships are used to defray team costs—as much as $400,000 per race—for pit crews, race cars, travel to and from races, and related expenses (Coble, 2012). NASCAR analysts have compared the earnings of NASCAR drivers to competitors in other individual sports such as tennis and golf, and noted the disparities. Winning a Grand Slam tournament or PGA TOUR event translates into multimillion-dollar earnings, without the danger of driving a race car 200 miles per hour. In NASCAR, only the Daytona 500 and All-Star Race pay winners more than $1 million, whereas most PGA TOUR–winning prizes exceed $1 million. Men's tennis players also have multiple opportunities each year to earn $1 million playing in a single event. Although NASCAR drivers can earn sizable prize amounts, large gaps still exist when comparing the top NASCAR potential earnings to those found in other individual sports (Caraviello, 2008).

ORGANIZATIONAL STRUCTURE. In 2003 Bill France Jr.'s son, Brian France, became the third NASCAR Chairman of the Board and Chief Executive Officer (Clarke, 2008). Reporting to him are the President, Executive Vice President, Chief Financial Officer, legal and secretary personnel, and licensing and consumer products personnel (The Official Board, 2012). As shown in Exhibit 13.7, the executive leadership team continues to remain primarily a family operation. Under this leadership, the governing body has placed a heightened emphasis on safety and innovation, working to ensure the safety of drivers, pit crew, and spectators at sanctioned events. The organization issues specific guidelines and safety measures regarding modifications race car owners and mechanics are allowed to make on their vehicles. NASCAR officials monitor alterations closely and quickly issue citations to drivers and owners running afoul of the rules (Clarke, 2008). NASCAR also introduced numerous safety innovations, including racetrack walls comprised of steel and foam and in-car driver restraints to minimize physical injuries during crashes (Clarke, 2008).

NASCAR acts as a sanctioning body, and race car owners and drivers operate as independent contractors. As of 2012 approximately 175 team owners compete to race in NASCAR-sanctioned events (Mickle, 2012b). They gain entry by entering race cars into lower-level series races and eventually moving up to higher profile races as they attain more experience and earnings (Martin, 2011). Prior to each of these races, NASCAR drivers must demonstrate their on-track skills. Qualifying laps are typically held in two days before each race. Drivers are given two opportunities to par-

NASCAR executive leadership structure.

exhibit **13.7**

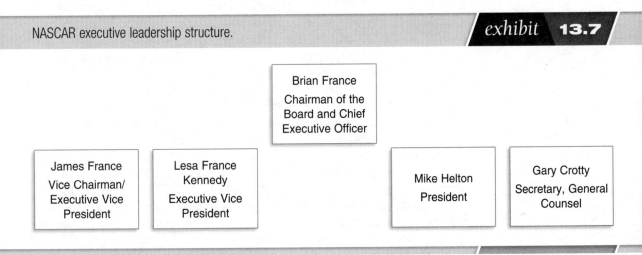

Brian France
Chairman of the Board and Chief Executive Officer

James France
Vice Chairman/ Executive Vice President

Lesa France Kennedy
Executive Vice President

Mike Helton
President

Gary Crotty
Secretary, General Counsel

ticipate in these laps, and the driver with the fastest lap time receives the pole position, or first-place slot, on race day. The remaining 42 of 43 drivers are slotted based on their qualifying times and their accumulated points earned over the season (NASCAR, 2012a). As independent contractors, team owners and drivers must secure revenues through purse winnings, sponsorships, endorsements, title sponsorships, and ticket sales. NASCAR does not participate in revenue sharing with its television contracts (Mickle, 2012b). Furthermore, drivers also must obtain their own insurance and create personal retirement plans (Martin, 2011).

Current Policy Areas

NASCAR leaders are constantly focused on innovation and ways to improve their products and organization. Currently, they face challenges in three key areas: addressing declining viewership, identifying new leadership, and securing corporate sponsorships.

Declining viewership

For the first half of the 2012 NASCAR season, automobile racing industry analysts reported a 20 percent decline in NASCAR viewership among its 18- to 34-year-old demographic, a key market for the sport industry in general and NASCAR in particular (Mickle & Ourand, 2012b). The organization reported a similar decrease in 2010, when viewership in the same demographic group dropped by 29 percent from the previous year. NASCAR leaders attribute the declines to the capricious nature of sports fans, weather conditions, and competition from other sports. The NASCAR season begins in February and extends through November, crossing paths with sports such as professional and collegiate basketball, professional baseball, and professional football. For example, the March 11, 2012, Las Vegas Sprint Cup race competed against the Atlantic Coast Conference (ACC) and Big Ten basketball championship games, and witnessed a viewership decline in popular NASCAR-viewing states such as North Carolina and Ohio (Mickle & Ourand, 2012a). The NASCAR leadership team believes it has initiated some important changes, such as promoting interesting driver story lines and changing the championship point system, but acknowledges the need for additional ways to retain this important demographic group (Mickle & Ourand, 2012b).

To help reverse viewership declines, NASCAR has connected with its target demographics through social media. In 2012 NASCAR's official Twitter followers increased from 339,347 to 801,019, and the NASCAR hashtag received more than 2.25 million tweets, contributing to a 60 percent increase in fan interest (Jessop, 2012). NASCAR driver Brad Keselowski frequently uses Twitter to connect with fans, and he gained over 100,000 new followers after tweeting from his race car during the Daytona 500. Race officials later revised their social media policies, which now prohibit drivers from carrying and using smartphones in their race cars (Ryan, 2012).

The launch of NASCAR's interactive mobile application has proven successful with race fans, who logged a 43 percent increase in usage from 2011 to 2012 (Jessop, 2012). The app enables fans to follow drivers as well as the Sprint Cup race action, including race day coverage. NASCAR hopes these innovative efforts will continue to attract and retain fans. However, whether the efforts will actually contribute to an increase in viewership and attendance remains to be seen.

Higher costs and shrinking owner pool

NASCAR also faces challenges with its race car cost structure. Race car owners have expressed difficulties due to exponential cost increases. One longtime owner noted that fielding a car in 1983 cost $250,000 while placing the same car in the Sprint Cup Series today may cost an estimated $40 million (Mickle, 2012b). Higher costs have forced some owners out of the market, while others have joined forces and consolidated. The number of Sprint Cup race car owners has shrunk from 37 in 1996 to 20 in 2012, and more owners are relying on multi-car ownership to spread costs over two or more race cars (Mickle, 2012b). Several owners with multiple race cars have remained in the industry for many years, but have started looking for successors. Concerned about the sport's future, they have met with NASCAR officials and offered cost suggestions, including moving away from the independent contractor system to a franchise system or revenue sharing model similar to the National Football League and National Basketball Association (Mickle, 2012b).

Corporate sponsorships and driver endorsements

Coupled with rising costs, NASCAR owners and drivers report challenges with securing sponsors to offset their expenses. For example, longtime Sprint Cup driver Matt Kenseth failed to identify a primary sponsor at the beginning of the 2012 season despite his career successes. Some attributed the lack of sponsorship opportunities to the driver's age—Kenseth was 40 at the time—and corporate sponsors are interested in younger, newer drivers. Lack of sponsorship funds can severely limit a driver's and owner's ability to field a successful race car (Blount, 2012). Beyond identifying sponsors, drivers have noted challenges with securing personal endorsements, which slumped considerably during the 2008 recession. Some corporate sponsors shied away from stock car racing during the time period and never returned. Others observed their growing sponsorship inventory and questioned whether driver endorsements and race car sponsorships made financial sense (Mickle, 2012a). NASCAR historically has tied its successes to attentive fans, longstanding leadership, and sponsorship revenues, and addressing these challenges will prove critical to the organization's future.

SUMMARY

Many individual sports share some governance elements with sports that operate as leagues. For example, both have commissioners, boards of directors, and owners. The governing bodies for individual and league sports are responsible for setting rules and regulations, developing policies, and responding to current issues. Membership in the organizations is well defined. One aspect that is different, particularly with golf and tennis, is the emphasis on grassroots development of the sport. For these sports, the professional aspect is just one part of what governing bodies attend to. Cultivating grassroots participation is also of the utmost importance in order to identify and train the next generation of elite athletes. In this way, these sport organizations resemble National Governing Bodies in the Olympic Movement, which stress both elite athlete development and grassroots participation.

A major difference between individual sports and league sports is the absence of unions and collective bargaining agreements. Also, the qualifying process differs markedly from the drafting process for league sports. From a spectator's perspective, team sports usually create a sense of community by encouraging spectators to be fans of a team. In individual sports, spectators often focus on a specific event (e.g., the Masters, Wimbledon) rather than a single player. Furthermore, the majority of the individual sports include senior tours or senior events promoting longevity in the careers of their individual athletes. It is important to recognize these organizations that work with individual sports and realize that sport governance in professional sport is not just about the Big Four.

case STUDY

FUTURE CHALLENGES FOR THE GOVERNING STRUCTURE OF GOLF

The IOC voted 63 to 27 with two abstentions to return golf to the 2016 and 2020 Summer Olympic Games. Male and female golfers competed for the first time in the Olympics in 1900, where men played 72 holes, and women played 9 holes (Little, 2009). At the St. Louis Olympic Games in 1904, only individual men and 10-men teams competed. In the 2016 Games in Rio de Janeiro, the game will be held as a 72-hole stroke-play event for men and women. Golf in the Olympic Games will be the biggest event golf organizations such as the International Golf Federation (IGF) and USGA will face in the upcoming years.

The IGF is the governing body responsible for arranging international amateur competitions in golf. The organization is located in the USGA's offices and comprises 125 federations from 118 countries. Although the

IGF promotes and acts as the golf federation for the Olympic Games, it is not the ultimate governing and rule setting body for golf. Those responsibilities are shared jointly with the R&A and USGA, and the current IGF committee includes joint chairs from the R&A and the USGA. Furthermore, the IGF Women's Chair is the president of the Royal Spanish Golf Federation, and not the joint president of the LPGA (IGF, n.d.).

Unlike other organizations where international federations represent the ultimate governing bodies overseeing regional and local governing bodies, golf organizations are dispersed and independent. Each golf organization serves different roles with players at different levels across the sport. The complexity of this organizational structure poses potential problems for golf in terms of who is responsible for the rules regarding player eligibility and other issues. Decisions about whether the rules from the USGA and R&A will remain the same could become an unavoidable debate among the organizations and for the IOC. The IGF's role and the decisions on rules and responsibilities likely will be questioned as we get closer to the Olympic Games.

1. What are your thoughts about the addition of golf to the Olympic Games program?
2. How should Olympic competitions "fit" into the regular PGA or LPGA Tours? Should they count as tour events? Should Olympic golf model Olympic tennis?
3. What are possible benefits of having joint chairs for the IGF?
4. What other possible challenges might IGF may face, as they are not solely responsible for rule setting and rule governing?
5. Who should be responsible if a major issue arises at the Olympic Games in 2016?

CHAPTER questions

1. The USTA has three important divisions but limited funds to support them. As the USTA leader, which division would you emphasize and why? What are the advantages and disadvantages of highlighting one division versus another?
2. NASCAR currently uses an independent contractor system, but team owners have suggested a franchise system and/or revenue sharing. What are the advantages and disadvantages of these proposals for the teams and NASCAR?
3. Professional tennis, golf, and stock car racing rely heavily upon sponsorship revenues. In challenging economic times, how can the three sports ensure ongoing support from sponsors? What alternatives can they pursue in the event of sponsorship declines?

REFERENCES

Amato, C. H., Peters, C. L. O., & Shao. A. T. (2005). An exploratory investigation into NASCAR fan culture. *Sport Marketing Quarterly, 14,* 71–83.

Blount, T. (2012, June 27). Money—or lack of it—talks. ESPN.com. Retrieved from http://espn.go.com/racing/nascar/cup/story/_/id/8098182/nascar-matt-kenseth-ouster-not-surprising

Caraviello, D. (2008, May 14). Sometimes, $1 million isn't quite as much as it seems. NASCAR.com. Retrieved from http://www.nascar.com/2008/news/opinion/05/14/dcaraviello.allstar.paycheck/index.html

Clarke, L. (2008). *One helluva ride: How NASCAR swept the nation.* New York: Villard Books.

Coble, D. (2012, February 16). Pit road to money pit: Costs to field a NASCAR team are staggering. *Florida Times–Union.* Retrieved from http://jacksonville.com/sports/racing/2012-02-16/story/pit-road-money-pit-costs-field-nascar-team-are-staggering

Crouse, K. (2011, September 7). Challenges would come with building a roof. *New York Times.* Retrieved from http://www.nytimes.com/2011/09/08/sports/tennis/2011-us-open-building-a-roof-would-come-with-many-challenges.html?pagewanted=all

Futterman, M., & Blackmon, D. A. (2010, January 25). PGA TOUR begins to pay a price for Tiger Woods's transgressions. *Wall Street Journal.* Retrieved from http://online.wsj.com/article/SB1000142405274870369920457501755026124550
6.html

Hambrick, M. E., Simmons, J. M., Greenhalgh, G. P., & Greenwell, T. C. (2010). Understanding professional athletes' use of Twitter: A content analysis of athlete Tweets. *International Journal of Sport Communication, 3,* 454–471.

Hinton, E. (2005, December 08). NASCAR reaches $4.5 billion TV deal. *Daily Press.* Retrieved from http://articles.dailypress.com/2005-12-08/sports/0512080247_1_nascar-s-deal-abc-sports-espn-international-and-espn

Homestead Miami Speedway. (2013). History of NASCAR. Retrieved from http://www.homesteadmiamispeedway.com/Going-Away/History-of-NASCAR.aspx

Hoy, P. (2008, August 22). The business of tennis: Economics of the U.S. Open. *Forbes.* Retrieved from http://www.forbes.com/2008/08/22/tennis-open-economics-tennisbiz08-biz-sports-cz_ph_0822economics.html

Iacobelli, P. (2011, June 24). 2012 PGA Championship to have big economic impact. *USA Today.* Retrieved from http://www.usatoday.com/sports/golf/2011-06-24-4108016794_x.htm

IGF. (n.d.). About IGF. Retrieved from http://www.internationalgolffederation.org/about/administrative_committee.html#admin

Jessop, A. (2012, Nov. 17). NASCAR's innovative social media approach leads to significant growth in fan base. *Forbes Magazine.* Retrieved from http://www.forbes.com/sites/aliciajessop/2012/11/17/nascars-innovative-social-media-approach-leads-to-significant-growth-in-fan-base/?utm_source=twitterfeed&utm_medium=twitter

Kaplan, D. (2010, August 30). CBS is ready to renew deal with U.S. Open. *Sports Business Daily.* Retrieved from http://www.sportsbusinessdaily.com/Journal/Issues/2010/08/20100830/This-Weeks-News/CBS-Is-Ready-To-Renew-Deal-With-US-Open.aspx

Kaplan, D. (2011, August 29). USTA signs Smith for another 4 years as executive director. *Sports Business Journal.* Retrieved from http://www.sportsbusinessdaily.com/Journal/Issues/2011/08/29/Leagues-and-Governing-Bodies/Smith.aspx

Little, W. (2009). Golf returning to the Olympics. *Golf Digest.* Retrieved from http://www.golfdigest.com/golf-tours-news/2009-10/golf_olympics_ap_1009

LPGA. (n.d.a). About the LPGA. Retrieved from http://www.lpga.com/corporate/ladies-golf/about-the-lpga.aspx

LPGA. (n.d.b). Directory of marketing partners. Retrieved from http://www.lpga.com/corporate/ladies-golf/directory-of-marketing-partners.aspx

Martin, B. (2011, March 21). Drivers, officials support NASCAR's nearly strike-proof labor system. *Sports Illustrated.* Retrieved from http://sportsillustrated.cnn.com/2011/writers/bruce_martin/03/21/NASCAR.NFL.lockout/index.html?eref=si_latest

McCormick, G. (2012, June 12). U.S. Open's return to SF Bay Area highlights game's economic contributions. *San Francisco Examiner.* Retrieved from http://www.examiner.com/article/u-s-opens-return-to-sf-bay-area-highlights-games-economic-contributions

Mell, R. (2011, October 13). Money title not what it used to be. Golf Channel.com. Retrieved from http://www.golfchannel.com/news/randall-mell/money-title-not-what-it-used-to-be/

Mickle, T. (2012a, May 28). Driver deals running on empty. *Sports Business Daily.* Retrieved from http://www.sportsbusinessdaily.com/Journal/Issues/2012/05/28/Marketing-and-Sponsorship/NASCAR-drivers.aspx

Mickle, T. (2012b, February 20). Who will fill their shoes? *Sports Business Daily.* Retrieved from http://www.sportsbusinessdaily.com/Journal/Issues/2012/02/20/In-Depth/Lead.aspx

Mickle, T., & Ourand, J. (2012a, June 18). FOX making strong bid to keep NASCAR. *Sports Business Daily.* Retrieved from http://www.sportsbusinessdaily.com/Journal/Issues/2012/06/18/Media/Fox-NASCAR.aspx

Mickle, T., & Ourand, J. (2012b, June 11). NASCAR: No panic over dip in 18–34 demo. *Sports Business Daily.* Retrieved from http://www.sportsbusiness daily.com/Journal/Issues/2012/06/11/Media/NASCAR-Fox.aspx

Miller, S. (2012, January 21). Trying to appeal to U.S. Under-10 generation by shrinking the game's scale. *New York Times.* Retrieved from http://straightsets.blogs.nytimes.com/2012/01/21/trying-to-appeal-to-u-s-under-10-generation-by-shrinking-the-games-scale/

Monson, G. (2012, June 11). Is American tennis dead? *Chicago Sun-Times.* Retrieved from http://www.suntimes.com/sports/13118366-419/is-american-tennis-dead.html

Mullen, L., & Smith, M. (2012, May 21). Changes may affect future pros' equipment deals. *Sports Business Daily.* Retrieved from http://www.sportsbusiness daily.com/Journal/Issues/2012/05/21/Marketing-and-Sponsorship/PGA-Tour.aspx

NASCAR. (2012a) Fan guide. Retrieved from http://www.nascar.com/kyn/

NASCAR. (2012b, February 2). Major sponsor deals indicate economy is turning. Retrieved from http://www.nascar.com/news/120202/sponsorship-deals-indication/index.html

NASCAR. (2012c, June 28). NASCAR announces diversity program internships. Retrieved from http://www.nascar.com/en_us/news-media/articles/2012/06/28/nascar-diversity-internships.html

NASCAR. (2012d, October 15). NASCAR, FOX Sports agree to new eight-year deal. Retrieved from http://www.nascar.com/en_us/news-media/articles/2012/10/15/nascar-fox-sports-multi-year-multi-platform-deal.html

National Sporting Goods Association. (2012). Ten-year history of sports participation. Retrieved from http://www.nsga.org/i4a/pages/index.cfm?pageid=3479

Ourand, J. (2011, June 6). How high can rights fees go? *Sports Business Daily.* Retrieved from http://www.sportsbusinessdaily.com/Journal/Issues/2011/06/06/In-Depth/RightsFees.aspx

PGA. (2012a). History. Retrieved from http://www.pga.com/pga-america/history

PGA. (2012b). Member classifications. Retrieved from http://www.pga.com/pga-america/member-classifications

PGA. (2012c). Partners. Retrieved from http://www.pga.com/pga-america/partners

PGA. (2012d). Bevacqua named new CEO of PGA of America, Crall promoted to COO. Retrieved from http://www.pga.com/pga-america/pga-feature/peter-bevacqua-named-new-ceo-pga-america-darrell-crall-promoted-coo

PGA. (2012e). Bishop, Sprague and Levy elected to highest offices at PGA of America. Retrieved from http://www.pga.com/pga-america/pga-feature/ted-bishop-derek-sprague-paul-levy-elected-highest-offices-pga-america

PGA Links. (2012). Mission. Retrieved from http://www.pgalinks.com/diversity/index.cfm?id=missionstatement

PGA Links.com. (2012) "Annual Report" by Professional Golf Association of America, 2011. Retrieved from http://images.pgalinks.com/vmc/pressReleases/AnnualReport_2011.pdf

PGA TOUR. (2012a). About PGA TOUR. Retrieved from http://www.pgatour.com/company/about_us.html

PGA TOUR. (2012b). Commissioner's office. Retrieved from http://www.pgatour.com/company/executive_bios.html

PGA TOUR. (2012c). PGA TOUR 2012 official retail licensees. Retrieved from http://www.pgatour.com/company/retail-licensees/

PGA TOUR. (2012d). Tournaments. Retrieved from http://www.pgatour.com/r/schedule/

PGA/Turner Sports Interactive. (2012). Adapted from "Annual Report" by Professional Golf Association of America, 2011.

Pucin, D. (2012, March 28). Things are looking up for the LPGA. *Los Angeles Times.* Retrieved from http://articles.latimes.com/2012/mar/28/sports/la-sp-lpga-kraft-nabisco-20120329

Ross, H. (2010, October 26). Q-School primer: Answers to key questions. Retrieved from http://www.pgatour.com/2010/qschool/10/18/2010-primer/index.html

Russo, R. D. (2012, June 14). USTA plans massive makeover for U.S. Open facilities. *Businessweek*. Retrieved from http://www.businessweek.com/ap/2012-06-14/usta-plans-massive-makeover-for-us-open-facilities

Ryan, N. (2012, November 17). NASCAR chairman says social media policy evolved. *USA Today*. Retrieved from http://www.usatoday.com/story/sports/nascar/2012/11/17/brian-france-says-nascars-social-media-policy-evolved/1711163/

Schorn, D. (2009, February 11). The real NASCAR family. Retrieved from http://www.cbsnews.com/2100-18560_162-919340.html

Schupak, A. (2012, August 18). Youth golf thrives, but not in high school. *New York Times*. Retrieved from http://www.nytimes.com/2012/08/19/sports/golf/junior-golf-tours-cater-to-youths-pursuing-scholarships.html

Smith, M. (2012, February 27). FedEx: PGA TOUR deal a winner. *Sports Business Journal*. Retrieved from http://www.sportsbusinessdaily.com/Journal/Issues/2012/02/27/Marketing-and-Sponsorship/FedEx-PGA-Tour.aspx

Starr, R. (2012, April 30). Marketers use creativity, technology to reach new golf audience. *Sports Business Journal*. Retrieved from http://www.sportsbusinessdaily.com/Journal/Issues/2012/04/30/Opinion/From-the-Field-of-Marketing.aspx

The Official Board. (2012, May 14). NASCAR organizational chart. Retrieved from http://www.theofficialboard.com/org-chart/nascar

"Top Athletes on Facebook." (2012). Fan page list.com. Retrieved from http://fanpagelist.com/category/athletes/

Tuohy, B. (2011, March 10). Federal judge upholds ruling on five ATP tennis players suspended for gambling. *Examiner*. Retrieved from http://www.examiner.com/article/federal-judge-upholds-ruling-on-five-atp-tennis-players-suspended-for-gambling

Twitter. (n.d.). Tweeting-Athletes. Retrieved from http://www.tweeting-athletes.com/index.cfm

USGA. (2012a). About the USGA. Retrieved from http://www.usga.org/about.aspx?id=7881#show=d1615101-00df-42fe-97f1-bb9cd1de416c

USGA. (2012b). Club membership. Retrieved from http://www.usga.org/clubs_courses/club_history/Club-Membership/

USGA. (2012c). Mission statement. Retrieved from http://www.usga.org/about_usga/mission/Mission/

USGA. (2012d). 2011 Annual report. Retrieved from http://www.usga-digital.com/usga/20120125?sub_id=JggDrvBjPGjv#pg1

USGA. (2012e). Final results and prize money. Retrieved from http://www.usga.org/news/2012/USGA-News/

USGA. (2012f). Leadership. Retrieved from http://www.usga.org/about_usga/leadership/Leadership-Committees/

USGA. (2012g). Allied organizations. Retrieved from http://www.usga.org/Content.aspx?id=24125

USTA. (2008). History. Retrieved from http://www.usta.com/Archive/News/Community-Tennis/Volunteers/95424_USTA_History/

USTA. (2011). Consolidated financial statements years ended December 31, 2010 and 2009. White Plains, NY: Author.

USTA. (2012a). About the organization. Retrieved from http://www.usta.com/About-USTA/Organization/Organization/

USTA. (2012b). Organizational memberships. Retrieved from http://membership.usta.com/section/Organizational-Memberships/122.uts

USTA. (2012c). Player development. Retrieved from http://www.usta.com/About-USTA/Player-Development/player_development_home/

USTA. (2012d). Staff management team. Retrieved from http://www.usta.com/About-USTA/Organization/Board-of-Directors/Bio/ExecutiveStaff/

USTA. (2012e). Individual and family memberships. Retrieved from http://membership.usta.com/section/Individual-Family-Memberships/101.uts

USTA. (2012f). Consolidated financial statements years ended December 31, 2011 and 2010. http://assets.usta.com/assets/1/15/USTA_2011_Consolidated_Financial_Statements_-_Signed.pdf

Vasquez, D. (2010, July 19). Your client sponsoring the U.S. Open. *Media Life Magazine*. Retrieved from http://www.medialifemagazine.com/artman2/publish/Out_of_Home_19/Your-client-sponsoring-the-U-S-Open.asp

Zinser, L. (2011, Sept. 6). Rain washes out play at U.S. Open. *New York Times*. Retrieved from: http://www.nytimes.com/2011/09/07/sports/tennis/us-open-rain-washes-out-play.html?_r=1

Professional Sport
Leagues Beyond North America

When you think of professional sport, the first leagues that come to mind are often the NBA, the NFL, the NHL, and MLB. However, in many parts of the world, the topics of discussion at the office the day after a game are very different. Perhaps a debate rages over the upcoming football match involving Manchester United and Amsterdam Ajax, the ongoing rivalry between Olympiakos and Panathanaikos, or whether anyone can catch Sebastian

Vettel in the next Formula 1 Grand Prix. If you are wondering what these examples refer to, then welcome to the exciting world of professional sport beyond North America, where *football* means *soccer,* basketball has a few different rules, motor sports does not mean NASCAR, and baseball is often completely unknown!

The sport industry is truly global in nature. Similar to other global products, such as Coca-Cola or McDonald's, sport transcends borders. The North American way of organizing and managing sport is not the only—and certainly not always the best—way to organize sport. Sport managers working in an international environment must learn to be respectful of local cultures, norms, and expertise. According to Apostolopoulou and Papadimitriou (2005), "it is imperative for sport managers to understand the international environment in which they operate. Sport professionals must be aware of the opportunities that are available on a global scale, as well as the challenges that arise from conducting business in this new, global market" (p. 170).

This chapter introduces the basics of selected international sport leagues and events. For the most part, people in North America have a relatively narrow view of professional sport—the Big Four, NASCAR, golf, and tennis. Hopefully, this chapter will expand your horizons to professional sport around the world. The chapter focuses on two particular examples—football and motor sports—that are extremely popular around the world, as witnessed by the enormous numbers of fans who follow the World Cup and the Formula 1 World Championship.

The governance of professional sport internationally is very different from that in North America. Relationships among several levels of sport governing bodies are involved. Specifically, leagues are tied to the national governing body (NGB) for the sport in each nation, the international federation (IF) for each particular sport, and sometimes to a regional governing body. For example, the Premier League in England has ties to the Football Association of England (FA), the Union of European Football Associations (UEFA), and FIFA (Fédération Internationale de Football Association) (Premier League, 2011a).

Another striking difference between professional leagues in North America and Europe is the system of promotion and relegation used in European leagues (Szymanski & Valetti, 2003). Briefly, this system operates as follows: "While there are several ways in which this scheme can operate, the most commonly used format is one where the worst performing teams in a league during the season, measured by the number of points won (a measure that is close to win percentage) are demoted to an immediately junior league to be replaced by the best performing teams in that league" (Szymanski, 2006, p. 685). As a useful comparison, what might this system look like if applied to Major League Baseball?

Let's say that in a given year the team with the worst record in the National League was the Miami Marlins, and the team with the worst record in the America League was the Kansas City Royals. Next, let's say the team with the best record in the AAA-level International League was the Louisville Bats, and the team with the best record in the AAA-level Pacific Coast League was the Memphis Redbirds. Applying the European scheme, the Bats would be promoted to the National League, while the Redbirds would be promoted to the American League. Consequently, the Marlins would be relegated to the Pacific Coast League, and the Royals would be relegated to the International League. "That sounds crazy," you say. "What about stadiums and season tickets and corporate sponsorships?" Although you may wonder how it could possibly work, promotion and relegation is a common practice in professional sport leagues outside of North America and has worked successfully for many years.

First we analyze soccer, though we in this chapter we use the term *football,* as the sport is known internationally. In this section we will concentrate on two professional leagues—the Premier League in England and the J. League in Japan.

FOOTBALL: PREMIER LEAGUE AND J. LEAGUE

As an organized sport, football has been around for an extremely long time. Professional football has a shorter past. In this section, we briefly trace the history of the Premier League and the J. League; then we focus more directly on league operations and governance.

Before discussing specific leagues, let's look at the overall governance of international football. The IF for football, FIFA, is the international governing body for the game. FIFA consists of six regional organizations, including the Asian Football Confederation (AFC), the Confédération Africaine de Football (CAF), the Confederation of North, Central American and Caribbean Association Football (CONCACAF), the Confederación Sudamericana de Fútbol (CONMEBOL), the Oceania Football Confederation (OFC), and the UEFA. Within these regions, every nation has its own FIFA-recognized national football governing body, such as the U.S. Soccer Federation, Canadian Soccer Association, and Hellenic Football Federation. Professional football leagues within specific nations must belong to their FIFA-recognized national football governing body to be eligible to advance in international play. For example, in the United States, MLS belongs to the U.S. Soccer Federation. The U.S. Soccer Federation, in turn, is a member of CONCACAF, which is the regional division of FIFA that includes North America. Because of this arrangement, MLS, or any FIFA-recognized professional football league in any nation, must follow the rules and regulations set forth by FIFA. Although the leagues have their

WWW

Premier League
www.premierleague.com

J. League
www.j-league.or.jp/eng/

Fédération Internationale de Football Association
www.fifa.com

Asian Football Confederation
www.the-afc.com/en/index.phpConfederation of African Football
www.cafonline.com

Confederation of North, Central American and Caribbean Association Football
www.concacaf.com

Confederación Sudamericana de Fútbol
www.conmebol.com

own individual league governance systems for daily operation, they must follow many basic policies handed down from FIFA on issues such as drug use, match scheduling, and player transfers.

History

In the late 1980s, English football was in need of restructuring. A 1985 fire at a match at Bradford City Valley's Parade Grounds cost 56 lives when flames engulfed the wooden stadium (Conn, 2010). Around this same time, a number of violent incidents involving fans occurred. The game's image was in tatters, and it also suffered from a lack of financial investment. Establishing itself as a business entity separate from the nation's FA allowed the FA Premier League to negotiate its own television and sponsorship contracts, sources of income that have helped the league transition to its current success. The FA Premier League was formed in 1992 and took over as the top professional league in 1992 and 1993 (Premier League, 2011b). The league attracts players and fans from all over the world and is a successful business entity. In 2007, it changed its name to simply Premier League.

In Japan, football became more popular after the 1964 Tokyo Olympic Games and the nation's bronze medal finish in the 1968 Mexico City Olympic Games. The sport was played on a national league level as the Japan Soccer League (JSL). This was an amateur league until professional athletes were officially admitted to the Olympic Games in 1984 and the JSL officially recognized professional players in 1986. The JSL established an action committee that discussed ways to grow the game and suggested formation of a professional league. The Japan Football Association (JFA) accepted the committee's recommendation. Thus, the J. League officially began in 1992, with a game in Tokyo before 59,626 spectators. By 2004, the league's aggregate attendance reached 7.4 million fans (History of the J. League, 2012).

Governance

Many nations large and small around the world have professional football leagues. Some of the most notable, in addition to the Premier League in England and the J. League in Japan, include the Bundesliga in Germany, La Liga in Spain, Serie A in Italy, and MLS in the United States. This is in addition to multination leagues, such as the UEFA Champions League. To illustrate governance structures, this section focuses on the Premier League and the J. League. Both are the top-level leagues in their nations, with lower leagues beneath them. These lower leagues are not technically minor leagues as we know them; they are separate clubs, not affiliates of the top division clubs. For example, the J. League technically consists of two leagues—J1 and J2. J1 is the top league, the one we refer to as J. League in this section.

MISSION. The Premier League mission statement is found in Exhibit 14.1, and the J. League's mission statement is presented in Exhibit 14.2. While both mention the development of the game, the Premier League presents more information concerning the business aspects of the league.

Mission statement of the Premier League.

exhibit **14.1**

The Premier League must:

- Manage, continually improve and be regarded as the world's best league football competition—on and off the field
- Increase interest in our competitions, promote accessibility to live games and ensure that media exposure is used to optimum effect
- Generate increased commercial value, using the resulting revenues to further enhance our competition and strengthen the long-term future of the Premier League and its clubs
- Use our power and influence responsibly to improve the game in this country and abroad through partnership with the FA, UEFA and other bodies
- Create a quality of competition that provides a platform from which our member clubs can achieve unparalleled success in European or World competitions
- Use our resources to develop playing talent that will provide for international success with the England team at all levels—with the status of World Champions being the realistic goal

Source: Premier League (2011a).

Mission statement of the J. League.

exhibit **14.2**

- To raise the level of Japanese football and promote the diffusion of the game through the medium of professional football
- To foster the development of Japan's sporting culture, to assist in the healthy mental and physical growth of Japanese people
- To contribute to international friendship and exchange

Source: J. League (n.d.a)..

MEMBERSHIP. The members of these two professional leagues are the teams themselves. The Premier League is owned by 20 shareholders—the member clubs (e.g., Blackburn Rovers, Newcastle United, Liverpool, and 17 others) (Premier League, 2013). The J. League's 16 member teams/shareholders include Gamba Osaka, F.C. Tokyo, and the Urawa Red Diamonds.

The J. League has very specific conditions of membership. These conditions fall into the following categories:

1. *Incorporation.* Each club must be a registered corporation specializing in football. This condition is stipulated to ensure that each club provides a secure management base.
2. *Hometown.* Each club must designate a particular locality as its hometown. It must cooperate in sports activities conducted in the area to grow as a club that takes part in activities in the community and promotes sport in the region.
3. *Players and coaching licenses.* First division teams must have at least 15 players who have signed the standard professional contract approved by the Japan Football Association (JFA), while second division teams must have at least five such players. Coaches must possess the appropriate coaching license approved by the JFA.
4. *Team structure.* Each J1 club must have at least a satellite team, a U-18 team, a U-15 team, and a U-12 team. Each J2 club must have at least a satellite team and a U-18 team. J2 clubs without a U-15 and/or U-12 team must organize football schools and conduct other activities targeting children of these age groups and organize these teams within three years of joining the J. League.
5. *Stadium facilities.* For both J1 and J2 clubs, stadiums must possess an evergreen natural grass field with, in principle, a size of 105 meters by 68 meters. The stadiums must also have floodlights of an average 1,500 lux or more. Stadiums for J1 clubs must hold 15,000 spectators or more. Stadiums for J2 clubs must hold 12,000 spectators or more. ("About the J. League," 2012, para. 14)

To determine ongoing membership, these leagues use a "ladder system." As previously discussed, this system, common in international sport leagues, works as follows: The teams that finish last and next to last in the J. League (or J1) one season are relegated to J2 the next season. Simultaneously, the two top finishers in the J2 are elevated to J1 status the next year, assuming they meet the above criteria for J1 membership.

FINANCIALS. The sources of revenues for these leagues are similar to those in North America; they include merchandising programs, broadcast revenues, and corporate sponsorships, in addition to ticket sales. The Premier League is also known as the Barclay's Premier League, because Barclay's banking and financial services is the official title sponsor for the league.

Other official partners of the Premier League are EA Sports, Lucozade, Nike, and Topps. In fiscal year 2009, the J. League produced revenues of over ¥12 billion, which is approximately US$150 million or €113 million (J. League, 2011). Some of the J. League's official sponsors include Calbee Foods, Canon, Coca-Cola, Konami, AIDEM, McDonald's, Fuji Xerox, and Yamazaki-Nabisco (J. League, n.d.a).

ORGANIZATIONAL STRUCTURE. The Premier League is a private company and, as mentioned earlier, is owned by 20 shareholders—the member clubs. According to the league:

> Each individual club is independent; working within the rules of football, as defined by the Premier League, The FA, UEFA and FIFA as well being subject to English and European law.
>
> Each of the 20 clubs is a Shareholder in the Premier League. Consultation is at the heart of the Premier League and Shareholder meetings are the ultimate decision-making forum for Premier League policy and are held at regular intervals during the course of the season.
>
> The AGM [Annual General Meeting] takes place at the close of each season, at which time the relegated clubs transfer their shares to the clubs promoted into the Premier League from the Football League Championship.
>
> Clubs have the opportunity to propose new rules or amendments at the Shareholder meeting. Each Member Club is entitled to one vote and all rule changes and major commercial contracts require the support of a two thirds vote, or 14 clubs, to be agreed. Substantive rule or policy changes generally only take place at the AGM in order to preserve the integrity of the competition during a season.
>
> The Premier League Rule Book serves as a contract between the League, the Member Clubs and one another, defining the structure and running of the competition. (Premier League, 2011a)

The organizational structure for the J. League is illustrated in Exhibit 14.3. The J. League has a Board of Directors, with directors and auditors elected at the regularly scheduled General Meeting. The Board of Directors, the J. League's ultimate governing body, oversees two Executive Committees, one for J1 and the other for J2. According to the J. League (n.d.b), "The Executive Committees put the league's aims and policies into effect and deliberate and decide on matters entrusted to them by the Board of Directors. Each Executive Committee is made up of the chairman, directors with specific responsibilities, and one representative selected from each club" (para. 1). The Board of Directors also determines the authority and responsibilities of the Disciplinary Committee, Technical Committee, Legal Affairs Committee, Match Commissioners' Committee, Consultative Committee on Management, and Marketing Committee (J. League, n.d.b).

The Premier League and the J. League offer us interesting information about the operation of international team sport leagues. Another well-pub-

exhibit **14.3**   Organizational chart for the J. League.

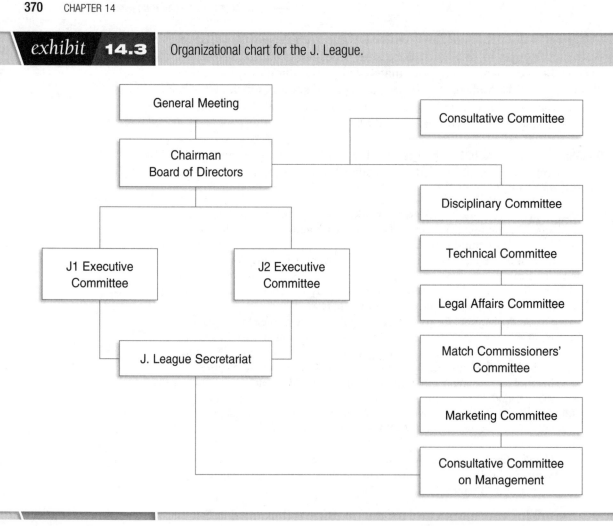

Source: J. League (n.d.b).

licized and highly regarded international professional sport is motor sports. Let's take a look at the most prominent of these—Formula 1 racing. It will be interesting to compare Formula 1 to NASCAR.

MOTOR SPORTS: FORMULA 1

otor sports take on many forms, including stock car racing, as in NASCAR; open-wheel racing, as in the Indy Racing League (IRL); and drag racing, sponsored by the National Hot Rod Association (NHRA). However, the form of motor sports reaching the largest number of fans around the world is none of the above. The most widely watched motor sport is Formula 1 racing. But what exactly is Formula 1 and how is it governed?

History

The IF governing motor sports is the Fédération Internationale de l'Automobile (FIA), which organizes Formula 1 World Championships as well as all other international motor sports (FIA, 2011a). FIA not only governs motor sports but also oversees issues concerning traffic safety and automobile safety in general. Created in 1904, today FIA is "a non-profit making association. . . . [that] brings together 227 national motoring and sporting organisations from 132 countries on five continents" (FIA, 2011a).

Formula refers to a certain combination of car specifications, including minimum and maximum weights, fuel consumption, and cylinder capacity. In the early days of racing, no *formula* designation existed. The first basic formula, introduced in 1904, simply restricted maximum car weight. The term *Formula 1* did not appear until after World War II. Created in 1950, the Formula 1 World Championship is the oldest of the FIA championships. According to FIA (2002), *Formula 1* is defined as

> a set of technical regulations for single-seater racing cars, which is published annually by the FIA. The regulations specify maximum and minimum dimensions, engine capacity, what is permitted technically and what is not permitted and, perhaps most important of all, a large number of safety measures to be incorporated in the car with a view to protecting the driver. (What Is Formula 1? section)

The 2012 FIA Formula 1 World Championship consisted of 20 Grand Prix events in the following locations: Australia, Malaysia, China, Bahrain, Spain, Monaco, Canada, France, Great Britain, Germany, Hungary, Belgium, Italy, Singapore, Japan, South Korea India, the United Arab Emirates, the United States, and Brazil. Two World Champion titles are awarded—one for drivers and one for car constructors. Points are awarded for order of finish, and the driver and the constructor with the most points after the season series are awarded their respective titles.

Governance

MISSION. The FIA is the governing body for Formula 1. Its mission statement, according to the statutes adopted by the FIA General Assembly in 2002 and modified in 2006, is presented in Exhibit 14.4. In contrast to the mission statement for the Premier League, FIA's mission statement describes its organization as a nonprofit, serving as an umbrella IF for activities in addition to racing.

FIA also lists a number of objectives, one of which is "promoting the development of motor sport, enacting, interpreting and enforcing common rules applicable to the organization and running of motor sports events" (FIA, 2011b, p. 2). Formula 1 racing falls under this particular objective.

| exhibit | **14.4** | Mission statement of the FIA. |

> The Fédération Internationale de l'Automobile (FIA), a non-profit-making world organization and an international association of national Automobile Clubs, Automobile Associations, Touring Clubs, and National Federations for motoring and motor sport, was founded in 1904 and enjoys consultative status with the U.N. It has its headquarters in Paris, or in such place as the General Assembly may determine.
>
> The FIA shall refrain from manifesting racial, political, or religious discrimination in the course of its activities and from taking any action in this respect.

Source: FIA (2011b).

MEMBERSHIP. The voting members of the FIA include the following:

WWW

ASN Canada FIA
www.asncanada.com

Deustche Motor Sport Bund e.V.
www.dmsb.de

- national automobile clubs and national automobile associations (for example, American Automobile Association and Canadian Automobile Association)
- clubs, associations, or federations covering road traffic, touring, or camping
- clubs, associations, or federations whose activity concerns motor sports (for example, ASN Canada FIA, Deustche Motor Sport Bund e.V. [Germany]). Once admitted as members, these clubs, associations, or federations exercise Sporting Power. (FIA, 2011b)

Clearly, the governance and operation of Formula 1 racing falls under "Sporting Power" in the third category above.

WWW

Canadian Formula 1 Grand Prix
www.formula1.com/races/in_detail/canada_870/

FINANCIALS. Formula 1 Grand Prix events are multimillion-dollar or -euro events. For example, the 2008 Formula 1 event in Singapore increased tourism spending by $100 million that year. Over 100,000 people attended the race, over half of whom were tourists from outside of Singapore. For a country that was struggling from high inflation and a down international economy, the Formula 1 race provided a boost to the local economy. Hospitality, food and beverage, and entertainment sales rose 20 to 30 percent, demonstrating the overall positive effect of the race ("Others May Seek to Emulate," 2008).

In 2009, 105,000 fans watched the Australian Formula 1 Grand Prix in person, 128,000 attended the UK Grand Prix, and 106,000 attended the 2008 Hungarian event (Grand Prix Cities, 2010). In addition, Formula 1 attracts roughly 500 million television viewers per year (Sylt, 2013). Formula 1 racing is heavily driven by corporate sponsorship. Formula 1 racing receives the second highest amount of euros spent by corporate sponsors on sporting events in Europe, second only to football. Major corporate sponsors include companies such as Federal Express, Allianz, Petronas, Gulf Air, Petrol Ofisi, Fuji Television, and Sinopec.

ORGANIZATIONAL STRUCTURE. Because Formula 1 is governed by FIA, we must first look at the governance structure of that organization to see where Formula 1 fits in. FIA's highest level of authority is the General Assembly, composed of delegations from the FIA member clubs, associations, or federations. The General Assembly elects two World Councils—the World Council for Automobile Mobility and Tourism (for all nonsporting activities) and the World Motor Sport Council, which governs all international motor sport (FIA, 2011b). Each World Council, in turn, is governed by its respective General Assembly and the FIA Articles describe the membership of these Councils. Exhibit 14.5 illustrates the governance structure of the FIA.

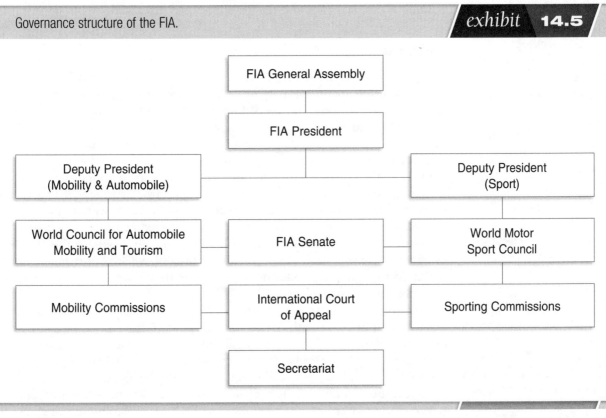

Governance structure of the FIA.

exhibit **14.5**

Source: FIA (2011c).

The World Motor Sport Council has numerous Sporting Commissions that assist in its tasks. Some of these Commissions include the Medical Commission, Volunteers and Officials Commission, Off Road Commission, Safety Commission, Manufacturers' Commission, Women in Motor Sport Commission, and of course, a Formula 1 Commission (FIA, 2011b).

In Formula 1 racing, a Formula 1 technical group consists of the technical directors of each team who "make recommendations to the FIA Formula 1 Commission on which the teams, race promoters, engine manufacturers, sponsors, tire manufacturers and, of course, the FIA are represented. Decisions of the Formula 1 Commission then go to the FIA World Motor Sport Council and ultimately the FIA General Assembly for approval" (FIA, 2002, How Are These Regulations Made section).

CURRENT POLICY AREAS

Just as with professional sport in North America, international professional sport faces a broad range of policy issues. These issues include racism and goal line technology in football and the fallout from the Bahrain Formula 1 race and the 2007 Formula 1 scandal.

Racism in Football

The past years have seen an increase in the number of incidents involving racist behavior on the part of football fans. Unfortunately, racism is still quite alive in some sectors of European football. "FC Barcelona stars Ronaldinho and Samuel Eto'o are taunted with monkey noises at Spanish matches. AS Roma fans display banners with neo-Nazi and anti-Semitic slogans. Gypsies are targeted by Romanian supporters" (Mackey, 2006, para. 1). Superstar Thierry Henry has been insulted by an opposing coach. An Italian footballer gave a fascist salute to spectators. At the EURO 2012 tournament, members of the team from the Netherlands were taunted by monkey chants from fans, and Spain was subjected to racist taunts from opposing fans (CNN, 2012). Mario Balotelli of Italy was also the target of chants. Racism is a complex matter in today's world. Sport managers will need to continue to educate the public with messages until the racist behaviors at sporting events end.

So what have sport organizations done to deal with this issue? At the 2010 World Cup in South Africa, the "Say No to Racism" message was expressed often and visibly. FIFA dedicated all four of the quarter finals to spreading the word against racism. Players and officials held banners on the field reading "Say No to Racism" before these games, and team captains read pre-match pledges against racism. In addition, all the stadiums where matches were played were equipped with a racism monitoring system using trained security personnel (FIFA, 2011).

www

Football Against Racism
in Europe
www.farenet.org

Unite Against Racism
www.uefa.com/multimediafiles/
download/uefa/keytopics/
448328_download.pdf

UEFA has joined with Football Against Racism in Europe (FARE) in a campaign called Unite Against Racism, and has produced a booklet describing racism and how to respond to racist fans. UEFA (2006) offers the following 10-point program for football associations and clubs:

1. Issue a statement saying that racism or any other kind of discrimination will not be tolerated, spelling out the action that will be taken against those who engage in racist chanting. The statement should be printed in all match programmes and displayed permanently and prominently around the ground.

2. Make public address announcements condemning racist chanting at matches.

3. Make it a condition for season ticket holders that they do not take part in racist abuse.

4. Take action to prevent the sale of racist literature inside and around the ground.

5. Take disciplinary action against players who engage in racial abuse.

6. Contact other associations or clubs to make sure they understand the association's or club's policy on racism.

7. Encourage a common strategy between stewards and police for dealing with racist abuse.

8. Remove all racist graffiti from the ground as a matter of urgency.

9. Adopt an equal opportunities' policy in relation to employment and service provision.

10. Work with all other groups and agencies, such as the players' union, supporters, schools, voluntary organisations, youth clubs, sponsors, local authorities, local businesses and the police, to develop proactive programmes and make progress to raise awareness of campaigning to eliminate racial abuse and discrimination. (p. 18)

Goal Line Technology

Germany v. England in World Cup 2010. Ukraine v. England in EURO 2012. Was it a goal or not? Both of these high-profile matches involved disallowed goals in which, upon review, the ball clearly had crossed the goal line in its entirety, but the referees on the field ruled otherwise. With pressure mounting to take advantage of the technology now available, FIFA officials finally decided to allow goal line technology to aid with these calls (The National, 2012). This was not without opposition, however. Some officials believed positioning another official behind the net was a better solution, while others felt countries able to institute the technology the earliest would have priority in hosting major international matches. Premier League officials have indicated they would like to implement the new technology as soon as possible (BBC, 2012). German league officials also welcomed the change and anticipate implementing the technology as early as feasible (Bundesliga, 2012). League officials will be following the lead of some North American leagues that have instituted the use of technology to assist the officials with critical calls. The NFL has used replay for a number of years and Major League Baseball has more recently adopted limited use of replays. This is a major move for a governing body, one that reflects the ability to realize the advantages of such technology. Of course, there will always be nay-sayers and the human element is always part of a game. With literally millions of euros and dollars riding on referees' decision, however, these governing bodies are trying their best to make sure the officials "get it right" when it counts.

Formula 1 Racing in Bahrain

Formula 1 racing came under a hailstorm of protest when they decided to run the 2012 Grand Prix event in strife-torn Bahrain after the 2011 event had been canceled. According to Mekhennet (2012, para 1), "The Sunni monarchy [had] been hoping that the Formula 1 Grand Prix, its showcase annual event, would restore Bahrain's stature as a stable Persian Gulf kingdom, blighted after months of antigovernment protests by the Shiite majority that led to the cancellation of the race [the previous] year." However, observers commented that the opposite effect occurred as thousands of protesters swarmed the streets in the days surrounding the event. The protesters, mainly members of the Shi'ite majority who felt they were being oppressed by a Sunni ruling family, staged major confrontations with police. Many media members who were non–motor sport reporters were also denied visas and were unable to report from Bahrain (Baldwin, 2012). In response to the questioning, FA released the following statement the week before the race (FIA, 2012, p. 1):

> The FIA is the governing body of motor sport and therefore of Formula One. As such, it sets the season's calendars following the proposal of the Commercial Rights Holder (CRH) in accordance with the local national authorities in all matters relating to safety.
>
> Within that context, the FIA ensures that any event forming part of an FIA World Championship is organised in compliance with the FIA Statutes and the relevant Sporting and Technical Regulations and that the safety of the public, officials, drivers and teams is secured at all times during an event.
>
> The FIA must make rational decisions based on the information provided to us by the Bahraini authorities and by the Commercial Rights Holder. In addition we have endeavoured to assess the ongoing situation in Bahrain.
>
> President Jean Todt led a fact-finding mission to the Kingdom in November 2011, meeting a large number of decision-makers and opinion

formers, including elected Shia members of parliament, the president of the Bahrain Independent Commission of Inquiry, ambassadors from the European Union countries, the Crown Prince, the Interior Minister and many members of the business community.

All expressed their wish for the Grand Prix to go ahead in 2012, and since then, the FIA has kept in close touch with all these stakeholders. Away from the public eye, the FIA has received regular security briefings from the most senior diplomatic officials based in the Kingdom as well as from other independent experts.

The 2012 calendar, as presented by the CRH, was ratified by the World Motor Sport Council (WMSC) in September 2011. Since then no request from the F1 Commission or the CRH has been made to the WMSC to either postpone or cancel the Bahrain Grand Prix.

Based on the current information the FIA has at this stage, it is satisfied that all the proper security measures are in place for the running of a Formula One World Championship event in Bahrain.

Therefore, the FIA confirms that the 2012 Gulf Air F1 Grand Prix of Bahrain will go ahead as scheduled.

This case is presented because it shows the interconnectedness of sport, politics, and sport governing bodies. Thinking back to the SLEEPE principle, one can clearly see where sport managers in international sport governing bodies must consider all implications of their decisions. Never before have sport and politics been so intertwined as in the 21st century.

Formula 1 Scandal

In the summer of 2007, Formula 1 was rocked by a scandal of epic proportions. In an attempt to gain a competitive advantage, "McLaren chief designer Mike Coughlan was found in possession of a 780-page dossier of Formula 1 rival Ferrari's technical data. The information allegedly had all the data on the Italian team's 2007 car" (Maphosa, 2007, para. 2). With a backdrop of espionage and intrigue, the punishments levied were newsworthy. Ultimately, the McLaren Mercedes team was eliminated from the constructors' standings and fined $100 million (€65 million) in a scandal that cast a shadow over the racing season (Spurgeon, 2007).

FIA issued the following statement regarding the penalties, after a special session of the World Motor Sports Council (WMSC):

The WMSC has stripped Vodafone McLaren Mercedes of all constructors' points in the 2007 FIA Formula One World Championship and the team can score no points for the remainder of the season. Furthermore, the team will pay a fine equal to 100 million dollars, less the FOM income lost as a result of the points deduction. However, due to the exceptional circumstances in which the FIA gave the team's drivers an immunity in return for providing evidence, there is no penalty in regards to drivers' points. The WMSC will receive a full technical report on the

2008 McLaren car and will take a decision at its December 2007 meeting as to what sanction, if any, will be imposed on the team for the 2008 season. (Formula 1, 2007, paras. 7–10)

Despite this scandal, and a number of others that followed (race-fixing allegations in the 2008 Singapore event, a bribery scandal involving organizational leaders), Formula 1 continues. According to Walker (2012),

Formula One is resilient, thanks in no small part to its large and passionate fan base. But it is also heavily dependent on public investment, thanks to the governments who pay the sport's hefty hosting fees. As a consequence, a worst-case scenario outcome of an F1 corruption scandal could see race contracts cancelled as governments kow-tow to public opinion. (para. 17)

SUMMARY

The world of international professional sport is complex. The interrelationships among professional leagues, IFs, regional federations, and NGBs are unlike any in North America. Despite these differences, similarities exist, particularly when it comes to player movement between teams and corporate sponsorship concerns. What is important to realize, however, is how global a product sport really is.

case STUDY

INTERNATIONAL PROFESSIONAL SPORT

The time for you to start planning your internship is quickly approaching. After reading this book (especially this chapter), you realize opportunities exist for you to pursue internships in nations outside of North America. The opportunities include professional sports, national sport organizations, IFs, and major games and events.

1. List a number of nations where you would like to live or visit.
2. List a number of organizations, sports, or events you would consider.
3. How can you find out more detailed information about these sport organizations?
4. Ask if any of your classmates have either visited or lived in other parts of the world. What questions would you like to ask them about their experiences?
5. What are three specific industry experiences an international internship could offer you that a domestic internship could not?
6. How do you see the global face of the sport industry changing in the next 10 years?

CHAPTER **questions**

1. Choose another professional sport league outside of North America and research its history, mission, membership, financials, and governance structure.

2. Choose a nation outside of North America. Research the different professional sport opportunities available in that nation.

3. In addition to the governance structures described in this chapter, some nations also have a governmental agency that oversees all sports, including professional sport, in that nation. Sometimes this agency is named the Ministry of Sport. If such a structure were created in the United States, who should serve on it, and how should it be organized?

REFERENCES

About the J. League. (2012). *The Rising Sun News*. Retrieved from http://www.the-rising-sun-news.com/news/index.php?option=com_content&view=article&id=613&Itemid=99

Apostolopoulou, A., & Papadimitriou, D. (2005). Global sport industry. In A. Gillentine & R. B. Crow (Eds.), *Foundations of sport management*. Morgantown, WV: Fitness Information Technology.

Baldwin, A. (2012, April 21). Formula One lives in Bahrain bubble. Retrieved from http://www.reuters.com/article/2012/04/21/us-motor-racing-prix-atmosphere-idUSBRE83K0H720120421

BBC. (2012, July 6). Premier League could use goal line technology in 2012–2013. Retrieved from http://www.bbc.co.uk/sport/0/football/18719396

Bundesliga. (2012, July 7). FIFA approve goal line technology. Retrieved from http://www.bundesliga.de/en/liga/news/2011/0000216250.php

CNN. (2012). Croatia faces fresh Euro 2012 racism probe. Retrieved from http://edition.cnn.com/2012/06/20/sport/football/euro-2012-croatia-racism-new/index.html

Conn, D. (2010, May 11). Bradford remembered: The unheeded warnings that led to tragedy. *The Guardian*. Retrieved from http://www.guardian.co.uk/football/david-conn-inside-sport-blog/2010/may/12/bradford-fire-david-conn

FIA. (2002, April). FIA Formula One World Championship FAQ's. Retrieved from http://www.fia.com/mediacentre/f1_faqs/2003/f1_faqs.html

FIA. (2011a). About FIA. Retrieved from http://www.fia.com/en-GB/the-fia/about-fia/Pages/AboutFIA.aspx

FIA. (2011b). FIA statutes. Retrieved from http://www.fia.com/en-GB/the-fia/statutes/Documents/Statuts-FIA-2012.pdf

FIA. (2011c). Structure. Retrieved from http://www.fia.com/en-GB/the-fia/governance/Pages/structure_1.aspx

FIA. (2012, April 13). Formula One World Championship—Bahrain Grand Prix. Press release. Retrieved from http://www.fia.com/en-GB/mediacentre/press-releases/f1releases/2012/Pages/f1-bahrain.aspx

FIFA. (2011, March 2). FIFA against racism: A decade of milestones. Retrieved from http://www.fifa.com/aboutfifa/socialresponsibility/news/news-id=1384919/

Formula 1. (2007, September 13). McLaren fined and stripped of constructors' points. Retrieved from www.formula1.com/news/headlines/2007/9/6767.html

Grand Prix Cities. (2010). Race attendance figure numbers. Retrieved from http://www.grandprixcities.com/raceattendances.html

History of the J. League. (2012). *The Rising Sun News*. Retrieved from http://www.the-rising-sun-news.

com/news/index.php?option=com_content&view=article&id=80&Itemid=54

J. League. (n.d.a). Mission. Retrieved from http://www.j-league.or.jp/eng/mission/

J. League. (n.d.b). Organisation. Retrieved from http://www.j-league.or.jp/eng/organisation/

J. League. (2011, March 21). Financial stats of J. League clubs in the 2009 financial year. Retrieved from http://www.j-league.or.jp/eng/data/2011/03-21.pdf

Mackey, S. (2006, January 31). European soccer's anti-racism conference. Retrieved from http://www.romea.cz/english/index.php?id=servis/z_en_2006_0046

Maphosa, T. (2007, September 13). McLaren fined in Formula-1 scandal. Retrieved from http://www.voanews.com/english/news/a-13-2007-09-13-voa51.html

Mekhennet, S. (2012, April 20). Bahrain protests intensify before Formula One race. *New York Times*. Retrieved from http://www.nytimes.com/2012/04/21/world/middleeast/bahrain-protests-intensify-before-formula-1-race.html?pagewanted=all

Others may seek to emulate Singapore's Formula One success. (2008, October 4). *Bangkok Press*. Retrieved from http://www.istockanalyst.com/article/viewnewspaged/articleid/2683915/pageid/1

Premier League. (2011a). About us. Retrieved from http://www.premierleague.com/en-gb/about/who-we-are.html

Premier League. (2011b, November 24). History of the Premier League. Retrieved from http://www.premierleague.com/en-gb/about/history.html

Premier League. (2013). Who we are. Retrieved from http://www.premierleague.com/en-gb/about/who-we-are.html

Spurgeon, B. (2007, September 30). After spying scandal, embarrassing results. *New York Times*. Retrieved from www.nytimes.com/2007/09/30/sports/othersports/30prix.html?fta=y

Sylt, C. (2013). Formula 1 audience declines in U.S. Retrieved from http://www.autoweek.com/article/20130220/f1/130219849

Szymanski, S. (2006). The promotion and relegation system. In W. Andreff and S. Szymanski (Eds.), *Handbook on the economics of sport* (pp. 685–688). London: Edward Elgar.

Szymanski, S., & Valetti, T. (2003). Promotion and relegation in sporting contests. Retrieved from http://law.psu.edu/_file/Szymanski%20Valetti%20promotion%20relegation.pdf

The National. (2012, June 20). Sepp Blatter calls for goal line technology after Ukraine blunder. Retrieved from http://www.thenational.ae/sport/football/euro-2012-sepp-blatter-calls-for-goal-line-technology-after-ukraine-blunder

UEFA. (2006). *Tackling racism in club football: A guide for clubs*. Retrieved from http://www.uefa.com/MultimediaFiles/Download/uefa/KeyTopics/448328_DOWNLOAD.pdf

Walker, K. (2012, July 3). What does the Gerhard Gribkowsky affair mean for F1? Retrieved from http://en.espnf1.com/f1/motorsport/story/83023.html

The Future of
Sport Governance

15

A future without change would be pretty bleak. Imagine if everything always stayed the same—the same people, same events, same physical layout, same schedule. Consider a professional basketball franchise: What if the rosters and schedules never changed, the competition was always the same, and the arena was never upgraded? For fans, this scenario would be boring and lack energy, and over time it simply would be no fun. While

381

an unchanging situation can be problematic, the exact opposite—rapid or unplanned change—can be equally difficult. Rapid change can be unsettling, creating confusion and uncertainty. Suppose the roster of the basketball team was shuffled every week, so that no one could follow who played for which team. NBA fans would find it impossible to feel loyalty for a team that changes players so quickly. A world without change is inconceivable, and a world in constant, rapid, and unplanned change can be chaotic.

Change is nonetheless important and inevitable. Change is often a component of progress; viewed with hope, it provides not just different, but better, ways of doing things. Sport organizations are perfect illustrations of the importance of change and the negative results accruing from overly rapid or poorly planned change.

To grow and thrive, a sport organization must be able to change and adapt to its environment. Factors in the environment include its size, members, competition, strategy, and technology (Chelladurai, 2009; Slack & Parent, 2006). As the size or membership of an organization grows, it changes to best serve its constituents. The organization defines strategy based on its competition and adapts to effectively utilize technology. Consider the NOCs in Chapter 10. The COC is a good illustration of an NOC that changed its operating structure to effectively deliver its mandate. As the Olympic Games evolved from a world festival of sport into a multimillion-dollar extravaganza and a stage for political agendas, the COC changed to accommodate this new environment, while still effectively delivering services to its members. The importance of winning Olympic medals as part of the national political agenda of Canada was one factor providing impetus for organizational change. This organizational change involved a new name, a new internal structure, and new criteria for funding Olympic sports within Canada.

One major concern to sport organizations as they undergo change is the pressure of future economic survival. The world economy fluctuates. During a recession, government spending on high school and college or university athletic and recreation programs is in jeopardy, as well as funding for city and municipal recreation programs. Professional sport, as well as Olympic and Paralympic sport, which rely on corporate sponsorships, also feel pressure as corporations make decisions about how much to invest in sport properties. Increased financial pressure, coupled with changing economic environments, present sport managers with a complex future.

This chapter completes our look at the governance of sport organizations. Its purpose is to look at the future of governance in the sport industry segments described in this text. Predicting the future, of course, is risky business. However, the future surely involves the continued evolution of sport organizations to meet the needs of their various stakeholders. The globalization of business practices, including the business of sport, has resulted in unprecedented change evolving faster than ever before (Moorhead & Griffin, 2007). We hope such change will be planned change, as opposed to forced change.

CHANGE WITHIN ORGANIZATIONS

Structures and governance policies of sport organizations evolve to improve effectiveness. The importance of change for sport organizations is in keeping with business and other organizations worldwide. As Beer and Nohria (2000) point out, "The demands of an ever competitive and changing environment are increasing the need for knowledge about how to lead and manage organizational change rapidly, efficiently, and effectively. The management mantra as we enter the 21st century is 'lead change'" (p. ix). Change should be planned and strategic, not some revolving door, constantly shuffling in new ideas while bouncing out the old.

According to Slack and Parent (2006), planned change can occur in four different areas of a sport organization: (1) the structures and systems of the organization, (2) the conduct of the organization's personnel, (3) the products and services delivered through the organization, or (4) the technology supporting the organization. So where do the pressures for change originate?

Pressures for Change

Pressure for organizational change may originate from three sources (Brill & Worth, 1997):

1. events occurring within the organization
2. factors arising outside the organization
3. an interaction of external and internal factors.

For example, the NCAA membership provided the impetus for restructuring the organization into divisions based on the changing philosophical perspectives of its members. In the past, changes in legislation and rules were made at the organization's annual meeting, where members from all divisions met together. When voting on issues, every school had one vote, and all divisions voted on all issues. Today the Division I, II, and III categories are taken for granted in the governance structure of the organization. The changing perspectives of various institutions within the organization provided the impetus for this change.

NCAA sanctions on Penn State as a result of the Jerry Sandusky child abuse case is illustrative of change resulting from outside the organization. In 2012 Jerry Sandusky, former assistant football coach at Penn State, was convicted of 45 counts of criminal child sex abuse, with some aspects covered up over the years by university officials. The NCAA fined the institution $60 million, banned competition in all postseason play for four years, reduced initial scholarships, vacated the institution's 112 wins from 1998 to 2011, and served the university with a five-year probationary term.

For an example of a combination of internal and external pressures, one could look at the decision to institute an NCAA Division I national football championship play-off with four teams. Many people, including fans, some lawmakers, and even the President of the United States, were unhappy with the Bowl Championship Series (BCS) system to determine a national champion, and there was a continued outpouring of sentiment to have a play-off. The NCAA thus moved, albeit slowly, to implement a four-team, three-game playoff that incorporates the major bowl games. The new format will take effect for the 2014–2015 season, incorporating two national semifinal games that will rotate among the major bowl games, and a national championship game hosted at a neutral site.

Sport organizations work within fairly complex environments, both internally and externally. What are the goals of planned organizational change?

Goals of Planned Change

Planned change involves the systematic development and initiation of new modes of operating to gain competitive advantage. As stated above, it may be prompted by the need for action resulting from events internal or external to the organization or both. The goal of planned change within a sport organization likely involves either matters of finance or organizational capability (Beer & Nohria, 2000). The impetus for change often results from financial belt-tightening within an organization. Specifically, a goal often involves increasing revenues or decreasing expenditures, or both, in an effort to balance the budget or enhance organizational services. When finances are not at the root of planned change, improving the organization's effectiveness usually is. In this case the purpose of planned change is to enhance the organization's capacity to respond better to its environment. Furthermore, the goal might be to move from *responding* to the environment to proactively *shaping* the environment. Achieving this second goal allows an organization to exercise more control over future directions and be on the cutting edge of the industry. Understanding the goals of planned change within an organization is important in determining a strategy for change. How is such change initiated, and what procedures are used to invoke organizational change?

Procedures for Organizational Change

Planned change occurs when several stages of activities result in organizational action (Slack & Parent, 2006). Change carries the most influence when it comes simultaneously from sources both within and outside the organization. Often the request for change is blocked by senior management because this group has a tendency to downplay organizational problems (Brill & Worth, 1997). First, a consultant may be used to overcome such hesitancy. Second, the specific problem prompting change is diagnosed and recognized throughout all the levels of the organization. Third, solutions to the problems are proposed, and a commitment to a

Organizational change process.

exhibit **15.1**

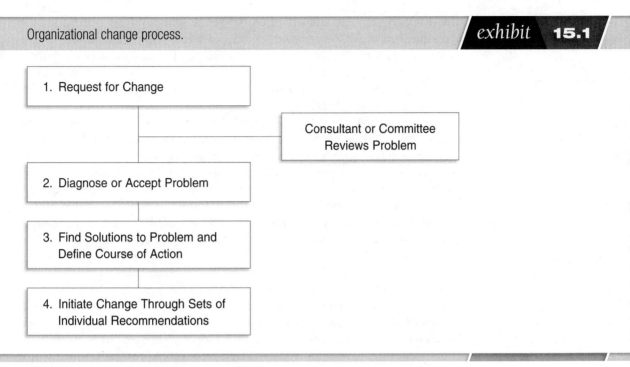

course of action is sought by testing several possible solutions. Finally, change is implemented through a number of small-scale decisions serving to reinforce a course of action and acceptance of larger-scale associated changes. This change process is presented in Exhibit 15.1.

FUTURE INDUSTRY SEGMENT ISSUES

Change within organizations is often slow and difficult. The previous chapters of this book outlined governance structure and policy development for several segments of the sport industry. Let's look briefly at some of the issues that might cause change within those segments.

Scholastic Sport

Today's youth has more opportunities than ever to participate in organized sport, from year-round traveling soccer teams, to sports offered in the European club model, Little League Baseball, summer camps, and more. While having such opportunities to participate is very positive, it also creates a more competitive climate for scholastic sport. Should a child play on a year-round soccer team or for the local high school team? Club sports, particularly AAU volleyball, soccer, and basketball, are becoming increasingly popular and are often the venue where young athletes showcase their talent for college coaches. Should a young athlete specialize in one sport all year, or change sports every season? Often these choices are driven by the thought that the more visible the competition level is to college coaches, the more likely it is that the young athlete will have an opportunity for a college scholarship.

These considerations lead to another key issue—what is the purpose of high school sport? Is it participation, healthy activity, and socialization, or is it preparation for intercollegiate athletics? A college education is a basic expectation, but these days as tuition costs rise and the economy stumbles, parents are looking for alternative ways to finance their children's education. Although the odds are against it, many parents in the United States see athletic scholarships as a way to cover these costs, and they see high school sport as the platform for their child's future success.

Sometimes high school sport becomes an even higher platform. Increasingly, high school athletes consider jumping directly into the professional ranks. National high school rankings and national high school All Star tournaments are now commonplace. High school sport governing bodies must make decisions about which types of tournaments to sanction and must examine more closely their definitions of *amateurism*. Athletes in baseball and hockey have the opportunity to sign professional contracts directly out of high school and then move on to the minor leagues to hone their talents. This is not the case with football or basketball. The NBA's rule on higher age restrictions for rookies has stemmed the tide of high school athletes trying to go directly to the NBA. In the future, high school sport governing bodies, in concert with college and professional sport organizations, will continually revisit important philosophical questions about the basic nature of high school sports.

The Dear Colleague Letter issued in early 2013 by the U.S. Department of Education has also opened the doors for high school students with disabilities to have competitive opportunities. As mentioned in the chapter on high school sport, these guidelines have been hailed as the Title IX for individuals with disabilities. It will be interesting to see how state high school athletic associations, school districts, and individual schools creatively respond.

Finally, the issue of funding for high school sports needs to be addressed. More and more corporate dollars are being invested in interscholastic sport. In addition, some individual high schools are selling naming rights to their stadiums and entering into deals with companies such as Nike and Under Armour. In many ways, the intercollegiate financing model is trickling down to high school sport. The implications of high school sport becoming more commercialized and reliant on outside funding through sponsorship are twofold. First, it will impact the competition for sponsorship dollars as sponsoring organizations have another sector seeking external funding and sponsorship beyond amateur, collegiate, and professional sport. Second, it may result in elevating high school competitions to levels expected of entertainment properties such as professional sport, which involves high costs and may further contribute to potential budget crises for administrators. Some may question this increasing commercialization of high school sport and whether it will influence the basic premise for why high school sport exists, which is to augment the education experience. Yet without these alternative funding sources, some students may lose out on the opportunities for these experiences.

Amateur Sport in the Community

Amateur community sport is the grass roots of competitive athletics. However, individuals in administrative positions will very likely be challenged to maintain the current breadth of programming. This challenge comes from competition for resources. Regardless of age group or type of sport, it takes significant human and financial resources to deliver programs. Competition for facilities is fierce. Finding people to coach, officiate, and organize programming is becoming more and more difficult. While public sport organizations will continue to strive to deliver recreational sport leagues, a lack of funding coupled with deteriorating infrastructure will create a major impetus for change. Policy decisions at the municipal or state level might well be enacted to create larger sources of funding to renovate facilities, allowing sport organizations to focus on program delivery. Current user fees will likely be increased to produce a larger revenue source. Personnel recruitment will be given higher priority, along with volunteer training. Competition among public and private groups will create an environment more accepting of change, spurred on by the importance of making use of every opportunity. Programming innovations and offerings will need to adapt to changing demographics, as the populations of seniors and racial and ethnic minorities continue to increase in North America. The future success of the Y, YWCA, JCC, Boys & Girls Clubs, and city parks and recreation departments will depend largely on their leadership and the ability of their boards of directors to understand the competition, to harness new forms of financial and human resources, and to enact policy that will take advantage of and accommodate shifting interests and trends for amateur athletes.

Campus Recreation

The leaders of campus recreation programs will oversee unprecedented change in the next decade. The future will be one of balancing service and customer-care issues in state-of-the-art facilities, while managing all user groups. In the past, campus recreation programming and facilities were primarily for constituent groups of the campus, including students, staff, faculty, and perhaps immediate family members. This mandate will continue to broaden as programs include members from the community. This might well involve parallel changes to organizational structures to include representatives from the community and their interests in campus recreation governance. It will surely include changes to campus recreation policies aiming to involve and protect the interests of an expanded group of constituents. Service will be the mantra, and unprecedented growth will create opportunities and challenges. Constructing additional facilities, expanding the numbers of professional staff, and increasing programming will be balanced with maintaining firm priorities so that the interests of university users, especially students, are not lost. The ongoing struggle over shared facilities at smaller institutions among campus recreation, intercollegiate athletics, and physical education departments will also continue. However, at larger institutions, the development of state-of-the-art recreation facilities for non-athletes will result in the need to include various user groups, especially as the demographics of the dwindling college-age population become better understood. The governance structure and policy-making procedures of future campus recreation programs, especially relating to risk management and access for people with disabilities, will be more important than ever before.

Intercollegiate Athletics

Although the commercial mandate of recreation programs on campus is generally accepted and supported, intercollegiate athletics policy makers will continue to confront negativity associated with commercialization in college football and basketball in the United States. It is unlikely, however, that any real change will occur. The issue, of course, will revolve around the role of college athletic programs in higher education. Are athletes at Division I colleges playing football and basketball really "students"? This is being called into question even more with the NBA's age restriction for rookies (minimum of 19 years of age), which has resulted in the so-called "one and done" basketball players who play their freshman year and have no intention of staying any longer. To encourage athletes to stay in school, the NCAA recently granted universities permission to award student-athletes an additional $2,000, although this decision is still under scrutiny (Nocera, 2011).

NCAA Division I athletes more closely resemble professionals, except they are not directly paid to play. Why not? Colleges and universities make significant sums of money from their athletes. How is it that our colleges and universities, supposed collectives of truth and light, have created a system so incongruous with their mandate and their purpose? The questions go on and on and include issues of fairness, equity, corruption, and control. The issue is articulated well by Duderstadt (2000), Professor Emeritus at the University of Michigan:

We are obliged to ask the difficult question of whether it makes sense for the 21st Century university to conduct commercial activities at the current level of big-time college football and basketball. Is there any logical reason for an academic institution, with the fundamental mission of teaching and scholarship, to mount and sustain a professional and commercial enterprise simply to satisfy the public desire for entertainment, and the commercial goals of the marketplace? Why should the university squander its resources, distract its leadership, and erode its most fundamental values and integrity with these commercial activities, particularly at a time when it will face so many other challenges in responding to the changing educational needs of our society? (p. 8)

Although the debate will continue, change is not on the horizon.

The Major Games in Amateur Sport

Managerial activities associated with major games policy development will receive considerable attention and will be the focus of governance activities for hosting events in the future. Two important issues are at stake. First, organizers will focus on the development of policy to ensure the safety and security of participants and spectators. World events such as the Pan American Games, Commonwealth Games, Special Olympics, World University Games, and the FIFA World Cup are major events, receiving considerable attention from the media, spectators, and television. Organizers must plan for every contingency to ensure security and safety are not compromised by any group attempting to use the event for political gain. Major games administrators must be prepared to deal with issues of security, given the events confronting the world in the 21st century. Second, the governance structures in place for organizing major games must be able to deliver effective policy to manage the issues of the day in a timely manner. The committee structures are considerably large, requiring massive support to make change and allowing only a few members to effectively block the ability to move on issues quickly. Also, the procedures for developing policy and initiating change are unwieldy; inertia resists change, and thus the old, conservative way of doing things prevails. Organizers of major games will be forced to manage issues such as security, and it will be paramount that they have the governance structure and technology in place to set policy in a timely manner.

The Olympic Games

The IOC will continue to evaluate the future of the Olympic Games. Currently, the IOC suggests the four Olympic Movement cornerstones under future review to include (1) assessing the Olympic Programme of sports and events; (2) studying the cost and complexity of the Games; (3) continuing to implement recent reform; and (4) auditing operation and financial administration (IOC, 2012). A major policy area demanding considerable attention of IOC members involves the size and "greening" of the Games. The current Olympic Games are considered by some the "overgrown Games," which have too many sports and too many athletes, and cost too much money to deliver, not to mention the Games' large ecological footprint. In 1948 the Summer Olympic Games involved 17 sports, 140 events, and 4,099 athletes (IOC, 2008), whereas the London 2012 games had 26 sports, 302 events, and 10,800 athletes (BBC Sport, 2012).

Given the four issues for reform mentioned above, reviewing the actual sport program may enact policy and create reform that might, at least in part, address the other areas of concern. In 2002 the IOC moved forward and created policy to systematically review the composition of the sports program after every Games to ensure its relevancy for future sporting generations. This work is undertaken by the IOC Olympic Programme Commission and the IFs. According to the Olympic Charter, the total number of sports on the program cannot exceed 28 (IOC, 2011). Sports can be voted on for inclusion on the program at the Sessions. For a sport to become an Olympic sport, a simple majority vote is needed at an IOC Session. Managing sports in the Olympic Programme through this policy will continue to be an item on the IOC's agenda. An assessment of the overall governance structure of the IOC should parallel that process. Moving sports off the Olympic competition roster, however, will continue to be challenging and controversial, as seen by the 2013 vote on wrestling.

One more issue of importance to the Olympic Movement is environmental sustainability. The IOC has now deemed the environment as the third fundamental objective of the Olympic Movement, alongside sport and culture (IOC, 2012). Efforts are made to ensure each Olympic Games operates with a minimal carbon footprint. In London, sustainability was part of the plan from the start and included areas such as carbon management, sustainable transport, food vision, and waste management (London 2012, n.d.). The environmental impact of the Games will be continually monitored and reported to the public.

The Paralympic Games

The Paralympic Games are gaining international recognition as an elite sport product. Along with this growth, numerous questions will arise regarding the Paralympic Movement. One of the first issues deals with integration of athletes with disabilities into mainstream able-bodied sport. Some IFs and events have already integrated competitions and rules (Grevemberg, Hums, & Wolff, 2001). For example, the Boston Marathon has included wheelchair athletes as competitors for over 25 years (DePauw, Driscoll, Fay, Hums, & Joukowsky, 2003). The International Tennis Federation website has links to information on tennis for athletes with disabilities. The Commonwealth Games holds events for athletes with disabilities, and there is a Paralympic arm to the Pan American Games called the Para-Pan Games.

Should athletes with disabilities be fully integrated into mainstream sport organizations, or should they remain separate with their own unique identities? With Oscar Pistorius claiming a spot on the South African Olympic squad, more attention will be focused on elite athletes with disabilities.

Another major issue facing the Paralympic Games involves illegal performance enhancement. Just as this is an issue in the Olympic Games, so too is it an issue in the Paralympic Games; elite athletes are always looking for an edge over the competition. Cooperation between the IPC and organizations such as the WADA will be critical in this area.

Advances in technology will also impact the Paralympic Games. As the technology of prosthetics advances, this will be reflected in the performances of athletes with disabilities. Racing chairs will be made out of lighter-weight materials, and prosthetic limbs will be made stronger and more flexible. Athletes will begin to achieve performances never seen before, and world records will be broken, establishing new standards. While examining the impact of technology, one must ask three questions: (1) Is the technology safe? (2) Is the technology fair? and (3) Is the technology accessible to all? These questions pertain not just to the Paralympic Games, but also to the policy-making bodies of any sport governing body dealing with advances in technology.

Finally, just as with the Olympic Games and professional sport, security will continue to be important for the Paralympic Games. Whenever there are large gatherings of elite athletes from many nations, security and risk management become critical for the athletes, spectators, and workers.

As the Paralympic Games continue to grow, the governing bodies associated with the Games, including the IPC, NPCs, and IFs, will need to adjust to an ever-changing environment. They will need to be responsive to governance decisions made by able-bodied sport organizations that may impact events, rules, and eligibility for athletes with disabilities.

Finally, the UN General Assembly's adoption of the Treaty on the Rights of Persons with Disabilities will have long-term effects on the Paralympic Movement. The Treaty contains language specific to sport in Article 30.5, thus sport and physical activity clearly fall under the umbrella of this Treaty. It may take some time for the document to be put into practice, but the long-term result will be increased opportunities for athletes with disabilities (Wolff, Hums, & Roy, 2007).

Professional Sport Leagues in North America

Professional sport leagues, teams, and players associations need to step up their stances on misconduct by athletes, coaches, and officials. Incidents

www

Boston Marathon
www.baa.org/races/boston-marathon/participant-information/athletes-with-disabilities.aspx

International Tennis Federation
www.itftennis.com/wheelchair/home.aspx

www

UN Treaty on the Rights of Persons with Disabilities
www.un.org/disabilities

such as the New Orleans Saints' Bounty Gate; the New England Patriots' videotaping the practice of an opponent; and athletes being arrested for driving under the influence of alcohol, domestic abuse or sexual assault, or firearm possession seem to be in the news almost every day. The seemingly rampant behavior problems, ranging from boorishness to unlawful activity, beg for leagues to take truly strong stands against misconduct. We have already seen this with NFL commissioner Roger Goodell's strong stance regarding the New Orleans Saints.

Although many people seemed to believe the professional sport industry was relatively impervious to the twists and turns of the economy and world events, those notions were swept away on September 11, 2001. In the wake of that day, professional sport has had to face the reality of unstable international economies and environments. The value of the U.S. dollar has continued to decrease in relation to the euro. The worldwide economic downturn in 2008 has continued to impact individuals, sport organizations, and governments around the world. The word *austerity* is commonly linked to economic predictions, and reduced revenues from luxury suites, premium seats, and sponsorships due to reduced corporate spending are problems facing professional sport managers. Reduced financial capacity for fans across the sports industry, and heightened competition for a share of that revenue stream is a significant issue for sport managers.

In an unstable economy, professional sport sponsorship is sure to be affected. Not only is the struggling economy an issue for sponsors when trying to negotiate long-term deals, the conduct of the players or teams associated with sponsors is also a major issue in sport today. With more and more athletes getting in trouble with the law and receiving subsequent bad press and a tarnished image, sponsors have to be very careful in choosing players with whom to associate.

Many security measures implemented in stadiums and arenas for professional sport events have remained in place since September 11, 2001 (Slezak, 2002). Stadiums continue to ban coolers and backpacks, and armed security personnel remain a visible presence. These are the changes visible to fans. Behind the scenes, the Big Four has increased measures to protect teams and players when they travel, and teams are required to carry special insurance plans as well. Security at sporting events has become one of the top issues facing industry executives (Hyman, 2002). Governing bodies, specifically leagues, have had to create and enforce new security policies and procedures in a somewhat uncertain environment.

While security and the economy remain at the top of the list, other issues are constant in professional sport. Leagues and PAs will continue to debate collective bargaining agreements. Labor issues in sport will always be with us, and leagues and PAs will continually hammer out new policies regarding everything from performance-enhancing substances to athlete misconduct. For example, prior to the 2011 NFL season a labor dispute between league owners and players resulted in the players being locked out for over 18 weeks, threatening the postponement or cancellation of the season. A range of issues were in dispute, not the least of which was how to divide up $9 billion in annual revenues. The NFL opened its 2012–2013 season with replacement officials, a move many saw as putting players' health and safety at risk at a time when the NFL had been making a stand about player safety and concussions. Similarly, the NBA lockout for 161 days delayed the 2011–2012 regular season for nearly two months. As in the NFL lockout, division of revenues and salary caps were the main issues in dispute. The 2012–2013 NHL season was postponed more than three months due to a labor dispute and subsequent lockout that ultimately shortened the season from 82 to 48 games. At issue was the terms of a new collective bargaining agreement. Collective bargaining and labor relations will continue to surface within professional sport, for both men's and women's teams.

Women's sport brings forth another issue—the future of women's professional sport. WNBA officials report that merchandise sales are up 20 percent and season ticket renewals are up 10 percent for the upcoming 2013 season, despite the fact that average attendance fell to 7457 in the 2012 season (Rhoden, 2012). If all indicators remain the same, the league which was founded in 1997, will be moving into its 20th season in 2017. Additionally, in 2012 the Women's Professional Soccer (WPS) league folded after only three seasons. The WPS debuted with seven teams, eroded to six, and then shrank to five before succumbing to full closure. Financial instability, low television ratings, and internal legal disputes each contributed to the league's demise.

Professional sport in North America has begun to take on a more international flavor. The number of athletes from around the world is increasing, with numerous athletes from South America, Central America, and Japan playing MLB and many European players filling the rosters of the NHL and the NBA. In fact, many of today's biggest pro sport stars come from outside North America, including Ichiro Suzuki (Japan) and Albert Pujols (Dominican Republic) in MLB; Dirk Nowitzki (Germany), Steve Nash (Canada), and Pau Gasol (Spain) in the NBA; and Daniel Sedin (Sweden) and Zdeno Chára (Slovakia) in the NHL.

League and play-off games are being broadcast to different nations and in different languages, as the professional leagues become a more global product. Each of these leagues is taking further advantage of this relatively new global market by scheduling regular season games in international cities, such as the NFL holding a 2012–2013 regular season game between the St. Louis Rams and the New England Patriots at Wembley Stadium in London, England. The Buffalo Bills play one home game 100 miles to the north in Toronto, Canada, each year. In addition, interna-

www

MLB Players from around the World
http://mlb.mlb.com/mlb/official_
info/dbp/about_players.jsp

tional "best-on-best" tournaments such as the World Baseball Classic and FIBA World Basketball Championship showcase their respective games to the world, helping the game to grow even more.

Individual Professional Sport

Individual professional sports and athletes have also faced challenges. Following his highly publicized personal problems in late 2009, Tiger Woods's image plunged, and some of his sponsors, including AT&T and Gatorade, dropped their contracts with him (Associated Press, 2010). Woods's absence from golf for eight months following the scandal had a negative effect on the PGA TOUR as TV ratings dropped almost 50 percent, and event organizers witnessed attendance declines at major events (Klayman, 2009). Woods returned to the sport in 2010, and the emergence of rising stars such as Rory McIlroy and Bubba Watson helped reignite spectator interest in the sport. Fans now await the sport's inclusion in the 2016 Summer Olympic Games (Davenport, 2012).

While women's team sports continue to struggle, individual female athletes are thriving; some of them are even making inroads in male professional sport. Both the LPGA and the Women's Tennis Association (WTA) have prize money approaching the levels of their male counterparts, and tennis players Maria Sharapova ($25 million) and Caroline Wozniacki ($12.5 million) were top 2011 earners. Golfer Paula Creamer earned $5.5 million in 2011, and NASCAR driver Danica Patrick competed against men, earning $12 million. It will be interesting to see if these or other women will be able to achieve consistent financial success compared to men in the future and to observe how sport governing bodies in women's sport continue developing. The WTA appears to be a model organization forging the way forward for women's professional sport.

Grassroots development remains a focus for individual sports. These sports rely heavily on an athlete's ability to master the skills necessary to reach the highest level of competition. The missing components of camaraderie, team support, and sport popularity in individual sports are challenges to attracting young fans and athletes. The number of beginning golfers ages 6 and over decreased from 2.4 million in 2000 to 1.5 million in 2011 (National Golf Foundation, 2012). The United States Tennis Association seeks to increase the sport's popularity among youth by introducing the 10 and Under Tennis program, in the hopes of making the sport more welcoming to children (Miller, 2012). Similarly, NASCAR promotes its Drive for Diversity program to bring more women and minorities to the sport. The organization also promotes its events as family entertainment, and these efforts may help attract potential drivers.

Finally, the financial requirements associated with some individual sports represent another significant challenge. Golf and tennis are costly endeavors, given the need for equipment, coaches and lessons, club memberships, and tournament entry fees. The financial investment in NASCAR is even greater as drivers may require one or more vehicles, support staff and personnel, plus the expenses associated with traveling to and entering races. The ultimate rewards remain high for successful athletes who receive millions in prize earnings, yet the initial costs of the sports may represent a barrier to entry for interested athletes.

Professional Sport Beyond North America

It is interesting to speculate on the future of professional sport internationally. Political and economic factors will no doubt impact the sport industry. International sponsors will continue to reexamine their choices for investing in sporting leagues and events. Accordingly, the sport governing bodies for these sports will have to make decisions regarding financial matters in order to maintain and improve operations in the coming years. Because of the interrelationship of IFs such as FIA or FIFA to the operation of international professional leagues, these organizations will be considering policies related to garnering sufficient financial resources, just as the professional leagues in North America will. Internationally, professional sport will continue to grow. Soccer will remain the most popular sport globally and a viable investment for corporations despite ongoing problems with racism and scandals involving high level officials. Formula One racing will need to find a way to recover from the McLaren-Ferrari scandal that resulted in a US$100 million (€65 million) fine for stealing trade secrets. In addition, sports such as lacrosse and cricket are coming onto the scene rapidly, bringing with them new fan bases and new sponsor opportunities to get their products in front of people around the globe. It seems that people in the United States are tuning in and slowly becoming more interested in and knowledgeable about international sport leagues. Current technologies and the proliferation of social media for transmitting sport allow for easier access and greater consumer choice, resulting in opportunities for some sport leagues, while presenting obstacles for others.

SUMMARY

The future of sport will be full of changes! How sport governing bodies respond to these facts will determine their success in the future. Some people resist change, while others welcome it. In each segment of the sport industry, sport governing bodies will face change. Some of these changes will be unique to one industry segment, while others will cut across a number of segments.

As a future sport manager, how will you choose to face this future with all its uncertainties, questions, and changes? As they say, "The ball is in your court."

CHAPTER**questions**

1. Choose three industry segments from the textbook and identify two additional future issues for each.
2. Using the model presented in this chapter, analyze the steps for change for one of the following:
   a. a professional athlete being accused or convicted of criminal behavior
   b. a state high school or provincial association creating a wheelchair division for track-and-field competition
   c. a campus recreation program facing declining participation numbers
3. Choose one sport organization you would like to see experience changes in membership, eligibility, or organizational structure. Describe the changes you would like to see take place and how these changes will improve the organization.

REFERENCES

Associated Press. (2010, February 27). Gatorade cuts ties with Woods. Retrieved from http://sports.espn.go.com/golf/news/story?id=4950137

BBC Sport. (2012, August 13). Olympics. Retrieved from http://www.bbc.co.uk/sport/olympics/2012/countries

Beer, M., & Nohria, N. (2000). *Breaking the code of change*. Boston: Harvard Business School Press.

Brill, P. L., & Worth, R. (1997). *The four levers of corporate change*. New York: American Management Association.

Chelladurai, P. (2009). *Managing organizations for sport and physical activity: A systems perspective* (3d ed.). Scottsdale, AZ: Holcomb Hathaway.

Davenport, G. (2012, June 16). Tiger Woods: Resurgence of golf's biggest draw is great news for PGA Tour. Retrieved from http://bleacherreport.com/articles/1224308-tiger-woods-resurgence-of-golfs-biggest-draw-great-news-for-pga-tour

DePauw, K., Driscoll, J., Fay, T., Hums, M. A., & Joukowsky, A. (2003). The Boston Marathon: Breaking barriers. Paper presented at the Disability Sport Symposium, Boston, MA.

Duderstadt, J. J. (2000, October 18). Some observations on the current state and the future of intercollegiate athletics. Remarks presented to the Knight Commission, Washington, DC. Retrieved from http://milproj.ummu.umich.edu/publications/knight_commission/knight_commission.pdf

Grevemberg, D., Hums, M. A., & Wolff, E. A. (2001). Integration of Paralympic Sport into International Sport Federations: Comparative international models. Paper presented at the Annual Meeting of the North American Society for Sport Management, Virginia Beach, VA.

Hyman, M. (2002, April 29). Security issues rise to the top of the docket for sport lawyers. *Street & Smith's SportsBusiness Journal*. Retrieved from http://www.sportsbusinessdaily.com/Journal/Issues/2002/04/20020429/This-Weeks-Issue/Security-Issues-Rise-To-The-Top-Of-The-Docket-For-Sports-Lawyers.aspx?hl=security%20issues%20rise%20to%20the%20top&sc=1

IOC. (2008). Facts and figures of Beijing Olympic Games. Retrieved from http://en.beijing2008.cn/media/usefulinfo/

IOC. (2011). *The Olympic charter.* Lausanne, Switzerland: Author.

IOC. (2012). Sport and Environment Commission. Retrieved from http://www.olympic.org/sport-environment-commission

Klayman, B. (2009). Tiger's troubles seen swiping sports sponsorship market. *International Business Times.* Retrieved from http://www.ibtimes.com/tigers-troubles-seen-swiping-sports-sponsorship-market-353348

London 2012. (n.d.). Our responsibility. Retrieved from http://www.london2012.com/about-us/sustainability/our-responsibility/

Miller, S. (2012, January 21). Trying to appeal to U.S. Under-10 generation by shrinking the game's scale. *New York Times.* Retrieved from http://straightsets.blogs.nytimes.com/2012/01/21/trying-to-appeal-to-u-s-under-10-generation-by-shrinking-the-games-scale/

Moorhead, G., & Griffin, R. W. (2007). *Organizational behavior: Managing people and organizations* (Canadian Ed.). Boston: Houghton Mifflin.

National Golf Foundation (2012). Golf participation in the United States. Retrieved from http://matt campbellgolf.com/?p=1575

Nocera, J. (2011, December 30). Let's start paying college athletes. *New York Times.* Retrieved from http://www.nytimes.com/2012/01/01/magazine/lets-start-paying-college-athletes.html?pagewanted=all

Olympic Golf News. (2012). Barra region to be Olympic golf site. Retrieved from http://olympicgolfnews.com/

Rhoden, W. C. (2012, October 7). Amid success, WNBA is still facing challenges. *New York Times.* Retrieved from http://www.nytimes.com/2012/10/08/sports/basketball/amid-successes-wnba-is-still-facing-challenges.html?pagewanted=all&_r=0

Slack, T., & Parent, M. (2006). *Understanding sport organizations: The application of organization theory* (2d ed.). Champaign, IL: Human Kinetics.

Slezak, C. (2002, September 8). Sporting a different look. *Chicago Sun-Times,* p. 123.

Wolff, E. A., Hums, M. A., & Roy, E. (2007). *Sport in the United Nations Convention on the Rights of Persons with Disabilities.* Boston, MA: International Disability in Sport Working Group/United Nations Office of the Special Advisor of the Secretary-General on Sport for Development and Peace.

Index